This is the best book ever written on American schools and teenagers. With thorough research across many kinds of schools, Milner spells out a general theory that explains why high school kids create their own caste system.

> —Randall Collins, author of *Violence: A Micro-sociological Theory*,
> Professor of Sociology, University of Pennsylvania, and
> Past-President of the American Sociological Association

Milner's work takes teenagers seriously as social actors. Rather than hand-wringing about "what's wrong with kids today," *Freaks, Geeks, and Cool Kids* offers discerning, theoretical analysis that reveals the broader social processes that animate contemporary teen culture. With the second edition, Milner brings his keen insight to understanding the new status pressures faced by teens growing up in an era of ubiquitous social media and high stakes testing.

> —Markella Rutherford, Associate Professor of Sociology, Wellesley College,
> author of *Adult Supervision Required: Private Freedom
> and Public Constraints for Parents and Children*

Through up-close observations of the day-to-day lives of high school students, Milner deftly demonstrates how complex and persistent systems of status buttress a culture of consumerism, both consistent with and at odds with the broader society. The book joins a distinguished set of sociological studies of teenage culture, while being accessible to a broader readership.

> —David Bills, College of Liberal Arts & Sciences, The University of Iowa

Freaks, Geeks, and Cool Kids is as fresh and informative today as it was when it was first published. Murray Milner's incisive analysis of American teen culture and practices remains an indispensable reference point for anyone seeking to take the study of status, hierarchy, and exchange in contemporary life forward into new directions.

> —Daniel Thomas Cook, author of *The Commodification of Childhood*, Professor of
> Childhood Studies Department of Childhood Studies Rutgers University-Camden

One of the rare academic books that is both theoretically rich and easily readable for both academics and students, this detailed study of high school culture shows that for youth who have little individual economic or political power, cultural tastes and experiences become the basis for status distinctions.

> —Paul Kooistra, Furman University, author of
> *Criminals as Heroes: Structure, Power, and Identity*

Freaks, Geeks, and Cool Kids provides a rare glimpse into the world of high school students. Understanding their behaviors as resulting from a near-constant pursuit of status, Milner not only explains teens' obsession with peer relations and being "cool," he also describes their role in the development and maintenance of consumer capitalism. Methodologically rigorous and theoretically elegant, *Freaks, Geeks, and Cool Kids* is a modern sociological masterpiece.

> —James Hawdon, Professor and Director, Center for Peace Studies
> and Violence Prevention, Virginia Tech

Freaks, Geeks, and Cool Kids is an insightful analysis into the lives of American teenagers and why they behave the way they do. Murray Milner uses engaging narratives to skillfully bring into focus how teenagers, with no real economic or political power, carefully cultivate status systems to maintain their position amongst peers, in school, and consumer capitalism. It should be required reading for anyone who wants to understand youth culture in the twenty-first century.

> —Bhavani Arabandi, Assistant Professor of Sociology, Ithaca College

Teenagers in an Era of Consumerism, Standardized Tests, and Social Media

Second Edition

In *Freaks, Geeks, and Cool Kids: Teenagers in an Era of Consumerism, Standardized Tests, and Social Media, Second Edition*, award-winning sociologist Murray Milner tries to understand why teenagers behave the way they do. The first edition drew upon two years of intensive fieldwork in one high school and 300 written descriptions of high schools across the country, where he argued that consumer culture greatly impacts the way our youth relate to one another and understand themselves and society. Milner now expands on that concept with a new year of fieldwork fifteen years after he began. He shows that the significance of consumerism has changed, that social media have altered the nature of fashion and "keeping up," and that standardized tests shape not only what happens in the classroom, but the nature of romantic relationships.

Murray Milner, Jr. is Emeritus Professor of Sociology and Senior Fellow at the Institute for Advanced Studies in Culture, University of Virginia. His book *Status and Sacredness* received the American Sociological Society's Distinguished Book Award. His most recent book is *Elites: A General Model* (Polity Books 2015).

FREAKS, GEEKS, AND COOL KIDS

Teenagers in an Era of Consumerism,
Standardized Tests, and Social Media

Second Edition

MURRAY MILNER, JR.

Routledge
Taylor & Francis Group

LONDON AND NEW YORK

First edition published 2006
by Routledge
Second edition published 2016
by Routledge
711 Third Avenue, New York, NY 10017

and by Routledge
2 Park Square, Milton Park, Abingdon, Oxon, OX14 4RN

Routledge is an imprint of the Taylor & Francis Group, an informa business

Library of Congress Cataloging in Publication Data
Milner, Murray.
Freaks, geeks, and cool kids : teenagers in an era of consumerism, standardized tests, and social media / by Murray Milner, Jr.
  pages cm
Earlier edition published in 2004.
Includes bibliographical references and index.
1. Teenagers. 2. Teenagers--United States. 3. Teenage consumers. I. Title.
HQ796.M493 2016
305.2350973--dc23
2015011690

ISBN: 978-1-138-01343-8 (hbk)
ISBN: 978-1-138-01344-5 (pbk)
ISBN: 978-1-315-79513-3 (ebk)

Typeset in Ehrhardt MT Pro Regular
Integra Software Service Pvt. Ltd.

Printed and bound in the United States of America by
Edwards Brothers Malloy on sustainably sourced paper

For Shelton and Ashley

OTHER BOOKS BY MURRAY MILNER, JR.

Police on Campus: The Mass Police Action at Columbia University, Spring 1968 (with others)

The Illusion of Equality: The Effects of Educational Opportunity on Inequality and Conflict

Unequal Care: A Case Study of Interorganizational Relations in Health Care

Status and Sacredness: A General Theory of Status Relations and an Analysis of Indian Culture

Elites: A General Model

CONTENTS

PREFACE: FIFTEEN YEARS LATER

By the time this book is published I will be eighty years old. This means my day-to-day life and experiences are quite different from the key actors this book describes, American teenagers. This is one of the reasons I was ambivalent about and even reluctant to agree to the publisher's request to update the book. But if age is a handicap, it is also an asset. It means I have seen a significant number of changes in my lifetime. Through no virtue of my own, it gives me an existential "sense of history" that young people and younger colleagues do not have. Close-up views of social reality are useful, but so are more distant perspectives. They each tend to see things that the other misses.

What motivated me to put aside my reservations was that shortly after the completion of the first edition a major cultural transformation had begun and is continuing. This change may turn out to be as important as the shift from preliterate to literate societies. It was what I will call a shift to a "digital culture." By this I mean a culture in which everyday people get much of their information, carry out many of their interactions, conduct many of their economic transactions, and entertain themselves via the Internet. A digital culture has also increased the importance of pictures and images and eroded the centrality of texts. This is somewhat analogous to the way written texts reduced the importance of poetry as a mnemonic device used to remember long narratives.

Young people are especially adept at dealing with this new culture and tend to use the new technology and media even more than adults. Hence, to have a view of the same school just before and shortly after the digital transformation seemed like a worthwhile project.

New technologies and the emergence of a digital culture were not, however, the only changes. Several attempts at reforming the educational system have occurred. The most obvious of these is the adoption of various forms of a required "common core" and the use of standardized tests to measure people's competence in communicating and acquiring the content of such curricula.

Despite these important changes, much remains the same. Teenagers are still very concerned about how their peers view them and the kind of status they acquire. But the changes described above have altered many of the ways teenagers acquire status and relate to one another—and this is the focus of the new material in this enlarged edition.

PREFACE

Intellectually, I came of age during the late 1960s and early 1970s in New York City. It was a time when radical thought, especially various forms of Marxism, stressed the fundamental significance of material factors—property and force—for the organization of social life. I was not persuaded. While I had no doubt that control of these played a crucial role in shaping what went on in the world, these seemed to me to be derived from a more fundamental form of power. To effectively exercise force or to control property you need the moral support of significant numbers of people. That support may come from only a small minority, but it is crucial.

I saw this most vividly during the students' occupation of the buildings of Columbia University in the spring of 1968, and the resulting police action to remove them.[1] Force or economic resources were of little importance in the students' ability to bring the university to a standstill for a week and to cause it to cancel one of its major construction projects. Nor did these play a role in gaining the attention of much of the world, or in eventually bringing about the removal of the university's president and provost. More striking was that once the police action to remove the students began, university, city, and police officials often had little control over what the lower-level officers did. The result was the indiscriminate beating of anyone who happened to be in reach, including conservative students who were protesting against the occupation of the university's buildings, press reporters, and people who just happened to be coming out of the 116th Street subway station. When superior officers were complicit, they were usually ignoring or violating the orders that were being given by their superiors. That is, at some level those who supposedly were in charge had no moral authority over their subordinates—and whatever force or economic sanctions they could exercise on their own were irrelevant.

This experience and other things caused me to focus much of my intellectual efforts on trying to understand the nature of the residue of power that was not directly due to force or material sanctions. I came to see that this form of power was rooted in the fact that individuals cared about the approval and disapproval of some people and were indifferent to the opinions of others. That is, some people had a status that made their expressions of approval and disapproval important to others. This book is another effort in my attempt to expand my understanding of status and its consequences for social life.

If it is not a surprise that I would focus on the operation of status systems, it is a surprise to me that I chose to focus on American teenagers. I did not much like teenagers when my wife and I were teenagers—we both attended the same high school. My enthusiasm for the age group was not improved when I worked with youth groups in both upscale Fairfield County, Connecticut, and downscale East Harlem in Manhattan.

I chose to conduct research on teenagers because I thought their status systems were particularly relevant to my analytical concerns. Therefore, I was a bit amazed when I came not only to respect these young people, but also to enjoy them. Nonetheless, the primary reason for focusing on teenagers is because of their strategic importance for my intellectual concerns and for the operation of our society. Understanding teenage peer status systems is crucial for grasping the nature of the economic and political processes that shape our times, including the education of our young people.

This book is intended for several different audiences, including scholars, college students, educators, and those interested in educational policy. I have minimized, but not eliminated, discussion of scholarly literature and methodology in the regular chapters. Therefore, those interested in these matters will need to read the Appendices and, on occasion, refer to the endnotes for further information about what is being discussed in the main text.

ACKNOWLEDGMENTS

One of the consequences of research and writing projects that extend over several years is that you are indebted to many people. One of the ironies of much of social research is that those to whom you owe the most—the people you studied—must remain anonymous. I came to admire and appreciate the members of the faculty and staff of the institution I call Woodrow Wilson High School. The principal, assistant principal, and dean of students were especially helpful. With very few exceptions, students at this school treated our research team with courtesy and were extremely patient in educating us into the ways of their society. The lunch group I personally observed for two years holds a special place in my heart. The 300 college students who wrote descriptions of their high schools made a crucial contribution to this book.

Some can be publicly acknowledged and thanked, though often their role must be left unspecified to honor the pledge of anonymity given to both the individuals and the institutions that were studied. In the research phase Jordi Comas, Savonne Ferguson, Ryan Pavlicek, David Sciulli, Mary Ann Clawson, and William Holt gave me vital assistance. I am especially indebted to the thirty-five undergraduate students who served as fieldworkers. Their level of commitment to the research process and their maturity and thoughtfulness frequently impressed me. At various times the following people served as research assistants: Glenn Dillon, Carrie Faulkner, Katrina Gaus, Susan Hamsher, Shana Pearlman, and Noa Taffet. With her usual good humor and efficiency, Joan Snapp transcribed my field notes. Jennifer Beyer and Annette Morris were especially helpful and efficient in assisting with the editing of the manuscript.

Much of the writing was done when I was a visiting fellow at Downing College, Cambridge University. It was a delightful setting, and my wife and I want to thank the fellows and staff of the college for their generous hospitality. Richard Stibbs not only took us into his weekly wine club, but also assisted us in numerous other ways. The hospitality of sociological colleagues Christel Lane, David Lane, Eileen Richardson, and Bryan Turner was especially appreciated.

I benefited greatly from the feedback and criticism that resulted from presentations at the European University Institute, Cambridge University, the London School of Economics, the University of British Columbia, Yale University, and several sessions I participated in at the American Sociological Association meeting. I am grateful to the many who provided hospitality during these visits, especially to my old friend Gianfranco Poggi.

At different stages of the project a variety of people read all or parts of the manuscript and offered helpful suggestions. These include Markella Rutherford, Syed Ali, William Lockhart, Paul Kingston, James Hunter, Jeffrey Alexander, Phillip Smith, several anonymous reviewers, and many of the graduate and undergraduate students who took my courses. I also benefited from the thoughtful editing of Ilene Kalish of Routledge.

The Institute for Advanced Studies in Culture, and the Center on Religion and Democracy has been one of my intellectual homes in recent years. I am indebted to the members and the director James Hunter for financial, moral, and intellectual support.

As always, the physical and emotional sustenance of Sylvia Milner was crucial to the project, and to all that I do.

FIFTEEN YEARS LATER

As is the case with most social research my deepest debt is to the students, faculty, and administrators who let us look at their lives or shared their thoughts. They were promised anonymity and hence cannot be named.

Of those who can be named I owe the greatest debt to Julia Ticona and Megan Quetsch, who conducted the great bulk of the observational fieldwork and student interviews. They did these jobs with outstanding dedication and competence, and were truly colleagues.

I am also grateful to the students at the four colleges and universities who provided descriptions of their high school experiences, and to the faculty and teaching assistants who assisted in the collection of this kind of data. They too must remain unnamed to reduce the chances that any of the people quoted or described can be identified.

James Hunter and Joe Davis of the Institute for Advanced Studies in Culture provided both encouragement and funds that made the research possible, as well as a most hospitable and stimulating place to work.

Those who read drafts of the manuscript and gave very helpful criticisms and suggestions include Jeffrey Guhin, Josipa Roksa, Megan Quetsch, and Julia Ticona. Longtime colleague and friend, Paul Kingston, has a long history of reading, critiquing, and suggesting improvements on my work and he is owed a special word of thanks. My undergraduate research assistant in the final stages of this project, Vincent Lam Ting Luk, was diligent and timely finding and checking relevant citations.

As always my deepest debt is to my wife of fifty-seven years, Sylvia Milner.

INTRODUCTION: FIFTEEN YEARS LATER

The first edition of this book was based on research conducted primarily in 1998. A new study was undertaken in the Fall 2013 and Spring 2014. That is, the second study was approximately fifteen years after the initial research. This second research effort was less extensive, but used essentially the same methods as the first, including ethnographic observations at "Woodrow Wilson High School," the same school that was studied in 1998. The purpose of the new study was not replication per se, that is, a rigorous retesting of the initial hypotheses and arguments. Rather the focus was on change or lack of it. That is, on what's old, and what's new in the life of American teenagers.

WHAT'S OLD

An obvious, but significant finding is that there was little change in the basic organization of high schools and the day-to-day structure of teenage peer culture. Most adolescent students spend the bulk of their day in high schools—rather than working full-time or being taught by parents, private tutors, religious gurus, guild masters or via Massive Open Online Courses (MOOC).[1]

High schools are organized pretty much the way they have been since the first quarter of the twentieth century: mostly classes of about thirty students (plus or minus ten), usually about fifty minutes long, focusing on a specific subject (history, math, etc.), supervised by a professional teacher, who is supervised by a principal, who answers to a superintendent, who reports to a school board. Adolescents are still legally required to be in school and most have relatively little choice about which school they attend, the content of the curriculum, or the hours they must be in school.[2]

That is, the main structure of their lives is determined by adults. The primary kind of power adolescents have is still the power to express approval and disapproval of their student peers. Hence, peer relationships and culture are still very central to their concerns. As in earlier periods, what happens during lunch and other periods of "free time" is especially important in shaping teenage student culture. Though, as we shall see, new technologies have opened up other times and forms of interaction.

To say that the main structural features of high schools are roughly the same is not to say that nothing has changed. In earlier periods such things as the telephone and the automobile certainly had an effect on teenage culture—even though the basic structure of schools did not change. The same can probably be said about the introduction of radio, movies, and TV programs aimed at teenagers. So there have been significant changes in the past, even if the basic organization of secondary education was largely the same.

WHAT'S NEW

A ubiquitous "digital culture" has emerged, rife with cell phones, digital tablets, and social media sites. These are typically linked via the Internet. This has produced significant social and cultural changes in schools and in the broader society. One of these, "Enterprise Systems," has affected many adults. These typically measure performance quantitatively. For example they may record how many key strokes a data entry clerk makes, the number of shipments a warehouse employee completes, how frequently a person buys a given item at the supermarket, or the number of "billable hours" generated by a member of a law firm—and how each of these vary for different times of the year and times of the day. Stated another way the micro minute-by-minute actions of people have become more visible via such systems.

Such quantification is not limited to the adult work setting, but has also affected schools. The increased reliance on standardized tests, usually linked to "core curricula" or "a common core" or "standards of learning" (SOLs), has affected high schools in a number of ways. Vocal proponents and opponents debate the benefits and costs of such changes. Evidence can be mounted for either side of this question.

More testing is by no means the only way this digital culture has affected schools. It has also impacted the informal peer culture and interpersonal ties between students. While student cliques or friendship circles are still important, the nature of these relationships has changed in some significant ways. There are, for example, larger social networks and there is less talk in general, more talk about grades, more gossip, less dating, less romance, about the same amount of sex, but a more carnal or profane ambiance.

The first edition of this book emphasized the important link between high school status systems and consumer society. High schools were a key place where young people "learned to consume." Occurring at a stage of life when core personal and social identities were being formed, an acquisitive consumerism became part of young people's taken-for-granted assumptions about what was "normal." This is now less the case. The "obsession" with fashions and owning the latest has lessened, though it has certainly not disappeared. I suggest explanations for why this has occurred.

The new concluding chapter will explore both the possible sources and the consequences of these changes. In order to appreciate change, there must be a baseline, a picture of how things were in the past. That is the reason I have left most of the chapters of the first edition unchanged except for minor editing to improve clarity.

The exception is chapter one, which deals with what factors help explain why teenagers behave the way they do. Is it because of parenting styles, socioeconomic backgrounds, what happens in schools, or the effect of peers (i.e., who people hang out with)? I have added an addendum to each of the original sections that deals with the research that has occurred in the last fifteen years that is relevant to the effect of that factor. I have also added a new section on the teenage brain—a topic that was nearly nonexistent fifteen years ago, but which has generated much new research and public discussion.

Hopefully the new chapter will provide a useful description of key changes, and at least tentative explanations of why these changes have come about.

Part I

THE PUZZLE AND THE TOOLS

INTRODUCTION

To paraphrase Marx, we must understand that teenage peer groups make their own history, but not under circumstances of their own choosing.

—Jay MacLeod, 1995

A great deal has been written about American teenagers. The first task is to make clear the particular focus of this book.

THE QUESTIONS

I ask two sets of interrelated questions: First, why do American teenagers behave the way they do? Why are many teenagers obsessed with who sits with them at lunch, the brand of clothes they wear, what parties they are invited to, the privacy of their bedrooms, the intrigues of school cliques, who is dating or hooking up with whom, what is the latest popular music? Why have alcohol, drug use, and casual sex become widespread?[1] Why has the status of cheerleaders and football stars declined in many but not all schools? Why do students in some schools rigidly segregate themselves by race and ethnicity and yet get along together reasonably amicably? Even more frequently students from different crowds and cliques shun one another with all the determination of orthodox Brahmans avoiding Untouchables: Why their penchant for caste-like divisions? Why are teenagers frequently mean and even cruel to one another? Why do the girls see one another as more petty and catty than the boys? How does the experience of being a teenager vary for urban, suburban, and small-town settings, for private schools, religious schools, and military academies? These are some of the questions this book asks—and answers. The usual explanations of teenage behavior tend to focus on the importance of hormones, psychological development, parenting styles, and social background characteristics (e.g., class and race). It is my contention that these factors are much less important than is usually assumed. Rather, a clearer understanding of adolescent behavior requires that we focus on the way adults have used schools to organize young people's daily activities, and the teenage status systems that result from this way of structuring their lives.

7

The second set of questions focuses on the connections between teenage culture and the broader society, especially the link between teenage status systems and consumerism. Teenagers have long been preoccupied with the clothes they wear, how they fix their hair, the cars they drive, the latest music, and what constitutes being "cool." Adults have been complaining about teenagers in general and their materialism and consumerism in particular for more than fifty years. Why has little been done to change these patterns of adolescent behavior? Certainly in other societies and in other historical periods in our own society adults have exercised more control and authority over young people. If so many adults are critical of teenage behavior why have they hesitated to exercise more control and authority? Why have the numerous attempts at curriculum revision and school reform had so little impact on these patterns? Why do adults both bemoan the consumerism of teenagers and yet do many things to encourage it? The answer to this second set of questions has relatively little to do with family values, liberalism, or progressive education. Rather, it has to do with the benefits that adults, especially parents and businesses, gain from the present way of organizing young people's lives.

SOME HEADLINES

The full answers to these questions require an extended description and analysis of the way adolescents behave and the nature of the social world in which they live. But let me give some telegraphic hints about where we are headed.

A teenager's status in the eyes of his or her peers is extremely important to most adolescents. Why this near obsession with status? It is because they have so little real economic or political power. They must attend school for most of the day and they have only very limited influence on what happens there. They are pressured to learn complex and esoteric knowledge like algebra, chemistry, and European history, which rarely has immediate relevance to their day-to-day lives. They do, however, have one crucial kind of power: the power to create an informal social world in which they evaluate one another. That is, they can and do create their own status systems—usually based on criteria that are quite different from those promoted by parents or teachers.[2] In short, the main kind of power teenagers have is status power. Predictably, their status in the eyes of their peers becomes very important in their day-to-day lives.

But why do their status concerns seem so obsessive, superficial, and often mean-spirited? The answer has to do with the nature and sources of status. Let me give three examples of characteristic behaviors and briefly explain why they occur.

DATING AND EATING

A teenage girl from northern Virginia says, "Another huge part of association ... is dating, the importance of which cannot be overstated." She continues: "Where and with whom one ate was [also] a huge decision to make,
particularly during one's freshman year [when] status roles were so uncertain. The cafeteria was a decent place to eat if one was eating with 'cool'
people, as everyone could see you, ... but if one was eating alone or with
those who were not deemed 'cool,' then eating outside or some other place
not so in view was preferable ... Eating maintains its importance throughout
[the] high school years ..."[3]

Why are adolescents so concerned about who "goes out with" whom and who
eats with whom? It is because they intuitively know that who you associate with
intimately has a big effect on your status. In all societies food and sexuality are
key symbols of intimacy. Where status is important, people try to avoid eating
with or marrying inferiors—as executive dining rooms, upper-middle-class
dinner parties, debutante balls, and the marriage and eating restrictions of the
Indian caste system all indicate. In contrast, if the occasion is purely instrumental, status concerns are much less important: The beautiful cheerleader
can work with a bright nerd on a class project, the Brahman can supervise
Untouchables working in the field, the company president can spend all day
in a meeting with subordinates and even share a "working lunch"—but when
work is done, they go their separate ways.

CLOTHES AND FASHIONS

A New Jersey girl comments, "Clothes during high school were extremely
important. Clothes measured how much money a person had, and how well
that person could keep up with the ever-changing fashion world. It was
always important to know brand name clothes if you were popular."[4]

Why are the latest fashions so important to teenagers? To gain status in any
group you have to conform to their norms. But this means that insiders, and
especially those with high status, have an interest in making conformity difficult for outsiders. Hence, they frequently elaborated and complicated the
norms. The elaborate social rituals and dress styles of aristocracies and upper
classes are obvious examples. In pre-modern societies, copying your social
superiors was often forbidden. Woe to the commoner who tried to dress like a
king or the Untouchable who donned the sacred thread of the Brahman. But
in contemporary societies most formal constraints on copying superiors have
been removed. Hence those at the top must constantly change and complicate the norms. Among teenagers this results in rapidly changing fashions in

clothes, music, and the "in" words and phrases. This obsessive concern to have "the latest" is not adolescent irrationality, but a very reasonable response to the power structure within which they must live.

PUT-DOWNS AND MEANNESS

> A male from a small Texas town says, "The ... gossip was either bashing some jerky guy, someone of the lower economic status, or even back stabbing one of their own ..." Another school 1500 miles away: Robert, the only Latino in the group, becomes the ... target. "First [Kate] asked him [in a snide voice] if they had chairs in Mexico, and then she made a similar comment concerning pizza. Robert shrugged off the chair comment, but when Kate brought up the pizza comment he seemed irritated."[5]

Why are teenagers frequently mean and petty toward one another? It is because status is relatively inexpansible. If everyone receives A's or has a cell phone, these have little value as status symbols. Because status is relatively inexpansible, if someone moves up, someone else will have to move down. But the reverse is also true; you can move up or stay on top by putting others down. Hence when adolescents are placed in a situation where they have little real economic or political power, and where they can only divide up an inexpansible resource like status, it is not surprising that "put-downs" and "small cruelties" are all too common.

As we shall see these three telegraphic explanations are based on a systematic theory of status relations. This will help to understand a much wider array of teenage behavior, as well as consider each of these examples in more detail later.

EDUCATIONAL REFORM

> Unfortunately, too many current school reform efforts are beside the point. They are often based on a fundamental misrecognition of the realities both of schools and teachers' lives, and even more damaging on an ignorance of the daily realities of the children who come to these schools (Michael W. Apple).[6]

Why is it so hard to change things? If both teenagers and adults often express dissatisfaction with many aspects of adolescent life—and they have done so for many years—why does little change? The matter is, of course, complex, but the basic answer is relatively simple. The patterns of behavior characteristic of teenagers result from segregating young people into schools until they are at least seventeen or eighteen and greatly limiting the kind of power they have. Adults and most young people like this age-based form of segregation. Young people are less subject to the supervision of their parents. Parents have the time and energy to do other things with their lives. Competition in the full-time job market is reduced. The direct cost to businesses of training employees is lowered. Students also form a large pool of part-time laborers that can be hired at low wages, with no benefits or job security; moreover, they spend nearly all of their money on immediate consumption items. Certainly, extended schooling and the related social arrangements provide important benefits, and hence they are not easily changed. But they also create the structural basis for an oppositional youth culture that many adults find offensive. The conclusion to be drawn is not that nothing can be done to address the complaints of both adults and youth. It does mean that reforming the curriculum and teaching techniques—however much these may be needed—will not change the structures that produce and sustain the patterns of behavior we associate with teenagers. This is the case for well-to-do students in good schools; it is even truer for young people from disadvantaged neighborhoods and families.

CONSUMERISM

> A girl from an East Coast high school: "Clothes are not used as an important status distinguisher because many groups wear expensive clothes …"[7]

> Proms are not what they used to be. The prom has gradually moved from the high school gym to the luxury hotel. Many students now rent limousines or expensive luxury cars (e.g., BMWs, Porsches, or Range Rovers) to go to the prom … Proms epitomize the expansion of a distinct youth consumer culture and the spending power of youth … [T]he process of being schooled can no longer be separated from commodity culture … Buying french fries from McDonald's to eat during study hall, drinking Diet Coke bought from the soda machine, or listening to music on a CD Walkman on the way to class … [C]onsumerism has become part of the everyday dynamics of school life … [8]

As the first quotation above indicates, in some schools expensive clothes are so much the norm that the cost of clothing is not what differentiates many of the peer groups. Of course, clothes and their cost are important in some schools, but the more general point is that consumerism in high schools is not only about clothes, but also a broader array of expensive items, such as the limousine to go to the prom or the hotel suite that is rented for the all-night party afterward, or where you will fly to for spring break.

The effect of consumerism is a two-way street. Teenagers are targeted as an important market by businesses and are strongly influenced by consumerism and commercialization. On the other hand, the success of many businesses can hinge upon whether they can predict the fashions that will appeal to teenagers— who are often style setters for those who are both younger and older.

The links between the organization of secondary education, the resulting youth culture, and American consumerism are not trivial or secondary matters. These are key features of American consumer capitalism. By consumer capitalism I mean simply the kind of societies characteristic of the contemporary U.S. and most developed countries. The term "consumer capitalism" is not pejorative, any more than terms such as "industrial capitalism," or "merchant capitalism." Rather the phrase distinguishes the particular type of society in which we live at the beginning of the twenty-first century. One implication of this phrase is that while innovative and efficient production is still important, much of the energy of businesses and the government is focused on stimulating consumption.

Our secondary schools are one of the important mechanisms for accomplishing this. Perhaps the thing that American secondary education teaches most effectively is a desire to consume. This is not primarily accomplished via the formal curriculum, but through the status concerns and peer groups that intensify during adolescence. The teenage preoccupation with status and status symbols creates inclinations and perspectives essential to contemporary consumer capitalism. We cannot adequately understand the contemporary world of high school teenagers apart from the context of consumer capitalism. Conversely, we cannot understand the dynamics of twenty-first-century American capitalism if we do not see the important role that secondary school status systems play in stimulating consumer demand.

In Max Weber's famous essay, *The Protestant Ethic and the Spirit of Capitalism*, he argues that the Calvinist version of seventeenth-century Protestantism played a vital part in providing the impetus and legitimation for the development of early bourgeois capitalism. He does not claim that this is the cause of capitalism or even a logically necessary condition. The Protestant ethic happened to be an available ideological and moral framework, which encouraged hard work and saving. This greatly contributed to the particular form of capitalism that emerged in Europe. My argument, though narrower in scope, is similar: The status systems of high schools were and are an important contributing factor to the creation and maintenance of consumer capitalism.

WHAT'S NEW?

Many books and articles describe and attempt to explain teenage behavior. Some of these emphasize status concerns and peer relationships. What is new here, however, is the description and organization of these patterns in terms of a general theory of status relationships. This enables us to see the sources of a wide array of adolescent behaviors, their interrelationship with one another, and how these processes are not unique to teenagers, but also shape behavior in quite different historical and cultural settings. But what insights do the theory of status relations offer that are not already available in existing theoretical frameworks? The answer is twofold. First, most existing theories point to and describe the differences between types of social formations, such as political parties, social classes, and status groups. Previous theories do not, however, provide systematic explanations of why these are different from one another; that is, why a particular kind of social formation has the one set of attributes and another has other characteristics. For example, why are the details of behavior different in status groups than classes? Second, existing theories of status groups do not indicate why status differences are very important in some contexts, but not in others. Why are these concerns so intense during the teenage years and less important before and after this? Why are some adolescent next-door neighbors perfectly pleasant to one another in their homes, but act as if they do not know each other at school? Why can preps and punks work together on a class assignment, but shun each other in the halls and lunchroom? In short, my theory specifies more clearly than previous frameworks the details and dynamics of status systems. (The differences between the theory of status relations and other theories are discussed in more detail in Appendix I.) One important result of my approach is that behavior of teenagers comes to be seen not as the result of immaturity or poor parenting and teaching, but rather quite reasonable behavior—given the social context they have been provided by adults.

A second contribution is to more clearly explain the links between youth culture and consumerism. This link has been pointed to many times before.[9] What is new here is that the theory of status relationships helps us see why adolescents are so susceptible to the siren call of consumerism. These susceptibilities are not primarily due to the manipulative attempts of marketers or the biases of the mass media because of their dependence on advertising—though these certainly exist and should be of acute concern. Neither does the teenage attachment to fashion and consumption result primarily from poor schools, bad parents, and ineffective teachers. Rather, the main roots of this connection are in the way that adults organize good schools, strong and stable families, and a robust economy. What is "wrong" with our teenagers is not due primarily to our failures, but rather to our supposed successes.

WARNING LABELS

Even when products are reliable and effective, they have known limitations and dangers that should be made public. The same is true for social research, and so I will sketch out some of the biases and limitations of this particular analysis.

Theories, like most tools, are useful, but potentially dangerous. All theories focus on some features of the concrete world and ignore others; they enable you to see important processes that are obscured if you try to look at everything. This selectivity is their virtue and their limitation. In addition, particular theories have particular biases. This book will focus on status relations and status processes. This means many aspects of high school life will be neglected or played down. Certainly students' experiences in high school are not solely about competing for status. Most students develop important friendships that give them both social support and emotional gratification. Many are frequently caring and thoughtful toward one another. Substantial numbers of teenagers are good citizens in their schools and their communities—volunteering to participate in a wide array of service activities. Most actually learn things from their classes and books. My goal is not to portray the full complexity of high school life. It is to highlight an aspect of behavior especially characteristic of teenagers and explain why these patterns of behavior emerge and are so salient in this context. To document widespread drug use is not to say that everyone uses drugs, or that all users are addicts. Likewise, to describe and explain the status processes that shape teenage behavior is not to capture the totality of teenage experience. Describing and explaining status processes is, however, a crucial prerequisite for understanding teenage behavior, and the significance of this behavior in the wider society.

Similarly when I describe adult behaviors and motivations, I will be drawing a selective portrait of American society. My story will draw attention to the centrality in adult life of earning income in the labor market and acquiring consumer commodities. Certainly making money and the mindless pursuit of the latest "hot" consumer products is not the sum total of most people's lives. Nonetheless the problems in contemporary schools cannot be understood without taking into account the prevalence of these kinds of behavior in consumer capitalism.

Social scientists draw the distinction between micro and macro analyses. Having or not having a job is an individual-level, micro characteristic; the percentages of blacks or whites unemployed are collective-level, macro characteristics. Why a particular student becomes obsessed with the latest fashions and another does not is a micro question. Why fashions are important to American teenagers is a macro question. My analysis focuses more on macro questions, though there is no absolute line between these.

Both the analysis and the data pay special attention to the middle-class adolescents and to the professional and managerial class of adults. This is deliberate. I have three reasons for this focus. First, students in poor schools or from disadvantaged backgrounds are already well represented in ethnographic and qualitative work.[10] Second, there is some evidence that even though lower-class students have fewer resources, they are even more oriented to consumption than those who are better off. Hence, a focus on middle-class students probably understates rather than exaggerates the connection between status concerns and consumption.[11]

Third, and most important, major changes in American education are likely to come about only if middle-class parents see that the "good schools" in "good neighborhoods" have problems that require a substantial restructuring of secondary education. My data and analysis are not limited to middle-class students, but they are front and center in this account.

Other approaches that could be used to analyze teenagers, as well as more details about the limits of this study are discussed in Appendix I. To state these various restrictions and boundaries on what I will discuss is not to say that this is a narrow technical study; it is to acknowledge that even studies of broad scope necessarily leave out much of the complexity of social life.

CHAPTER ONE

Why Do They Behave Like That?

[W]hat children learn derives as much from the nature of their experiences in the school setting as from what they are taught.

—**Robert Dreeben, 1967**

FROM THE LUNCHROOM: Donald said something [derogatory] about one of the boys at [another] table ... Tina immediately jumped up and told the boy ... The boy charged over and insulted Donald calling him a "fag" and other [names] ... Donald did not say anything to him except "Shut up" and "Go away." But as soon as the boy left Donald began to bad mouth the boy. He said he was a child molester because he was dating a freshman and he was eighteen. The boy continued to talk about Donald at his table. Tina made a point of relaying the messages back and forth.

Throughout the entire first half, most everyone [ignored] the [football] game. The girls and guys were flirting with each other ... [T]he announcer constantly would tell the crowd to yell ... On one occasion, the group started ... singing songs. The first song was "Apples and Bananas," an elementary school song that ... teaches kids the vowels. [Then] a girl sang a vulgar song that the whole group started to sing. "Hey Hey, Ho Ho, this penis party's gotta go!" They all thought this was very funny ... [1]

What factors shape teenage behavior? Many of the things people assume are important in influencing young people's behavior—parenting, social class, and schools—have only a limited impact. A key factor that often gets less attention is the organization of peer relationships—and this is often crucial to understanding why teenagers act the way they do.

ARE PARENTS IMPORTANT?

To ask whether parents are important seems impertinent. Obviously they are essential. Parents have primary responsibility for directing the lives of their children, even their adolescents. Most people think their parents shaped their lives. Some have had years of psychotherapy to supposedly overcome the poor parenting they received. Most parents believe that their child-rearing will play a crucial role in shaping their offspring. A long line of research starting with the famous 1966 "Coleman Report" on *Equality of Educational Opportunity* argues that family background is a stronger determinant of educational attainment than most other things. Therefore if we are dissatisfied with how adolescents behave, perhaps parents are at fault. The conventional wisdom advocates stronger "family values," more "authoritative parenting," and spending more time with our children. In contrast, an influential and controversial book argues that the impact of parents on children is much less than we think. Judith Harris's *The Nurture Assumption: Why Children Turn Out the Way They Do* draws on the scholarly literature from developmental psychology, behavioral genetics, ethology, and anthropology. The book points to extensive evidence that the way parents raise their children has much less effect on their personalities and later behavior than is normally assumed. The genes children inherit make a difference, but child-rearing practices have a very weak effect on how children turn out. For example, there is *no* measurable correlation between the personality of adopted children and their parents. On the other hand, children's playmates and the crowds they identify with are very important in shaping how they turn out. As one reviewer says, "This book has a second subtitle: 'Parents Matter Less Than You Think and Peers Matter More.'"[2] As Harris notes, the strong effect of social environment and the relatively weak effect of parents is seen in the children of immigrants. Their language, their values, their tastes, their understanding of the world are often much closer to the social environment in which they grow up than they are to those of their parents. According to Harris, parents do play an important role in certain aspects of early childhood development, but beyond this point parenting styles seem to have little to do with how children turn out.[3] Consequently, poor parenting is unlikely to be the main source of most of the teenage behavior that adults tend to find objectionable.

The notion that correct parenting would produce good teenagers is made even more questionable by Ann Hulbert's *Raising America* (Hulbert 2003).[4] The book recounts the history of what experts from G. Stanley Hall to Benjamin Spock to recent successors have advised parents about how to raise children. She finds that the experts have differed and do differ greatly on what they recommend and that often this advice is at best loosely connected to substantiated research findings.[5] Even if parenting styles do have a big impact on how teenagers behave we have little evidence that there is clearly one correct way to produce the outcome that parents intend.

As we shall see, parents may contribute to some of the outcomes they bemoan, but in ways that are much more indirect than child-rearing techniques.

Fifteen years later: First a word about what I mean by the effect of parenting. Clearly parents have an effect on their children in a variety of ways: the parents' education, occupation, income, where they locate the family, how attentive they are to their children's school activities—and numerous other ways. Here, however, I am referring to a narrower range of effects that focus on parenting styles or approaches. Often these variations are summarized as authoritarian, indulgent, neglectful, and authoritative (Steinberg et al. 2006). There is evidence that authoritative parenting is generally the most effective style. It combines affection and sensitivity to the children's desires with firm guidelines and expectations—and the consistent enforcement of these.

There continues to be research attempting to relate parenting behavior to their children's outcome. These studies look at a variety of concerns: juvenile delinquency (Chung et al. 2011; Steinberg et al. 2006), eating habits (Savage et al. 2007), whether young people exercise (Trost et al. 2003; Anderssen et al. 2006). Clearly styles of parenting and the models they provide for their children are important at the extremes: abusive or neglectful parents can severely reduce the chances that their children become mature, happy people. It certainly seems to be the case that authoritative and even authoritarian parenting is more effective than indulgent or neglectful parenting in preventing delinquent behavior (Steinberg et al. 2006). But for an array of other outcomes the impact of parents' behaviors is more mixed and modest.[6]

As noted above Hulbert's history of child-rearing in America shows there has been wide variability in what was considered the proper way to raise children. David Lancy's *The Anthropology of Childhood* (2008) is even more nonchalant about what constitutes good parenting. He surveys the great variety of ways that different cultures raise their children and concludes that in most cases children turn out just fine—at least in the eyes of that culture. This is not to say that the techniques in one culture will work in another, but rather that there is no one correct way to turn out adolescents who avoid becoming criminals and turn into responsible, competent adults.

None of this is to suggest that parents are not important, but the variations in the different styles of parenting often have a weaker effect on how adolescents behave than conventional wisdom assumes.

ARE BRAINS IMPORTANT?

Fifteen years later: This question seems even more bizarre than asking whether parents are important; brains are obviously necessary to survival and flourishing. I ask the question because since the first edition of this book there has been a significant amount of research showing that brains mature much later than was previously thought. Much of this research has been possible because of new techniques of imaging the brain and its processes, especially more sophisticated forms of magnetic resonance imaging (MRI).

This research has been widely discussed in the popular press, drawing varying and sometimes questionable implications for what this means for parenting, schools, and public policy.[7] For the most part the research literature behind this discussion is more tentative and guarded, both in its findings and their implications.[8] For example, it is still ambiguous how much of risk taking is due to immature brains versus other factors such as opportunity. By several measures risk taking is not greatest among teenagers, but young adults of college age who have more mature brains (Willoughby et al. 2013). There are even more radical skeptics who see much of this research as largely another way to negatively stigmatize adolescents—and as failing to adequately deal with the effects of socioeconomic factors (e.g., Males 2009). Other researchers (Johnson et al. 2010 and Shulman et al. 2013) have presented strong rebuttals to such scepticism.

Lawrence Steinberg (2008), a social psychologist and a recognized expert on adolescent development, argues that there is strong evidence that two and perhaps three forms of brain maturation are a source of increased risk taking during adolescence. This is complicated, however, because there are also biologically based reasons that adolescents become much more sensitive to peer pressure and to socio-emotional situations. So while there are good reasons to think that teens' risk taking is related to a stage of brain development, the proclivity to risk taking varies by individuals, the presence of peers, and the nature of the social situation.

Generally, leading brain researchers such as Johnson et al. (2009: 216) warn that we must be cautious about translating images of the brain into "objective truth" and correlations into causal effects.

They continue:

Neuroimaging technologies have made more information available about the structure and function of the human brain than ever before. Nonetheless, there is still a dearth of empirical evidence that allows us to anticipate behavior in the real world based on performance in the scanner. Linking brain scans to real-world functioning is hampered by the complex integration of brain networks involved in behavior and cognition. Further hindering extrapolation from the laboratory to the real world is the fact that it is virtually impossible to parse the role of the brain from other biological systems and contexts that shape human behavior. Behavior in adolescence, and across the lifespan, is a function of multiple interactive influences including experience, parenting, socioeconomic status, individual agency and self-efficacy, nutrition, culture, psychological well-being, the physical and built environments, and social relationships and interactions. When it comes to behavior, the relationships among these variables are complex, and they change over time and with development. This causal complexity overwhelms many of our "one factor at a time" explanatory and analytic models and highlights the need to continually situate research from brain science in the broader context of interdisciplinary developmental science to advance our understandings of behavior across the lifespan (Johnson et al. 2009: 216).

Other researchers (e.g., Segalowitz et al. 2010) provide similar warnings.

It does seem clear that across cultures and historical periods, adolescents are more likely to seek novelty, engage in risky behavior, and be influenced by peers. But constants cannot explain variations—and there are significant, even enormous, variations in how different cultures handle immaturity and these related inclinations. Some societies spend enormous resources in the form of advertising, marketing, and media coverage of fashions, encouraging adolescents to be concerned about novelty and "the latest"; others try to repress this. Some societies rigidly segregate by gender and encourage early marriages to avoid premarital sexual activity that risks pregnancy; others are relatively nonchalant about adolescent sexuality and premarital pregnancy. Some societies expect adolescents to be "young braves"; these societies often see their relative insensitivity to risks as a personal virtue and military resource. Other cultures send adolescents off to monasteries for both protection and discipline. Some societies increase adult authority and restrict peer influence as in the case of guild-based master–apprentice systems; others require adolescents to attend schools where they spend most of their time with age peers supervised by a relatively small number of teachers. My own research on Indian teenagers (Milner 2013) shows that there are not only very significant differences in the behavior of contemporary American and Indian teenagers, but there are significant culturally based differences within India. Variations in brain maturity are relatively irrelevant to understanding this array of differences.

In addition to the significant variations in how cultures handle biologically based inclinations, it is important to keep in mind that the behavior of others toward adolescents also shapes brain development. In sum, while it is certainly a mistake to be dismissive of the new scientific findings about brain development, it is also a mistake to think that MRIs of adolescent brains or the physiological immaturity that they have pointed to are sufficient to explain teen behavior.

IS SOCIAL CLASS IMPORTANT?

Perhaps what is wrong with young people is simply a reflection of the class structure of the society and discrimination against minority groups. Poor kids come to school ill-prepared and are soon alienated by their academic failures and their prospects for the future. Richer kids are indulged and become self-centered and narcissistic. (Obviously racial and ethnic minorities are disproportionately represented in the first category.) Several lines of social research emphasize this theme, including what is called "reproduction theory." According to this perspective, the availability of equal opportunity is greatly exaggerated; the basic structure of capitalist societies and the positions of the privileged (and underprivileged) tend to be reproduced across time by cultural as well as economic processes. Pierre Bourdieu, probably the best-known French sociologist of his generation, provided the dominant framework for this type of analysis.[9] Bourdieu's own empirical work centers on how those at the top maintain their privileges. I will, however, discuss two influential studies in this tradition that specifically analyze lower-class teenagers and stress the cultural basis of the reproduction of inequality.[10]

In his highly influential *Learning to Labour*, sociologist Paul Willis studied a group of British adolescents in the 1970s, referred to as "the lads."[11] They had rejected the norms of their school because they "penetrated," that is, saw through, the conventional ideology and recognized that what they learned in school was largely irrelevant to what they would wind up doing. The supposed career choices that were held out to them by counselors and teachers all amounted to the same thing: low paid unskilled labor that offered little or no chance for upward mobility. Willis sees their anti-school subculture as a creative response that at least gives them a sense of social support and a bit of fun. Yet, at the same time, this further undermines their educational and occupational prospects and places what he calls "limitations" on their ability to transform their deviance into politically relevant action. While Willis attempted to avoid a Marxian economic determinism by his emphasis on the cultural creativity of "the lads," he nonetheless stressed how industrial technology had largely eliminated relevant differences in skill. In the Marxian terminology he draws upon, the "concrete labor," which had been characteristic of a particular type of production, had been replaced by "abstract labor." Abstract labor was largely interchangeable from one industry or job to another, was more boring and alienating to the workers, and made them more vulnerable to declines in the economy. A combination of these techno-economic factors, and "the lads" creative but self-defeating cultural responses to these realities, perpetuates, that is "reproduces," their subordination and supposedly that of much of the British working class.

In his widely cited book *Ain't No Makin' It*, Jay MacLeod studied two groups of U.S. teenage boys in the same housing project.[12] "The brothers," who are black, believe they can "make it" through education and hard work. "The hallway hangers," who are white, reject the relevance of school and claim there "ain't no makin' it." The latter group is racist, sexist, and frequently in trouble with school officials and the police. In his follow-up study eight years later, he finds that most of the hallway hangers regret many of their past behaviors and have few prospects for the future; similarly many of the broth-ers have found that their confidence in the achievement ideology has not paid off nearly as much as they had hoped. At the core of MacLeod's analysis is an attempt to capture the interplay between what social scientists refer to as "structure" and "agency." People's actions are limited by the structure of their social situation, but they are also active agents, selectively drawing on cultural resources to, in part, shape their futures. There is "cultural autonomy within structural constraints." He concludes, "How poor youths react to an objective situation that is weighted heavily against them depends on a number of medi-ating factors and ultimately is contingent."[13] That is, he seems to be saying that the odds are stacked against such young people, but no one knows why some are able to overcome the odds and others are not.[14]

Most analysts in the reproduction tradition are interested in increasing equality and opportunity. However insightful these studies, they have two cru-cial limitations. The first limitation is the implicit assumption that the primary goal should be equal opportunity.[15] The whole notion of the reproduction of inequalities from one generation to the next implies that if the children of the poor had the same opportunities as the children of the rich, all would be right with the world.[16] *I reject this assumption.* Even if there were complete equality of opportunity—if the power and rewards of adults were unrelated to their social origins and based solely on merit—inequality could still be a serious social problem. Even in a complete meritocracy the extent of inequality—that is, the distance between the top and the bottom—is important. Families do not reward their children solely or even primarily on the basis of performance and merit. In most developed societies those who make the highest grades do not get more food and better clothes, or even a significantly bigger allowance. This is because most parents know that this would have a very negative impact on relationships between siblings and between parents and children. Societies are not families, but the extent of inequality is an important issue affecting many aspects of a society's life—even if everyone initially had an equal chance to be rich or poor. I am not advocating some kind of complete egalitarianism, but I do want to stress that the reproduction of inequality across generations (i.e., inequality of opportunity) is only one aspect of social inequality.

The second limitation of many studies in the reproduction tradition, including Willis and MacLeod, is that they focus on a question that, polit-ically speaking, is of secondary importance.[17] They try to find out why the working classes and disadvantaged are either politically passive or supportive to the basic structure and ideology of advanced capitalism. The assumption is that the political mobilization of the disadvantaged is the crucial prerequi-site to change. In contrast, I believe that if we want to understand the ongoing legitimacy of advanced capitalist societies we need to focus primarily, not on the disadvantaged, but on the broad middle classes. It is their support that

is crucial. Protests during the 1960s were powerful not because they mobilized the poor, but because they mobilized the youth of the middle classes
and many of their parents. Middle-class women were the key actors in the
feminist movements. Even the Civil Rights movement was highly dependent on the black middle classes. The animal rights and anti-war movements
are overwhelmingly made up of members of the middle classes. While the
stories of how privileges of the upper classes and disadvantages of the lower
classes are reproduced are important to understand, they are secondary to the
politics of consumer societies. The crucial story is what the middle classes
support and why.

So while differences in social class, race, and ethnicity certainly affect what
goes on in our high schools, and our society in general, the most important
story is *not what disadvantaged students* fail *to learn, but what most students do
learn*.[18] Obviously high school students pick up some of the information that is
imparted through the formal curriculum. Many also develop certain levels of
discipline and an ability to cope with boredom and bureaucracy—things that,
in Paul Willis's terms, will help them "learn to labor."[19]

Fifteen years later: In the first edition of this book I claimed that a primary
feature in American high schools was *learning to consume*. Students from the
broad middle classes are an especially important part of this story because it
is the purchasing power and political support (or resistance) of these students
and their families that most shape educational and social policy. High schools
still play a role in inculcating young people with assumptions, motivations, and
norms needed for a consumer society. This is the theme that is highlighted in
chapters eight and nine. The data collected in our later study, however, suggests that the significance of high school peer culture for sustaining a consumer
society has declined.

In my discussion of the effect of social class on education in the first
edition I concluded, "Social class is important. Nonetheless, concentrating
exclusively on how the social background of students affects their academic
performance (and supposedly their later occupational attainment) misses an
even bigger story about the nature of education and consumerism in contemporary America." I still believe that this is the case—but less so.

There is increasing evidence that class background and the tendency to
reproduce inequality across generations have not improved and may have even
become stronger in the last fifteen years. As one study says,

> Both cross-country comparisons and the underlying trends suggest that
> these drivers [i.e., the interaction between families, labor markets, and
> public policies] are all configured most likely to lower, or at least not raise,
> the degree of intergenerational earnings mobility for the next generation of
> Americans coming of age in a more polarized labor market (Corak 2013).

Another elaborate study shows that 42 percent of those born into the lowest fifth of the income distribution are likely to end up there and only 6 percent of them are likely to wind up in the highest fifth of the income distribution. In contrast, 39 percent of those born into the top fifth are likely to remain there (Isaacs 2007). Census Bureau data indicates, and it is widely acknowledged by most scholars, that the distribution of income has become more unequal and that it is those at the top that have most benefited and those at the bottom *and the middle* have become relatively worse off. There is also increasing evidence that the gap between the academic skills of those from lower and higher socio-economic backgrounds has increased.[20] The intergenerational transmission of poverty, however, is a complex issue. As Susan Mayer points out, "It is impossible to reduce the future poverty rate appreciably by correcting the behavior of current parents because most children who will grow up to be poor do not live in poor dysfunctional families" (Mayer 2010: 26). In sum, while the significance of social class background on opportunity can be overemphasized, there is little reason to think that equality of opportunity has increased and at least some evidence that it has declined.

Both the decline in teens' relevance to consumerism and the significance of social class differences will be discussed in chapter eleven.

ARE SCHOOLS IMPORTANT?

If parents, brains, and social class are not the primary determinants of how teenagers behave, maybe the problem is with our schools. A common perception is that our schools are doing a poor job in educating many of our young people. Why are our schools failing us? Schools are in some respects like factories, good at taking uniform raw materials and turning out a standardized product.[21] But when the quality of the input becomes highly variable and the number of products that are produced becomes manifold, the routinized procedures of factories are more problematic. In part, this is what has happened to our schools. A larger and larger percentage of young people are attending school for longer and longer periods. The educational system as a whole has become less selective. In most respects this is very good news. Stated positively, education has been significantly democratized over the last hundred years, at least with respect to the time young people spend in classrooms. Yet, as with any manufacturing process, the more raw material processed and the more variable the characteristics of that raw material, the more difficult it is to maintain the uniformity and quality of the output. The education system is required to process more students for longer and to affect many more dimensions of their life: computer literacy, driver education, drug prevention, sex education, multicultural perspectives, bilingual education, morals and values—just to mention some obvious examples of expanded responsibilities. Yet, during the same period that responsibilities have been expanding, our society has shifted public spending from the young to the old.[22] The techniques of social control that are available to school authorities have also become more restricted and exercising authority is more problematic. In most schools the paddle and the strap are gone and expelling students requires complicated and time-consuming processes. There are many positive things about such changes, but they also have their costs. If the factory model is no longer working well, how else might we organize our schools? One answer has been to make them like shopping malls.[23]

Obviously, a crucial difference between a factory and a school is the nature of the raw material. Wood, coal, and ore have no "mind of their own"; they do not actively resist being transformed; students often do. Consequently, if the mix of students admitted to school is more variable, and if the content of the education remains the same for everyone, we can predict with confidence that resistance will increase. Since coercive means of suppressing resistance have been banned or significantly restricted, schools have had to find other remedies for maintaining order. In part, they have done this by expanding the variety of options available to students—attempting to have something of interest for everyone. If schools have similarities with factories, increasingly they also resemble shopping malls. This was the thesis of Arthur G. Powell and his colleagues in an influential book entitled *The Shopping Mall High School*.[24] Modern high schools have significantly increased in size (though these trends are complex) and in the array of courses and services they provide.[25] In addition to the wide array of course offerings,[26] a great variety of non-academic activities are available: sports teams, computer clubs, debate teams, drama, dance and singing groups, drill teams, cheerleading, editing school newspapers and yearbooks—and more. The service curriculum includes counselors who advise about course selection and college admissions, and nurses who provide medical services. Special programs are offered for students who are pregnant, have young children, are abused by parents, or are addicted to drugs—to mention only a few of the services offered. Because of the wide array of courses, activities, and services offered, "choice" becomes central to adolescents. They must decide what selection and combination of these alternatives will receive their time, and perhaps, their attention. In this respect, the modern high school is often like a shopping mall.[27] Schooling becomes another form of consumption. What Powell refers to as a "treaty" emerges: if students are reasonably orderly and do not cause trouble, they can choose to be engaged in the educational process or to largely ignore it.[28] Those who are intellectually engaged and make wise choices often receive an excellent education. Others mainly kill time. As in the shopping mall, some are real customers and others simply window-shop or hang out.[29]

Given this context, it is hardly surprising that, by both objective and subjective measures, our schools are not performing as well as we think they should.

Whether they are performing worse or better than they have in the past is less clear—because they are doing more and more things for more and more people. The average level of learning, as measured by standardized tests, has not increased very much.[30] Even though the level of violence committed by students in schools has generally decreased since the 1990s, horrific school shootings like those at Columbine High School in Littleton, Colorado, have contributed to the perception that our schools are not only ineffective, but unsafe.[31] The result is that Americans are increasingly dissatisfied with public schools.[32]

But are schools the real source of our dissatisfaction? Three respected scholars of adolescence, Laurence Steinberg, B. Bradford Brown (1990), and Sanford M. Dornbusch jointly conducted extensive research and collaborated on a book entitled *Beyond the Classroom*.[33] They argue that the primary problem is not the schools, but who students are and what they do outside of the formal educational process. Hence, school reform by itself—whether shaped by conservative premises or liberal premises—will not accomplish much. The book is controversial and certainly is not beyond criticism.[34] The following excerpts from their book provide an outline of some of their key arguments:

> Our research indicates that a profitable discussion about the declining achievement of American youngsters should begin by examining students' lives outside of school[35] … School reform is not doomed to failure, but … changes in other facets of students' lives must occur before school reform is to yield any major benefits … The discussion has focused on schools, when it should have focused on students[36] … What has changed in the past three decades—the period during which our achievement problem became most severe—has not been our schools, but our students' lives outside of school[37] …

Also important are the way time is allocated and the non-academic aspects of school life:

> The most time-consuming activity is "hanging out" with friends. A close runner-up for many is working at a part-time job[38] … It is clear that for a large proportion of students school is little more than a place to congregate with friends. Within the context of this marvelous party, classes are annoyances to be endured, just so many interruptions in the course of a busy day of socializing[39] … American youngsters spend far more time than students in other countries on non-academic activities—such as part-time work, extracurricular activities, and socializing with friends—and far less time on school-related affairs such as homework, studying, and reading. The ultimate source of our achievement problem may be how students spend their time out of school.[40]

Moreover, peers are perhaps the most important factor affecting school performance:

> Our research indicates that peers shape student achievement patterns in profound ways, and that in many respects friends are more powerful influences than family members are. For a large number of adolescents, peers—not parents—are the chief determinant of how intensely they are invested in school and how much effort they devote to their education[41] ... How does [good parenting] stack up in comparison to the "power of the peer group"? At least by high school, the influence by friends on school performance and drug use is more substantial than the influence of parents' practices at home. Parents may influence their children's long-term educational plans, but when it comes to day-to-day influences on schooling—whether students attend class, how much time they spend on homework, how hard they try in school, and the grades they bring home—friends are more influential than parents.[42]

Steinberg argues that improving the education of our young people requires a focus not only on how educational authorities organize schools, but on other aspects of young people's lives. This is obvious for students in the inner city who must negotiate the dangers and pressures of "the street,"[43] but it is also true for students who attend effective schools in "good" neighborhoods.[44]

In sum, the usual ways of trying to change the basic patterns of adolescent behavior are not promising. Better parenting styles, compensatory education for those from disadvantaged backgrounds, and reforming schools are likely to have only modest effects on teenage behavior. This conclusion is congruent with sociologist Randall Collins's more general analysis of power. In *The Credential Society* (Collins 1979), Collins argued that significant social power is primarily rooted in the extensiveness of the informal social network one is able to maintain.[45] In his terms, power is rooted in political labor rather than productive labor. (He is using "political" and "productive" in a very broad sense and not restricting politics to the government or productivity to the economy.) Stated in more concrete terms, who you know and how you relate to them is often more important than your technical skill or any objective measure of productivity. Adolescent status groups are often the starting point for learning "political" skills and building social networks.[46] Many teenagers seem to have an intuitive sense of this and accordingly they care more about their friendships than they care about their grades. If this is the case, then perhaps drawing on this insight points to a more promising path.

Fifteen years later: Since the above was written there has been a reaction against the "shopping mall school" in the form of efforts to institute a "core curriculum" or "SOLs" (i.e., standards of learning) that all students would have to master in order to graduate from high school. This has usually been accompanied by various standardized tests that all students would have to pass in order to receive credit for their work. The details of these developments vary from state to state, but clearly there has been a national movement in instituting such changes. Now there is increasing criticism of and resistance to overly demanding and rigid curricula and especially to the frequency of standardized tests and the weight given to these tests in evaluating students, teachers, and schools. This will be discussed at greater length in chapter eleven. The key point is there have been extensive efforts to make schools more academically demanding and effective. Nonetheless recent research seems to indicate that both the orderliness and effectiveness of schools are strongly and even primarily shaped by contextual factors such as the supportiveness of families, the socioeconomic backgrounds of students, and the neighborhoods from which they come. Teachers and school officials have a limited ability to affect the factors that seem to have the strongest impact on academic outcomes. After an elaborate multivariate analysis of the effect of family characteristics, socioeconomic background, and neighborhoods Woolley and Grogan-Kaylor (2006: 103) warn, "that school outcomes are the result of multiple factors from multiple contexts. Thus, schools should not be held solely responsible to effect change. Schools alone are simply not in the position to change many of the significant factors."[47] This is not, of course, to say that we should be indifferent about what happens in schools, but that variations in the quality of schools are in large part due to the nature of the students, families, and communities they serve, and the teachers they attract. Therefore it is naïve to think—and disingenuous to claim—that schools can be the primary means of erasing the long history of gender, racial, and ethnic inequality and the economic inequality that has been increasing since the 1970s.

ARE PEERS IMPORTANT?

If parents, social class, and schools all have less impact than is usually assumed, what shapes teenagers' behavior? Steinberg and Harris both see peers—other teenagers—as playing a very important role. Studies of younger children have also found that peer cultures develop quite early and are an important feature of children's lives. William Corsaro, one of the foremost sociologists of children, emphasizes that we should not study childhood as simply a period of socialization and training—a prelude to adulthood. Rather the social lives of children and adolescents need to be studied in their own right, and their role in the wider society analyzed. Much of children's socialization results from interaction with peers. The peer cultures that emerge are not iron scripts that are simply inherited and determine young people's behavior. Rather, according to Corsaro, children engage in "interpretive reproduction." This involves innovation and individual adaptation, as well as reproduction of what has been socially inherited.[48]

I think the emphasis that Harris, Steinberg, and Corsaro place on young peoples' peer relationships and cultures is especially warranted in the study of adolescents. Adolescents spend more time with each other and less time with adults than younger children do and hence the importance of peer cultures almost certainly increases.[49] In some situations the impact of peers seems to outweigh the impact of family influences, in shaping economic and occupational goals and opportunities.[50] Teenagers themselves clearly think peer relations are crucial. When teenagers phone hotline peer counseling centers, what they most commonly discuss is not family problems, a lack of money, academic stress—or even sex and drugs—but their relationships with other students.[51] In the first edition of this book I claimed that the influence of peers is very important. I did *not* attempt to measure the *relative* impact of peers compared to the effect of parents, socioeconomic class, and schools—and there was very limited research that addressed this question.

Fifteen years later: There has been a body of research that has attempted to quantitatively measure the relative effects of peers on teen behavior. Virtually all of this research has focused on various kinds of "risky" behavior or what, from adults' point of view, is undesirable behavior: binge drinking, use of drugs, early initiation of sexual intercourse, truancy, cigarette smoking, dropping out of school, various forms of delinquency, and the eating of high calorie snacks by overweight youth. Just as it is difficult to measure the impact of parenting and school effects, measuring peer effects is problematic. This is because of the number of relevant factors, the complexity of the causal mechanisms, issues related to measurement and statistical modeling, and the limitations of experiments conducted in relatively artificial contexts. Nonetheless an array of studies—carried out primarily by economists and psychologists—has repeatedly reported significant peer effects accounting for between five and forty-five percent of the variation in risky and undesirable behaviors.[52]

It should be kept in mind, however, that virtually all of this research focuses on behaviors that most parents would consider troubling and problematic—and usually attempt to discourage. It seems reasonable to assume that peer effects might be even stronger for adolescent behaviors that most parents and adults are indifferent to or might consider immature or annoying, but not dangerous: fixing hair in a "strange" way, "weird" nail polish, being "obsessed" with the latest clothing fashions, adopting the latest teen lingo, playing loud "bizarre" music, etc.

There is room for argument about *how* influential peers are, but the argument seems to range from quite important to extremely important. Given that peers are very significant, *my focus is on why and how teenagers organize themselves when they are left more or less to their own devices.* Much of adolescent social life takes place within school facilities, even if it is not part of the formal educational program.[53] Some of this happens outside of school hours. (As we shall see new technologies have probably increased the importance of "outside" activities.) Whether inside or outside of the school proper, teens' behaviors are significantly shaped by their peers.

To help us understand central features of this informal system of peer relationships, I will draw on another metaphor: the Indian caste system.

STATUS GROUPS: ADOLESCENCE AS A CASTE SYSTEM

Status groups: The German sociologist Max Weber used the term *status group*, which he contrasted with notions of class and political party, to refer to social formations that were based on differences in status and lifestyle.[54] According to Weber, the most extreme form of status group was Hindu castes. In traditional India, members of one caste did not usually marry or eat with members of another caste. The higher status castes tended to minimize their contact with lower castes and expected to be treated with deference by those from lower castes. These patterns are common for teenagers. Other status groups such as the Boston Brahmans, the New York Social Register, or a local country club set are less intense forms of this pattern. Still other status groups may be even more amorphous with indistinct boundaries, as much a subculture as a concrete group. Examples include Latinos, Italian-Americans, and wine connoisseurs. Instead of sharing simply a common economic or political location, members of a status group share a common lifestyle, that is, elements of a common culture that may include a common language or religion, shared symbols and rituals, or similar patterns of consumption.[55] Wealth or political power may be a prerequisite, but they are not sufficient. The new multimillionaire who smokes big cigars and brags loudly about his wealth is not likely to be accepted into exclusive upper-class social circles. A teenager may be rich, handsome, and knowledgeable about punk bands, and still be shunned by local punks if he wears khakis, button-down dress shirts, and a "Just Say No" button.[56] Both the new millionaire and the preppy teenager are rejected because they have not adopted the appropriate lifestyle.

Crowds and cliques: I will argue that teenage *crowds* are another example of status groups. Because they are a status group and a subculture, they show an enormous concern with lifestyle and acceptance by peers.[57] Often they engage in behaviors that are highly reminiscent of castes. Crowds are often composed of multiple overlapping cliques. In contrast to crowds, *cliques* are relatively small numbers of individuals who interact with one another regularly.[58] Crowds are a social category, a type of subculture, a reference group, and a status group; cliques are small groups that embody, transmit, and transform such subcultures. Categories that have become broadly established in the wider society are *societal categories*. They are often widely discussed and portrayed in the media. For example, most high schools have few if any skinheads, but most high school students will know that skinheads are stereotypically associated with adolescence, shaved heads, racist attitudes, and aggressive behavior.[59] Sometimes these societal categories are borrowed or adopted to create local social categories and cliques.

When people talk about these matters they sometimes say "crowd" when they mean "clique" and vice versa, but usually the context indicates whether they are referring to a clique or a more amorphous crowd or societal category.[60] For teenagers, acceptance or rejection by peer cliques and crowds—preps, jocks, nerds, etc.—is often perceived to be much more important than academic success. Some become virtually obsessed with social distinctions made by their peers.

In addition to clarifying the nature of the teenage crowds and cliques, let me summarize some of the characteristics and variations in teenage behavior that need to be explained:

1. Why do contemporary teenagers behave in the various ways mentioned in the introduction, including their intense concern with appearance, clothing, music, privacy, gossip, peer relationships (especially who they eat with in the lunchroom and who "goes out with" whom), partying, athletic events, television, etc.?
2. Why do teenagers' behavioral patterns seem quite different from patterns of earlier or later stages of life?
3. Why are contemporary teenagers in many respects quite different from those of earlier historical periods and other societies?
4. Why is this pattern spreading to other societies?
5. Why is the American pattern changing toward greater diversity?
6. Why is the pattern being extended to both younger and older age groups?[61]

Fifteen years later: Some new questions have emerged; these include:

1. Why do teenagers spend so much time on their mobile phones and tablets and are anxious and frustrated when these are not available?
2. Why has the significance of dating declined?
3. Why is fashion less important than in the past and why are teenagers less important to a consumer society?
4. Why has the gap between the best performing students and the lowest performing students probably increased rather than decreased?

Learning from the caste system: As strange as it may seem, I believe that I have found the answers to some of the above questions by studying the Indian caste system.[62] The results of this earlier study are reported in my book *Status and Sacredness*.[63] The classic Indian caste system is characterized by (1) avoidance of intimate associations with those of lower status, (2) conformity to the norms characteristic of one's particular caste, (3) elaborate rituals and symbols to mark social boundaries, and (4) prohibitions against cross-caste mobility, marriage, and dining.[64] Both Indian castes and adolescent subcultures are systems in which status is the key resource. My argument is not that there is some vague parallel between Indian castes and high school stratification systems. Rather, I am claiming that what I have learned about how status systems operate from studying castes, significantly clarifies what goes on in our high schools. The pre-modern Indian caste system is arguably the most elaborate status system in human history. The intensity of status concerns in the Indian context makes it easier to see social processes that shape the status system. My argument is that these same processes are present, but more obscure, in other historical situations. Therefore a key to understanding American high schools is to understand why status systems operate the way they do. This means seeing that there are similar social processes that are relevant to both Indian castes and American high schools—as well as other social systems. Of course, the precise ways these processes operate are shaped by the specific historical and cultural contexts in which they occur.

Are Indian castes and teenage crowds important? The Indian caste system is rapidly changing and in important respects disappearing even in village India. Other historic social structures in which ascribed statuses were central have largely disappeared. Except for a few faint cultural echoes, European feudalism is long gone. Even the apartheid of South Africa and the racism of the American South were dramatically transformed in the last quarter of the twentieth century. The feminist movement has significantly reduced gender inequality. If rigid status systems are disappearing as a central mechanism for organizing whole societies, they are nonetheless present in important pockets within twenty-first-century societies. The fact that these are limited enclaves does not mean that they are not important to the larger society. In the nineteenth century both the British aristocracy and the racially segregated American South were bounded enclaves, but they had enormous importance for the societies in which they were located. Both shaped the national culture of which they were a part in ways that still profoundly affect these societies.[65] High schools are places where status is very important and, as we shall see, this has important implications for the broader society. Thus our next task is to understand what it is about the social situation of teenagers that produces such an intense concern with peer status. I touched on this in the introductory chapter, but now we need to elaborate the story.

WHY IS STATUS SO IMPORTANT TO TEENAGERS?

If peers are so influential, how do they exercise this influence? A primary means is through creating status differences. Of course, all social systems create some kinds of status differences. So why are these so important for teenagers? In all societies, as individuals mature they develop some level of independence from their parents; their autonomy increases. Schoolchildren in modern societies, in effect, "go off to work" and spend most of their day away from their parents. Teachers and administrators supervise them, but the scope of these adults' authority is much narrower than that of parents. The ratio of supervisors to subordinates also decreases significantly. This new autonomy and reduced control by adults usually means that the influence of peers is amplified dramatically.[66] All of these processes are further intensified when students reach high school. They move to larger, more complex schools, gain increased mobility (often by driving cars), and greater communication facilities (via the telephone, e-mail, and the Internet). Not only school time, but most leisure time is spent in the presence of peers or in communication with them. "In a typical week, even discounting time spent in classroom instruction (23% of an average student's waking hours), high school students spend twice as much of their time with peers (29%) as with parents or other adults (15%)."[67] The separation of school and peers from family, the increased mobility, and the independent communication networks mean that the actions of students are less visible to adults, and hence less subject to supervision and control.

As noted in the introduction, adolescents have more autonomy, but little economic or political power. They cannot change the curriculum, hire or fire the teachers, decide who will be admitted to their school, or move to another school without the permission of adults.[68] At the time of life when the biological sources of sexuality are probably strongest, in a social environment saturated with sexual imagery and language, they are exhorted to avoid sex. In many situations they are treated as inferior citizens who are looked upon as at best a nuisance. They are denied the right to buy alcohol or see "adult" movies and are subject to the control not only of parents, teachers, and police, but numerous petty clerks in stores, movie theaters, and nightclubs who "check their IDs."

In one realm, however, their power is supreme; they control their evaluations of one another. That is, the kind of power they do have is status power: the power to create their own status systems based on their own criteria. Predictably, the creation and distribution of this kind of power is often central to their lives. Therefore, what is needed to understand the patterns of behavior that emerge in such social systems is a theory of status relations. This is the subject of the next chapter.

Fifteen years later: Teenagers are still very concerned about how their peers evaluate them, that is, about their peer status. In large degree this is because the basic structure of high schools and the life patterns of adolescents have not changed much. Accordingly the kind of power they have is still largely status power. But as we shall see, who are their relevant peers, and the content of these relationships, has to some degree shifted. These changes are correlated with increased academic pressure and the new ways of communicating via digital technology.

CHAPTER TWO

The Tools for Understanding

... since the main features of an educational system do reflect the main features of the society in which it is embedded, any criticism of education is at the same time a criticism of the wider society.

—Donald Arnstine, 1987

FROM THE LUNCHROOM: When I introduced myself they seemed excited and pleased that I wanted to sit with them. I think we should be considering our effect on the students [we are observing]. The groups that we visit are going to feel "honored" that we find them "worth observing." The freshman group that had been visited so often said to me, "I guess we're a really interesting group or something ..." I think we should be really careful about observing as many groups as we can to avoid this problem.[1]

Like most jobs, sociological analysis is easier if you have some tools to work with. Theories and concepts are intellectual tools. They help to organize data and make visible connections between things that might otherwise seem unrelated. Similarly, research methods are the tools used to collect and analyze data. This chapter will outline the theory of status relationships and define the concepts of social structure, social formation, ideal-type, and hierarchy-pluralism. These will be the tools we use to understand American teenagers. (Don't worry if this string of notions sounds like impenetrable jargon; I will explain what these mean and why they are useful as we go along.) Finally the chapter will briefly describe the nature of the data and how it was collected.

SOCIAL FORMATIONS: COMBINATION, SEPARATION, AND LINKING

A key focus of this book is a set of closely related social formations: high schools, high school peer groups, and, more specifically, cliques and crowds. They are part of a broader social structure.[2] The clusters of people who share a common identity are what I refer to as social formations. Social formations vary in the degree to which they have well-defined patterns of interaction, a common culture, and social solidarity. Some are little more than categories created by an analyst (e.g., 13- to 19-year-olds throughout the world); others are an identifiable but informal subculture (e.g., American teenagers); still others are formally organized (e.g., those attending the same high school). That is, formations vary in the extent to which they are a group, community, or organization rather than simply a category. Terms such as "group," "community," and "organization" usually imply that a social formation has relatively high levels of interaction, shared culture, and organization.[3]

Social formations are the result of three processes: separation, combination, and linking. *Separation* can be due to such things as physical separation, different activities, different experiences, or mutual dislike. Hence, social differentiation and segregation may occur by space, function, experience, sentiment—or numerous other factors. To give an obvious example, students in the same neighborhood, with comparable grades and similar tastes are more likely to attend the same high school and be in the same crowd than dissimilar students. *Combination* results when people come together by intent or luck. This may be due to common interests (e.g., playing tennis), functional interdependence (e.g., working for the same company), or close proximity (e.g., living on the same block). They may create mechanisms to strengthen their ties such as an organization with a formal identity (e.g., a tennis club, a union, or a neighborhood association), and common symbols and rituals (e.g., a club jacket, a union song, or an annual neighborhood picnic). Conversely, they may create mechanisms to separate themselves from others (e.g., membership requirements, dues, and negative stereotypes of outsiders). That is, they define, mark, and police their boundaries.[4] Yet, rarely are groups self-contained. *Linking* occurs through interaction across boundaries (e.g., personal friendships), mobility from one group to another (e.g., changing employers or neighborhoods), overlapping membership (belonging to a union and a neighborhood association), and the use of common elements of culture (e.g., listening to the same music or using the same computer program). Students who take different courses, play on different teams, and like different kinds of music spend less time together (i.e., separation). Those who spend time together are likely to take on a distinctive identity: "the preps," "the jocks," "the skaters," "the band nerds" (i.e., combination). Yet, these different identities are often linked. A few "preps" are in the band; some jocks date preps or band members; some members of all these groups get their drugs from the skaters (i.e., linking).

Another way of saying this is that the amount of variation within a social formation is reduced and its differences with other formations is increased.

Not many punks wear button-down collars; gender does not vary in a girl's school.[5] Much of the analysis will look at how and why teenagers tend to form groups with those they consider to be similar to them—and hence reduce within-group variation.[6] What is especially characteristic of high school peer relations is the importance of status differences. Hence what we need to understand the behavior of teenagers, and how and why they separate and combine themselves into various crowds and cliques, is a theory of status relations.

THE THEORY OF STATUS RELATIONS

WHAT IS STATUS?

Status is the accumulated approval and disapproval that people express toward an actor or an object. As used here, it is more or less synonymous with notions of prestige and honor-dishonor—though of course each of these terms has gradations of meaning and numerous connotations. Status is the sum of the evaluations that are "located" in the minds of other people with whom a person interacts. Status is inherently linked to the process of the social construction of social meaning and evaluations.[7]

HOW IS STATUS RELATED TO POWER?

People can be influenced by three kinds of sanctions: (1) force, (2) goods and services, and (3) expressions of approval and disapproval. Each of these is the basic element of a type of power: political power, economic power, and status power. The president of the United States, the head of a large corporation, and the pope each specialize in a different kind of power. This is not to say that the pope has no wealth or that the president has no prestige. It is only to point out that the primary basis of their power is different. Similarly, institutions and societies differ in the relative importance of these three kinds of power. In the pre-1989 Soviet Union, political power was central. In most capitalist societies, economic power is central. In traditional India, caste status was a central form of power.

Typically, individuals and groups attempt to influence and control their environment by the type of power that is most readily available to them. Those who are physically strong but short on money and respect—like dictators in poor countries and young males in poor urban neighborhoods—use force more often than others. Those who are rich usually oppose moral or political restrictions on what can be bought and sold. Those who are cultured or pious disdain mere money or political power. Therefore, while in most social contexts status is important, it is more important in some contexts than in others.

WHEN DOES STATUS TAKE ON INCREASED IMPORTANCE?

One of the conditions under which status tends to increase in importance is when people are losing economic and political power. It is when the aristocracy or the old upper class are threatened by the newly rich that they emphasize their ancestry and gentility. In contrast, where groups are excluded from economic and political power and given little respect, they may build a new identity rooted in a new status system. The black power movement and most forms of multiculturalism emerged from this condition. Those who are not respected in terms of the dominant norms and values embrace norms that value the attributes they do have. Often they reject the values of the established order. Different values are emphasized: black is beautiful; Native Americans are sensitive to the environment and the spiritual aspects of life; women offer greater levels of caring and support to others. This is least likely to happen among those who have virtually no economic and political resources. Cultural resistance usually requires at least sufficient resources to organize and communicate a new identity. Often this occurs when the disadvantaged gain some minimum level of economic and political resources.[8]

As I indicated earlier, adolescents in contemporary societies find themselves in a version of this situation. They have growing independence from adults and increased levels of spending money, but they are largely excluded from the major economic and political decisions that affect their lives. Often adults criticize them. Many teenagers experience this as a form of ritual degradation. The combination of powerlessness and adult disparagement motivates many adolescents to adopt an alternative status system with values and priorities different from adults'.

To point out that teenagers commonly engage in certain levels of rebellion and create independent status systems is not to suggest that they are necessarily highly alienated from their parents or society in general. As we shall see, the level of alienation varies considerably by community, school, subgroup, and individual.

THE ELEMENTS OF THE THEORY

The main elements of the theory of status relations can be stated—in a very simplified form—in four points. First, one key source of status is *conformity to the norms* of the group. This is an obvious point, but its consequences are less obvious: Those with higher status tend to *elaborate and complicate* the norms. Primarily, they do this to make it harder for outsiders and upstarts to conform and thereby become competitors. (This is the analog of making it difficult to copy money in order to prevent counterfeiting and inflation.) They also do this to reassure themselves that they are accomplished and sophisticated, and hence deserve their superior status. Therefore, where status is important, there are usually complex, subtle systems of norms and rituals. These often concern behaviors that are learned early in life—accent, demeanor, body language, and notions of taste and style—because these are all very difficult for outsiders and upstarts to copy.[9] When high status norms can be copied with relative ease, an alternative strategy is to change the norms frequently, so those outsiders are always a step behind. This is the reason that keeping up with fashions is often central to status systems. When attempts at mobility are thwarted and some are consistently judged to fail to conform to the norms—whether or not that judgment is just—they usually reject the norms and establish alternative or counter norms.[10]

Second, the other key source of status is *social associations*: If you associate with those of higher status your status increases, and if you associate with those of lower status your status decreases. This is especially true for intimate, expressive relationships, such as close friendships, in contrast to impersonal and instrumental relationships.[11] The former imply mutual approval. Consequently, where status is important, publicly acknowledged romantic or sexual relationships, especially marriage, tend to be carefully regulated. Anthropologists refer to a strong tendency to marry within your own status group as endogamy. The endogamy of the caste system is one example of the tendency to regulate romantic relationships, but so are country clubs, debutante balls, and fraternity or sorority systems that encourage the children of the affluent to "run in the right circles." Not only do sexual partners affect one's status, but status increases sexual attractiveness. It is one of the reasons that status symbols are often linked to sexuality: The beautiful car will supposedly attract the beautiful women.

Eating is also a near universal symbol of intimacy. Where people are status conscious, they care about their dining partners. Hence, there are eating clubs at Princeton, corporate executive dining rooms, upper-middle-class dinner parties, and in traditional India, Hindus normally ate only with members of their own caste. Frequently, the process of regulating associations involves creating and maintaining social boundaries between groups and categories.[12] Associations with objects are also important. If those with new wealth want upper-class respect, they learn to buy art, antiques, and "historic" homes and to avoid kitsch. Teenagers associate themselves with the "right" brands and hang out in the cool places. On the other hand, *disassociation* is important: The status-conscious avoid people and objects that are low status, and may even try to publicly denigrate them. Where low-status groups are treated with disrespect or there is a history of such denigration they frequently reciprocate—avoiding contact with superiors unless it offers them clear instrumental benefits. In the U.S. African Americans are eager to have equal access to jobs, but they have generally chosen to maintain their own churches and social clubs—even when historically white institutions are open to them. Finally, status systems usually involve significant amounts of ritualized behavior, and especially when the relationships are intimate and expressive. Such rituals often reinforce and symbolize solidarity and mark boundaries. The "high fives" and other ritualized greetings of clique members are an obvious example.[13]

Third, status is relatively *inalienable*. It is "located" primarily in other peoples' minds. Hence, in contrast to wealth or political position it cannot be appropriated. Conquerors or parents may be able to take away your economic resources, but to change your status they have to be able to change the opinions of other people—often your peers. This relative inalienability of status makes it a very desirable resource. Those with new wealth or new political power nearly always attempt to convert some of these resources into status—in order to give them greater security and legitimacy. But inalienability is a double-edged sword: Other kinds of resources are not easily converted into status in the short run. Typically, it takes a generation for the newly wealthy to acquire the status associated with old wealth.

Once status systems become institutionalized they are relatively stable compared to other forms of stratification. Inalienability helps protect the status of those at the top. Conversely, it perpetuates the stigma of those at the bottom. This often motivates the excluded to create alternative, counter, or oppositional status systems.[14] While status itself is relatively inalienable, the markers of status vary in their degree of inalienability. Race and gender are not easily changed; clothes and cosmetics are. As we shall see, this variation in the inalienability of status markers will shape when and how they are used.

One of the implications of the inalienability of status is that it is not easily transferred from one person to another. Therefore the degree to which status can be exchanged for other resources is limited. To offer to sell your approval or to buy someone else's is to greatly devalue this approval. Consequently, in status systems most *exchange and conversion is implicit* or disguised. A public offer of money to let your child marry into a renowned family is likely to be rebuffed. Even if the proposition were accepted such crassness would reduce the status of both families. The high-status family's enthusiasm for the match may soar, however, if it is subtly made clear that a substantial loan for the son's financially stretched family firm would be available in order to ensure the couple's future. The same is true of conversion of other resources into status (or vice versa). The family that recently bought their way into the nobility or the individual whose diploma is from a degree mill tries to keep these facts hidden.

Fourth, status is relatively *inexpansible*. Per capita economic and political resources can be expanded: Some societies have a per capita income that is a hundred times greater than other societies. Some societies have only bows and arrows while others have rockets and nuclear weapons. In contrast, status is a relative ranking. If a thousand Nobel prizes were awarded each year or every soldier received a Medal of Honor, the status value of these would be greatly diminished. That is, the result would be status inflation. This is common for educational credentials and consumer commodities; as soon as most people have a high school diploma, a TV, a cell phone, or whatever, those items lose their value as a status symbol.[15] Because status is relatively inexpansible, when the status of some is increased, the status of others will eventually decrease; if someone moves up, someone will eventually have to move down.[16] Consequently, where status is the central resource, mobility tends to be highly regulated and restricted. Examples include the Indian caste system, the legally segregated American South, fraternities and sororities, the Social Register, the National Academy of Sciences, and high school cliques. To some extent, creating multiple status systems can expand status. Instead of one set of elites, there can be multiple elites. There is, however, a strong (but not inevitable) tendency to start ranking the different systems relative to one another, thus limiting the expansion of status. Few contemporary American sports stars are as universally admired as Babe Ruth was when baseball was the "national pastime." Adding soccer, lacrosse, and field hockey to a school's varsity sports gives more students the chance to earn an athletic letter or even become a "star." But the tendency is for the various varsity sports to become ranked. Being a star in football or soccer usually results in a higher status than being a star in field hockey. Nonetheless making status systems more multidimensional can expand status to some degree, but not in the same way that greater wealth can raise everyone's standard of living. Everyone can have a decent diet or a telephone; not everyone is going to be a widely admired "star" no matter how many dimensions of status there are.

In sum, the theory explains some of the key features of social organization and behavior when status is a central resource.

WHAT DOES THE THEORY ADD?

A long line of sociological analysis, beginning with Max Weber[17] and more recently including work by Frank Parkin[18] and Raymond Murphy,[19] described the tendency for groups to create boundaries and close themselves off from outsiders. In recent years special attention has been paid to the importance of status differences, symbolic markers, and lifestyles.[20] What the theory of status relations adds is that it explains (1) why status groups take on the characteristics that differentiate them from other types of social formations such as classes and parties, and (2) why the same individuals and groups vary in the intensity of their status concerns as the time and social situation vary.

A fuller understanding of the theory of status relations and its contributions to sociological theory requires elaboration of the scope of the theory, the relationships between closely related concepts such as visibility and status, conformity and innovation, groups and categories, and how the theory is similar to and different from other theories that have dealt with status and related issues. Readers, especially scholars, who have questions about these issues, should turn to Appendix I.

HIERARCHY AND PLURALISM: IDEAL-TYPES

Status systems vary in the degree to which evaluations are shared across groups or only apply within a certain group. In more traditional schools most students envy the popular crowd and, at least begrudgingly, acknowledge their high status. In other schools, however, the punks or the brains or the drama students may well consider themselves the cool people and the so-called popular crowd to be superficial snobs, deserving derision rather than envy. In short, some status systems are relatively hierarchical (i.e., there is relatively widespread agreement about how individuals and groups are ranked), and others are more pluralistic (i.e., little agreement about ranking and even the rejection of the relevance of ranking).

The extreme versions of hierarchy and pluralism are ideal-types, to use a bit of sociological jargon derived from Max Weber.[21] An ideal-type is not a description of an actual concrete case, but rather a list of the characteristics that would be found if the phenomenon existed in its most thoroughgoing and consistent form. For example, the notions of a complete vacuum or a perfectly competitive market are ideal-types. So are the pictures and descriptions provided by breeding associations, for example, of the ideal Cocker Spaniel or Hereford bull. Few actual markets or real bulls match all of the characteristics included in an ideal-type description. Rather such a model is a useful benchmark against which to analyze concrete cases and a method for summarizing and organizing our information. In this context "ideal" does not mean good or best. There can be ideal-type notions of villains, disasters, tragedies, injustice, or evil.

In both the sociological literature and the popular media, high school students have been portrayed as highly status-conscious—ranking one another in terms of status and popularity. This image approximates an ideal-type notion of hierarchy. Chapters three through six will focus on high schools that seem to have significant elements of hierarchy. In chapter six more pluralistic high schools will be the focus. There is, of course, no clear line between these two ideal-types, many of the processes described in the next three chapters are also relevant to understanding features of more pluralistic schools and vice versa.

DATA AND METHODS

Most readers of this book have been in high school and already know a lot about how teenagers behave—or at least how they behaved when they were teenagers.

Both the popular press and fiction also provide many accounts of teenage behavior. A vast scholarly literature is devoted to adolescence. Moreover, the basic pattern of peer groups is not that difficult to discern. As Laurence Steinberg, one of the leading scholars of adolescents, notes, "In most high schools, it is fairly easy to see the split between cliques—in how people dress, where they eat lunch, how much they participate in the school's activities, and how they spend their time outside of school."[22] Consequently, while I will identify particular crowds and cliques and provide descriptions of how teenagers behave, this is not the primary purpose of this book. Rather it is to provide a set of systematic explanations—not simply to describe how teenagers behave, but to explain why they behave this way. Another way of saying this is that the rationale for this book is as much theoretical as empirical.

Nevertheless, good theories organize and explain concrete patterns of behavior. I use two kinds of data to provide such concreteness. One source of data is 304 papers written by undergraduate students describing the status structure of the high schools they attended. (Each paper was given a number and when it is quoted its number is cited in the endnotes, for example, "SP31.") These college students were enrolled in three universities in different parts of the country They attended 251 different high schools in twenty-seven different states. The second source of data was derived from three years of observing students in one high school. This institution is given the pseudonym of Woodrow Wilson High School (WWHS). I conducted observations once or twice a week for two years. Three graduate students and thirty-two undergraduates also served as fieldworkers and observed the behavior of WWHS students. (Each observer has been given a number and when their field notes are quoted, this is cited in the endnotes, for example, "FW16.") This use of multiple observers had two key advantages. First, a large number of different groups could be studied. Second, it provided observers who were both quite different from those being observed—I am a white male who was sixty-three years old when the fieldwork began—and some first-year college students who were very similar to the WWHS students being observed. The details about the nature of these data and the methods used to collect them are given in Appendix II.

The goal of this research is not to rigorously test the theory. That would be premature since this is the first time it has been used to analyze teenagers. Rather, the intent is to show the usefulness of the theory in making sense of what, for the most part, we already know. The qualitative data presented is mainly used to illustrate and interpret patterns of adolescent behavior that are familiar to most observers of high school students. Some new and unanticipated findings emerge, but the key aim is to provide a new understanding of familiar phenomena.

Part II

EXPLAINING TEENS' BEHAVIOR

CHAPTER THREE

Fitting In, Standing Out, and Keeping Up

Taste classifies, and it classifies the classifier.

—Pierre Bourdieu, 1984

FROM THE LUNCHROOM: There were about ninety black kids hanging out and rapping freestyle. A few of the boys were making beats on the table so the others could rap ... [T]he kids were having a great time. One at a time the kids would step up and show off their talent by rapping to the beat. There was one ringleader who kept calling out to the crowd to "do their thing." A few of the kids were really good and a few others were really funny. One smaller kid was imitating the rapper Too Short and was making the crowd laugh. Another was "representing" the West Coast rap scene by "calling out" some Death Row. Death Row is a major rap label ... A girl was imitating the rapper Foxy Brown. She was pretty good ... and was using a lot of profanity ... but that goes hand in hand with rap music. After the bell rang they dispersed.[1]

The boys were either wearing Airwalk or Nike sneakers, baggy blue jeans, and several had on Tommy Hilfiger and Billabong tee-shirts and fleece pullovers ...[2]

The next three chapters will look at processes that are common in most status systems, but are most easily identified in relatively hierarchical status systems. The material is organized around the key notions of the theory of status relations: conformity, association, inalienability, and inexpansibility. This chapter focuses on conformity. Those who wish to have high status not only attempt to conform, but they often try to control the content of the norms. They do this by elaborating and complicating the norms in ways that give them an advantage in the competition to conform. Paradoxically, high levels of conformity often require that students be very sensitive to changes in the norms. They must "keep up" with their competition and changing fashions in the broader society. Often conformity to the norms of one group requires that you reject, or at least distance yourself from, the norms of other groups. Before I attempt to explain the patterns of behavior, I need to describe the crowds commonly found in high schools and their relationships to one another.

SOME CROWDS AND THEIR RANKINGS

In the majority of the schools analyzed, students were stratified by status, and most had variations on a common structure. A female student from the Tacoma, Washington, area provides a typical description:

> The ideal of a social status was clear to all incoming sophomores ... [T]here
> were six primary groups on campus which followed a specific hierarchy:
> the "Preps" (image-conscious types), the "Jocks" (highly athletic-oriented;
> usually involved in at least two sports), the "Rockers" (alternative grunge,
> skateboard types; Pacific Northwest version of the California "surfer"
> stereotype), the "Nerds" (academic-oriented; studious), the Punks/Weirdos
> (seen by the other groups as nonconformists; apathetic to [the school's]
> social hierarchy), and the "G's" (gangsters, "wannabe"[3] gangsters) ...
> [E]veryone agreed that two groups in particular distinguished themselves
> from the rest—the "Preps" and the "Jocks" ... [Our] high school had a
> deeply-embedded tradition of school spirit and sports—especially football.
> The closer associated one was with this tradition, the more popular one
> became. Therefore, members of the sports teams, the cheerleading squad,
> and the dance team were considered the "royalty"...[4]

In other schools there were fewer distinctions—for example, everyone who was not a prep, a jock, or a nerd might be labeled "alternative."

As the above quote indicates the "popular crowd"—those who were "cool"—were usually composed of a combination of male preps and athletes and the most attractive females in the school. Usually most of the female cheerleaders were core members of "the royalty." One young man from a small Texas town provides a stereotypical description:

> All cheerleaders have a nice golden, crispy tan and it is so obvious during the
> winter that they have unlimited tanning at the local tanning salon. If a guy
> got up the nerve to ask a cheerleader out then that was the talk of the week
> for their clique ... The cheerleaders are very snobbish and feel too good to
> talk to anyone but themselves and people on a high economic level. Since the
> cheerleaders did a lot of jazz/dance, they listened to pretty much anything
> that had a fast beat so they could shake any body part they got a chance to.[5]

In some schools female members of the drill team were less exalted members of the popular crowd.[6] Star athletes were well known not only in the school but were community celebrities.

The dominance of a popular crowd is not a West Coast or Southern or a small town phenomenon. A boy from a high status and very historic Boston suburb reports:

> The social scene ... was split broadly into two extreme groups commonly called the "jocks" and the "freaks" ... The jocks were not necessarily all athletes ... rather they were the "cooler" and more popular students ... Although the different cliques ... were not openly ranked, most people would agree that the jocks were the more prestigious, popular, and "cooler" students by the traditional high school standards ... A "cooler" or more popular student rarely formed a friendship ... with a less popular student ... The strict barriers around different cliques made it very hard for students to get to know students well from other social groups.[7]

If there is a "top," there is also a "bottom." Toward the bottom were the "geeks" or "nerds." Sometimes a distinction was made between "nerds" who were openly preoccupied with academic success and an even lower strata referred to variously as "dorks," "trash," or "geeks." These students were considered hopelessly inept when it came to social events, dress, and style. Often they also had low grades and were poor athletes. In academically oriented schools a distinction was made between "brains," who were moderately high in status, and "nerds," who were simply socially inept or too publicly studious.

In all but the smallest schools, there was usually an "alternative" group. The name or names used for this group included "freaks," "weirdos," "druggies," "hippies," "deadheads," "punks," "goths," and "the chain gang." (The last term refers to the practice of attaching their billfolds to their belts with a silver chain or wearing such chains in connection with items of clothing.) It should be noted that some of these terms are what groups call themselves; other labels are created by outsiders. In various ways these groups rejected many conventional middle-class values. They tended to be especially critical of what they saw as the hypocrisy of the preps, who were often sexually active and used alcohol and drugs, but were careful to keep this behavior hidden from adults. The more alienated of these alternative groups often flaunted their deviance.[8] Contrary to popular stereotypes, such groups were not limited to California or the East Coast. A male from Alaska reports: "[The radical group] would wear black combat boots, bell bottomed pants, and ragged tee-shirts with sarcastic messages such as 'I love Cops.' These students were more likely to have pierced ears, eyebrows, noses, and belly buttons. One of the main ideals which the radical group wanted to be associated with was individuality."[9] Even elite Catholic girls' schools have such groups: "The 'freaky' girls danced to a beat different than the rest of the cliques at St. Mary's.[10] They wore pale makeup with dark lipstick. They seemed to all have dyed hair colors and wore knee-high socks. Most of them wore Dr. Seuss or windsock hats to school. They were quiet and usually kept to themselves."[11]

Often there were important internal distinctions within the alternative category. Skaters sometimes formed a distinct subgroup. This group in turn could be divided between those who specialized in "boards" (skateboards) and those who used "blades" (straight-bladed roller skates attached to boots). In many schools, skaters were associated with drug use. In at least one school, cigarette smokers were seen as a nonconforming semi-hippy group.[12] Hippies were often considered as quite distinct from groups that had more aggressive styles such as punks, goths, and metalheads.[13] Often these subdivisions were based on a preferred style of music: hard rock, punk, ska, blues, etc. Alternative groups may or may not have actually used drugs, but they were characterized by what others considered bizarre dress, hairstyle, and body ornamentation such as nose rings. These symbolized their rejection of both adult authority and the cultural dominance and superior status of the popular crowd. The status of alternatives—or at least the less extreme versions of it—was frequently characterized as neutral—that is neither high nor low, but for the most part outside of the system. In some respects, they seem to be analogous to monks or ascetics in pre-modern societies. (In more hierarchical schools, these groups represent latent or embryonic pluralism.) In situations where such styles were associated with poor academic performance or openly defiant and aggressive behavior, these groups were seen as low-status "losers."[14] One of the most cohesive of these alternative groups is the "straight-edgers." Their distinctive characteristic is that they eschew drugs, alcohol, or promiscuous sex. Many of them are vegetarian or even vegans, who also avoid the use of all animal products such as wool clothes or leather shoes.[15]

In many non-metropolitan schools there is a contingent identified as "country," "cowboys," "rednecks," or "kickers" (which is short for "shit kickers"). They are usually from families of working class or rural backgrounds. Country music and various forms of "Western" dress, such as cowboy boots, are preferred. Large pickup trucks are their key status symbol. Where these groups are present they tend to be looked down upon by others—though they do not necessarily accept their lower status. Many of these students are alienated from academic endeavors.

A number of schools identified groups known as "hoodlums,"[16] "dirtbags,"[17] "hoods," "gangstas," "thugs," etc. They were identified with gangs who were willing to threaten and use force. In the schools for which we have data they have low status, though they may be feared.[18] In many schools, especially those with significant numbers of racial or ethnic minorities, there were often "pretend hoodlums." These were students who might dress and walk like those associated with gangs, but who were in fact reasonably well-behaved students concerned about their academic performance.

Most students modeled themselves to a significant degree after the popular crowd, but were not members of the core clique or cliques; they were respectable members of the community who have not been banished to "nerddom," but they were neither social stars nor members of the other groups mentioned. Frequently they were referred to as "normals," "regulars," or "average students." Most schools also had "drifters" or "floaters." These students manage to participate in more than one group. There is some evidence that as students mature more of them focus on particular friendships and liaisons rather than clique membership.[19] Floaters are probably an example of this tendency. Usually floaters were not the highest-status individuals in a group, but they were accepted members. Ordinarily they had a primary group, but significant associations with other groups as well.[20] A suburban Dallas student remarks:

> At my high school, people normally had to choose a group that would be
> the most important to them … Even if a person was a member of multiple
> groups, they almost always had one that they were the most loyal to. Race
> was often the most important [characteristic]. After all there was no way to
> get around what race you were but you could always drop out of other clubs
> and groups.[21]

Someone from a small Gulf Coast city agrees, "any member of any group could be a member of a certain club, academic achievement group, or team, but they usually classified themselves as members of the group that contained most of their colleagues or friends."[22]

As is the case in most stratification systems, the top and the bottom groups are usually more clearly defined than those who rank in the middle.[23] Those at the top must avoid classmates of only modest status if they are to maintain their superiority; students of modest rank must shun those of even lower status to avoid becoming outcasts themselves. As we shall see, where there are significant numbers of African Americans or other distinctive ethnic groups, the structure becomes even more complicated. This will be discussed below. In sum, most high school students are organized into sets of crowds and cliques with distinguishable identities and most students are associated with one of these particular identities.[24] The details of these groups and their styles can vary from school to school and year to year, but the basic structure is common to most hierarchical high schools.

Of course, these identities and groups do not have the same relevance in every situation. Just as the occupation of an adult does not shape all interaction with other people, neither does the participation of an adolescent in an identifiable crowd shape everything else teenagers do. Moreover, the boundaries of both occupation and crowd are often fuzzy. Some people have more than one occupation and some teenagers associate with more than one crowd. Nonetheless, occupation powerfully shapes the experience of most adults, and crowd membership is central to the experience of most teenagers. In the next chapter I will say more about when and why the boundaries of these crowds are more rigid and salient in some contexts than others.

ASPECTS OF CONFORMITY AND ELABORATION

First, we will examine some of the obvious norms of teenagers and how they are important in shaping the student status structures in schools. These include norms about beauty, athletic ability, clothes and style, athletic uniforms and letter jackets, speech, body language, collective memories, humor, ritual, popular music, dancing and singing, and space and territory. It is not news to point out that these concerns are often important to adolescents. The important thing to see is how they are all variations on the same themes: seeking status through conformity in order to fit in, that is, to gain a sense of acceptance and belonging. The paradox is that in order to be successful in the "conformity game" students must constantly change, elaborate, and complicate the norms in order to gain a competitive advantage. This is not the case for most traditional status systems and, as we will see, even a few aspects of high school life.

BEAUTY AND ATHLETIC ABILITY

Let's begin with the obvious. In many schools the most important factors influencing a teenager's status are largely inherited: athletic ability for men and good looks for women.[25] A male from a suburb east of Oakland, California, says, "Social rank was determined largely by physical attractiveness, and to a lesser extent by cheerfulness, [and] a willingness to 'party' (with alcohol and marijuana) …"[26] A woman who attended a Catholic school said, "Females received high status if they were pretty. In fact, all the 'cool' girls had to be at least reasonably attractive.[27] A young man from the Washington, DC, area observed, "The best looking girls were always invited [to parties] first."[28] He elaborates: "For females, appearance was the single most important factor … Girls who were considered attractive dated the popular males and were invited to the cool parties, and therefore gained high status."[29] Of course, beauty is not simply determined by biology. Norms concerning makeup, hairstyles, body weight, and clothes affect the definition of what is attractive. Often significant amounts of time are spent applying makeup and styling hair.

Men's status was also affected by their looks. The women we observed at our fieldwork site frequently discussed or pointed out which boys were "cute" and told various stories about them. A female field observer[30] who was sitting at lunch with a group of girls who were members of the orchestra reports the following:

> The girls once again began gossiping about Morris, supposedly one of the cutest guys in the school. Laura had spotted him in the parking lot the afternoon before changing [his clothes] in his car. She had gotten a quick glimpse of his boxers and began to describe them to the whole group, "They were so cute with green and white stripes …" Then all of a sudden Morris walked by and the group got silent. After he was far out of sight, everyone breathed … [31]

Athletic ability is usually a highly respected quality for men.[32] This is especially true of small towns, but is often also the case in urban and suburban schools. Teachers and administrators frequently accentuate the status of sports. A student from Fairfax County, Virginia, which contains a high percentage of professional families who work in the District of Columbia and is noted for its strong academic programs, reports that teachers and administrators heighten the status of those who participate in sports. This emphasis was related to the politics of the community:

> Teachers also inflated the status of athletes by asking about particular plays from games over the weekend … [W]hen our football team made it to the quarterfinals of the state competition … the hype surrounding this success was nearly unbearable. For an entire week straight, on the morning announcements we had to listen to the [song] … "We Are the Champions"—and again in the afternoons. In the case of our men's basketball team we heard the same song twice a day everyday beginning with district play all the way through until we lost in the quarterfinals … This type of recognition … and encouragement was never given [to] our state champion forensic team nor [to] our nationally ranked [drill] team … I recall a student [who was] actively involved in these clubs pointing this issue out … [T]he principal of our school said that it was not intentional [and] that they did not have a theme song or battle cry for science oriented teams. But as [the principal] put it, "It goes much further than just the individual team. We have got to get the whole community excited about these next couple of games."[33]

There is some evidence that being a good student has gained in importance, even though in many schools the importance of athletic accomplishment has not diminished much. The new ideal for men in some schools is to be both a strong student and an outstanding athlete. Obviously, not very many students are actually excellent at both, though there is evidence that on average athletes make better grades than non-athletes.[34] This is, of course, another example of the elaboration of the norms that must be conformed to in order to achieve high status.

There is often less encouragement for women to become athletes and the consequences of doing so are less predictable. In some schools women athletes had considerable status, while in others they were referred to as "brutes."[35] An African-American female attending a predominantly white school says, "[I]f a girl was too good at a particular sport she was often labeled butch or lesbian."[36]

CLOTHES AND STYLE

Close behind these relatively inherited characteristics were clothes and sensitivity to style. A fieldworker notes that the girls at her table, "[C]ommented on what everyone was wearing, especially the guys. 'Can you believe he is wearing that awful shirt at school,' as they pointed out a guy in a lime green shirt."[37] As one student from Pennsylvania said, "The easiest way to identify different groups in high school was simply to look at them."[38] A northern Virginia woman reported, "Without the cool clothing, a girl had no way of becoming popular, and her movement into the dating sphere would also be extremely limited … [M]y friends and I were always very conscious of where we were shopping, making sure that everything had its correct label with respect to what others were wearing."[39] A female athlete who was a student in a Virginia high school commented, "If a kid doesn't play a sport then the next thing that kids look at is their clothes. If they wear cool clothes then usually they're all right."[40]

What it took to be fashionable was highly dynamic and competitive. A girl who went to a Catholic school in the Mid-Atlantic notes, "The problem with conformity in my high school was that the norms were always changing."[41] A California woman laments, "I remember going out countless times to a dance club thinking that I looked great in my new outfit … until I saw someone else that had on an even trendier outfit than I did [and] suddenly my status … seemed to fall …"[42]

Once a person's status was established, the norms about clothing (and most other things) became more flexible and relaxed. A student who attended a Catholic girls' school in a large Texas city reports, "You had to look a certain way to become popular (nicely and neatly groomed and preppyish), but once you became popular, you could dress sloppy and no one cared."[43] The effect of high status and self-confidence in relaxing the pressures to conform is not limited to differences between individuals. Class and ethnicity can also affect this. Groups who are most confident about their status can be more relaxed about conformity while those whose status is less secure are often preoccupied with fashions. Minority groups are frequently quite concerned with fashion.

This is reported for a variety of such groups. Well-to-do predominantly Jewish suburban communities in Philadelphia,[44] New Jersey,[45] and New York[46] often had groups of "JAPS" (Jewish American Princesses and Princes) who were very fashion-conscious.[47] Similarly, the Asian cliques in a Houston, Texas, school were careful to have designer labels.[48] Black students seem to be especially fashion conscious. In part, this has been a matter of establishing a special identity for themselves through the adoption of hip-hop clothes. But their concern seems to involve more than establishing a distinctive identity. A Hispanic male in a Philadelphia suburb—who hung out almost exclusively with African-American students—comments:

> Dress was very important for the black crowd. We were almost always trying to stay on top of the latest hip-hop fashions. Baggy, somewhat flashy clothes were the norm … but the influence of the white students was clearly also present. We would wear "preppie" or nice, dressy clothes often, just as the white students, regardless of the group that they fell in. Shopping at the Gap, Structure, Eddie Bauer was practiced by almost everyone. I can say, however, that we dressed better than the popular, smart, or the two other groups. We would wear the dressy clothes, but always remain faithful to the hip-hop style, which back then was not as glamorous as it is today. None of the other groups would ever dare cross over to wear our clothing style. My friends and I always wondered about why we [sometimes] conformed to [the preppy] dress style, but it was never the other way around.[49]

A black female who went to school in an upper-middle-class suburb of Washington, DC, with twenty-five percent minority students observes: "There did not appear to be a major emphasis on clothes in terms of brand names within the majority group of cool kids … [F]or African-American boys in particular things like Nike, Timberland, or Fila shoes were factors in social acceptance within the smaller peer group."[50] In the pluralistic school where we carried out extensive observations, African-American students tended to be more concerned with dress. An African-American observer reports that the group of black women she observed didn't wear brand names, but were well dressed. They said that if someone who was dressed "bumified"—like the hippies—tried to hang out with them, they wouldn't talk to them.[51]

UNIFORMS, JACKETS, AND EMBLEMS

Armies have for centuries worn distinctive emblems or uniforms to identify friend and foe. The uniforms worn by sports teams are a similar example. But in addition to being worn during a game, uniforms and quasi-uniforms are also used to signify distinctive identities in other situations. A most obvious example is the custom of sport teams wearing their game jersey to school the day of a game. The explicit intent is both to honor them by setting them apart and to create solidarity within the team. Some teams wear matching outfits during classes, especially women's teams or those who play less established sports.

After battles, armies give citations and decorations. This is true in high schools as well. The "letter jacket" is an especially significant status symbol. These jackets, emblazoned with the school's initials, indicate special accomplishments. As a woman from Corpus Christi, Texas, reports, "Most members of a school-related subgroup showed their status by wearing the school letterman jacket ... The jacket was the symbol of a winner."[52] A student from a rural area in the Shenandoah Valley of Virginia reports: "A letterman's jacket ... gave the individual a chance to show that they were an athlete anytime, not just on the day of the games, [and] also gave the wearer the prestige of being a veteran ... There was even a school club for jacket wearers called the Monogram Club ..."[53] This last sentence refers to an especially interesting phenomenon: The jacket club was not a pre-existing group of outstanding students nor was the group based on a common activity. Rather the very basis and raison d'être of the group was a common status symbol.

Jackets are an especially useful form of status symbol because they are highly visible and supposedly have a practical purpose, which makes wearing them legitimate. In contrast, students who wore a medal to school all of the time would be considered pretentious. Jackets not only make their owners visible to others, but they make the wearers visible to one another, and hence contribute to elite solidarity. In this context jackets are a rudimentary form of "ethnicity"—a solidarity based on visible status markers.[54] Here clothes literally make the group.

Historically, jackets were awarded at first only to accomplished athletes in high-profile sports like football and basketball. Most schools now give these for accomplishments in a wide variety of activities, including band, choir, debate, student council, and academic performance. Students reported that, while it was acceptable for non-athletes to wear jackets, they were often teased if they wore championship patches. Only participation on important athletic teams warranted displaying patches. This indicates the strong tendency of high status groups to differentiate themselves from upstarts. In theoretical terms they are trying to prevent status inflation that would result in a decrease in their own status.

SPEECH AND LANGUAGE

Non-material aspects of style were also important. Each clique tended to develop its own vocabulary. A Washington, DC, suburbanite recounts, "I can remember when some of the popular males, including myself, decided to create a word with no meaning and start using it to see if people tried to copy us. Within a few weeks, we could hear people using this word, although they had no idea of what it meant or what context to use it in."[55] A student from a small town in Appalachia recalls:

> [S]tudents ... would come up with a saying or an original way for a word to be used. Only those in that particular crowd knew the meaning and the correct way to use a word or phrase. For example, to say "relish," meant that something was really cool or awesome. Nonsense and made-up words were ... important. Examples included "carbeeb" which translates to "that is stupid," and "smedus beadus," which refers to a nerd.[56]

Note that "cool," "awesome," and "nerd"—originally innovative word usages—have become so conventional that they now require updated synonyms, even in small-town Appalachia.

As the theory would predict, higher status groups sometimes attempted to make copying more difficult: "When the preps talked they ... used the highest vocabulary they knew, like 'euphemism' or 'supercilious.' "[57] But slang and new words can be learned relatively easily so more subtle markers are introduced. A boy from the Dallas area reports, "Many of these slang words made it into everyone's everyday language at my school. It was how the words were said that made the difference."[58]

COLLECTIVE MEMORIES AND HUMOR

Groups often elaborate their cultural distinctiveness by referring to events and experiences that only members of the group have shared. These can be evoked by cryptic references, sometimes a single word. Typically, these events are humorous and are underlined by the ritual incantation, "It was *so* funny!" Another common marker of group distinctiveness is the inside joke. A young woman in a Catholic girls' school reports, "[A]ll groups had inside jokes. These were jokes that only they understood and could use and see the humor ... The thing about inside jokes is that they are not funny when you are on the outside and this excluding of others is exactly their point."[59] As we shall see later, inside jokes seem to be especially characteristic of groups that others see as deviant or weird. Of course the memories and jokes are not norms, per se. Rather, the norm is that a full member of a group must be familiar with the group's collective memories—whether or not they were actually present at the events. They must also "get it" when inside jokes are told.[60]

RITUAL

Even more elemental than languages and inside knowledge are various forms of ritual. Animals often engage in elaborate forms of ritualized behavior including mating displays, dominance-subservience signals, and grooming rituals of solidarity. These are easily observable when you walk your dog, your cat has kittens, or you observe behavior at your bird feeder. But unlike these examples, most human rituals are much less rooted in genetic programming and are primarily learned behavior. Nonetheless, many rituals are pre-linguistic forms of communication and are often extremely important mechanisms for expressing solidarity. Obvious examples are a smile or a handshake.

Some of the most obvious rituals associated with high school life are the routines led by cheerleaders and drill teams. This usually involved a mixture of verbal phrases and routinized physical movement. As Emile Durkheim pointed out early in the twentieth century, participating in common rituals is a primary means for creating social solidarity.[61] High school cheers, which engage large crowds in simultaneously producing the same movements and sounds, are an obvious example. Rituals were, according to Durkheim, likely to be especially effective when they were oriented toward some transcendent being or object. The differences between members of the community seemed inconsequential compared to the "otherness" of the god or totem. Durkheim focused on the otherness of the sacred and the solidarity and effervescent spirit that emerged from its ritualized worship.

Such solidarity and spirit can, however, also be produced by the otherness of a common enemy. This is, of course, precisely what military parades and high school cheers at sports events are intended to produce: solidarity in the face of a common enemy. The enemy is in some respects the analog of the devil or even more accurately foreign gods. But the solidarity produced at the high school ballgame is not solely rooted in antipathy directed toward a common enemy. A positive dimension is also present: the honor and prestige of the school community. This is a form of sacredness and, sociologically speaking, an analog of the "true god." Just as in many societies, these sacred notions are given a more concrete form by adopting a totem. Typically these totems are powerful animals that it is wise to treat with respect and even fear: lions, tigers, bears, wolves, cougars, eagles, etc. (Schools rarely adopt totems that are associated with weakness, dirtiness, or other low-status attributes, for example, flies, buzzards, rats, pigs, or lambs.) The solidarity and spirit needed to gain victory is created by ritualized behavior directed toward honoring the local gods and rejecting the foreign gods. Just as churches honor gods by singing hymns of praise, schools have songs and anthems. Taking part in such rituals usually has an impact on the way participants feel, resulting in a heightened state of emotion. Durkheim referred to this as effervescence. "School spirit" is, of course, a particular example of such ritually induced effervescence.

Ritual leaders of the community, whether they are priests or cheerleaders, usually have relatively high status. In part this is because of their close association with what is especially sacred for a particular community. In the case of high schools this is honorable combat with enemies, hopefully victory over them, and the honor this victory brings to the whole school. Cheerleaders have no direct role in the games played, but they are the key people who organize "moral" support for the teams. This moral support is expressed through public rituals. In addition to their close association with what is sacred, cheerleaders are ritual specialists who have mastered the ceremonial techniques of the community and can lead others in carrying these out.

Ritual is not only important in producing school-wide solidarity, but also in creating the solidarity, and hence the boundaries, of the various crowds and cliques that make up the student body. Special handshakes or greetings such as a "high five" or "low five" are common. Hugs are frequently exchanged by girls and occasionally by boys to express friendship or solidarity. This rarely occurs between members of different groups, unless they have been close friends in the past. Explicit in most of these interpersonal rituals is the positive affirmation of a common social identity, and the implicit distancing—at least for the moment—from other identities. When football players greet one another by keeping their elbows bent and gripping one another's hand and then each making a fist—instead of shaking hands in a more conventional manner—they set themselves apart from other students and affirm their identities as members of a team. When these same individuals apply for summer jobs, however, they usually shake hands with the interviewer in the more conventional manner. They want to affirm their identity as responsible young adults who are capable of assuming a different identity than the one they adopt on the football field. The particular ritualized greeting selected depends on whether they are greeting close friends, casual acquaintances, parents, or the school principal. In each case, rituals are used to affirm particular identities and, implicitly, to downplay alternative identities.

BODY LANGUAGE AND DEMEANOR

Closely related to ritual is body language: the way people communicate by the way they carry and use their bodies. This is an even more implicit form of symbolization and communication. The marionette motions of the military drill team communicate obedience, preparation, and skill. The formal dress and demeanor in the corporate office communicates a tend-to-business seriousness that is inappropriate in the family room or neighborhood bar.

On average, American teenagers use a less formal demeanor than adults. Frequently they are "laid back," "cool," or "chilled out." Demeanor is also used to communicate status and mark different subgroups. Students' off-handed comments make this clear: "Preps walk with pride..."[62] "When these [popular] people walked, they had a certain air about them."[63] "The guys all walked really stiff (trying to look as muscular as possible), flexing almost as they walked, taking up a lot of space, and showing little emotion."[64] "The jocks were very noticeable … They would walk around with erect posture and their chest pointed toward heaven."[65] "Many of the ["kickers," i.e., "cowboys" or "rednecks"] walked bow-legged …"[66] "Some black students walked … as if they had an ankle injury and limped on every other step."[67] Each of these remarks may have been derogatory in intent, but they report widely observed patterns of behavior. These patterns are not primarily unconscious habits. Rather they are rooted in social norms about how the members of a certain crowd are supposed to portray themselves in public.

POPULAR MUSIC

In addition to language, ritual, and demeanor, music is often a central medium of expression and communication and this is especially the case for teenage Americans. Music communicates primarily by sound rather than bodily motions. It is often used to create social solidarity, for example, religious hymns, national anthems, and labor union songs. Predictably, teenagers want their own music. Each generation or cohort seems to embrace new forms of music as a way of distinguishing its identity from older generations. The emergence of rock 'n roll at the end of the 1950s is the most dramatic example, but, both before and after this, each generation has been associated with a relatively distinctive genre or set of genres.[68] Music sets off teenagers from adults, but also distinguishes various adolescent subcultures. Country and western, ska, West Coast rap, East Coast rap, classic rock, acid rock, hard rock, and techno rock, not to mention older forms like jazz, rhythm and blues, and swing, are only a few of the distinctions that were significant in the last decades of the twentieth century. Most large high schools have some devotees to each of these genres and often this shared appreciation will serve as the basis for friendships and cliques.[69]

DANCING AND SINGING

Dancing and singing use multiple media. Dancing involves music and ritual movements. Singing involves music and language—usually in the form of rhyming poetry. Dancing is frequently used to suggest sexuality—a special preoccupation of adolescents. Predictably, each generation and subculture of teenagers adopts at least some relatively distinctive dances. Frequently, older generations find these crude or overly suggestive. Each generation also seems to adopt particular songs.

Dancing seems to be especially important in creating solidarity across relatively large groups. Many can participate simultaneously in the presence of others. This is, of course, also true of hymns or anthems sung in unison, such as the school song. For teenagers, however, songs seem to be especially important in creating links between small groups of friends and romantically involved couples. Friends often have a favorite song. Many couples have "our song." In addition to being a means of creating internal solidarity, dances and songs are another way of elaborating and complicating the norms in order to create boundaries between insiders and outsiders.[70]

PHONES, BACKPACKS, AND CARS

While clothes are an important status symbol, so are other physical objects. One male from a small West Virginia city noted, "Now maybe 50 percent of the higher status crowd have pagers."[71] In many schools, pagers were associated with gangs and drug dealers. By the end of the 1990s, mobile phones had become an important status symbol. In some schools in upscale neighborhoods they were so common that they lost their value as a positive status symbol, but not having one could cause you to be looked down upon. Backpacks could be important, but it was not just a matter of having the right kind, but how you wore it: "When the popular kids started to wear their backpacks with both straps as opposed to wearing their backpacks with one strap, [other students] eventually followed by wearing their backpacks with both straps even though wearing your backpacks with both straps had traditionally conveyed strong images of the 'nerd.' "[72] In yet another school, how men wore their hair was an important marker. "Most preps had neatly trimmed hair; most redneck males made a half-hearted attempt to grow facial hair."[73] Some of the most potent status symbols are associated with cars. The first crucial distinction is whether a student has a driver's license. The second is whether they have a car they can regularly drive to school. The third is whether it is a cool car. In the 1990s, the highest status cars were new four-wheel-drive sports utility vehicles commonly referred to as SUVs. Among "rednecks" and "cowboys," large pickup trucks were cool. Most of these vehicles cost in the range of $20,000 to $40,000. Forty thousand dollars is 115 percent of the total annual median household income for this period.[74]

SPACE AND TERRITORY

Because students tend to associate with members of their own group, space tends to become segregated. This is obvious in the halls, before and after school, and even between classes. A girl from a prestigious high school in suburban Boston reports, "The major way that virtually everyone—students, teachers and administrators—identified cliques ... was tied to where people gathered on the school's main hallway in their free time ... Each locker area was associated with a particular social group, each with its own identity."[75] This is especially the case at lunch. A female who attended a large private school reports: "At lunch, 'cool' kids sat at the front of the cafeteria. This allowed for … all the 'cool' people to sit in one place. Not to mention, it gave [them] … a chance to be seen." Space was also segregated at out-of-school hangouts; unwanted students were often teased and even harassed if they showed up at the wrong place. Even small spaces become important symbols, for example, seating in classrooms, cafeterias, and school buses. Who was seen with whom in cars was a crucial status symbol. In one community, not having someone to drive you home was humiliating: "The bus was the ultimate ride of shame …"[76] In other communities, however, most people rode the bus, but seating quickly became stratified. High-status students sat at the back because it was harder for the driver and others to see them, and because they paraded by everyone else as they made their entries and exits. But even where it was not possible to actually segregate space, who one was seen with in certain public places was important. A male student remarks, "Who a person came with to the mall was very important."[77] This was even more the case for school events like football games or concerts. Some privileges in the use of space are officially sanctioned. Seniors usually have the most desirable lockers and often have their own lounge.

For some groups, "their space" seems almost crucial to their identity. One group of freshmen[78] we observed at WWHS hung out in the courtyard even in the coldest weather. Often they complained about the cold, but they rarely moved into the cafeteria only a few feet away. A field observer records the following incident. "It was quite cold outside today, and since he [James] is only wearing a short-sleeved shirt, he is especially freezing. He yells out loud, 'I can't take it anymore. It's just too cold.' Wilson answers back in jest, 'Oh shut up, you baby' They remained in the courtyard."[79] Later in the lunch period:

> [Bill's girl] friend pretends to cry and whimpers aloud to him, "It's so cold. I don't want to stay out here anymore." Everyone stands up and moves closer together because Wilson said, "Let's move together for body warmth."
> Soon, Wilson says, "It's too cold out here. I think we should all go inside until the bell rings." No one has any objections to this idea since the wind is making everybody especially cold. Each of the students picks up their backpacks and begin to head inside … I went in with the group but as soon as we got inside the cafeteria, everyone went their separate ways.[80]

It is noteworthy that when they leave "their space," they disperse—almost like a congregation leaving church.

Just as individuals and groups have a status, spaces are assigned different identities and different statuses. One's status and group membership is signified not only by a particular style of dress, but by the physical spaces one uses. Failure to conform to these practices violates norms that can result in sanctions from one's own group and from other groups as well.

This is not unique to teenagers. Physical distance is frequently used as a metaphor for social distance. The rich tend to live on top of the hill or in penthouses; the offices of top executives are never in the basement; the powerful have larger offices, desks, and cars. Similarly, social boundaries are represented by physical boundaries. The "well-to-do" live in "exclusive" neighborhoods and in "gated communities"; the lowly live in "the ghetto" or on "the wrong side of the tracks." Some of these patterns have practical roots: The view is better from the penthouse than the basement; gated communities probably are safer. But these patterns are also a way to symbolize status differences. Predictably, high school students also relate physical space to status. Later we will take up subtler and less-well-known examples of how space is related to social structure.

THE FLEXIBILITY OF NORMS AND STATUS SYMBOLS

Obviously, conforming to some norms is easier than conforming to others. Wearing a fashionable tee-shirt is not hard; making an A in calculus is more difficult. The ease of conformity affects whether a cultural item will be used to symbolize differentiation or solidarity. Language and popular music illustrate this.

LANGUAGE AND MUSIC

Though language and music can be used to create social boundaries, they can also be used to create links across these boundaries. Interestingly, for adolescents this seems to be truer for language and music than it is for clothes or other physical objects. As noted above, a student from the Philadelphia area reports that in his school, whites would never dare copy black hip-hop dress, though blacks would on occasion dress preppy. But he goes on to say:

> Music was a little more flexible because there was acceptance on both sides for different types of music listened to by the white and black crowds. White students listened to some rap and hip-hop, and black students (which included myself) listened to some of the top 40 and alternative music the white students listened to. The status walls were nonexistent when it came to music and language. We all listened to pretty much the same music, and talked the same.[81]

The tendency of music to be shared across groups was not restricted to this eastern urban setting. A boy from a small Texas town reports, "Music was a universal characteristic that was not a major difference in any certain group, other than the 'cowboys.'"[82] A girl from the same school says, "Ironically, [music] was a common bond … Music that transcended the social boundaries included alternative rock, rock 'n roll old school style, and rap music …"[83]

These differences are special instances of variations in the inalienability of status markers, and how this affects their use in creating social differences and social solidarities. If you come to school wearing preppy clothes, it is not practical to slip into other clothes when you encounter acquaintances dressed in hip-hop or punk fashion. But with a little effort, you may be able to express solidarity by speaking their lingo. Similarly, you can go to a party and, without too much difficulty, feign appreciation for the kind of music that is being played—even if it is not your favorite. This is in contrast to objects such as clothes, cars, and where you live. These may create divides that are much more difficult to bridge because these goods are simply not available to some.

This is not to say that symbolic, in contrast to material, markers are always more alienable and hence more flexible. Picking up a few words and phrases of an argot is one thing; speaking a second language like a native is quite another. The latter is nearly impossible after early adolescence. Consequently, where status groups are especially determined to maintain their boundaries these more complex symbolic systems often serve as barriers that are the last line of defense. In Britain, an Oxbridge accent is still a distinctive class marker. In numerous historical contexts, groups that speak essentially the same language go to considerable lengths to maintain differences in vocabulary, accent, and even the alphabet they use. The relevant point for understanding contemporary high schools is that where people seek to develop links across social boundaries—as different groups of adolescents frequently do—language and music may be a more available medium than consumer goods.

ATHLETIC SHOES AND LETTER JACKETS

When status symbols are used primarily to differentiate individuals and groups the ease with which they can be acquired or copied is an important consideration. For most consumer commodities the only limitation on acquiring them is having the money to pay for them. This is, of course, one reason that the status values of these commodities change relatively rapidly. At the end of the twentieth century athletic shoes were a good example. The major manufacturers brought out new models of shoes about every six months. Since there were several major manufacturers, what was considered cool among young urban males changed even more often. In order to gain status by this, it meant you had to regularly discard one style and acquire another. These concerns have also spread to both male and female suburban students.

Letter jackets, which are a prized status symbol among many of the very same adolescents, illustrate the opposite tendency. Letter jackets are not subject to rapid changes in fashion—and the theory of status relations explains why this is so. The distribution of these status symbols is controlled and allocated by an authority structure. An attempt to buy look-alike jackets by someone who had not earned a letter would be derided and looked down upon. Conversely, those who have earned a letter jacket would be considered crass or even despicable if they agreed to sell their jackets to the highest bidder. Hence, the pressure to stay ahead by having the most up-to-date version is largely removed. Rather, there is even some value in keeping them largely the same since this places people in an honored tradition. Of course, styles eventually change over time, but like the military services—where drastic changes in uniforms are nearly always controversial—uniforms and letter jackets change relatively slowly.

Since some status symbols are commodities that can be purchased, a brief note is needed to clarify the link between money and status symbols—and some of the consequences of this link.

MONEY AND STATUS SYMBOLS

To acquire significant status usually requires more than money; you must acquire the appropriate status symbols. Athletic uniforms of officially sponsored school teams cannot simply be purchased and worn at will, and hence money is not directly relevant to acquiring this kind of status. This is obviously not the case with many kinds of status symbols, including most kinds of clothing. Consequently, the preoccupation with fashionable clothes and other status symbols creates an acute need for money. This sometimes creates conflicts with parents. On the other hand, some parents take pride in their children's ability to be popular and willingly provide them significant amounts of money. Students who do not receive much money from their families often hold part-time jobs so they can buy the status symbols they feel they must have to be accepted or popular. A female from a very well-to-do community in New Jersey observes, "A number of the 'popular students' who were not all that rich and could not afford the name brand clothes, somehow managed to work many hours while going to school to obtain nice clothes."[84]

Some research suggests that the pressure to have fashionable things is also one of the factors that have contributed to the high rate of shoplifting among teenagers. Teenagers, however, deny that their friends in any direct way pressured them to engage in such activity. Rather, it was more a matter of keeping up with one's peers both in terms of exciting behavior and the acquisition of status symbols.[85] Such social and economic pressures may also increase the probability that students will sell drugs.[86]

Being a cool teenager and more generally the acquisition of status is frequently associated with conspicuous consumption. Ironically, coolness can also be a form of asceticism.

COOLNESS AND BOREDOM

For a number of years the word "cool" has been used to describe characteristics that were envied or at least admired. Like most widely used terms it has relatively specific roots but over time has taken on a number of more general and figurative meanings. According to Marcel Danesi in his book, *Cool: The Signs and Meaning of Adolescence*, the notion emerged from the early jazz movement. The initial participants were mainly black men who were subject to all sorts of discrimination and oppression. It is not accidental that the notion and term emerged among an oppressed group. Open resistance to white authority could bring severe penalties, including death by lynching. In such a context, self-respect is found and a modicum of power gained, not by being aggressive, but by taking on an air of seeming indifference. The oppressiveness of the broader social context is mitigated by creating a separate world that does not openly threaten the-powers-that-be, but resists them in subtle ways. Especially important is the creation of new cultural forms. These forms usually express indifference and thinly disguised disrespect of established conventions and authority structures. Jazz was initially such a cultural development. This resistance is communicated not primarily by explicit content, but implicitly by style. According to Danesi:

> First and foremost, coolness implies a deliberately slow and lackadaisical
> form of bodily locomotion; accompanied by a nonchalant and unflappable
> countenance ... Being cool involves a control over emotionally induced body
> states. Losing one's cool, as the expression goes, is to be avoided at all costs
> ... [T]he sum and substance of coolness is a self-conscious aplomb in overall
> behavior.[87]

Unsurprisingly, adolescents, who are subject both to the authority of parents and school officials, adopt this style as a means of expressing resistance to adult authority. Obviously, a typical teenager's social location is significantly different from that of early jazz musicians. For most teenagers, their relationship and attitude toward those in authority is ambivalent. Most adolescents love their parents and respect most of their teachers. Nonetheless they are seeking greater autonomy and often disagree with authority figures about the norms that are appropriate for their situation.

A male from suburban Burlington, Vermont, says, "A sense of self-confidence, [a] lack of respect for authority, and occasional recklessness were all crucial in becoming part of the cool group of people ... For females, coolness came from attitude and dress ... If a girl acted self-confident, reckless, and also dressed somewhat provocatively, she would immediately become popular with the boys ..."[88] Similar criteria are mentioned in Virginia: "An air of invincibility seemed to surround the popular guys. They drove fast, often under the influence of alcohol …"[89] A female from a small town says, "The cool kids were effortless and that was their number one resource. They didn't seem to try."[90] A crucial aspect of conformity to peer norms is to feign rebellion or at least non-conformity to the norms of adults in general and school officials in particular. Numerous students testified to these aspects of coolness.[91]

The precise stylistic content of the conformity varies from time to time and from subgroup to subgroup.[92] The commonality, however, is resistance to some set of norms that are seen as imposed—usually by parents and schools. Ironically, some students use the term to describe resistance, not to adult authority, but to peer pressure—especially those that produce failure in school. In some schools, it is cool to be smart, as long as one shows resistance to adults in other ways. For some, ambivalence toward authority is transformed into alienation and open hostility. These are the wild teenagers who are described in many movies and books.[93] While some may still aspire to conventional notions of success, the patterns of behavior they engage in are almost certain to produce a different outcome. Many are openly cynical about conventional norms and have few hopes for the future. These levels of alienation are not restricted to minority students in urban ghettos, but involve substantial numbers of white teenagers in suburban areas.

The key theoretical point is that "coolness" expresses resistance to established authorities or conventional customs and involves the creation of a set of alternative or counter norms. Not surprisingly, in resistant subcultures—whether they are teenage cliques, Communist Party cells, or persecuted religious sects—high levels of conformity are demanded to the norms of the deviant group.

For students who still are committed to conventional notions of success—a college education, a good job, etc.—behavior that would get one thrown out of school or barred from further education is not a viable option. If one cannot be cool by being daringly deviant, the next best thing is to be blatantly bored. Adolescents characteristically complain about how boring their school or hometown setting is. "Nothing ever happens." A fieldworker reports, "One boy came up to me and said, 'Lunch is so boring for us; I can't imagine how boring it is for you.'"[94] A second observer reports: "Today, I spent more time observing my group … I watched them and they sat there absolutely bored. They sat there for a while like that and then finally Scott came out and admitted that their lunch was totally boring … They sat there for the rest of lunch doing nothing."[95] Such complaints may have substantial validity, but in addition, it is a way to distance one's self from the authorized patterns of behavior without having to engage in serious forms of deviance, which might result in serious sanctions. These expressions of boredom are frequently associated with behaviors annoying to authorities—throwing food, jokes in class, a surly manner—but are not serious enough to bring significant retribution.

Finally, coolness needs to be put in a broader historical and comparative perspective. Coolness is a variant of asceticism. Asceticism is a means of seeking power by being indifferent to the usual worldly sanctions. Typically this involves a form of "otherworldliness." Usually it is associated with those who are highly religious and seek to express their religious commitment by eschewing worldly forms of power and privilege. The power of the saint or holy man is not of this world, but of a different realm. Certainly, the otherworldliness of American teenagers is not that of the religious monk or the self-denying sect. Nor is it the asceticism of early capitalism described by Max Weber, which praised disciplined hard work and rejected the lavish forms of consumption and status pretensions of the feudal nobility.[96] What teenage coolness and these other forms of asceticism have in common, however, is resistance through the cultivation of an alternative lifestyle that advocates indifference to what is valued in the existing dominant culture. They do not usually attack existing authority, but subvert it by inverting its values and symbols. Blessed are the meek and the poor. Cool are the nonchalant and the bored.

Let me summarize the argument. A key source of status is conformity to the norms of the group. This creates a tendency for those who want to protect their status or identity to elaborate and complicate the norms in order to make it hard for outsiders to copy. In situations where members of a group cannot prevent others from copying them, they change the norms frequently and emphasize keeping up with the fashions they set. A result is that peer norms are created, elaborated, and regularly changed in a wide variety of areas.

While teenagers often want to set themselves off from others, at other times and in other contexts they want to create connections and establish solidarity with those who are not members of their immediate status group. This is often done by affirming norms and symbols that other groups share such as certain forms of popular music or shared slang or argot. Because symbols vary in the ease and flexibility with which they can be adopted, some symbols are more likely to be used to create cross-group solidarities and others to symbolize differences.

Though modern status processes are closely tied to high levels of consumption, the essence of coolness is a form of asceticism, that is, the resistance to adult norms and authority through the adoption of an alternative lifestyle. These tendencies are not due primarily to the biological and developmental peculiarities of a particular age group. Their obsession with status and status symbols and their conformity to peer norms are a perfectly reasonable response to the social setting in which they live—a situation that has been created largely by adults.

CHAPTER FOUR

Steering Clear, Hanging Out, and Hooking Up

*I saw that the students' most active and alive moments, and indeed
the great majority of their school time, was spent not with teachers and
subject-matter affairs, but in their own small group interactions …
I frequently asked informants, "Which would you rather do, flunk a test or
eat alone in the cafeteria?" Invariably the answer was, "Flunk a test!"*
—**Philip Cusick, 1973**

FROM THE LUNCHROOM: Tandi started talking to a guy named Dwayne.
They started arguing. Apparently she used to date him and he did
her wrong. They were yelling at each other. At first Jamar stood next
to Tandi, but then she came back to stand by me and watched them.
Tandi walks away from the boy and starts crying. Jamar said, "I told
her he was bad news, but did she listen to me?" … Tandi was crying
and in a bad mood the rest of the period. She walked over to a group
of all black people in courtyard No. 1 and they asked her what was
wrong. She said, "People runnin' their mouths." They finally guessed
that it was Dwayne. Another black boy came up twice and put his arm
around Tandi and asked if she was all right. Jamar said, "He's no good
either. He used to date my cousin. I'm not even going to get into that
story."[1]

Tracy spent much time discussing a boy named Randall, who I believe
is older, and is her boyfriend. She wanted to plan a party for Randall's
birthday, which is two months away. She said he wanted a "drink till you
drop" party … I got the impression that Tracy's mother does not approve
of Randall.[2]

Adolescents are acutely aware that who they associate with affects their own
status. Often disassociation is a prerequisite to desirable associations. In early
adolescence, disassociating yourself from your parents, in at least some ways,

is virtually a prerequisite for associating with high status peers. A girl from a Catholic school notes, "Those freshmen who were driven by their parents occupied the lowest status, because it was very 'uncool' to be associated with your parents in public, no matter where you were."[3] Avoiding low status peers is also important. A New Jersey male reports, "It was critical to one's status to be seen talking only to people in your own status group. By talking to someone who was beneath you, you ran the risk of lowering your own status."[4] These avoidance concerns obviously restrict interaction between groups.

Even within some groups, the willingness of others to associate and inter- act is associated with rank. A field observer studying a group of sophomore preppies at WWHS reports the following incident:

> One boy I watched for some time, Adam, is not a leader, but not really an
> outsider either. Today he seemed a little uncomfortable—self-conscious.
> He asked Morris a question and Morris was pretty short and to the point.
> Adam looked as if he wanted to converse longer with Morris, and he seemed
> slightly distressed that Morris showed so little interest. Adam almost
> immediately began looking for something in his book bag and cursing ... as
> he rummaged.[5]

Adam tries to disguise even this seemingly trivial incident of rejection. He acts as if he stops talking to Morris because he needs something in his book bag, rather than because he has been "dissed" by Morris. Moreover, he immediately tries to literally increase his centrality in the group: "At first ... he was sort of [sitting] on the outside [of the group]; it looked like he really thought about it and made a big effort to make himself move closer into the circle."[6] His intense concern with association and acceptance is made apparent by his attempts to move physically to a more central position in the group in order to offset Morris's rejection. Apprehension and distress about rejection are common.[7]

A girl from suburban Washington, DC, says:

> Bad grades and fights with my mother were nowhere near as traumatizing
> as not being included in some social activity, a disagreement with a friend,
> or not having a date for homecoming. Acceptance within my peer group
> and a feeling of belonging were the key to my happiness. As superficial as it
> sounds, being elected to the homecoming court my senior year ... was the
> highlight of my four years ...[8]

Close associations are so important that for some they shape academic and non-academic contexts. "Who you walk into the pep-rallies and who you sit with make the whole world of difference. In fact, you will often see cliques (preps in particular) meeting outside so that they may walk in together."[9]

A student reports, "It was amazing that year after year, the popular group managed to have almost identical class schedules so they could literally be together every minute. This particular group sat together and associated with few outsiders unless they required help with homework."[10] More typically, whether people are willing to associate is conditioned by the purpose and context of the interaction.

Associations are not simply an individual concern. Groups care about who their members hang out with; the status of all is affected. How carefully each other's associations are monitored depends when, where, and why they occur. When you are with your own group, others should be tuned out. At other times, ties with non-members are acceptable. As is often the case, these "rules" are usually applied less rigorously to those who already have high status. Now let us turn to a crucial factor affecting the status relevance of associations: whether they are instrumental or expressive.

INSTRUMENTAL AND EXPRESSIVE RELATIONSHIPS

Instrumental relationships are formed for some specific purpose or goal; expressive relations are those that have no specific purpose but focus on companionship. Strictly instrumental relationships usually limit or restrict emotional intimacy. Judges should not try cases that involve friends or family members; teachers should not have romantic relationships with their students. *Expressive relationships*, on the other hand, necessarily involve emotional intimacy and attachments. Detached, emotionally uninvolved individuals may be co-workers or acquaintances, but they are rarely considered friends. Obviously some relationships are a mixture of instrumental and expressive elements. The theory of status relations predicts instrumental relations will be treated differently from expressive relationships. In India, Brahmans can supervise low-caste workers in the fields, but they do not fraternize or eat with them. The boss may work closely with subordinates, but does not normally socialize with them—except perhaps at a few official social functions. Parallel processes are clearly at work in high schools. A guy from a small Texas town observes, "During regulation school hours a student would 'hang' or 'chill' with his or her own clique and not express more than a 'hello' to members of other cliques. This was especially a trend of preps … One can converse with members in different groups in classrooms, but outside classes, conversation ended."[11] The taboo against associating with those in other cliques did not apply when it came to schoolwork; you could be friendly to people not in your strata as long as it was required or advantageous. This same process is seen in a wide range of schools. A student reports that in her Hispanic Catholic school, "Everyone gets along in class, but it's very segregated outside."[12] A girl from Corpus Christi, Texas, says: "The real test for most of the friendships formed [in class] came after school. If apparent friends hung out together beyond the school and [extracurricular] activities realm, then it was typically a sign of true friendship."[13] The very same people are treated quite differently at different times; those treated as friends in one context are ignored or shunned in another. "I found myself unable to say 'hi' to many in the hallways who had been my friends at the start of the year, because they were not 'cool.'"[14] Other research has indirectly pointed to the difference between instrumental (goal-oriented) associations and expressive (companionship-oriented) associations. Professor of Education Pamela Bettis reports, "White honors students often noted that their after-school friendships were more homogeneous than their in-school friendships."[15]

The more intimate an expressive relationship, the more associations are socially regulated. Sex and eating are near universal symbols of intimacy. Consequently, nearly all societies have rules about with whom one can sleep and eat. In the Indian caste system, where status differences are crucial, marrying and eating with members of your own caste (or a closely related one) are central features of the social structure. Especially important are publicly visible relationships. Covert indiscretions may be tolerated; conspicuous ones are not. Teenagers are no exception. More concretely, they are preoccupied with who "goes out with" (or "hooks up with") whom and who eats with whom in the lunchroom. These are the kinds of associations that most affect and symbolize one's status.

Adolescent women usually show more concern about expressive relationships than men. One study notes, "On the whole, females appeared more 'expressive' than males with greater emphasis on being pleasant and caring in interactions."[16] This gender difference is due in part to the greater importance of associations as a source of women's status. As we will see later, this concern can also lead to some very mean-spirited behavior by women toward other women.

If intimacy can express approval, *forced intimacy* can express disapproval. Perhaps the most degrading kinds of relationships are those that involve unwanted intimacy. Sexual harassment, rape, torture, cannibalism, and the forced feeding of those on hunger strikes are examples. In these cases one actor forces intimacy upon the other. As we shall see, milder forms of forced intimacy are also found in high school settings.

TYPES OF ASSOCIATIONS AND RELATIONSHIPS

DATING AND HOOKING UP

For teenagers perhaps the most crucial form of intimate expressive relationship is dating. As one girl noted, "Another huge part of association ... is dating, the importance of which cannot be overstated."[17] The archetypal tales are about dating female cheerleaders and male athletes. In a study of a South Texas high school the men were ambivalent about cheerleaders, but dating them was clearly a means of raising one's status.

[T]hey saw "going with a cheerleader" as guaranteeing their coolness and masculinity. Particularly the less attractive males plotted the seduction of these young women and reveled in the idea of having them as girlfriends. When expressing their views publicly to other males, however, they often accused the cheerleaders of being "stuck up" or "sluts" … These highly prized females become, therefore, dangerous, status-confirming creatures that were easier to "relate to" in rhetorical performances than in real life. Only those males with very high social status could actually risk relating to and being rejected by the cheerleaders …[18]

Similarly, girls can increase their status by dating star athletes. A young lady from Vienna, Virginia, recounts the "tragic" story of a classmate who dropped a very good-looking soccer player in order to date the quarterback of the football team. The quarterback soon sustained an injury and could no longer play. The status of both declined and they soon broke up.[19]

In most schools, race and ethnicity are an important consideration in forming romantic relationships. A young woman from the same county, but a different school, reports that an African-American guy and an Asian girl were assigned seats next to one another and got along well. Nobody made a big issue of it. "But when they went to a football game together, rumors started to spread and the black girls started to question the black guy's status and loyalty to their race."[20]

Of course, age and grade (i.e., year-in-school) influence dating patterns. One of our field observers at WWHS reports, "I asked Lacey if the date worked out with the guy she was supposed to ask. She said she called him, but he wasn't interested because she is a freshman. He is a junior and although he did not have a date, he did not want to go with a freshman."[21] On the other hand, there is a clear tendency for men to date slightly younger women. As a young female from rural Pennsylvania notes, this has an important consequence for dating opportunities: "As we got older … the girls' dating pool of acceptable partners shrank as they progressed through the grade levels, while boys actually had wider options, both due to the common belief that the boy should be the older partner, especially to maintain status [and if boys] wanted to still have that submissive partner required by the stereotype …"[22]

Being involved in an ongoing romantic relationship tended to increase your status within a group. One of the observers at WWHS reports:

[A couple] often became the center of attention. Many times, others from the group would crowd around these two and attempt to engage in conversation with them. It was a frequent occurrence for several of the boys to tease the male or try to wrestle with him. Clearly, dating was seen in a positive light for the individuals in my group and being part of a couple tended to improve a person's status.[23]

But the other side of the story was that one's group limited who one could date. Trying to date someone of a different group or a different status may lead to rejection and ridicule, as the following story by an observer at WWHS indicates.

> The conversation … around the table was [about] a love letter that one of the group's members, Dana, received from a member of another group, Cecil. The incident was discussed first [and] then the actual letter made the rounds and was read aloud to the shrieks and delight of all. The letter was first an apology (for some incident I don't know about), then a statement that the author liked her friends and that he hoped that they liked him, then the statement that Cecil liked Dana the best and thought she was beautiful. Dana showed great disdain and the rest of the group laughed about the note.[24]

The emergence of romantic relationships is obviously rooted in puberty and biological maturation as well as psychosocial development.[25] But this does not explain why adolescents are so preoccupied with *other* people's relationships, and especially who is "going out with" whom. Only by under-standing the centrality of status and the nature of status relationships can we make sense of these patterns. Often students who go out together have relatively shallow emotional attachments and are primarily conforming to an expected social form that provides them respect and status.[26] As we shall see later, where status concerns are less intense, the significance of dating tends to decline.[27]

In some schools traditional dating is passé or limited to very special events, like the senior prom. Students often go to places in groups, but they do not usually have an explicit "date" with another individual. In the course of such social events, or following them, couples may "hook up." This is a deliberately ambiguous and variable term. It implies some kind of sexual relationship, but does not necessarily mean that a couple had sexual intercourse. The exact con-notation differs by crowds, schools, and communities. This pattern is more characteristic of younger students. Older students with steady boy- or girl-friends are more likely to go out as a couple on occasion, even if it is not defined as a formal date.

FOOD AND FOOD FIGHTS

In some respects, whom you eat with has even more importance than dating because this occurs every day. A male from suburban Northern Virginia says, "[There was] a great deal of concern as to what the lunch arrangements would be. As freshmen, people scurried around the lunch room, searching desperately for friends to sit with, so that they would not have to suffer the ultimate embarrassment of eating alone or sitting at an uncool table."[28] A young man from Boulder, Colorado, says, "Eating alone wasn't cool, and [since my school had] three different lunch periods, I couldn't always find a friend who I'd want to eat with … And when I sat with friends in the cafeteria I always felt that my level of coolness was being judged by the respective status of each individual I was with."[29]

Eating can be an important symbol in other settings. Going on a date to an expensive restaurant symbolizes the importance of the event, especially if others know about it.

> Raquel was having trouble deciding what restaurant to go to for prom. She and her date Tommy had decided upon Chili's as a possibility. Jenna said, "You want something fancy" … Todd said, "Chili's isn't fancy … if you want a fancy restaurant you should go to Harrington's" … Rachael wrote all the restaurants down on pieces of paper … She put the slips of paper in the hat and drew out Steak Barn. Laughing, she said, "I'm going to draw again." She drew out Harrington's, which made Todd gleefully shout, "I told you!"[30]

Even the parking lots of fast food establishments have significance:

> Another important place to show off your status was the McDonald's parking lot. I know it sounds weird, but the parking lot would be full of teenagers just eating and hanging around on any weekend night. I had the privilege to witness this phenomenon many times, as I used to be an employee of this prestigious firm. People would go there and smoke and try to look cool, with their fancy cars and cool clothes. It was very important to look cool just standing … outside McDonald's.[31]

Keep in mind that not any parking lot will do. The most frequented are those associated with food and drink. Part of this is a practical matter; teenagers do get hungry. The significance of these locales cannot be comprehended, however, unless the significance of food as a symbol of expressive intimacy is also understood.

Two other interesting phenomena make more sense when seen in the context of a theory of status relationships. One is the tendency of lunch groups to share food. In some groups people will literally reach over and take food from someone's plate without asking. In other groups, people go through the ritual of asking, but it is usually considered inappropriate to refuse. Bargaining may go on about what is to be given in return, but in the groups that have high solidarity, anything more than playful bargaining is looked upon as inappropriate.

Often what is being shared is very common and the amounts are small; the main thing that is going on is clearly symbolic rather than practical. In the closest groups, sharing food comes close to being a form of communion, a sacrament in the religious sense. A fieldworker reports, "The group [nine sophomores, one senior; six girls, four boys; seven whites, two African Americans, one Asian Indian-American] ... shared food communally ... it was placed in the middle of the table and everyone took what they wanted. I also noticed there was no real leader of the group."[32]

This use of food to express intimacy helps to make sense out of what may seem to be a completely different phenomenon: throwing food. One field observer at first thought her group of second-year students was especially immature because of the frequent food fights. "When I learned later that such food fights were common in many cliques, I decided these were 'normal' soph-omores."[33] A different observer reports:

> Brian brought grapes ... He began throwing them at Jessie, who then in turn
> threw them right back. There was definitely a little flirting going on between
> the two ... Jessie turned to me and explained that she was going skiing over
> the weekend with her boyfriend. Her boyfriend went to ... the school she
> had transferred from just a few months before ... It was funny to watch
> the ways in which the boys acted around the girls. If they felt they were not
> getting enough attention they would start throwing grapes at them.[34]

Obviously, one of the reasons that students throw food instead of other things is because it is at hand. But other potential projectiles are sometimes even more available—wadded paper, used drinking and eating containers, and—for the many groups that eat outside—sticks, small rocks, dirt, etc. Yet, our observations show that food is clearly the projectile of choice. The most common kind of food throwing is between friends. Usually this involves mock conflict that is more an expression of solidarity than of hostility. Sometimes it is an expression of romantic or sexual interest, of desired intimacy.

Because food implies intimacy, it is also a useful symbol of aggression or hostility; thrown food can symbolize unwanted or forced intimacy—like sexual harassment. A black female observer at WWHS reports the following incident involving a group of African-American girls: "A senior female threw orange peels at a group of 'hippies' seated on the ground not far away. Seemed to be ritual harassment. They did not respond. Another girl wrote things on the table [that] she did not like about some other groups. Others added to the list."[35] The combination of the food throwing and listing what is not liked about other groups makes it clear that this is an act of disrespect.

Throwing food seems to be more insulting than another kind of relatively harmless projectile. Throwing a hard object or spitting on someone—not to speak of urinating on someone[36]—would be too hostile an act that would clearly bring negative sanctions from both peers and school officials. Throwing food is "appropriately hostile." If school officials intervene, the sanctions are likely to be relatively mild. The ambiguity about the precise meaning of food throwing is also useful. The recipient can ignore the insult without losing face or return it in kind without escalating the conflict. Some groups eat lunch together, not so much because they are attracted to each other, but because other groups reject them. A group known as "Don and Company" was observed by a field-worker. He concluded that they did not really like one another very much. He happened to note that they mainly threw food but rarely shared it.[37] This is what the theory would predict. While food throwing combined with food sharing can express intimacy, trust, or desire, when there is only food throwing it is much more likely to express underlying hostility.

In many high schools, seniors are allowed to leave the school grounds for lunch while other students must eat on the school premises. Underclassmen may have "their own table" in the school cafeteria, but seniors can have "their own place" off campus. In some schools going to another group's place can result in harassment and even fights. The privilege of having lunch off school grounds is highly valued by seniors, and is sometimes used by teachers as a means of social control. In one school seniors who were caught smoking on school grounds were forced to eat lunch in the cafeteria. The sanction was quite effective.

Food not only symbolizes already established intimacy and solidarity, but also can be a means to establish these. When middle- and upper-class Americans want to get to know someone better, they invite them to dinner. In her book about teenagers entitled *A Tribe Apart*, Patricia Hersch reports how she went about establishing rapport with students after school hours:

> My passport into their private lives was food. Lots of it. I ate subs by the lake with Jessica while she expounded her theories of love and friendship; I had M&M's with Courtney while she told me about her new boyfriend; leftover Chinese with Ann while she went on about her parents. Charles and I discussed race over pizza. Chris and I consumed Chicken McNuggets at McDonald's while dissecting the seventh grade. I had more McDonald's, Roy Rogers, Taco Bell, and Pizza Hut in the years of this book than during the previous decade.[38]

In other words, sharing food was the means of lowering her status to establish the intimate rapport she needed for good reporting. For similar reasons eating lunch with students was the primary form of my fieldwork.[39]

In sum, the teenage preoccupation with who eats with whom in the lunch-room is not primarily due to developmental immaturity. Rather, this is one

aspect of the much broader issue of symbolizing intimacy in expressive relationships when status is an important consideration. While ninth grade lunch
cliques, adult dinner parties, Holy Communion, power lunches, Princeton eating clubs, and reporters taking their informants to lunch are different in detail,
all are ways of affecting people's status because sharing food is a near universal
symbol of intimacy.

KNOWLEDGE, SECRETS, AND RUMORS

If sex and food are the common physical symbols of intimacy in social associations, knowledge about another person is a less material form of intimacy.
Intimacy is even more strongly implied when only a few are privy to the information; that is, when there are *secrets*. Teenagers and pre-teenagers sometimes
seem to be obsessed with secrets. Sharing secrets with someone is a sign of intimacy and trust. Conversely, those not let in on the secret are kept at a distance.
Often secrets involve some kind of deviance. The most obvious example is the
secrets that adolescents do not want parents, teachers, and other adults to know.
Frequently these involve forms of sexual behavior and use of drugs or alcohol.
A key thing that separates adolescent from adult culture is the information
that is not supposed to be shared with adults. Such secrecy is not restricted to
matters of sex, alcohol, and drugs, but to the very nature of their peer society:

> Status didn't matter when accompanied by parents. When parents were
> around two individuals would act as though they had been friends all of
> their lives even though they didn't hang around each other during school.
> The biggest reason is that students didn't want to let their parents in on
> what went on during school. To them school was their time and what went
> on was on a need-to-know basis, and parent's didn't need to know.[40]

This is a report from a small town; other individuals in other settings might be
less concerned about secrecy from adults, but the general tendency operates in
most communities.

Secrets also divide teenagers; they should be shared with friends and
members of your clique or crowd. As we shall see shortly, keeping secret information about the time and locale of social events is a key means of status differentiation. On the other hand, breaking a confidence is a form of disrespect, and
frequently is associated with rejection and exclusion. The incident described
earlier in which Dana shows Cecil's love letter to everyone (p. 76) is a clear case
of violating confidences in order to create social distance. Dana passes Cecil's
love letter around and ridicules his interest in her. Not only is he rejected, but
his attempts at intimacy in the form of a love letter are transformed into public
knowledge.

Too much association with those of another crowd is problematic; secrets may be revealed to outsiders. A fieldworker reports the following incident: "I saw one of the [black] girls that used to sit at their table and I noticed that she was hanging with an all white group and her and Tandi didn't even speak to each other. I asked Tandi about it, and she said she found out that the girl ... had been 'telling all their business' to Tazy, and suddenly started hanging with white girls."[41] The offense is not just racial disloyalty, but sharing secrets with outsiders. Another significance of secrecy as a form of intimacy is to be able to claim that higher status people share secrets with you—that you are one of the high status crowd who is "in on" everything.[42]

If there are secrets, there will be *rumors*.[43] A lack of reliable knowledge can be remedied by speculation or fabrication—by "making it up." Not sharing rumors—keeping them secret—can be interpreted as a lack of intimacy and trust: "Liz and Bill are definitely a couple, still sitting in each other's laps and holding hands. They also were having a disagreement today, something involving Bill having heard a rumor about her and refusing to tell her what it was."[44] I will discuss gossip later, but it is clear that rumors can be an integral part of gossip. Sometimes rumors are used as gossip in order to maintain group interest and solidarity: "The only topics of conversation were the fact (or rumor) that a girl named Tammy ... is pregnant. They seemed very knowledgeable about the subject, but when I asked who the girl was, they said they didn't know her."[45] Sometimes the "knowledge" is deliberately distorted, that is, there is rumor mongering, intended to harm others: "I asked them where the other girls were that they used to sit with. The response was, 'They are all two-faced. They were spreading rumors and trying to instigate fights. They are hoochies. They tried to start fights between us and other people.' "[46] Even when the motives are not specifically malicious, the tone of rumors and gossip is usually negative. Since the most common motivation for secrecy is to hide various forms of transgression, rumor and gossip tend to focus on deviance. Hence, the characterization of secret behavior is seldom positive. Later I will discuss gossip and say more about why rumors and gossip tend to be negative.

To summarize, secrets and rumors are crucial mechanisms in the competition for status. Therefore they are especially characteristic of social systems in which status is a central resource—as is the case in American high schools. Of course, most people intuitively "know all of this." The theory of status relationships enables us to see the parallel between the different kinds of intimacy, for example, between food fights and spreading rumors. Both are expressions of intimacy that can be used to express either solidarity or hostility.

Now let us shift from secrets about personal experiences to an activity that by its very nature must be a shared group experience: the party.

PARTYING

A fieldworker at WWHS recorded the following account:

> Mora told them that her parents were going away for the weekend and she
> was going to be home alone. Lacey and Macy got excited and decided that
> they should have a party. Cassic exclaimed, "This is a chance of a lifetime!"
> Emily chipped in that she wanted to come. Mora said that her parents said,
> "We can trust you now," and that she can have "a couple of friends over."
> They were very excited to think of what they could do this coming weekend.[47]

The most important event for displaying and acquiring status is the party. This
is a purely expressive event, the essence of which is associating with others.
A party is more public than a date, but can still be relatively exclusive. Often
parties involve some form of deviance from adult norms. This most typically
takes the form of drinking alcoholic beverages and in some cases using drugs.
Moreover, it nearly always implies and often involves romantic or sexual liaisons. Being invited to the right parties is a mark of high status. This frequently
requires keeping secret the time and location of such parties—so those who
are not wanted do not show up. A source of upward mobility is providing an
attractive location for parties or a supply of alcohol. Cooperative parents or an
older sibling who can legally buy the needed beverages is a great asset.

In most high schools, frequent partying is the essence of being part of the
"popular crowd." The significance of parties in most high schools is captured
well by a male from Vermont:

> The principal social activity of the "cool" group was having parties at vari-
> ous people's houses or at random outdoor locations. Because everyone was
> under 21 and alcohol and drugs were usually in abundance, the location and
> times of these parties were kept secret ... [S]imply finding out the location
> of these parties was difficult unless you knew someone in the cool group ...
> These parties were not so exclusive that someone would be asked to leave ...
> However, if you had no friends or people to talk to, you could probably not
> help feeling out of place. Still, despite an implicit exclusivity, these parties
> represented the most universal social scene for my high school ... [W]hile
> there was a central group ... who were always at these gatherings, numerous
> groups of other people could come and go without seeming out of place.[48]

In many high schools, there are different kinds of parties. The relatively exclusive parties of the popular crowd are usually by invitation only. "Crashing"
such a party can provoke conflict and fights. Those from relatively well-to-do
backgrounds also have more formal versions of the exclusive party, which are
usually sponsored by adults: debutante balls, coming out parties, and country

club dances. In contrast to these, some parties emphasize solidarity and togetherness as well as displaying status differences. A student from a small Texas town says, "A healthy percentage of all cliques would be equally represented at weekend beer bashes and countryside parties. This is the one place that preps, skaters, band members, and blacks all converge into one melting pot of new-generation culture …"[49] This joint conspiracy and solidarity at beer bashes is in part because this involves illegal behavior. But even functions that are more official can involve multiple groups. This is often the role of the Homecoming Dance and the Junior-Senior Prom. A wide variety of the cliques and subgroups usually participate—though some do not. (In many schools gay and lesbian couples may be discouraged from attending.)[50] On one level, these events emphasize class and school solidarity—or at least solidarity among a substantial cross-section of the students. On the other hand, considerable differentiation occurs in terms of singles and those with dates, who dates whom, what pre- and post-dance parties are attended, and who sits and dances with whom. Whether the emphasis is on solidarity or status differentiation varies by school. Size seems to be a significant factor here. In small to medium size institutions, school-sponsored public events are likely to be seen as times of "togetherness." In large high schools, however, the solidarity of particular subgroups seems to be strengthened.

The key point is that the preoccupation with partying is not simply a matter of adolescent exuberance rooted in "hormones"—though this clearly plays a role. Other status-conscious groups have also been preoccupied with partying. This includes most aristocracies, small-town upper classes, the various Social Registers, and the entertainment world's "glitterati." When status is a crucial form of power, the skillful display of expressive activity and relationships is a crucial determinant of rank.

Obviously the instrumental-expressive dimension is relevant to partying. Less obvious is its importance for friendships in sports teams.

SPORTS TEAMS AND RACE

Students on the same sports team were often friends, even though they had little else in common. That is, they hung out with one another at times other than in class or during practice. In most schools, sports teams that involve significant numbers of African Americans and whites—football, basketball, baseball, and track—were usually some of the most socially integrated subgroups in school. Undoubtedly, some of these friendships are the by-product of working together to win games. Another reason that cross-race friendships are more common on sports teams is that the membership on such teams gives them relatively high status.[51] This enables minority students to resist the considerable pressure that exists in many schools against "acting white"—or in other ways undercutting racial or ethnic solidarity and loyalty. A student from a southern urban school with considerable racial and class divisions says: "There were some students that were able to break the rules of the rigid structure within the school. Those affiliated with sporting events were able to belong to more than one group ... they were accepted by the other groups and accepted by each other ..."[52]

Athletic team solidarity is not sustained when the season is over. A woman from the Tidewater area of Virginia observes:

> During any particular season, the members of a team tended to hang out with other members of their team, but these friendships rarely seemed to carry over into the off season [when] members would return to their usual groups. For example, during my time, our wrestling team was ranked number two in the nation. During the wrestling season, wrestlers would hang out primarily with each other, but ... when wrestling season was not in session the wrestlers would hang out with whichever of the ... groups they were a part of.[53]

The key theoretical point is that the common instrumental activity of the team and the relatively high status of the athletes made it possible to sustain expressive friendships across well-established social boundaries, including race. When the instrumental activity ceased, so did the expressive activity—not necessarily because the individuals were no longer personal friends, but because the instrumental shield that allowed the crossing of racial and crowd boundaries was removed and the salience of other associations and status groups prevailed.

CLUBS AND ASSOCIATIONS

The mix of instrumental and expressive elements also affects clubs and associations. This mix produces differences in who participates and the extent to which the boundaries of the club are open or closed. In a number of communities, some school organizations and some sports teams, which supposedly had various instrumental goals, were in effect near-private clubs. They tended to be dominated by one clique and others were discouraged from joining. Trying to be where you were not wanted was considered more degrading than rejection per se. A student notes, "Staying in high status school clubs ... where you were not wanted gave you the title of 'wannabe.'"[54] In short, whether an organization was primarily instrumental or expressive depended upon whether it had a relatively concrete goal that involved more than concern about social relationships within the school. Where this was not the case, the ostensibly instrumental purposes were often a fig leaf for more expressive concerns. In such situations, cross-group relationships were problematic. This was often true of golf, tennis, and lacrosse teams; they were frequently the domains of white upper-middle-class cliques. Similarly, particular cliques often dominate the staff of the school yearbook. In a school in the Houston area, "The popular girls also occupied the high positions on the yearbook staff (editors), and so the yearbook contained many more pictures of them than people from other groups."[55] This is a rudimentary example of how elites not only have special privileges, but also bias the historical record. On the other hand, in many large high schools, clubs and associations tend to create links across groups. This is especially the case if these are high status organizations like the National Honor Society. But, the extent to which a social group's activity is actually expressive or instrumental, or involves closed or open boundaries, is shaped by the particular historical and cultural context. As we will see from the analysis of music and drama groups, this will also be affected by the extent to which the activities are inherently expressive and ritualistic.

BANDS, ORCHESTRAS, DRAMA GROUPS, AND CHOIRS

In larger schools musical and drama groups offer an interesting contrast to sports teams. Clearly, artistic groups are engaged in a common purpose and often this involves competition with other outside groups. Nonetheless, these activities tend to create their own distinctive subculture and crowds, rather than integrating those from different social groups. Usually most members of the band and orchestra have low to moderate status in the eyes of other students and have relatively few ties to non-band members. A female from the Norfolk, Virginia, area comments:

> Another group that tended to isolate themselves from the general student body was the Band/Orchestra/Chorus. This group spent a lot of time outside of class with one another. The three segments of this group shared a lot of the same characteristics, but were pretty separate from one another. They spent an enormous amount of time with their respective unit, and they had a unique solidarity and strong group identification.[56]

A male from North Carolina says, "Participation in the school marching band or orchestra oftentimes served as a way for some students to develop [an] ... identity. There were always those kids who talked about famous composers perpetually and hung out in the band room during lunch and after classes."[57] But in many schools this identity was not seen in a positive light and, as a student from New Jersey reports, they are "commonly known as 'band fags.'"[58] A Texan who went to a large suburban school says: "Members of the band associated primarily with other band members ... For example, band members dated only band members, and frowned upon their peers that did otherwise. In addition, if a band member did not fully dedicate their time to band, and the band only, they were not accepted."[59] A guy from California says, "I remember there were cliques for whether you were a band member or not. The band/choir all hung out together ... The people who were interested in drama all hung out together and dated each other."[60] I have fewer reports that specifically mention orchestras, but they seem to follow a pattern similar to that of bands. Clearly, this tendency of music and drama groups to be relatively self-contained is very widespread, especially in large schools.

Drama groups are an especially interesting case. They often adopt distinctive and extreme styles of dress and behavior. Hence the terms "drama freaks" or "drama queers." A girl from a Washington, DC, suburb reports:

> Another obvious clique ... was the DQs or drama queers. This ... contained all of the people that put on plays and any other type of theater-related production. This group was mainly recognized by the fact that many of them wore black all the time (some even wore black capes). This group usually ate lunch together in front of the theater—located at the opposite end of the school as the cafeteria. I think if you asked anyone in my class what their impression of the "DQs" was ... they would probably answer, "Weird" ... [T]hey always seemed to have an inside joke going that no one outside of their group ever got. Members of this group would throw temper tantrums during class if they disagreed with a teacher.[61]

There are similar reports from a variety of public institutions as well as private prep schools and Catholic schools. In contrast, in schools that do not have formal drama programs, solidarity among drama participants seems much more transient. While particular crowds may be overrepresented, student actors are often drawn from a variety of groups. The cast is often very close during the course of preparing and presenting a performance, but like sports teams, the solidarity declines when the "season" is over.

Compared to bands and drama groups, choirs seem more varied in the degree of insularity. Sometimes they follow the pattern of bands and drama groups. In some schools, African-American students are disproportionately represented in the choir. In other schools, however, choirs come closer to the model of major sports teams in that they draw people from an array of social groups. A student from a diverse school in central Virginia reports: "Another group that managed to combine the blacks, preps, nerds, and rednecks was choir. There was very little interaction between these people outside of class. For the most part people hung out with those in their own clique."[62]

How do we explain this tendency toward self-containment for bands/ orchestras, choirs, and drama groups, as well as the differences between them?

First, in contrast to sports teams, these groups are seldom segregated by sex. Consequently, they offer opportunities for heterosexual romantic relationships and this greatly increases the probability of self-containment.[63] Second, they spend a lot of time together on a common activity. But gender composition and intense common activity are not a sufficient explanation; the first does not explain why bands/orchestras, choirs, and drama groups vary from one another and the second factor does not explain the differences between artistic groups and sports teams.

Rather this insularity is affected by three additional factors that are particularly characteristic of status-conscious social systems. First, in the eyes of most other students, band (and probably orchestra) is seen as a low-status activity and this is often publicly expressed, as the well-known terms "band nerd," "band queer," and "band fag" indicate. This low status, reinforced by the use of homophobic labels, seems to derive from several factors.[64] To play a musical instrument even reasonably well requires years of disciplined practice under the supervision of adults, so it is not accidental that one of the derisive terms is "band nerd." Moreover, the activity is non-athletic and for the most part non-aggressive, and hence is defined as "unmanly," an activity for "sissies," or "fags and queers." That is, it deviates from some of the key norms of the dominant groups in most high schools. Second, amateur music and drama are culturally defined primarily as expressive rather than competitive or instrumental activities. (Of course, this notion of art for art's sake is an ideological exaggeration. Nonetheless most people learn to play a musical instrument because they enjoy doing it, not because they see it as the route to fame or fortune.)[65] Because music is a shared expressive activity, it creates and sustains an initial base of solidarity. This increases the likelihood that friendships, dating, and other forms of expressive association will occur within this group. Third, inherent in music and drama is ritual performance, which is a key source of social solidarity and closely associated with status processes. Subgroups or individuals may have special parts, but the key to a good performance is to carefully coordinate these efforts so that they produce a unified whole. The process of preparation involves going over the same material repeatedly until it becomes a complex but highly coordinated form of ritual performance. Bands engage not only in the rituals associated with music, but also marching, which is a highly stylized form of collective ritual. Similarly, drama involves learning stylized gestures and bodily movements. The combination of ritualized activities that increase solidarity, and the low regard and derision of other students motivates the creation of a counterculture that extols alternative values to those of more popular groups. When these second and third sources of solidarity are added to the first one of facing a common enemy (i.e., the majority of other students who hold this activity in low regard) we have a theoretical explanation for the insularity of these two groups.

Why are drama groups seen as even more "weird" than musical groups? Acting inherently involves taking on new and different social roles, that is, becoming other than one's conventional self. It involves ritual, but a weaker form of ritual than music. The script of the play offers a common sequence of actions and words that is roughly the same for each performance. But unlike musical groups, parts are not usually performed simultaneously in unison, but rather are normally distinctly different for each character. Moreover, in amateur drama the internal ranking of individuals is less stable than for musical groups. Actors have to "try out" for each play and who gets the leading role often changes from production to production. In contrast, rankings in a band—first chair, second chair, etc.—are usually more stable. Unlike bands and sports teams, drama groups have no official uniforms. Consequently, we should expect that drama groups would have less solidarity than musical groups—unless they develop additional mechanisms to maintain their boundaries. This is precisely what they do by wearing "weird" clothes, makeup and jewelry, and self-consciously taking on the stereotypical attitudes and behavior of the alienated artist.[66]

Why are choirs more variable in their degree of insularity? Singing generally requires significantly less sustained preparation to participate at the amateur level. Many students playing in a band or orchestra have taken several years of private instruction, but this is not often the case for high school singers. This also means that the status of this activity is more ambiguous, since one does not have to be a "music nerd" to participate.

In sum, both their insularity and variations in the degree and form of this insularity are due to structural factors largely related to the status position of the activity within the larger status structure of the high school. The theory of status relations predicts that when those of relatively low status experience disrespect, they will restrict their expressive associations (e.g., friendships and dating) to those of similar status and create boundary markers of their own. These processes are accentuated if the activities involve extended periods of intensive ritual-like activity. Bands, orchestras, drama groups, and, to a lesser extent, choirs illustrate this phenomenon. Sociologist Randall Collins's theory of ritual interaction is relevant here. Collins suggests that the degree of solidarity and hostility to outsiders is due to differences in (1) social density, that is, the number of other people who are physically present,[67] (2) common focus of attention and mutual awareness, for example, saying a prayer together or watching the same ballgame, and (3) common emotional mood, such as reverence in worship or elation when the team you support wins. These are high in bands, drama groups, and choirs, and accordingly the solidarity of the groups is high. The theory of status relations clarifies several additional points. First, Collins's theory does not address why these groups have relatively low status, and hence share a common emotion of suspicion toward outsiders. Second, it does not explain why some kinds of relationships with outsiders are more likely than others. Why will band members gladly work with and cooperate with non-band members in rock bands or events such as football games, pep rallies, or joint choir-band concerts—all of which have the characteristics Collins's theory points to—but not date or eat with non-band members in the lunchroom? It is because boundaries are especially rigid when it comes to purely personal expressive relationships. In short, the theory of status relations and the theory of ritual interaction usefully supplement one another in helping us to understand the characteristics of these types of groups. (For a more extended discussion, see Appendix I.)

This leaves one obvious question. Why does popular music often create cross-group ties, while participating in school artistic groups creates boundaries? This contrast is due to the difference between consumption and production. It is relatively easy for an individual student to consume a variety of musical styles—and hence share common cultural forms with others. It is much more difficult to produce the same variety of music. Hence, those who produce music, even amateurs, tend to specialize in particular types of music and to associate with those who have a similar focus.

THE EFFECT OF TIME AND PLACE ON ASSOCIATIONS

Whether people from different groups could associate with one another was not only affected by whether it was instrumental or expressive, but also by the time and place of the interaction. Especially important is whether such relationships are highly visible or conflict with times that are usually devoted to a particular clique. A student from St. Petersburg, Florida, comments, "Students from different popularity groups found it acceptable to talk early in the morning or late after school. This was a neutral time that it was acceptable for anyone of any category to talk to each other. In some cases this was the only time that students who were friends in elementary school would talk in high school."[68] In other cases, neighborhoods provided the basis for cross-group friendships. Someone who went to a Connecticut high school describes two neighborhood cliques, the "Kelly School group" and "Flanders Street group."[69] With respect to the first: "The kids in this group had grown up together and their parents were close, thanks to PTA and Little League. Members of this group would separate during the school day [and associate with] various groups ... However, after school they would come back home and would hang out together either partying, playing sports, playing video games, or just hanging out." He notes that the second group behaved in a similar way. In part, the continued solidarity of each of these groups was related to their longstanding rivalry. "The big thing was the weekly tackle football games between the two neighborhood groups who seemed not to like each other—for no particular reason."[70] Typically, such local groups maintain certain levels of friendship in the context of the neighborhood, or perhaps the school bus, but in the context of most school events, they would virtually ignore one another. What seems to be going on sociologically is that the saliency of the old neighborhood groups declines in significance in the newer and broader social context of the high school. The older relationships can, however, be activated in contexts where they are relatively invisible to the broader student body. But when outside associations are visible to school cliques—even though they occur in a completely different context—they may be denigrated. A girl from a small Texas town reports, "If you associate with someone outside of your clique outside of school it doesn't do any harm until you come back to school and are teased about it until you just can't stand it any longer."[71] She notes that how much teasing you received depended on your status in the group.

The point of this chapter has been to show the wide variety of situations in which students carefully regulate their associations and to explain the variations in the nature and dynamics of such associations. Groups care about their members' associations because it affects the status of all. How rigorously associations are regulated depends on the mixture of instrumental and expressive elements, and the purpose and visibility of the relationship. These latter factors are, in turn, strongly affected by the time and location of the interaction. In general, when one's group is "in session" and "on its own turf," others should be ignored. At other times, cross-group relations are acceptable. Groups that are high or low in the status order, or whose activities are inherently ritualistic and expressive (such as musical and drama groups) are more likely to develop strong boundaries and distinctive subcultures.

CHAPTER FIVE

Exchanges, Labels, and Put-Downs

My life has been full of incident: I have met well-known people, includ-ing Salvador Dali (mad, but shrewd) and Prince Charles (shorter than you would imagine), many exciting women (including an actress who almost received an Oscar), yet here in Hollybush [Michigan] my whole life is seen to be defined by the high school senior trip of 1966.

—Justin Cartwright, 1998

FROM THE LUNCHROOM: Melanie began telling stories about talent show auditions. Apparently, she is in charge ... of choosing the acts. She made fun of an [Asian] Indian girl who did a dance, saying it didn't even look like an Indian tribal dance at all, and standing up and imitating her. She said the girl had bells on her skirt and an Indian costume where you couldn't see her face ... She and two other girls "couldn't look at each other or else they would start cracking up." Melanie also talked about other acts ... including a freshman named Patrick who apparently wears a skirt to school. She said he played a guitar and sang. Then she imitated how horrible he was. She talked about a girl [singer] ... "She is the one who" and then made a gesture imitating big breasts. "They call her Foxy Brown." Boy #1 said, "No, they should call her Big and Brown." [The observer remarks]: "... they are probably one of the more popular junior groups ... They talked about people behind their backs; ritually insulted, and imitated people during most of the lunch period."[1]

The last two chapters have looked at the sources of status. Now we consider how status is different from other kinds of resources and how these distinctive characteristics shape peoples' behavior.

INALIENABILITY

If a robber says, "Your money or your life," most people hand over their cash. But if a robber says, "Your status or your life," people are likely to become very apprehensive—he must be insane. They could not give him their status if they wanted to. In this sense, status is inalienable. In high schools, the handsome football player or the beautiful cheerleader cannot give someone else their status—much less sell it to them. Stated in other terms, changing or exchanging status is difficult, and therefore converting other resources directly into status is problematic. One can, of course, gain or lose status by acquiring a status-relevant social position, but the status acquired is compromised if it is gained by illegitimate means. The nobleman who gains the crown by murdering the existing king and his heirs, the bourgeoisie who buys a title of nobility, or the candidate who wins by bribing election officials are looked upon with suspicion and disdain. Or conversely, the opposition leader or social critic who is imprisoned for obvious political reasons may officially be a criminal, but in the eyes of many becomes a hero. The point is not that economic and political resources are never used to manipulate status, but that the very nature of status makes this problematic.

This relative inalienability of status has several important implications for the nature of the social structure. First, it is the reason that social exchange in status systems is both limited and tends to be implicit or indirect. Second, it is one reason that status systems tend to be stable and have restricted mobility.

EXCHANGE, CONVERSION, AND MONEY

A note is required about the significance of exchange, conversion, and money. Clearly, having the resources to buy fashionable clothes, drive a cool car, and go to the "in" places is a big advantage. But it is important to see that economic resources are primarily a means and not the basis of status. The student who goes to school waving his bank statement around and bragging that he or his family has lots of money, only lowers his status. Wealth is an effective means to status only when converted into appropriate status symbols. Even then simply buying the right things is not enough. One must be able to develop the right personal style and the appropriate associations to be accepted. As one student noted, "Buying the right clothes did not automatically increase your status, but it served as one way to keep some people out. People who believed that they were cool simply because they wore expensive clothes were often the butt of many private jokes."[2] Moreover, exchanges between individuals must be implicit. The boy who is too blatant about wooing girls with gifts and lavish entertainment becomes suspect—not to mention the girl who is too obviously influenced by such things or resorts to such tactics herself.

In the case of exchange and conversion, approvals or disapprovals that are bought or coerced are greatly devalued if not meaningless. Those who hire yes-men and flatterers are looked upon with derision, as are those who sell their ser-vices in this way. The same is true of prostitutes and their clients, and regimes that use torture to get confessions or pay for false testimony. The motives of the beautiful young woman who marries the rich old man are suspect, and there is "no fool like an old fool." These various examples indicate that for status to be valuable, it must be rooted in relatively authentic expressions of approval and disapproval. Consequently, conversion of force or material resources into status is problematic. A well-known movie among teenagers is entitled *Can't Buy Me Love*.[3] Made and set in the 1980s, it is the story of the stereotypical nerd who hires the beautiful popular girl to go out with him. His status skyrockets and he becomes one of the coolest guys in the school. They begin to fall in love—transforming their "arrangement" into an authentic relationship—only to be disgraced when their peers discover how the whole thing started. Of course, in good Hollywood fashion, they work through this trouble and supposedly live happily ever after. Even the Hollywood versions of adolescent culture recog-nize the limitations on exchange and conversion of other resources into status.

None of this is to argue that wealth is not important or that the class and status of a student's family are irrelevant. Rather, I am arguing that the effect of these background resources on a student's status *within a given school status structure* are mainly indirect and mediated through conformity to the student norms in a particular school. Obviously, family resources play a crucial role on where you live and which school you are likely to attend. They also affect a student's ability to engage in implicit exchange with other students; the low-income student cannot offer friends a ride in a new cool car. Nonetheless the link between family background characteristics and status among one's peers is not especially strong and is largely mediated through lifestyle norms.

STABILITY AND MOBILITY

Once status systems become well established, they are relatively stable. Adolescents repeatedly report the difficulty of changing their status once their peers have categorized them. There is general agreement that "a per-son's rank was mainly determined during their first year" [of high school].[4] A girl from a District of Columbia suburb reports, "Social groups within the freshman classes started to be formed. These groups remained relatively sta-ble throughout all four years ..."[5] Another student qualifies this slightly: "By sophomore year, the [high-status group] had basically determined who was going to be 'cool' for the next three years."[6] A sophomore in high school says: "I don't really think that there is a way to change your status because who you start to hang out with when you begin high school is who you end up with at graduation ... Once you are labeled by the students and the teachers as belonging to one group or another group, that status does not change throughout your high school experience."[7] A student from an all-girls Catholic high school reports, "At the beginning of the freshman year there were not too many bonds formed, so mobility and change was widely accessible. But as the years passed, accessibility became more difficult for those few that wanted to change groups."[8] A student who attended an all-male Catholic school reports the same: "It is hard to think of how hard it was to move from one group to another."[9] Like in the caste system, and apparently most institutionalized status systems, mobility is highly restricted. Frequently, however, the stability and the absence of mobility are exaggerated. There were cases of women who "bloomed" or men who became star athletes rather late, and consequently experienced considerable upward mobility. Occasionally, popular students disgraced themselves. Most of the mobility that does occur involves movement from middle status categories to categories just above or below. As we shall see later, boundaries weaken as students move into higher grades and are less salient in certain more pluralistic schools. For the most part, however, after the first year or so, status is relatively fixed for most people in most schools.[10] What is even clearer is that many students perceive that changing identities and crossing boundaries is difficult.

There is an individual and psychological aspect of this tendency toward stability. The initial rejections that many adolescents experience in middle school and the early years of high school shape how these students see themselves. If someone is a late bloomer and not particularly attractive in their freshman year, this objective reality limits their opportunity to conform to the norms of their peers. Typically they are excluded from the highest status, most popular groups. This initial objective experience then shapes their subjective sense of themselves, which may in later years limit them as much or more than their own looks or the actions of others. In sociological jargon, the initial limits of the objective opportunity structure that shaped their earlier social identity become subjectively internalized and form part of their personal identity. One student describes how early social definitions become personal identities.

> Early definitions of the groups were hard to overcome. I know that by my senior year, I would have interacted well with the popular group, and I also know that they would have been fairly accepting. Despite these two facts, I never made much of an effort to break into that social crowd because I still felt a distinctive separation from it ... In my mind the popular group was inherently exclusive and I therefore did not have a chance of successfully interacting within it. Because I had this prejudice, I did not even try to break into the group. I ended up excluding myself.[11]

This is the report of a white middle-class student from Alaska. It seems likely that these effects are even stronger for those from lower-class or minority backgrounds, who have often experienced a long history of being rejected by those of higher status.[12]

This stability, however, involves more than limited mobility for individuals. Rarely are there dramatic changes in the relative status of different categories. In no school that we know about are cheerleaders and athletes the "in crowd" one year, only to be replaced by computer geeks and drama students the next year. The categories and the relationship between categories are relatively stable over time. None of this means that there is no mobility or that the rankings of social categories are natural or immutable. Nor am I suggesting that an individual's status cannot change quickly, for example, by being disgraced or winning a famous prize. In most situations, however, the inalienability of status makes status systems *relatively* stable.

INEXPANSIBILITY

In chapter two I noted that the total amount of status available to a group was largely inexpansible, in contrast to goods and services or force. Status is primarily a relative ranking. If everyone received A's or had Mercedes these would not have much status value.

MORE ON MOBILITY

The concept of inexpansibility of status further enriches our understanding of several of the key characteristics of high school status systems. First, in conjunction with the notion of inalienability, it helps us comprehend why mobility is so difficult in high school status systems. Because status is relatively inexpansible, those who initially gain high status are very reluctant to improve the status of inferiors by associating with them. Intuitively they know that allowing others to move up threatens their own position. So, the concepts of inexpansibility and inalienability help us to see why, in most high schools, very few people are able to change their status or their group ties after the first or second year.

This is not to say that people do not try to change their status. A few succeed as the following account indicates:

> My friend had been a member of the Brain groups since elementary school, but beginning in the eighth grade and continuing through high school, he persistently pursued acceptance by the Preps. His family background and dress were quite similar to theirs, yet they were reluctant to accept him. He was fairly good friends with a couple of Prep girls, but still not a group

member. In an effort to prove to them he could be like them, he changed his appearance slightly by wearing nicer shirts, such as polos and oxfords … He gradually distanced himself from his old friends and continually "kissed-up" to the Preps … He spent two and a half years striving to become one of the Preps. Surprisingly enough, he was successful and became one of them by the time we reached the end of junior year. His success became evident when he won a spot on the student council and was the student announcer for the morning announcements our senior year.[13]

Clearly one of the prerequisites of this success was a willingness to distance himself from old friends.

Another girl, in a quite different school, reports on a similar attempt that was less successful:

As we got older, about the end of the tenth grade, a group of girls began to move ourselves away from our normal crowd … My two best friends, Sarah and Mary, and I were getting bored with hanging out at the mall and going to the movies every weekend. The three of us and a few other girls felt the draw of the popular crowd. We were ready to drink and socialize with the popular girls and date the more attractive guys. Unfortunately, it was not easy to break into the popular crowd. We attended a couple of the popular crowd's parties because we would tag along with Mary's popular older brother John when he went out. But we never reached the stage where we felt that we could just show up at parties and be accepted as regular members.[14]

She goes on to recount how this attempt at upward mobility involved not only withdrawing from old relationships, but also denigrating former friends and contributing to their downward mobility.

For us to move up, we felt that we had to distance ourselves from our former friends and push them down. My friends and I would not defend our old friends when the popular kids called them dorks merely because they did not drink or because they attended the Governor's magnet school … for science. We just laughed … and agreed with their insults. We wanted to distance ourselves from our old friends so that the popular kids would see that we were nothing like them. In the end, I think my friends and I that broke away merely reestablished ourselves as the normal group and … downgraded our friends to the smart nerd category.[15]

This story of the betrayal of old friends is an example of a more general phenomenon and leads to our next question: Why are teenagers so frequently mean-spirited and even cruel to one another?

PUT-DOWNS AND "SMALL CRUELTIES"

The fact that status is inexpansible has an additional implication. If lowers moving up threaten those above, the inverse is true; you can move up by putting others down. This is one reason put-downs are such a common phenomenon among adolescents. In his book *Cool*, Marcel Danesi notes the prevalence of "small cruelties." He focuses on those that involve the criticism of someone's body, for example, "Hey, fatso."[16] While these "small cruelties" often refer to characteristics of the body, the phenomenon is much more general and fundamental. Terms like "put down," "make fun of," "trash," and "dump on" (a euphemism for "shit on") occur with considerable regularity in school settings. More accurately, most local adolescent cultures have more "up-to-date" synonyms for these concepts.

Both the observations at WWHS and the descriptions from other high schools provide many examples of this phenomenon. On the mild side was the treatment of low-status peers who showed up in public places frequented by the elite: "Those who were not 'cool', that showed up at the park, were not included, ostracized, and even teased."[17] The treatment of others is frequently much harsher. One girl from an East Coast metropolitan area reports, "The struggle for popularity was a harsh one, with back-stabbing by supposed 'friends' … and the banishment of one person by another based on the need to find one's own level of popularity."[18]

Most common is the tendency of friends and clique members to say snide things about those who are not members of their group. Even if the outsiders are not present, such put-downs lower their status and discourage those who are present from associating with them, or even treating them with routine respect. One of our field observers[19] recorded the following incidents:

> Kate and Ellen were joking with Robert about having found him a date for the dance. I did not catch the name of the girl they were making fun of, but they told him that he could go with "that big, fat, blonde girl." This inspired Robert to start making jokes about the trouble he would have wrapping his arms around the girl and to laugh about how she would roll over him.

This was a put-down of both the "fat blonde girl," but also a subtle dig at Robert. He ignores the innuendo by playing along with the "joke." While Kate may have been particularly inclined to put others down, it was by no means restricted to her. Our field observer continues, "There was an overweight girl whom I have never seen before who was sitting at the table for the first few minutes of the period. After she left, everyone expressed their gratitude that 'the bitch was gone …'" These incidents are reported from a school that, relatively speaking, is low on hierarchy and status differentiation.

Such behavior is not restricted to the inner-city or public schools. A student who attended a relatively small and well-to-do Christian academy in a major Southern capital reports:

> Ritual insulting was common. The most popular boys were capable of cleverly using language to formulate the perfect insult. They devised nicknames for everyone they did not like. These nicknames brought individuals into the spotlight and heavily influenced their status. "Betty Spaghetti" went on to a successful social career. "Yoshi" and "Salmon Boy" became isolates … Low-status boys … participated in ritual insulting in a more vicious and indiscriminate way …[20]

Nor was viciousness in this school restricted to the boys. The popular girls "practiced ritual insulting, mocking each other and those less popular, attractive, or fashionable." The former student of this Christian academy was struck by what she called "the brutality of their commentary."[21] Physical aggression was also used to keep people in their place. High-status boys would gang-tackle and rough-up others "in an isolated hallway out of the view of the administration …" "New football players were cruelly hazed and freshman boys tried to avoid locker rooms where they could be cornered and dunked in a toilet."[22]

Predictably the tendency is for those of higher status to insult those of lower status and this motivated the latter to minimize interaction. A young woman from a small coastal town in the East says, "If a higher status person talked to a lower status person then they were usually out to embarrass them. A lower status person usually avoided high status people for this reason."[23]

HARASSING THE WEAK

Preps often make fun of nerds. A northern Virginia female says, "The 'cool kids' had many ways of making themselves distinctive; the first and most obvious was labeling everyone else … with names like prude, dork, geek, dweeb, bamma … which instantly made you a social outcast."[24] More generally those who are most vulnerable usually receive the most verbal and physical harassment. In some situations, students officially designated as academically weak were stigmatized. A student from a small rural community says that the "slow" students

> … were made to attend classes separate from the rest of the students and were given various labels that coincided with each new trend developed by educators to make them feel less inferior … [T]hese labels were used by other students to demean the "slow" students and differentiate them from "normal" students. It is no surprise that many of these students eventually dropped out.[25]

One of the most troubling things is the aggressive harassment of the physically or mentally handicapped. A student from Texas reports:

> The retarded students socialized only with each other, and were pretty much made fun of by all the normal students. For example, during class changes, all of the retarded students stood outside their classroom and watched everyone walk by. The sad part is that they were oblivious to the fact that almost everyone passing by made fun of them in some sort of way. They tried to participate in extracurricular activities, such as going to the Homecoming Dance and football games, but yet again just hung around each other. Most students felt they had special needs and should not be in public schools as they were.[26]

In the relatively egalitarian school in which we conducted extensive fieldwork, an observer reports: "Then a mentally disabled boy walked by who Angela called 'Funky Butt' because of the way he walked. She then started to make up songs about him."[27]

A female with a physical handicap from a well-to-do community in New Jersey reports, "Those students with physical disabilities tend to be mocked … The learning disabled are not popular and are seen as stupid dorks who wear ugly clothes. Special education students have classes in a separate part of the school, and teachers assume they are troublemakers."[28]

On theoretical grounds, I would predict that harassment of the weak is more common from those just above them or those who are wannabes rather than from the highest status students. The top elites of a social system rarely carry out the persecution of the lowly—even though they may instigate it. One of the points of being elite is to have stooges do the dirty work for you. We did, however, observe cases where relatively high status students engage in this behavior. Overall our data is ambiguous on this point and further research is needed to clarify the matter.

In short, "small cruelties" and "meanness" are extremely common.[29] Why are teenagers so mean? This is due to the centrality of peer status in school settings and the competition that results for a largely inexpansible resource.[30] In the competition for status, people (especially leaders), often vacillate between being nice and being mean, depending on whether they see the other person as a supporter or as a threat. Conversely, followers are usually nice to those above them in the hope of being accepted as an intimate, and hence raising their status. At the same time, they often resent the deference they have to show. Frequently, those with high status are talked about and envied, but disliked.[31] From the leader's point of view, followers of high status are essential, but they pose a threat and from time to time must be "put in their place." This, of course, may turn them into enemies rather than supporters. To further complicate things, if those of high status hold others at too much of a distance, they run the risk of being labeled snobs. In sum, high status requires the careful management of social distance and intimacy. These contradictions and dilemmas often lead to treating others positively in one context and negatively in another. Often this involves two-facedness and backbiting. My key point, of course, is that such behavior is not primarily rooted in a particular stage of biological and psychological development, but is largely the result of the social context.[32]

But if teenagers are mean to those who are roughly equals because they are competitors for an inexpansible resource, why are they mean to those who offer no threat at all? Some of the most demeaning behavior is directed toward those who are the weakest and most vulnerable. Why does cruelty to the handicapped raise someone else's status? Beating a much weaker team does not raise the status of the victor much. I suspect that the primary motivation for picking on the weak is not because it directly raises the aggressor's status. One psychological and two social processes probably contribute to the victimization of the weak. First, in an atmosphere where put-downs and verbal aggression are common, there is probably a definite tendency to displace hostility by scapegoating the vulnerable.[33] This mechanism has been widely alluded to as a reason for the persecution of minority groups.[34] Second, in a context where verbal aggression is common and even admired, the vulnerable offer an opportunity to hone and display one's skills without risking significant retaliation. Third, in a system where the content of many of the norms is obviously highly arbitrary—as is the case with fashion and style—an even higher value is placed on conformity. Deviance must be persecuted lest it call into question the basic assumptions of the normative structure. Many handicapped students do deviate considerably from the norms of other students. Apparently, this is seen as highly threatening and is punished. These ideas are offered as tentative hypotheses to explain what seem like "senseless" cruelties. The broader theoretical point is that the inexpansibility of status has a number of direct and indirect consequences on behavioral patterns. None of this means that such cruelties are unavoidable or inevitable, but it does suggest that they are likely, given how we currently organize our schools.[35]

EXCLUSION AND INCLUSION OF THE WEAK

There is also a tendency for the weakest members of the group to be the most isolated. This is not limited to the handicapped. In August B. Hollingshead's classic study *Elmtown's Youth*, which was initiated in the 1940s, he reports:

> [P]ersons in each class try to develop relations with persons a class higher in
> the status structure than themselves. Conversely, the higher-class person, on
> average, tries to limit his contact with persons of lower status than himself
> in order to not be criticized for "lowering himself." This process operates in
> all classes, but it is especially noticeable in contacts with class V. This class
> is so repugnant socially that adolescents in higher classes avoid clique and
> dating ties with its members.[36]

The treatment of Untouchables in the Indian caste system is an even more extreme version of this. In the past they were forced to live outside the village, excluded from temples, forbidden to use the village wells, and forced to carry out the most menial tasks, such as removing dead animals and cleaning out latrines. In general, they were shunned by everyone else.

The isolation of the people at the bottom is largely a function of social location. If everybody "reaches up" and you are on the bottom, there is no one below attempting to establish relationships with you. But there seems to be an additional psychological or cognitive mechanism operating. Those at the bottom seem to be reprehensible to an extent that is disproportionate to their structural location. This seems to parallel the disproportionate rewards of those at the top. For example, sports stars, who usually out-perform their competitors by only marginal degrees, receive a highly disproportionate amount of praise and other rewards. Apparently, those at the bottom are seen as not only lowly, but degraded. Accordingly, they are avoided and often harassed and victimized. Whatever the sources and mechanisms of rejection and isolation of the lowest strata, the result in high schools is a social world in which the lowest status students are deprived of many of the things available to other students.[37]

On the other hand, rarely is the isolation of the lowly solely a matter of persecution; they often do deviate in ways that are at best insensitive to others. This is not infrequently true of handicapped students. A fieldworker reports on an incident involving a special education student who had some kind of mental handicap:

> One specific incident that occurred toward the end of the period while the girls were around was the ridicule of Louis. Louis was distinct in the group because he was the only black person and overweight. When I asked a girl who he was she said, "He is Louis. No one really likes him, but he always hangs around during lunch. He is foul." Louis had been the center of ridicule throughout lunch but he seemed to bring it on to himself. At one point, Louis pulled out a condom. He started to swing it around and got the girls worked up and the boys laughing. He then put his mouth to it and blew it up like a balloon. All of the girls shrieked and the boys thought that that was so funny. Word got around to the whole group, even those who were not watching the incident. Laura stood up and told a friend who was approaching the group to let her know what Louis had done. Louis then dropped the condom and walked away. An adult walked up to the area and Louis nonchalantly picked up the condom and threw it away in the trashcan. The adult remained standing in the area for most of the remaining lunch period.[38]

Hence, reducing the exclusion and isolation of the lowest strata—even handicapped students in schools—is rarely simply a matter of reducing inequality and changing the prejudices of higher status strata. This is, however, a crucial prerequisite to greater inclusion and solidarity.[39]

GOSSIP

Gossip is a particularly common and powerful means to inflict small cruelties. It is, of course, closely tied to secrecy and rumor, which were discussed earlier. Others have studied the content and structure of gossip in some detail.[40] Gossip is evaluative talk about a person who is not present. The findings indicate that the vast majority of incidents of gossip involve negative comments about someone not present. Unless a high status member of the group immediately contradicts a negative remark, it tends to be seconded and elaborated by other members of a group, both those of high status and those of low status. An obvious question is why gossip tends to be so negative and often malicious—even when it is about close intimates. Why do people rarely gossip about how well someone else did on a quiz or how pleasant he or she is? First, if one is inclined to praise someone, it can be done in public—even with the person present; it does not require their absence, as is the case with gossip. Second, because of the inexpansibility of status, praise of others tends to lower one's own status. Conversely, putting them down tends to accomplish the opposite—especially if others join in.

If the point is to raise one's own status, put-downs are most useful if they lower the status of those who are status equals or superiors. But publicly criticizing such people can be dangerous; it motivates them to retaliate. Precisely because they have equal or superior status their put-downs are as likely to be just as successful as the instigator's. Hence, secrecy is needed. This encourages people to be two-faced and go behind others' backs. If others really respect someone, criticizing them can be a risky act of deviance. Hence, the company of those who are likely to agree is needed. Consequently, most gossip occurs between those who are relatively intimate and considered trustworthy.

A very important kind of respect and status comes from one's close peers, and the rivalry can be intense. Sibling rivalry is the most obvious case, but gossip about close friends is another. The result is that gossip is often about another intimate who is not present, and is frequently associated with back-stabbing and backbiting. A fieldworker reports:

> This group almost always had gossip, often about their own members who
> weren't there at the time. This was not done only playfully, but often was
> somewhat malicious. For instance, when it was discovered that Karen had
> egged Kate's car, everyone turned against [Kate] and insulted her seeming
> inability to stand up for herself. Yet, the next week, Susan was talking about
> [Kate] as if they were great friends again. I found it sort of odd that so much
> backbiting went on within this seemingly close-knit group.[41]

Not all gossip is about close friends. Frequently, gossip is a form of forced intimacy, that is, people being intimate when it is not wanted. Gossip does not involve forced physical intimacy, as in the case of throwing food, but rather forced cognitive and emotional intimacy. But what is the motivation for such behavior? Why would people want to be intimate with someone who rejects them? There seem to be two key motivations. One is to reduce the status of someone by making public his or her deviant behavior. This is usually directed toward rivals or high status individuals who are viewed as snobbish and as needing to be "brought down a notch or two." An alternative motivation is to raise one's own status by publicly displaying one's intimacy with someone of higher status. Even if the person who spreads the gossip does not have direct contact with the high status person, it shows that they have their "sources"—that is, they are tied into the network of higher status people.

Web-based bulletin boards are becoming a new means of public ridicule popular among teenagers. This is, of course, a great magnification of gossip written on the walls of toilet stalls. These means of gossip do not require that it be restricted to trusted intimates because retaliation is unlikely since the perpetrator is anonymous. Such websites often amount to near-permanent public slander, which is potentially available to large audiences. It is becoming an increasing matter of concern to students, teachers, and parents.[42]

Gossip and storytelling are closely related. Having gossip or a juicy story to tell is also a way of gaining the group's attention and making one's self the center of the group's activities, as well as lowering someone else's status. I recorded the following in my field notes:

> About this time John asked Linda whether she likes Luke. She said, "Well, not really. He treats me nice but we're not really friends." John then said, "Well, you'll like to hear this because he's really 'going down.'" He repeated the theme of "going down" several times laughing about it. When they asked why, he said that Luke's girlfriend was going to beat him up. Apparently on a band [bus] trip … someone suggested … that they share their most secret fantasies [by writing them down] … Luke wrote down, "Every night I dream of fucking Sally [someone other than his girlfriend]." Predictably—and maybe this was part of a plot all along—the paper was grabbed and passed around the bus. John took great relish in recounting these various events of the bus trip. Jane expressed the general opinion of the group that anyone who would write down such fantasies was stupid and deserved to be embarrassed.

This incident illustrates in a slightly different way the significance of gossip and storytelling and how one blends into the other. Telling a good story is, in part, a source of status for the storyteller, but it is also usually a way to lower the status of someone else.

In sum, like earlier work, we found that gossip was common and usually negative. This is rooted in the struggle for status and respect—even among intimates—that is accentuated because of the relative inexpansibility of status.

GROUP MOBILITY: THE EFFECT OF AGE AND GRADE

Earlier I discussed the difficulty most individuals face in changing their initial status or crowd—due to the inalienability and inexpansibility of status. On the other hand, the distribution of status across grades, and the fact that most students will change grades each year, means that there are certain forms of built-in mobility.

David Kinney's study of "Nerds to Normals" looked at students' transition from middle school to high school.[43] In middle school, students were either members of the popular crowd or they were shunned and excluded and given a negative label such as nerds or geeks. But when these same students made the move to high school many of the former nerds were able to make the transition to normals. Because of the greater number and variety of both students and extracurricular activities there was a larger array of peer groups, while those who had been nerds could find friends that would treat them as normal. Moreover, high school students were generally less judgmental of their peers than middle school students. This same decline in the intensity of status differences seems to continue as students move through high school.

Not surprisingly, students are especially preoccupied with their status during the early years of high school. A girl from suburban Boston says:

> During the first two or three years of high school, students were very
> conscious of the status of the particular group to which they belonged, and
> various groups did very little intermingling. For instance, a "cooler" or more
> popular student rarely formed a friendship or even acknowledged a friend-
> ship with a less popular student … The strict barriers around different
> cliques made it very hard for students to get to know students [from other
> social groups] well.[44]

Even some freshmen are aware of this pattern:

> Susan began to explain to me how the freshmen class was very clique-
> oriented and that although the different groups sometimes associated with
> one another, there was often tension between them. She seemed very mature
> and said that, "By the time the students reached their senior year, the
> cliques became less apparent and the class interacted more as a whole." She
> said that she was friends with many upperclassmen, and that "on the whole,
> they were much more accepting of each other." She explained, "You don't
> have to look or act a certain way to be someone's friend by the time you
> enter twelfth grade."[45]

Part of this anticipated change will result from physical and psychological maturation.[46] In addition to physical and psychological considerations, the social status of freshmen is relatively fluid. Students see both great opportunity and danger, and hence are more concerned about their status. But these well-known factors are exacerbated by a structural consideration that is often overlooked: First- and second-year students as a group have low status relative to other students and so collectively these lower grades have less status to go around. This makes the competition for that status especially intense. As time goes on their status becomes crystallized and they become resigned, if not reconciled, to their social position. But in addition, the competition and emphasis on differentiation lessens as the status of the class as a whole gradually increases. A student from Pennsylvania makes the following observations about her senior year: "The senior class as a whole became such a high status group that even [vocational/technical students] and nerds were reassimilated back into the general fold of simply 'a senior' … [T]here was just less drive to increase individual status as the class as a whole was so high …"[47] This student attended a medium-sized, rural high school. The shift toward class solidarity may have been more extensive than in other settings, but students in most schools report these same tendencies.[48] In short, because status is relatively inexpansible, and because its distribution is skewed in favor of the upper grades, competition and preoccupation are especially acute in the early years of high school and less so in later years. Data dealing with a different aspect of school life supports this interpretation. Anthropologist Frances Schwartz found that students in high ability classes were much more cooperative and less hostile toward one another than students in low ability classes.[49] Obviously various things could contribute to this. Nevertheless, the relative inexpansibility of status and scarcity of respect for students in lower-status classes almost certainly adds to their competitiveness and aggressiveness.

The higher status of older students is probably the most important social factor affecting the declining significance of status. A second social factor is the extensive common activities and rituals of solidarity during the senior year: senior trips, senior-class gifts to the school, senior picnics, the senior prom, and usually a whole array of graduation-related events. A girl from an urban Catholic school in Texas recalls, "As senior year rolled around the groups became more welcoming and open because of the bonding events that the school sponsored, such as retreats, community days, and intramurals [i.e., competitions between the senior and junior classes]."[50]

A third important consideration is a shift in the types and arenas of power that are relevant. Most seniors have more money to spend than in previous years, in part because many have part-time jobs. Many become eligible to vote. Some are courted by colleges and offered scholarships. That is, status in their peer group is no longer the only kind of power that is available. A key assumption of the theory is that the patterns associated with status groups and caste will be especially strong where status is insulated from other forms of power. As this condition begins to break down, the power of these patterns declines accordingly. Stated in slightly different terms, seniors begin to both acquire and anticipate other forms of power, and hence the relevance of the high school status system declines.

To summarize, the behaviors characteristic of status systems in general and teenagers in particular occur because of the nature of status as a resource. Status is relatively inalienable. It cannot be easily appropriated or simply transferred from one person to another. Because status is relatively inalienable, status identities and status systems tend to be relatively stable once they have become well established. Therefore changing status or status groups after the first or second year in a school is difficult.

Status is also relatively inexpansible. If someone moves up in the status structure, someone else will have to move down. Similarly if a social category gains higher status, another category will lose status. Conversely, one way to move up is to put others down. These characteristics of status help explain a number of behaviors typical of status systems in general and teenagers in particular, including: extreme concern to maintain boundaries and limit mobility; the "small cruelties" toward those who are vulnerable, including the handicapped; the frequent use of negative and even malicious gossip—even about close intimates; and the greater concern with status and cliques. The theory of status relations, and more specifically the concepts of the inalienability and inexpansibility of status, offers systematic explanations for all of these phenomena in the sense that they can be seen as parts of a broader pattern rooted in the nature of status and status groups.

Part III

WHY SCHOOLS VARY

CHAPTER SIX

The Pluralistic High School

... I do believe that there is a plurality of values ... If I am a man or a woman with sufficient imagination (and this I do need), I can enter into a value system which is not my own, but which is nevertheless something I can conceive of men pursuing while remaining human, while remaining creatures with whom I can communicate, with whom I have some common values—for all human beings must have some common values or they cease to be human, and also some different values else they cease to differ, as in fact they do.

—Isaiah Berlin, 1997

FROM THE LUNCHROOM: A table of African-American students: Boyd said, "Let me tell you this joke a white boy sent me." The joke read as follows, "Why do black people stink?" "So blind people can hate them too." The table all laughed at the joke. Donald asked Boyd why he had to say it was a white boy and not just a boy. Boyd said that if he was to talk about Donald he would say black boy so it was the same. Tina jumped in and told Donald that Boyd needed to say white boy so we would know in what context the story was taking place. She jokingly called Donald white.[1]

Homecoming court [was] presented. Each class had two representatives (girls), except the senior class had four ... There were two whites and four black underclassmen and two whites and two black seniors ... [W]hen each senior was called, a certain crowd of students would cheer for her ... The [Monday] After Homecoming: Surprisingly, not one single conversation centered around homecoming—without my bringing up the subject.[2]

---

*An earlier version of this chapter was co-authored with Jordi Comas and presented at the 1998 meetings of the American Sociological Association.

Up to this point, I have focused on social situations and processes that are especially prevalent in school where there are tendencies toward hierarchy: the ranking of groups and individuals. With the exception of very formal hierarchies such as in the modern military, rankings are seldom clear-cut or unambiguous. Yet, even in informal hierarchies most people can agree on who and what is at the upper end, who is at the lower end, and who is neither. When we began our case study of Woodrow Wilson High School (WWHS), our research team expected to encounter a version of hierarchy with relatively strong group boundaries. After several weeks of observations and discussions among the fieldworkers, this assumption seemed inadequate and even misleading. The puzzle was how to document and understand the proliferation of status groups with minimal ranking, variations in the rigidity of their boundaries, and little inter-group conflict. Some previous studies of high schools have suggested that status systems may be less hierarchical and boundaries may be less rigid than is generally assumed.[3] There has not, however, been a systematic attempt to specify an alternative to the hierarchical ideal-type. Most studies of high school peer relationships have implicitly assumed a form of hierarchy.[4] The purpose of this chapter is to outline such a model and illustrate it with data from WWHS, supplemented by less detailed information about several other high schools scattered around the United States. This non-hierarchical pattern of peer relationships is an example of the new kinds of relationships that are emerging in postmodern society—relationships that tend to be more numerous, more diffuse, and less encompassing.[5]

PLURALISM

My notion of pluralism is contrasted with three other ideas: assimilation, hierarchy, and intolerance.[6] *Assimilation* means that one thing is absorbed into another; differences disappear. Complete assimilation means no pluralism because there is only one kind of identity. At some points in the history of the United States this has been the ideal—people would eventually be "just Americans." Therefore, the notion of pluralism at least implicitly rejects complete assimilation and homogeneity. Maintaining some forms of distinctiveness is a goal or value, but this does not necessarily imply the rejection of all, or even most, forms of commonality. Many white prep teenagers choose to listen to rap music. Even ardent supporters of a distinctive African-American subculture do not usually discourage black young people from learning algebra, using a computer, or aspiring to become a professional major-league baseball player. Nearly everyone is for some degree of commonality, but the notion of pluralism implies that this is not the only goal or value. *Hierarchy* implies different ranked social identities; social groups are not just different, but some are definitely better or worse, higher or lower than others. In an ideal-type hierarchy

the rankings are formal and not just a matter of opinion. Usually they are associated with enforced differences in power, privileges, and disabilities. In the
previously segregated Southern states of the U.S., the ranking and privileges
of blacks and whites was not simply a matter of opinion and choice; they were
backed by strong informal and legal sanctions. To the degree that different
identities are associated with such hierarchy, there is not pluralism.[7] *Intolerance*
means "refusing to accept people who are different or live differently," and
often implies enmity and hostility toward those that are different.[8] Tolerance,
however, does not necessarily imply camaraderie or mutual appreciation, but
rather, some minimal level of civility. The three dimensions of pluralism can
vary independently, though of course they are commonly correlated. In the
ideal-type case, pluralism means (1) distinctive social identities, (2) equality,
and (3) tolerance. Few social systems, and not many U.S. high schools, fully
match this ideal-type model of pluralism. Increasingly, however, some high
schools come closer to this ideal-type than the traditional hierarchical one.
This concept of pluralism is intended as a hypothetical benchmark useful for
characterizing and comparing actual high schools. Two forms of pluralism are
relevant.

RACIAL AND ETHNIC PLURALISM

The notions of race and ethnicity usually imply inherited characteristics
involving some mixture of biological and social reproduction. "Race" usually
implies the importance of biological factors, while "ethnicity" usually implies
social and cultural reproduction.[9] Racial or ethnic pluralism involves more
than the presence of individuals from different backgrounds; it consists of at
least two subcultures based upon inherited characteristics. This does not mean
that all those who might have the outward characteristics of a particular racial
or ethnic group will participate in the subculture associated with their apparent ethnicity. Many schools have relatively distinctive subcultures for blacks
and whites. Nonetheless, some blacks may primarily participate in the white
subculture, and some whites may primarily participate in the black subculture.
Pluralism, as used here, means that subcultures are relatively equal in status,
that claims of superiority are contested, and that tolerance of other ethnic and
racial groups is a social norm.

LIFESTYLE PLURALISM

"Lifestyle" is derived from Max Weber's discussion of status groups that was
outlined earlier.[10] lifestyle pluralism is a melange of relatively unranked groups
that have differing lifestyles and discernable social boundaries—though the
boundaries are often fuzzy and more relevant in some contexts than others.[11]

These differences are seen as largely a matter of "choice" and are not defined in the broader society as being inherently transmitted across generations, though these "choices" are clearly limited by income, cultural capital, family connections, and physical attributes (e.g., good looks, athletic ability, and disabilities). Stated in more concrete terms, lifestyle pluralism in a high school means that while people may draw distinctions between preps, brains, punks, jocks, skaters, nerds, or whatever, if members of any group publicly proclaim their superiority, or argue that everyone else should become like them, or were intolerant of other groups, they would be criticized or not taken seriously. Lifestyle pluralism can exist within a particular racial/ethnic group or can cut across these groups. Similarly, a given lifestyle group could be multiethnic. Obviously, racial/ethnic identity typically lasts for a lifetime, while the lifestyles of adolescents often change when they mature and move to another social context.[12] However, this very difference makes the other similarities of the two types of pluralism all the more notable.

THE RESEARCH SETTING

Woodrow Wilson High School (WWHS), where we conducted extensive observations, is a public high school of approximately 1,200 students in four grades. There are about the same number of black and white students with a few students from other ethnic backgrounds. Of a faculty of eighty-five, eighteen are African American and the rest are white. The school offers general academics, accelerated academics, and special education; it has a wide range of activities, an unusually strong fine arts program, and multiple sports, including football, volleyball, basketball, track, softball, wrestling, soccer, lacrosse, and swimming. WWHS is the only high school for a medium-sized city of close to 40,000 located in a metropolitan area of about three times that size. The schools in this state were officially segregated before the Civil Rights movement of the 1960s. While this is a relatively progressive community, most non-professional blacks still live in predominantly black neighborhoods and come from families whose incomes are significantly below the mean.[13] Hence, within the city itself, there are distinctive black and white subcultures. Socioeconomically WWHS is very diverse.[14] While interpersonal conflicts are common at WWHS, there is little or no interracial conflict. Some cliques are clearly interracial and many students have friends in the other racial group. Within the white subculture, there are identifiable status groups but relatively little ranking and little open hostility. Compared to its counterpart, the black subculture has more ranking, but even in this subculture it is less prevalent than in most high schools.

WWHS was studied intensely for two semesters and more intermittently for another year and a half. As indicated in the introduction, three graduate students and thirty-three undergraduates assisted me in making observations.

(For the details of the data collection techniques and the nature of the data, see Appendix II.)

RACIAL PLURALISM

SEGREGATION

At WWHS there are two large lunchrooms, each with an adjoining courtyard. One is called area No. 1 and the other is No. 2. When one enters these areas at lunchtime, it is obvious that most tables are segregated by race. Lunchroom and Courtyard No. 1 are predominantly white, while No. 2 is predominantly black. Predominantly does not mean exclusively. There are a number of black tables in No. 1 and white tables in No. 2. Moreover, about ten percent of the tables have a mixture of black and white students. In nearly all aspects of school life where spatial arrangements are voluntary—classrooms, hallways, parking lots, football bleachers, etc.—this same pattern emerges.[15] That is to say, the predominant pattern is voluntary segregation by race, but significant deviations from this pattern exist. Neither the dominant pattern of segregation, nor the deviations from this seem to be of much concern to anyone. Here are some typical comments by students and observations by fieldworkers:

> White freshman: "This school is pretty segregated. That's just the way it is." Interviewer: "Is there any hostility between black and white students?" Student: "Not really."[16]

> Fieldworker reporting on conversation with white sophomore: "On the topic of racial segregation, Carrie says that there is indeed segregation, but no tension. There may be racial jokes, but nothing serious, and certainly no violence between races. She says, however, that they separate themselves into different groups even in class. Her last comment was that she enjoys the egalitarian nature of the school."[17]

> Black sophomore: "Tonya Johnson said the white people and the black people were very segregated and formed their own little groups ... Courtyard No. 1 is mainly white people and Courtyard No. 2 is mainly black people. She said, 'Black people think they are too good to hang out with white people.' She said she doesn't understand why there is so much segregation because 'everyone should be treated the same.' "[18]

> Fieldworker reporting on conversation with black freshmen and sophomore girls: "They said the students segregate themselves, blacks with blacks, whites with whites, but overall there is racial harmony, everyone gets along with everyone else."[19]

As the above comments indicate, there is segregation, but it is by no means complete. Students interviewed were asked to agree or disagree: WWHS has high levels of segregation and low levels of racial conflict.[20] With a few qualifications, almost all agreed with this statement. Typical responses included: "There is not much I-hate-those-Mexican-people here" (black male). "People get with groups who are similar to themselves. They don't have a problem with other groups" (white female). "There is no racial conflict, everyone gets along … the cafeterias are more segregated, but it has always been like that" (black female).

TWO SUBCULTURES

The segregation is not simply physical; there are also two relatively distinct racially based subcultures here. Most black young men dress in hip-hop fashion: oversize casual pants, various oversize sweat and tee-shirts, and often loosely laced gym shoes. The dress of black women is more variable, but only a few could be characterized as preppy. A female black student says, "The blacks use slangish language. They say stuff like: 'hey,' 'yo,' and 'what you doing.' "[21] Our observations confirm this: though there is considerable variation among black (and white) students in the type of English they regularly use, the systematic use of "improper" English is more prevalent among black students. While many students listen to rap casually, this style of music is especially resonant and meaningful for most black students. In good weather, there is often an informal rap performance in Courtyard No. 2. People will take turns reciting the rap verses they have composed as several people beat out various complex tempos. We never observed white students performing, though a few would occasionally watch. Another indicator of race-related cultural differences is the atmosphere and noise level in the two lunchrooms. A white female field observer reports, "I changed lunchrooms and went to Lunchroom No. 2 today. The first thing I noticed was that students were much louder and more energetic … it was a huge difference."[22] An African-American male observer remarks, "Today I sat in what the students refer to as the 'quiet' lunchroom. [S]tudents were a lot quieter and things were more structured, as opposed to Lunchroom No. 2."[23]

The cultural divide is also evident in each group's perceptions of the social organization of the other group. Whites and blacks frequently refer to some of the same status groups; however, they tend to be aware of more differences within their own racial category and less aware of differences within the other race. White students identify between three and seven white status groups. When commenting on black status groups, white students typically draw a distinction between regular black students and a subcategory variously labeled as thugs, gangsters, or hoodlums. Black students also tend to identify the same difference, but they often draw a distinction between "real thugs" and "looka-likes" or "imitators"—those who try to act "hard" or tough, but for the most part conform to school norms. Blacks commenting on white status groups often identify two or three. For example, a black freshman identified athletes, preppies, troubled kids, and freaks. Some students of each race either seldom mentioned students of the other race or claimed that they did not know much about them. An African-American fieldworker interviewed a black student and notes, "She only talked about the black groups." A different interviewer says, "Rebecca, a white freshman, didn't say very much about the black students." These examples reveal a definite social distance between many black and white students and the presence of two distinct, but related, status structures and subcultures.

PERSONAL CONFLICTS

From an observer's field notes:

> Suddenly, I notice a lot of commotion outside. One white boy had been pushed up against the glass windows and three or four kids (white male and female, I think) were hitting him. When the teacher came to break up the beating, the … boy was left with a bloody nose. Not a minute later, another fight was about to occur. I saw two black boys, standing about ten feet apart, just staring at one another. One of the boys looked extremely angry, as if ready to attack at any moment. [Some administrators] noticed a crowd start-ing to form and began to approach the two boys. The angry one … suddenly ripped off his shirt and wanted to lunge at the [other] boy … Luckily his friends held him back and led him out of the courtyard. While all of this was going on, only one of the seven people at my table noticed the outside activities. The rest just went about their business. The lack of interest struck me. Tessy made the observation that most fights are the result of individual disputes and have nothing to do with the group with which the partici-pants are associated … [M]ost violence occurs between members of the same group … Kathryn [noted] tension between blacks and whites, stating, "Prejudice is getting really bad." Tessy felt the two races were separate, but not hostile … [24]

Public conflicts along racial lines are rare at WWHS. Except for the imme-diate friends of the combatants, other students do not consider a fight as having anything to do with them—though they may run to "watch the fun." According to students who had gone to other schools in the area, fights at WWHS are about as frequent as in the other schools. As one walks down the halls, there is not an atmosphere of hostility, though some are boisterous and less polite than others. The school has its share of bullies and groups that adopt a "don't mess with us" posture. While incidents do occur, for the most part, WWHS is generally a safe place, though not tension-free. Even in the incidents in which the combatants are from different races, they mobilize little racial solidarity per se.

CONFLICT AND SPACE

There are things students could fight about. Chairs and tables are often scarce in the lunchrooms, especially in bad weather because people cannot spread out into the courtyards. Here are some typical reports from fieldworkers:

> I asked the girl if I could join her for lunch. She said, "Yes, if you can find a chair; they're scarce around here." After several attempts and rejections—"That one's taken"—I found an unoccupied seat ...[25]

> "... Cafeteria No. 1 was loud and it was very hard to find a seat."[26]

> ... the group enthusiastically invited me to sit down. There were no chairs, so Carolyn asked a guy from a neighboring table if he had any extras (the people at his table were hoarding chairs). She said, "Come on you have, like, fifty."[27]

From time to time, there are arguments and students confront one another about being in "their place." If anyone were looking for a fight, they could easily find an excuse. Some (usually black) students may be rude to members of the other race if they hang around where they are clearly unwanted. Generally, however, people are not looking for a fight. Most of the time, the pervasive atmosphere is one of live-and-let-live and even mutual respect.

DEALING WITH SCARCITY: SENIORITY AND CIRCULATING

We observed two mechanisms that seem to reduce significance of the scarcity of space and that probably help to maintain the peace. Interestingly, one of these is based on hierarchy and one is based on pluralism. The first mechanism is an informal norm: If anyone had to do without a table, it would be the freshmen. One fieldworker reported: "Most of the freshmen groups in Lunchroom No. 1 sat either on the floor when the weather was poor or in the courtyard when the weather was nice. There were a limited number of tables and, as one of the girls put it, "We're freshmen! We can't get a table."[28] Another records the following: "Five girls were sitting at the back of the lockers ... I asked what grade they were in and they said ninth ... 'that's why we're sitting on the floor ... only older people get tables. We'll probably get one next year.' "[29] Giving freshmen last priority on tables and chairs reduces the scarcity and potential conflict between older students in general and blacks and whites in particular.

The second mechanism is more complex and less obvious; it is the contrast between walking and staking out territory. Essentially, walking consists of individuals or groups circulating among more stationary groups of individuals. Some form of this is common in many societies.[30] Territoriality is the claiming of space as a group's own, and the ability to enforce this spatial differentiation. Both are, in part, strategies to control visibility. Visibility is a prerequisite to a distinctive status—high or low.[31]

Walking was common among high status black men and lower status women of both races. A typical lunch period might consist of a quick meal—if they ate at all—followed by thirty or forty minutes of walking from group to group visiting, gossiping, and flirting. A field observer recorded the following:

> The group was very mixed, about three girls and seven guys, eight white and three black … The two black guys, Eddie and Omar, wore their football jerseys. They quickly got up from the table and began circling the room, talking to the group playing cards and then to the girls standing in the corner. The room started to get quiet as the football and basketball players made their lap around the lunchroom. Jessie explained to me that each day, at almost the same time, the players circled from Lunchroom No. 2 to Lunchroom No. 1 and then through the courtyard and then finally back to Lunchroom No. 2 … Melanie [who was white] was still in awe of the football and basketball players, "They are the hottest guys in school and they stay here at lunch even though they are seniors, just to strut their stuff."[32]

A black female fieldworker at a table of black girls reports, "They ate quickly so they would have ample time to walk around the courtyards and the lunchrooms. This increases their visibility and, most important, gives them the opportunity to flirt with boys." Walking was also common for a few groups of lower status white females, which many people identified as "rednecks." An observer sitting with a table of these girls: "Ayeisha returned to the table and announced that it was time to go walking … when I was invited … I followed them out to Courtyard No. 1." She notes this happened most days.[33] A woman fieldworker, who observed this same group the semester before, reported the same pattern.[34]

Walking is a logical strategy for high status men because it enables them to maximize their visibility among many groups and individuals who are all part of a contiguous social network. Since they are high status and recognized by many people, moving about helps to maximize their visibility and contacts. This would be much less the case for those of low status—unless they are trying to attract the attention of the high status men who are circulating, which, in large part, is precisely what many of the low status women are trying to do. Since these guys are unlikely to visit their table, they maximize their contact with them by circulating. They can at least observe them, and occasionally they "bump into them." It also increases the chances of them interacting with others of less exalted status.

Most of the various white status groups neither seek the admiration of all, nor compete with other groups for school-wide status. Rather they focus on defining boundaries, membership, norms, and styles of their group. Because of the de-emphasis of rank and the emphasis on boundaries, marking territory is important for many white subgroups. For example, in one courtyard, freshmen preps and alternatives always occupied one corner. Their loyalty to this space included sit-ting on backpacks or notebooks when the ground was cold or wet—even when they could have found at least floor space inside. A group of sophomore preps discussed painting their table—they were literally going to mark their territory.

These contrasting modes of operating have an important unintended consequence; they reduce the potential for competition and the conflict over space. The two mechanisms can operate simultaneously without competing for resources or involving each other.[35] An exception proves the rule. We noted above that a few groups of white women, usually labeled by others as "red-necks," do circulate. They also often try to flirt with the more attractive black men, creating further resentment among black women.[36] At WWHS there has been a history of hostility and fights between so-called redneck women and lower status black women. These groups use the same mechanism to compete for status, and are often hostile toward one another.

The key theoretical point is that in a pluralistic setting, the relevant status are-nas may vary for different groups as well as the modes of acquiring status. Where groups use the same arenas and mechanisms, conflict and hostility are more likely. I will discuss why pluralism, with its multiple arenas, emerges later in the chapter.

PERSONAL TIES BETWEEN BLACKS AND WHITES

Despite the predominant pattern of segregation, many interpersonal ties exist between blacks and whites. While most groups are segregated by race at lunch, a number are not. From our field notes:

Lunchroom No. 1, table at left back corner, across … from soda machines, three white males, one black male, eight white females, all freshmen.[37]

My table was composed of eight girls and four boys. All were sophomores except for one senior boy. Eight of the students were white, three were black, and one was from another ethnic origin, possibly Latino.[38]

There were six guys, five black and one white. The guy … with the Gap shirt on was a senior and the starting quarterback [on the varsity football team]. The guy beside me was Trey ... The guy sitting between the two was Matt ... The white guy, Mark, was on my right. He acted pretty cool and was really close with the other guys.[39]

Seven males, six white and one black ... The black boy and Aaron contributed the most to the conversation.[40]

Today, the group of twenty or so freshmen ... Sabrina [was] the only black girl in the group ...[41]

Several integrated tables had only one white or one black person; students do not need a second or a third person of their own race to sit at a table with members of another race. Some students see this as disloyalty to their racial community, but for most students it is "no big deal" if people chose to deviate from the predominant pattern of segregation.

In addition to racially mixed tables, we witnessed other examples of camaraderie and friendship between students of different racial backgrounds. Simple greetings to friends were not uncommon.

Tandi [African-American] waved to a white boy who appeared to be a member of the skater clique ...[42]

The [black] girls hardly ever remarked about racial tensions. Many white students, male and female, would regularly come by the table for various reasons ...[43]

The three black girls came over for a little while. Nicole hugged one of them and they chatted for a while. The other two were primarily talking to Kate ...[44]

Often, playful teasing and banter expressed intimacy.

At the beginning of the lunch period Alice (the white girl in the group) stood on the outside of the table and didn't sit down ... Deva said, "Why are you standing up? Because you need to lose weight?" Alice went over to Deva and pretended to hit her ...[45]

A medium-built black guy walked by carrying a backpack. He had his hand between his backpack and his back so that it was sticking out on the other side. Matthew [who is white] said to him, obviously as a friendly joke, "Hey, Nick, you have a hand behind your back." The boy smiled and stuck his middle finger up at him. Matthew returned the gesture ... The boy laughed and exited to the courtyard ...[46]

All white table: Lisa came back, and soon after, a group of three black males
came over to the table. They just sort of said hi to everyone, and Lisa, who
was standing next to them, eating her ice cream, got into a sort of play scuf-
fle with one of them.[47]

AN INTERRACIAL GROUP OF FRIENDS

For a limited subset of students, cross-race interpersonal ties are much more
intimate and longstanding. A group of students that I personally observed once
or twice a week during their junior year and more intermittently during their
senior year illustrates such relationships. The ostensible tie between most of
these students is that they were in the band, had been in the band, or had a
girlfriend or boyfriend in the band. When first observed, they were seated at
a round table in the following order—though the seating order changed frequently: *Melissa* (black junior), *Jane* (white junior), *Kim* (white sophomore),
Sue (white junior), *Rita-Mae* (known as *Mae*) (black junior), *Maggie* (black
junior), *Paul* (black junior), and *Linda* (white junior). During the course of
the observations the group was joined for extended periods of time by: *Tomika*
(black senior), *Marsha* (black sophomore), *John* (white freshman), and *Elie*
(black junior). Before the observations had ended, several members had left
the group. As we shall see, racial tensions between the students played virtually
no role in these changes.

Most were juniors the first year of observation. The core of the group was
Jane, Sue, Mae, Maggie, and Melissa. Paul and John were there by virtue of
being the boyfriends of Maggie and Elie respectively. All of these students were
middle class, though not affluent. At least six of them were not living with both
"natural" parents. All except the two youngest members had part-time jobs.
Mae, Jane, Sue, and Melissa were members of the National Honor Society.
Mae was class president both her junior and senior years. This is more than a
nominal honor since the holders of these offices are responsible for organizing
the junior-senior prom and several other events important to many students.

They readily acknowledged that as a group they did not spend a lot of time
together away from school, though this did happen on occasion for the core
group and for various smaller subgroups. It was clear from observing them
over a period of time that most of them were genuinely fond of one another.
Some were more compatible than others and the strength of ties varied over
time. To portray the quality of the interpersonal relationships we will describe
their discussions about "twinning":

> Twinning is the process of particular sets of individuals deciding to dress
> identically on the designated day [during Homecoming Week]. Some
> lengthy negotiations went on between different sets of people about what it

was that they were going to wear. Jane initially suggested that everyone wear black sweat pants and black jackets, but some complained that they didn't have these ... At this point Mae was negotiating with Linda about being twins whereas Jane had initially discussed the possibility with Melissa. At one point, Jane, who had started all of this, was left out of the negotiations in the sense that she was no longer a part of the possible pairs that were being discussed and she feigned pouting.

It was clear that who was going to twin with whom had little if anything to do with race—except perhaps that they wanted to make sure that there was cross-race twinning, though nobody ever said anything about this.

Personality conflicts developed between individuals of different races and no one defined it as a matter of race.

> I asked about Kim (white) ... Sue explained that she had had some kind of conflict with Tomika (black) and was no longer coming. Jane said they couldn't understand it ... everyone knew that Tomika was "mean" to everyone and that Kim seemed to take things too literally. They seemed mildly concerned about it, but not particularly angry with Tomika or Kim.

"Racial" characteristics could be discussed with nonchalance:

> Sue and Melissa and Jane began looking at a catalog of dolls ... something that they had been getting since ... the fourth grade ... They looked intently at these and were discussing the characteristics of the various dolls. The catalog contained dolls of a number of different skin complexions, eye colors, and hair types. Some of the dolls were clearly African American, some seemed to be Asian, and some seemed to be various mixtures. As this discussion went on, one of the copies was handed ... to Tomika and she began to intensely study the various dolls. Linda looked over her shoulder. Linda started joking about which doll Maggie looked like. (Maggie is a very light-skinned African-American girl.) They were teasing her about this. Maggie took it good-naturedly but with feigned pride said, "I'm the whole world; leave me alone."

Here "racial" features are clearly the focus of attention. The group openly discussed and joked about racial features, not just in the abstract, but also with reference to a particular member of the group.

As is often the case for teenagers, tensions and conflicts emerged over romantic relationships. Early in our observations I noticed Melissa, who was an attractive young woman, flirting in a rather sustained way with Maggie's boyfriend, Paul. Maggie seemed to ignore it. A few weeks later Melissa turned her attentions to John.

Melissa and John were in a fairly animated conversation. She began to explain that John and Elie, who is John's girlfriend and usually sits at the table, were having trouble. She matter-of-factly stated that John was attractive and a lot of the girls paid attention to him and Elie was very jealous of this. She continued, "John needs his own space. He is Elie's first boyfriend and she doesn't want to lose him." I asked John if this was an accurate description of the situation and he said, basically this was correct. (What makes this relationship especially interesting is that John is a white freshman and Elie is a black junior.) This was all discussed very openly.

A few days later I witnessed an example of John's apparent charm:

About that time three cute African-American girls came up to the table and began talking to John, asking him to use his "Scream voice." This was a reference to the movie *Scream*, a horror film. He acted shy, but obviously didn't mind the attention. He asked them to stand away from the table for a few moments and in the meantime the people at the table nagged him to practice. In a deep bass he gave an imitation of the background voice in the film, setting up a horror scene. He then got up … and did the same thing for the girls that were standing about fifteen or twenty feet away. They all giggled and thanked him and John came back to the table.

The next week:

I asked about Elie and John … and the girls giggled, making a comment about how the group was breaking up … The story supposedly is that Melissa and her sister and John, who are all in the band, were going to go to the movie together. Melissa makes the statement in front of a large number of band members that she and John have a date. Tomika … soon passed this information along to Elie, who was John's girlfriend. Jane and Maggie were quite clear that Melissa's behavior was inexcusable and stupid. "She shouldn't have been fooling around with Elie's boyfriend and if she was going to do so, she certainly shouldn't have told everybody in the band." According to them, to make matters worse, Melissa then acts as if she did nothing and doesn't understand why everybody is upset. In the meantime, Elie and John mutually agree to break up.

From that time on, Melissa was rarely if ever at the table. She was sent (or chose to go) into exile, though she had been one of the original core members. However, members of the group occasionally expressed concern about her, and hoped that she would "grow up."

The fact that John was white and Elie black never seemed to bother any-body at the table—though there were several snide remarks about the fact that Elie was a junior and John a freshman. The fact that Melissa was black seemed irrelevant to either her conduct or people's reactions. Maggie and Mae, who are black, seemed to be as critical of her conduct as Sue and Jane who are white. Clearly most students at WWHS are more mindful of race in their interper-sonal relationships. Some students of both races do not approve of interracial dating and may well have criticized John and Elie's relationship. This, how-ever, was not why they broke up. What I witnessed were the "normal" teenage romantic intrigues—and race was largely irrelevant.

Certainly, these kinds of relationships and attitudes characteristic of this group of friends were not the dominant pattern, though each grade has a few similar groups. The very fact that such groups can exist—without anyone outside of the immediate network paying significant attention—suggests that for some, WWHS is not "two different schools in the same building." The fact that a member of such a group can be elected president of her junior and senior class shows that even if most students do not participate in such groups, it is not a scandal that some do. There is plenty of white and black racism, but there is also a degree of genuine racial pluralism. Such interpersonal relationships both result from and contribute to this racial pluralism.

But developing and maintaining interracial friendships is not easy. There is even the question of whether the group I observed actually involved cross-race relationships. When Mae, who had been the class president, read a draft of this section three years after the fieldwork, she responded, emphasizing the impor-tance of having foreign-born parents. According to her, they do not define their identity as simply black Americans, but as immigrant African Americans in the literal sense. The question Mae raises is whether the group described actually involves relationship between white Americans and black Americans, or whether it is better understood as relationships between some second-generation immi-grants who happen to be black and some white Americans. This is an important aspect of what was going on. I pointed out to Mae that there were, however, members of her group and black members of other interracial lunch groups who did not have foreign-born parents. (This includes groups that contained "wiggers" from lower-class backgrounds, but also groups made up mainly of students whose parents were educated professionals.) Mae replied:

> Forgive me if I'm asking questions that seem closed-minded, but I'm really
> trying to understand how everyone could one day come to respect each
> other mutually, and though I know that you'd like to present WWHS as
> coming close to that, and it may look that way from the outside, but to be in
> it (at least to me) feels like you are passing by ghosts in the hall; they can't
> feel you, and you can't see them.

I quote this for two reasons. First, I want to make clear I am not trying to portray WWHS as some idyllic community of pluralism. The imagery of ghosts passing in the hall is a haunting one, and yet it is instructive. In many high schools and situations of racial and ethnic conflict, people do not pass one another as ghosts, but rather as all-too-present and real enemies. This is not usually the situation at WWHS. Greetings between blacks and whites who have a connection, and an ongoing social relationship are not uncommon. The ideal-type model of pluralism, which I claim WWHS approximates to some degree, is not of a community of love, understanding, and amity. Rather it is one of diversity, limited hierarchy, and tolerance, with people avoiding public expressions of disrespect. While the students at WWHS do not always measure up to even this very limited notion of the good society, they usually do. This is a modest goal but I believe a worthwhile one.[48]

LIFESTYLE PLURALISM

Racial and ethnic differences are not the sole source of pluralism. There are also identities and groups based on lifestyle that both cut across racial identities and create differences within racial groupings.

CATEGORIES AND GROUPS FOR WHITES

In chapter three I provided a composite description of the peer groups that were found in many high schools around the country. WWHS has many of these groups, but because my purpose here is to look at a relatively pluralistic high school in some detail, a more specific description is needed for this high school.

I begin with a description provided by a white junior girl:

> The groups definitely have different ways of dressing. For the rednecks, the girls wear tight jeans, lots of makeup, have frizzy hair, and wear lots of gold jewelry. They spend a lot of time and money on the way they dress. The redneck guys wear baggy clothes. The blacks, and the white people who try to be like blacks, wear baggy clothes, lots of gold, and new gym shoes practically everyday. The preps dress in khakis and polo shirts, and look nice, and the athletes just wear whatever, usually sweatpants and shorts and soccer sandals. The alternative group is into camouflage and baggy clothes. The skater group wears baggy pants and (Adidas) Gazelles and stuff.[49]

This captures the underlying structural features of the white status order. The contrasting poles of the status order are the *preps*, stereotypically from upper-middle-class suburban backgrounds, and the *rednecks*, usually from working and lower-class rural backgrounds."[50] Often the term *alternative* is used to refer to a broad array of other categories—hippies, freaks, weirdos, skaters, punks, goths, straight-edgers. The implied meaning is an alternative to being a prep or a redneck, though the term is sometimes associated with a particular style of music. While this three-category description identifies key structural distinctions, it leaves out the complexities. A white freshman girl gives a more complicated account of differences:

> *Drifters* can be almost anyone ... people who like to associate with many different groups rather than stick with just one group of people. *Preps* dress in preppy clothes, such as khaki pants, sweaters, and polo button down shirts. They act snobby and superior to the rest of the students ... The *freaks* tend to dress in all black and dye their hair unusual colors ... Some are violent and others are thought to do drugs. The majority [of freaks] are not very involved in school sports or activities. They do not get along with other groups, especially the preps and the homies. They often do poorly in school and pretend to be weird, scary, and bad. The *homies* are also known to drink and do drugs. They play loud rap music in the parking lot and dress in baggy jeans, basketball jerseys, and dark colors. Some are involved in football and basketball ... The *skaters* are very visible in this school, probably because there are not that many of them. They always look grungy and do not seem to care at all about their appearance. They are liked more than the freaks are. The *whiz kids* are the intelligent students. They dress in normal clothing, but they do not pay attention to brand names. They are often said to talk about computers and usually do homework during lunch. The *jocks* are mostly ... football players. The majority ... are black ... The *hippies* wear clothing that looks like it came from the 1970s. They always talk about folk music and sit at the picnic tables during lunch. They tend to ignore everyone else. I know that some do well in school, while others do not. They are not involved in many extracurricular activities. The *average students* are those who do not like to be seen as a part of any of these other groups. They usually do not pay much attention to brand names, so their clothing is wide ranging in style. They like punk and rock music. Some are involved in school clubs and many are in the marching band.[51]

Another student gives a very similar description, though she also uses the terms "goths," "yuppies," and "rednecks" and does not specifically mention the terms "whiz kids," "hippies," or "average."[52]

These descriptions add several significant complications. First, they allude to a number of differentiations within the broad term "alternatives." These students explicitly mentioned hippies, skaters, goths and freaks.

A second complication is suggested by the category whiz kids. The terms "brains," "intellectuals," or "AP'ers" (i.e., those taking Advance Placement courses) are common synonyms. Some socialize and lunch together, but some participate in other lifestyle groups. The third complication is that many white students do not belong to the preps, the rednecks, or one of the alternative groups, but are "average." A senior who was a straight-edge punk referred to these as the "typical Joe Schmoe." With respect to style, they dress, in their words, "comfortably," but without the intent of standing out or being dramatically different. Some may make a point of saying that they are not preps, but others will define themselves as "semi-preps" or even "yuppies." The fourth complication is suggested by the term "drifters." As we saw in the discussion of hierarchical schools, there are individuals who manage to participate in several groups. Usually they have a stronger tie to one than to others, but this does not mean they are not accepted members of other groups.

The final three complications have to do with whites' relationships to blacks. The category "jocks" refers mainly to male football and basketball players—though sometimes it refers to those active in other sports. About two-thirds of the football players are black. For the basketball team, one out of fourteen was white the first year we observed and three out of fourteen were white the second year. Despite the fact that most players on these teams are black, "jocks" is still a relevant social category for whites as well as blacks. There are ties of friendship between black and white players. Moreover, most players seem to realize they represent the whole school and care about the support and approval of both black and white students. Hence, "jocks" is a lifestyle category that is relevant to both race-based subcultures. In contrast, "homies" refers exclusively to black students.[53] Finally, there are the "wiggers" (a contraction of "white niggers"), a derogatory name for whites who listen to rap music and wear baggy hip-hop clothes. A few hang out with black friends, though many blacks look upon them disparagingly as "homie wannabes."[54]

While most students fall pretty clearly into one of the more generalized categories, there are many gradations and ambiguities. Students are often reluctant to label themselves or even their clique—though they seem to have little trouble categorizing others. Furthermore, the finer gradations, such as between skaters, punks, and goths, or between preps or almost-preps, are expressed through variable amalgams of fashion, music, mannerisms, and speech or slang. Moreover, like most social roles, lifestyle groups are more relevant in some contexts than others. As we have already seen, they are especially likely to be relevant when intimate expressive relationships are involved. What is not ambiguous is that the hierarchical ranking, which is often associated with such categories, is largely absent at WWHS.

LACK OF RANKING

Most white students claim that there is no ranking system. Alternatively, they think that their group is or should be the highest status, but recognize that most students would disagree.

> Seth (junior): *Q*: "Would you say that some groups are ranked or that some of the groups have a higher status?" *A*: "No. Each group pretty much does their own thing and thinks all of the other groups are stupid. But there is some mixing between them. People can have friends in different groups … At WWHS, there really is not a social hierarchy."[55]

> Beth (sophomore): "[E]veryone is pretty equal here." Since she transferred from St. Marks, she compared the two schools and said that at WWHS, nobody was really inferior like they were at St. Marks's. At St. Mark's there were definite rankings.[56]

> Jim (junior): "Here, it's like nobody's really popular, you know. Not like County and Northern [the other high schools in the area]. There it's like it was forty years ago … We can tell you who is popular with us, but I'm not sure we can tell you who is popular in the school."[57]

> Rick (senior): Rick … says he saw an article in the paper about different cliques, and who the "popular" cliques are. He says, "It's not like that here; there really is not a popular group …" Marty chimes in, "Yeah, there was a girl from [the research team] who sat with us earlier and she wanted to know who the cool kids were, and I was like, 'I don't know!' There really aren't any easily identifiable 'cool kids' "[58]

> Patrick (junior): *Q*: "Would you say these groups are ranked or that some groups have higher status than others?" *A*: "No, not really … [I]t just doesn't seem like people care about other groups. I mean there is no competition between groups."[59]

> Stephen (senior): *Q*: "Would you say these groups are ranked …" *A*: "No … There is not really one universal set of things that makes you cool, it depends on who you ask—because you can be cool in one group, and at the same time not cool in another."[60]

> Frank (sophomore): "I don't think that there's that much [of] a concept of 'coolness' here at WWHS—it's not really a big deal … *Q*: "Would a prep ever date an ['alternative'] person? *A*: "No." *Q*: "Would it create a big stir if that did happen?" *A*: "No, nobody would really care. It just wouldn't happen."[61]

In short, the stereotypical hierarchy is largely absent at WWHS, but claims that there is no ranking need qualification. Most students are negative about the group they usually call "rednecks."

> Steve told me to look out of the window and pointed out the redneck group to me. Everyone at the table laughed and this sparked a series of jokes targeted at the rednecks. Steve said, "They're so pre-primate!" Bill exclaimed, "They give chimps and apes a bad name!" Someone else said, "They all get facial hair at like twelve years old." They also joked that the rednecks must eat rabbits and other road kill.[62]

> Suddenly Nathan said (sarcastically), "Damn! I wish I were a redneck." I looked up and noticed that the rednecks had partitioned off a section of the courtyard for themselves. Jared said (sarcastically), "G-d, I wish I was that cool."[63] Nathan replied, derisively, "The rednecks are so cool, man. I can't even touch that." Laughing they turned their backs to the rednecks.[64]

> [A table of six white freshmen—half boys, half girls] ... despised the rednecks because "they are mean and have a very high opinion of themselves. They pick on a lot of other kids ..."[65]

Yet, despite the negative opinion of many other students, those whom others identify as rednecks often define themselves as the "popular students." At any rate, they certainly would not acknowledge their inferior status.

CATEGORIES AND GROUPS FOR BLACKS

There were, of course, also distinctions within the black student community. Friendship groups sometimes assigned themselves the name of a common street or neighborhood. An ongoing hostility existed between the Sunset neighborhood and City Housing Project. More commonly, there were references primarily to two broad categories. "Jocks" referred to football players, basketball players, and cheerleaders. Then there were the "thugs," "hoodlums," or "hard-core" individuals.[66] In fact, most black students did not fall into either of these categories. Popularity among black students, however, was primarily derived from participation in athletics and cheerleading. An observer reports: "She mainly talked about the cheerleaders and the other jocks and about how 'they think they are everything.' "[67] Most black and white students considered a few dozen black males "hoodlums" or "thugs." Black unwed mothers were an identifiable category who tended to have low status in the view of other blacks, especially the more middle-class black women. In short, there were de facto two broad categories of black students: "troublemakers" or "losers" and those who were not. Most of the jocks were the elite of this second category. Of course, people might differ over the details of what constituted being a trouble-maker and who should be so labeled. The distinction parallels the jock-burnout distinction that Penelope Eckert, a scholar of linguistics, found in two schools she studied in the Detroit area.[68] If there were fewer clearly identifiable and commonly used social categories among black students, there were nonetheless considerable variations in the nature and behavior of subgroups. I will portray these through the notes of African-American fieldworkers.

"NORMAL" STUDENTS

A male fieldworker observed a lunchroom table that was usually occupied by three black men, five black women, and one or two white women. "I would say the entire table was normal looking. They did not sport the name brand clothing and the entire lunch period they sat and talked."[69] These students were concerned about their grades and so were their parents: "The discussion turned to the topic of grades. The students … told their grade point averages … Most of the students had 3.0 or somewhere around there. Boyd did not tell his grade point but he did tell a story of how his mother thought he had failed a class. He told his mother, 'No, I ain't failed no class, I failed the exam!' "[70] A female observer reports on a similar group: "[The table was] … all females, occasionally visited by males … all African-American … three or four fresh-men, one sophomore, one junior, and one senior. Later visited by junior or sen-ior female basketball players … no obvious group identification." [Same group a week later] "Friendly reaction to my presence, open to conversation. Not as many girls at table today … Main topics of conversation: Driver's Education, [and] 'Squeaky,' [who] was supposed to bring food for Diana. No noticeable jargon/slang used."[71] In short, a number of African-American students have the usual characteristics and concerns of most adolescents, but there is nothing particularly distinctive about them and they are given no specific label by other students—black or white.

UNWED MOTHERS

A male observer recorded the following accounts.

> Girl A [was] seventeen years old in the tenth grade [and had] a one-year-old baby. [She was] the leader of the group. [She] talked about how her baby's father pays child support every month [and] takes care of her son while she is in school … [He] is a high school dropout. [S]he works at Boston Market to provide for her child. She was very excited because she had recently bought her son a new pair of Nike tennis shoes … One

girl would try and outdo the other by comparing how much they spent on each of their kids. Girl B was in the ninth grade and had a four-month-old son. [The] father is also a high school dropout [who] lives in Tennessee, and doesn't pay child support. Girl C was a ninth grader without kids ... The other girls made fun of her because she wasn't a mother like them ... She said she didn't want to wind up like her friends ... [She told] her friends that she was interested in a particular boy in her class. Her friends laughed at her, and called the boy a "faggot" and said he was gay. She smiled and laughed at it, but it seemed as though she was really hurt inside ...[72]

CHEERLEADERS AND BLACK PREPS

The same observer describes a quite different group:

> I sat at a table ... of seven African-American females. Four ... were juniors ... three freshmen. The four juniors were all on the varsity cheerleading squad. They played card games during the entire lunch period [and] would gossip about someone or something ... As opposed to the girls I sat with in the other cafeteria, these girls didn't curse, had a very pleasant attitude, and seemed to have a good head on their shoulders [sic]. The girls were also very bold and outspoken ... very articulate and seemed to be mature for their age ... [They talked about] their newly acquired driving experiences with their parents in the car. This was a big deal ... The bell sounded, and each one of the girls spoke to me before they left, threw their trash away, and left to take yearbook pictures.[73]

MALE JOCKS

One of our male fieldworkers developed very good rapport with a number of the football and basketball players:[74]

> I sat down at the boys' table. They asked me who I was and I told them why I was there ... [T]hey were all key players on the varsity football team. At first ... they were kind of hesitant ... simple yes/no answers ... Sam became more open with me after about 15 or 20 minutes. He started telling me about all different kinds of things: The girls from the basketball team sitting behind us were a hard-core clique; all the other girls in the school were scared [of them]. Shanika is the ringleader. She has most girls in the school very intimidated ... He [said the] vice-principal ... was a "dickhead" that nobody liked. He pointed out one guy on the boys' basketball team that all the blacks think is gay. He is a good player though. The right corner by

the courtyard was Sunset Avenue [a local black neighborhood] Crew. The [students from the city housing] projects were by the wall. On the left was a group of girls [he] referred to as the "hookers" of the school. He called one of them over to the table and asked her to suck my penis. She smacked her lips and she walked back. He said Lunchroom No. 2 was "the happening lunchroom" and Lunchroom No. 1 was the lunchroom for the gay guys and freshmen.

[One week later] Many of the people from the group today were in ISD (In-School Detention) … Sam … took me to the pathway behind both lunchrooms … introduced me to one guy who is supposed to be the main drug dealer in the school and … to some "pipehead" [drug user].

The observer summarizes and reflects on his time with these students:

They always made fun of Mason, the retarded guy, and talked about females … There was really no other topic of conversation. Even though they were on the football team, they never talked about it … These guys were always getting in trouble. Clothes [were important] even though they never talked about it … you could tell by the expensive, popular name brands they wore. Until the last visit, they never talked of aspirations of going to college or having a career … [They] did have goals and aspirations to go beyond high school, but they were afraid of rejection by their friends. It was not the cool thing. Smoking and drinking were a big deal … They all smoked marijuana and cigarettes. They said that was what they spent an awful lot of their time doing. They were afraid [of being] caught but were willing to deal with the consequences … One thing I have observed about the males is that they think they are hoodlums. They don't act like thugs, but they believe that they are hard.[75]

WOMEN'S BASKETBALL TEAM

The core of the women's basketball team sat at a table only a few feet away from the male jocks. The same fieldworker reports:

The females at the other table … started to come over … Shanika kept tapping my butt saying she was trying to fix my shirt … Shanika kept implying … that she wanted to have … sex with me. She even said to me, "You eat pussy good, don't you?" I just ignored her and started talking to the guys again … Guys from my other group say that she … has casual sex with older men. [S]he was quick to admit that she loves sex and only with men outside of high school.

[A week later] I sat down with Shanika and her crew and talked. They said
they were just "chillin'." They had a game the night before and Shanika
was happy because they had an article in the paper about her team with
her picture beside it ... Their women's basketball team is the school's prize
possession. They were on like a thirty-game winning-streak ... She started
asking me if I was going to stop "faking" on her ... I told her I was not
"faking" but I couldn't [call her or go out with her] because it was against
the rules ...

[Two weeks later] For the first time, I heard these young ladies talk about
goals. They said that they wanted to go to college and make something of
their lives. They said ... it is not the "cool" thing to talk about it and be a
"nerd." Even though they have goals, they all smoke ... weed, blunts, and
cigarettes ... [and] drink ... because it is the thing to do. I asked them who
were the more popular people in the school ... [They said] within the black
population there are two main groups that attract the most attention ...
their group and Sam's group ... they said that both groups were tight and
... many of them were sexually active with people [in] Sam's group.[76]

These field notes show considerable variation in lifestyle within the black subculture at WWHS. Add to this mix the African-American students at the racially
integrated table described earlier (and similar tables), and the range of variation is
even greater. Yet, other than the notions of "jock" and "thug," there are not many
distinctive social categories that differentiate groups of students. Those categories
that do exist at WWHS are primarily local terms, for example, the "Sunset Crew,"
rather than widely recognized cultural concepts like "punks" or "rednecks." This
is probably because the societal media pay less attention to differences within
black adolescent communities. The black subculture at WWHS is on average (1)
more "traditional," (2) more hierarchical and gradational, and (3) less culturally
segmented and pluralistic. Popularity is still closely tied to athletic prowess and
to physical attractiveness. At least a portion of the black subculture is much more
open about sexuality, and probably more sexually active than other students.[77] In
this school, many black students make good grades and are committed to academic
performance. Nonetheless, on average, WWHS's African-American subculture is
even more ambivalent about academic commitment than the white subculture.[78]

The differences between the black and white subcultures should not be
overstated. Both are relatively pluralistic. A male African-American observer[79]
noted:

I also found a high level of respect between the different groups of students
that you don't see in most schools ... no one tries to emulate someone else,
and everyone does their own thing ... The group of [African-American]

cheerleaders who I usually sat with could tell me information about each group. They also told me which groups they liked and those they disliked, but … they admitted that they had no problems with any other groups and that even though there might be a level of dislike, there is still a high level of respect for each group.[80]

Within each crowd and clique there are some individuals who have higher status than others, but their ability to lord it over others is limited. In a more egalitarian context, being too aloof from other members can erode your own status. None of this is to suggest that WWHS is a school without inequality, conflict, and tension. However, this data is better explained using the concept of pluralism than simply relying on notions of ranked hierarchy. I will return shortly to the question of why pluralism develops, but first I need to address a slightly different question.

WHY IS CONFLICT RARE AND SEGREGATION PREVALENT?

When most people seem to have genuine respect for others, and generally get along in a civil and peaceful manner, why is there so much racial segregation at WWHS?[81] The students tend to give two answers to this question. The most common answer is that "it is just natural" for similar people to "hang out" with one another. Of course, what this answer ignores is that only one type of similarity is being considered—skin color. Clearly some whites are much more similar in most respects to some of their black peers than to other whites, and the same is true for some blacks. Why is it not "natural" for these other similarities to produce association and solidarity? No simple notion of "natural" similarity can explain the pervasive segregation.[82]

A few students give a second answer. They claim segregation produces peace.[83] That is, people who live in two separate worlds that have little to do with one another, and hence they have little reason to fight. However, this overstates the degree of segregation and independence. Black and white students must and do interact with each other in a number of ways on a day-to-day basis—in classes, in the halls, on athletic teams, in student government. As noted earlier, the shortage of seats in the lunchrooms could easily lead to fights. Yet, there is little racial conflict. Some students may be hostile toward members of the other race, but they usually keep this to themselves or openly express it only with close friends. In our judgment, segregation, per se, is an inadequate explanation for the low levels of conflict.

So, what explains the apparent paradox of high levels of segregation and low levels of racial conflict, In part, it is the difference between micro and macro levels of social relations.

At the micro level, many WWHS students have known one another most of their lives; the micro history of their interpersonal interaction has not, for the most part, involved racist attitudes or behavior.[84] Nevertheless, the macro history—the collective memory and societal politics—of each group has not escaped the past. The move toward pluralism and equality may have equalized the legitimacy of different macro identities, but if anything, they have accentuated the boundaries of such identities. In terms of the theory, minority groups, and especially those that have long experienced domination and discrimination, create alternative subcultures through the adoption and elaboration of distinctive norms and styles. Minority members who have close expressive relationships with those of other races and ethnic groups or who are too preoccupied with conforming to the norms of the dominant groups are often seen as disloyal, as denying their macro identity. This is especially likely to be so for black students who "act white."[85] Thus, the paradox is that students "have no problem with" concrete fellow students of another race or ethnicity, but they have a problem being publicly intimate with someone who does not share their own macro identity.[86] Hence, the great paradox of pluralism is that it both reduces and increases the social distance between people.[87]

In WWHS and all of the pluralistic high schools for which I have data, race and ethnicity served as the initial starting point for most group formation: Most first sought to associate with students of their own ethnicity and then created differentiations within these ethnic enclaves. In more abstract terms the initial basis for separation and combination is race or ethnicity. This seems to be the pattern in most schools with significant minorities. In the context of most contemporary high schools, race and ethnicity are relatively inalienable characteristics. In recent years, the social sciences have tended to stress that ethnicity is not primordial, but socially constructed in particular settings.[88] From a historical perspective this is almost certainly the case. But from the point of view of most—not all—high school freshmen, this is irrelevant. For them, race and ethnicity seem inalienable.[89]

HOW COMMON IS PLURALISM?

WWHS is of greater interest if it represents a larger population of schools. In addition to the WWHS data, we have qualitative descriptions of four other high schools, each in different parts of the country, which describe ethnic and/ or lifestyle pluralism in these situations.

A student from a Texas high school with 4,000 students reports:

> My high school was very diverse; the school district kept reminding us
> how lucky we were to go to a school where over fifty-seven languages were

spoken, and how this is what the world is really like. This also helped each ethnicity to have their own cliques … Even though the cliques seemed seg-regated they really were not … People who were Asian had friends who were not Asian. There were also some … multiracial cliques.[90]

It seems clear that there were significant levels of racial and ethnic pluralism in this school, but he does not comment on lifestyle pluralism per se.

A girl from Maryland went to a magnet school with 3,000 students. She describes her school in the following manner:

[My school] is a very large, diverse school, where a student is almost guar-anteed to find some group or organization to fit his or her major interests. The status hierarchy is not so much a vertical one based on who is more popular than whom, but one where groups are based largely on interests and activities. Because of this structure the high status, medium status, and low status are not always easily defined. As in most schools, certain groups are labeled as "cool" or "nerdy," but there is not always a consensus on such labels. Instead, mixing among groups occurs frequently, and those who look down upon others are often the ones with whom most of the student body wishes not to associate.[91]

A male student who went to a high school in Alaska with 2,400 students reports:

My initial reaction to this paper topic was frustration … I considered the way social interactions occurred in my high school and believed that there were no clearly defined groups. However, after further thought, I reconsidered my position and realized that there were very specific social groups. The reason that they are hard to recognize is that the members of the groups often overlapped; for this reason, ranking the groups was not extremely prominent. However, groups definitely *were* there [emphasis in the original] … There wasn't a specific ranking of these groups. At times, the group which contained the supposedly "popular" people did hold a higher status among the student body … Once we move past the popular group, we see that the other groups do not fall into any particular ranking … There was very little deliberate exclusion in the groups. People simply hung out with whomever they happened to get along with.[92]

Students attending three different universities wrote these reports as part of class assignments. The authors had direct contact with only the student from Maryland. If there were any biases created by the nature of the assignments, it would have encouraged students to report hierarchy, not pluralism.

A fourth report is drawn primarily from press reports and information on the school's website.[93] In 1971 T. C. Williams High School in Alexandria, Virginia, underwent court-ordered racial integration as a white high school and a black high school—each with a strong football program—were merged. The Hollywood movie *Remember the Titans* is about the tension and conflict that emerges at the combined school and how the new integrated team goes on to win the state football championship.[94] The movie stimulated media interest in what was happening at T. C. Williams High School thirty years later. In 1999 the official figures for the school's ethnic composition were forty-five percent African American, eight percent Asian-Pacific Islander, twenty percent Hispanic and twenty-seven percent white.[95] These figures fail to do justice to the ethnic complexity of the school. The nearly 2,000 students come from 80 countries. When lunchtime comes the students split up into a multitude of ethnic enclaves, many speaking the languages of the country from which they came. The school principal observes, "There are no overt tensions, but sometimes it is a harder job to get to an understanding, to get the students to know each other." Many of the student clubs have an ethnic basis: the Asian Club, the South Asian Club, the All-Africa Student Club, the Somalia Club are some examples. "It's the coolest thing, because T. C. has everything," said … a member of the school's Gay Alliance. "There is a club for every person." In addition to media reports, one of our college students described this school in a class assignment well before the media reports described above. He reports that the school is not only multiethnic, but that the lifestyle groups were not clearly ranked: "No group could be seen as dominating or possessing a higher status than all the other groups because to make such a statement would be extremely subjective. T. C. Williams resembled more of a … system that was almost [horizontal] as opposed to vertical … The only group really looked down upon by the majority of the others was the gang bangers."[96]

This makes clear that pluralism occurs in other schools scattered throughout the country. With the current state of our knowledge, it is impossible to say how intense or common pluralistic structures are. On both theoretical and empirical grounds, it seems likely that pluralism is increasing, but obviously we need more research to clarify its frequency and extensiveness.

THE NEED FOR A MODEL OF PLURALISM

One purpose of this chapter has been to suggest a revision in the usual assumptions about the prevalence of hierarchy in high school peer relations. I am not claiming that all previous studies have been oblivious to pluralistic tendencies. Yet, much of popular culture and scholarly research have drawn on a hierarchical imagery that obscures the more complex status relations in many (and perhaps most) high schools in a postmodern society. A more adequate sociology of education needs to supplement the notion of hierarchy with an explicit notion of pluralism, and to empirically specify the nature of such pluralism, especially in high schools. I have suggested one such model, which I contrast to the concepts of assimilation, hierarchy, and intolerance. This is an initial conceptual model that is certainly open to criticism and revision—but it is a start. My aim is to increase sensitivity to the range of different social contexts that young people actually experience, and may eventually contribute to less stereotyped images in our postmodern popular culture.

EXPLAINING PLURALISM

RACIAL PLURALISM

With respect to racial pluralism at WWHS, I have already outlined the macro context that creates social pressures toward cultural differentiation and voluntary segregation. Whether pluralism develops in a particular school or community, however, is obviously affected by the *racial composition and structure of the community*. If only a very few people are identifiably "black" (Latino, Asian, etc.), pluralism is seldom well developed. Obviously, the likelihood of racial or ethnic pluralism depends on the presence of sizeable identifiable groups. Although the community surrounding WWHS is relatively progressive on issues of race and gender, there are distinctive black and white subcultures. These major cultural differences in backgrounds certainly reduce agreement about the dimensions and criteria of status that are important, and hence contribute to lifestyle pluralism as well as racial pluralism. But if the two race-based subcultures in the high school reflect the unequal economic resources and substantial (but not complete) residential segregation of the community, neither the community nor the high school are very polarized over the issue of race. Racial issues and even hostilities emerge, but these are usually handled by discussion and accommodation rather than more intense forms of conflict. Even though blacks are a relatively small minority and the city council members are elected at large, there have regularly been black members of the city council and there have been three black mayors. In short, WWHS pretty well reflects the community: segregation, some tension, but relatively little open hostility or conflict.

LIFESTYLE PLURALISM

Racial differences only account for certain aspects of pluralism. How might we use the theory of status relations to explain the emergence of lifestyle pluralism? First, status is relatively inexpansible and this interacts with *school size* to affect the degree of pluralism. The larger the school is, the smaller the proportion of the students who are highly visible to most other students. In a school of 250, ten percent is twenty-five—easily small enough to be a highly visible "popular crowd." In a school of 2,500, ten percent of the students is 250—far too many to be highly visible to most other students. Hence, if there continues to be only one kind of elite, for example, "the popular crowd," this means that larger numbers and proportions of students are not only excluded from the elite, but also excluded from any significant contact with them. In a small school, lower status students may not be able to date the cheerleaders, but they usually are in classes with them, ride the bus with them, or knew them in grade school. This is not the case in large high schools. Moreover, as the size of a student body increases, it is more difficult for those on top to control those below. In small social systems, elites can keep many in line by putting down and stigmatizing a few. As the size of the system increases, opportunities for deviance and innovation increase. Consequently, many able and ambitious students are motivated to either create or support other dimensions and realms of status competition, and hence form other groups who do not recognize the superior status of a traditional "popular crowd." They adopt or create other status systems based on different lifestyles. WWHS is not an exceptionally large high school, but it is large enough that these processes are operating. I suspect that it will be rare to find large high schools (1,500–4,000) without significant pluralistic tendencies.[97] In short, because status is inexpansible, increase in school size increases the likelihood of pluralism.

Second, *gender equality* contributes to greater lifestyle pluralism through the mechanisms specified by the theory. In more traditional hierarchical schools women's status was highly dependent upon their associations with men; they needed to be "popular" with high status men, but not "sluttish."[98] This put most women under great pressure to try to be part of the "popular crowd" or at least to aspire to this and copy their lifestyle. While this tendency is still there, feminist ideas have significantly weakened its power. To a greater degree than in the past women can gain status by being smart students, outstanding athletes, and leaders in student government. That is, new dimensions of status and different kinds of conformity are relevant. When fewer girls are obsessed with "being popular," the status of the popular crowd is reduced. Instead of being envied and copied, they may be dismissed as "superficial." This is not to say that good-looking, fashion-conscious women in the popular crowd are low status, but in many schools they are not the "goddesses" they once were. The status of this "popular crowd" as a whole is relatively lower than in prefeminist times. Since status is relatively inexpansible, the downward movement of the old popular crowd eventually means the upward movement of at least some of the other crowds.[99] By lowering the status of the popular crowd, the gender revolution has not simply decreased gender inequality within high school status groups, but has also contributed to a more general reordering of high school status structures. Of course, to point out the important effects of reduced gender inequality is not to argue there is full equality for women and men. While the data is largely impressionistic, it is almost certainly not accidental that in subcultures where feminism tends to be weaker—for example, in African-American, Latino, rural, and conservative religious groups—pluralism is usually less developed.

Another source of pluralism the theory points to is *multiple criteria for status*. Hierarchy will be more intense and unambiguous when only one or two criteria of status are relevant. It is usually clear which baseball player has the highest batting average. Who is the best all-around baseball player is usually much less clear. Who is the best all-around professional athlete is even much more debatable. Different groups will focus on different sports as well as different individuals. Many avid baseball fans do not know and do not care who is the top-ranked women's tennis player. One of the reasons that WWHS has a pluralistic status structure is that the school supports many different kinds of extracurricular activities. Part of this is undoubtedly due to pressures to provide women equal opportunity to participate in sports. Another reason may have been to provide athletic activities for white males once blacks began to dominate the football and basketball teams.[100] Whatever the motivation, WWHS has a wide array of "non-traditional" athletic activities, such as soccer, field hockey, tennis, wrestling, swimming, and lacrosse. The school system, of which WWHS is a part, has invested significant resources in band, orchestra, chorus, and drama. Several of these programs are outstanding and hence increase the status of those who participate in them. The result is students at WWHS have a wide array of extracurricular activities available to them. Consequently, while football, basketball, and cheerleading are still important activities for some, for many they are simply one of a possible array of activities. This factor partially explains why lifestyle pluralism is weaker within the black subculture than the white one. Activities such as orchestra, band, drama, lacrosse, field hockey, and tennis are still largely white middle- and upper-class activities. Consequently, the interest of black students still tends to focus on the more traditional activities of football, basketball, and cheerleading. Hence, the black status structure is less multidimensional and, accordingly, less pluralistic.[101]

David Kinney's study of the transition from middle school to high school identified two of these three processes at work.[102] Both the greater diversity of extracurricular activities and the larger social arena of high school made for a less hierarchical and more pluralistic social environment in high school. My argument is that these processes also help explain some of the differences between high schools. Undoubtedly, other factors affect the degree of pluralism such as the number of ethnic groups represented in the school population, the status of the school relative to other schools in the area,[103] and the commitment of the school administration and local officials to notions of equality, pluralism, and tolerance. My claim is not that the theory of status relations fully explains this pluralism, but it does generate suggestive hypotheses about when and where pluralism is likely to develop.

Let me summarize. In a number of high schools, peer relationships involve a pluralistic set of status groups, rather than a hierarchy, and status inequality is relatively muted. I outline an ideal-type model of pluralism—in contrast to the notions of assimilation, hierarchy, and intolerance—to assist in analyzing and understanding more pluralistic social settings. This model identifies two types of pluralism: racial or ethnic pluralism and lifestyle pluralism. At WWHS, two corresponding subcultures, largely segregated by race, exist and are further subdivided into different crowds and cliques. There is very little ranking of groups and little conflict or even competition between these groups—even though space is scarce—though tension, conflicts, and fights between individuals do occur. Friendly interpersonal relationships between blacks and whites are common and some cliques are multiracial. The segregation is due more to macro history than personal experience. For the most part these students have not and do not experience any blatant racism from each other, but they have not escaped the macro history of slavery and racism. Most peer groups are voluntarily segregated even when there is not significant hostility between most blacks and most whites.

The emergence of pluralism is due to several things. The relative inexpansibility of status means that as the size of schools increases, a decreasing proportion of students can be members of the traditional "popular crowd" or have any connection with them; hence, they create alternative lifestyle groups. Feminism and decreased gender inequality give women alternative means of gaining status than simply "being popular with the boys." This also decreases the pressures to be in the "popular crowd" and hence reduces this crowd's status and dominance. Because of the relative inexpansibility of status, this demotion increases the status of other groups, reducing hierarchy and increasing pluralism. This tendency toward pluralism is also stimulated by increases in the variety of well-funded extracurricular activities and a more varied racial and ethnic composition of the student body.

CHAPTER SEVEN

Other Kinds of Schools

... some speak of the way the "social atmosphere" of the school provides a "hidden curriculum," but the nature and influence of this "atmosphere" are at best nebulous ... [These commentators] proceed without any robust understanding of the nature, power, and dynamic of institutions ... [and] are thoroughly inattentive to the independent yet powerful moral influences of the media, the market economy, and the contemporary political culture and how they interact with the consciousness of children and the culture of the schools themselves.

—James Davison Hunter, 2000

FROM THE LUNCHROOM: Marsha [who is black] talked about the possibility of going to [a local conservative Christian academy or one of the county high schools]. She waxed eloquent about the beautiful pool at the new high school. Jane [who is white] said to her, "Think about who you would be with. There are going to be a bunch of racist rednecks in that school."[1]

Most students in the United States attend relatively large public schools; the focus thus far has been primarily on such schools. This chapter looks at schools that are atypical in some respect: military academies, a school for the upper classes, public schools in small towns, schools on small military bases, and religiously oriented schools. The point is to look for schools in which the pattern of status relations among students might be different from those that we have considered so far.

THE "MILITARY" ACADEMY

Some schools self-consciously create official and semi-official status differences and suppress attempts of students to create other kinds of status distinctions. Moreover, they encourage associations between those of roughly equal rank and discourage association between others. They also create status sequences in which people can count on gaining more privileges as they move through the system. For example, all seniors are given privileges that are not available to underclass students.

I refer to this as the "military" academy model, because the best-known examples are military schools usually modeled after colleges like the Virginia Military Institute, the Citadel, and the U.S. Military Academies.[2] In these schools, first-year students do not have an amorphous, yet-to-be-defined status; they are officially assigned a very low status and subject to constant status degradation and harassment. The intent and effect is to create solidarity among the members of a given class by repressing competition for informal status among peers. (Here "class" refers to students in the same grade, age cohort, or year-in-school—not to socioeconomic status or a particular group of students taking the same course in the school curriculum.) As students progress from one school year to the next they are given additional responsibilities and privileges denied to those less senior. Of course, some are given more responsibility than others; some seniors are captains, some are colonels, only one is corps commander. Nonetheless in most public situations, all seniors receive deference.

I put "military" in quotes because, while this form of organization is most characteristic of military schools, it is not restricted to them. The essential defining feature is officially organized status systems that de-emphasize informal status differences. Perhaps surprisingly, one school that fits this model is Springdale Academy, an elite girl's school in the Washington, DC, area. I will focus on this school precisely to show that the social mechanisms discussed are not relevant only to military institutions. A former student of this school notes, "The crucial factor was above all [an] emphasis on class unity from day one."[3] Some of the usual markers of individual status differences are eliminated. For example, the girls wear uniforms, and clothing seems to have little status relevance. Other common status markers become associated with different classes. While the tables are not officially assigned, class members eat together. The former student remarks that she could never remember an underclass girl having the nerve to sit at the senior table, unless she was specifically invited to do so. She goes on to recount how older students and especially seniors had considerable privileges and power over younger students.

This official differentiation by class is mitigated, however, by dividing the whole school into teams that cut across classes—the "Lions and the Tigers." One stays on the same team throughout one's time at the school. Obviously, this creates some cross-class solidarity and channels competitiveness into athletics and other approved forms of competition. Moreover, she specifically notes that the status differences between classes do not apply in academic settings, nor do they apply during athletic competitions. In these competitive, instrumental contexts most preexisting status differences, whether official or unofficial, are much less relevant.

I do not mean to suggest that this type of school is completely successful in reducing informal status differences, cliques, and crowds. Such schools are, however, relatively successful in doing so for reasons that the theory makes clear: (1) they create official status differences linked to seniority, (2) they suppress competition in dress, (3) they reduce competition for the attention of members of the opposite sex in the school setting, and (4) they organize academic and athletic competition so as to reduce their impact on expressive relationships. One's year-in-school is crucial. For military schools per se there are also the official military ranks. That is, these schools explicitly manipulate the content of conformity, association, and alienability. All of these factors contribute to a distribution of status by official social categories—that is, year-in-school and formal organizational position—rather than informal criteria based on personal differences. Cliques and informal status differences exist, but they are significantly muted.

Some additional indirect evidence about the relationship between class solidarity and status group differentiation and competition comes from two relatively small public schools. The first, a rural western Pennsylvania school, had a tradition of class-based privileges and of relatively high levels of class solidarity, especially for seniors.[4] While each class had an array of cliques, these were relatively unimportant. As the school attempted to "upgrade," academic tracks were introduced and students were grouped by their academic performance. This meant that privileges were less tied to the year-in-school and, consequently, class solidarity declined, status competition increased, and consumption patterns—dress, cars, etc.—became more central to status. Instead of creating mechanisms that increased class solidarity—as the "military model" does—this school's efforts to raise academic standards had the unintended effect of reducing class solidarity and increasing status group differentiation.[5]

The second case is a high school of about 400 students—an unusually small public school for the Washington, DC, suburbs. A graduate of this school says:

> Among all groups ... the group that had the most status (by far) was the seniors ... For freshmen, seniors are glorified images who are almost mystical ... Every student wonders what it would be like to be a senior in the same way a blue-collar factory worker wonders what it would be like to have enough money ... As far as achieving high status, if you were a senior you had it ... and if you were not a senior you had to wait your turn like everyone else.[6]

While seniors have an exalted status in many schools, the school administration supported the seniors' exalted status by giving them various special privileges. But lower classes were not officially ranked and privileged relative to one another. Hence, cliques, crowds, and status distinctions were more pronounced within the lower grades. Nonetheless, these seem more limited than is characteristic of most other "traditional" high schools of this size. The high official status of seniors is a more limited and weaker form of the "military" model.

Military academies reduce the variation within classes and increase the variations between classes—especially with respect to expressive forms of behavior. All first-year students are "rats" or "plebes"—no matter how brilliant they are or how they perform on the athletic field. All seniors are due deference. Uniforms, forms of address, and privileges highlight the within-class similarities and between-class differences. In the theoretical terms introduced in chapter two, this pattern is brought about by separation, combination, and linking. Freshmen are segregated and have special demands and expectations imposed upon them. Degradation at the hands of more senior students gives them a common set of intense and emotionally charged experiences. This shared commonality is an important mechanism of combination and solidarity. But this class solidarity, rooted in separation and combination, is linked to the larger system of planned (and anticipated) mobility and status sequencing: next year they can count on being sophomores with more responsibility and more privileges—and eventually being almighty seniors. Of course, in other schools, students usually progress from one class or grade to another, but the lines between classes are not so sharply drawn and these changes are not nearly so linked to uniform changes in privileges. The key point is that the significance of informal peer groups is minimized by reducing variations in informal social status within classes and increasing them between classes.

Linking privileges to year-in-school in some ways harks back to premodern societies. Those societies typically had mixed-age playgroups in which older children usually dominated younger children. But the younger children anticipated more power and a higher status as they grew older. Modern schooling systems sort children by age. The result is social groups that are relatively homogeneous and insular, eliminating the sequencing of status and power. Of course, there are younger and older students around, but they are not part of one's primary reference group—those who really count and with whom one compares oneself. Hence, high status requires dominance over those who are very similar to you. Being subject to domination by age peers is probably more demeaning than situations in which domination was more linked to age and physical maturity. The linking of privileges and status to year-in-school is an alternative form of linking status to seniority. I am not suggesting that the status sequencing, characteristic of the "military model," is always preferable. My key point is that the way contemporary societies group young people by age and allow those within a particular age group to compete with one another for popularity and status is in no way "natural," or necessarily the most effective way of organizing young people's education.

THE UPPER-CLASS "TOTAL INSTITUTION"

Sociologist Erving Goffman, famous for his studies of everyday life, introduced the concept of "total institution" to refer to organizations that attempt to regulate virtually all aspects of people's lives.[7] The classic examples are prisons and mental hospitals. Elite boarding schools have also been analyzed as total institutions; they were organized not only to socialize students into upper-class culture, but also to distance them from the conventional teenage culture.[8] One school in my sample— an elite private prep school in a mid-Atlantic state—is an interesting variant of a total institution. The Gates School was originally created to educate the children of one of the wealthiest families in the United States and it continues to educate the children of the well-to-do. These families are from a limited geographical area and are more or less from the same social circle. For example, about a fourth of the families attend the same Episcopal church and many have multiple business or social ties. Unlike the stereotypical prep school, it is not a boarding institution. Nonetheless, the children have very little contact with young people who go to other schools. Most of the students attended this same institution from pre-school through high school. The school has about 650 students in fourteen grade levels with about forty-five students in each grade. The students are required to wear uniforms. These "look like clones out of the world of J. Crew and Laura Ashley. It was the way ... our parents and the school expected us to dress. When one of the students asked an administrator why there was a dress code, he replied it was to make the students dress the way executives did on the weekends."[9] While students varied greatly in athletic ability, all were required to participate in sports; this was not the exclusive province of an elite subgroup of jocks. The school did not explicitly use mechanisms of the military model to build class solidarity. Students, however, spent years with largely the same set of individuals. "Since the class was so small, we all felt like brothers and sisters. Therefore, we watched out for each other like a family would."[10] During the ninth grade, there were three identifiable cliques: "the superb athletes, the really smart people, and the rest of us." These distinctions were less clear-cut before and after this grade. Much of the status competition and differentiation that is characteristic of most high schools was muted—though not eliminated—in this school.

The term "total institution" is not meant to imply that the school was like a prison. It was, however, a largely self-contained institution immersed in a rather small, local, and all encompassing upper-class culture, which produced very high levels of homogeneity and conformity among students. The former student observes:

> By constantly putting us together, our parents created an excellent check system. Due to the check system, very few people acted out in my school … If someone dressed differently, wore makeup, had strange looking hair, or acted differently, their classmates would make their lives miserable by constantly teasing them … The parents and the school liked this type of pressure because it kept almost everyone in line.[11]

Earlier studies point out how elite boarding schools force high levels of intimacy and hence at least certain forms of solidarity. As the theory of status relations would predict, sharing food and sexual experiences, such as group masturbation, often played an important role in creating this intimacy.[12] But what makes the Gates School an interesting case is that such intimacy and solidarity are developed even though it is not a boarding school. Social insularity, homogeneity, and conformity are created by other means. Undoubtedly such conformity is much easier to produce when students are already economically and socially privileged, and anticipate a prosperous and rosy future.

As in the military model, reducing the variations in conformity and association minimizes informal status differences. In most military schools, entering students do not know one another and have few common experiences. Consequently, an intense "baptism by fire" creates powerful common experiences and sentiments in a relatively short time period. In contrast, in this upper-class school initial selectivity and long-term socialization reduce the variations between students and provide a shared culture. All of the students are the same because they came from the same kind of families and have shared the same experiences all of their lives. Note I say here the "same" experiences not simply the "same kinds" of experiences.[13] They have grown up as members of a concrete community. Here the separation and combination operates not just at the level of a particular year in school, but also at the level of social class: The children of an upper class are systematically isolated from others and socialized into a particular upper-class subculture. If status sequences and future privileges make military discipline tolerable and enhance solidarity, these effects are probably even greater for the students in this school.[14]

THE SMALL-TOWN SCHOOL

This section focuses on public high schools in communities of less than 20,000 with a high school of fewer than 800 students. The one exception is a town that was a small town, but has grown rapidly in recent years and still retains much of the culture of its past. The question is how does the size of the community and high school affect adolescent status systems.

As suggested in chapter six, larger schools are likely to have more multidimensional status systems. Conversely, in small communities the "traditional" importance of athletics and good looks is particularly strong. A student from a small town in the Shenandoah Valley of Virginia reports:

> The field of athletics was the most important in the status structure … The easiest way to make friends and get noticed was to find some sport which best fit your athletic abilities. [The school's] small student population meant that most everyone knew who the athletes were … It was always better to be considered an athlete in some field than to be a non-participant.[15]

In a small town in north Texas the entire popular culture revolved around the high school football and basketball teams:

> [T]he football and basketball teams dominated the social scene … Athletes are pinpointed as early as the fourth grade, whether it be in Little Dribblers Basketball League or Little League Baseball. Parents are at each other's throats from the first time they hand their children balls to play with. Parents want their child to be the "star," and it is a very political and cut-throat style of rivalry. Much of the ranking is established in elementary school and is really well defined once the children reach the seventh or eighth grade. Even within the school system the parents [fight] for their child, and playing time is often the result of politics between parents, coaches, and school officials.[16]

Predictably, in a situation where most other dimensions of status recede into the background, intense competition for status and social differentiation developed between the two major sports teams. Two separate sets of cheerleaders and separate social circles revolved around each of the teams.[17]

Another tendency in small towns is for a student's status to be strongly influenced by the status of their parents. The central thesis of Hollingshead's classic 1940s study, *Elmtown's Youth*,[18] is that the differentiated social groups in the high school largely reflected the class structure of the community. This tendency was still present fifty years later. A girl from a town on Lake Erie says:

> I was treated well by others, but I did not agree with the way in which students and teachers at my school judged and grouped people … First of all, students had already been associated with certain status groups in junior high … People were also judged by their looks, how they dressed and carried themselves, the status of their parents in the community and how wealthy they were …[19]

In most large suburban schools, teachers' knowledge of families is more limited and plays a smaller role.[20] The relative status of parents is often less clear.

In the small town of the era Hollingshead describes, students easily recognized the status difference between the banker and the butcher. In the suburbs little is known about the parents of most peers and students have difficulty grasping the relative status of accountants, brokers, and computer programmers. Hence, family background is increasingly transmitted by the money students have to spend on clothes, cars, etc., the skills and tastes children learn at home, the educational credentials they bring to the larger impersonal world, rather than by the family's reputation in the community. Conversely, the status of young people in small towns is more rooted in family reputation, and hence more ascribed and inalienable than is the case in larger more impersonal settings.[21]

In addition to the effects of economic and cultural capital, influential families in small towns can use their personal influence to benefit their children.[22] Teachers and coaches treat some students differently than others. In a small "sports crazy" north Texas town, a parent's clout with the coaches and school officials could affect how much a student got to play.[23] A female from a small-town setting in Virginia, which is fast becoming suburbanized, reports:

> It is a well-known fact to residents … that many of the teams are selected well ahead of tryouts, making it nearly impossible for an outsider to break into the ranks … [O]n several occasions … spots on the team were held for students, including one of my friends, who did not even tryout … [S]pecial "private" practices, which were held for all those who eventually ended up making the team, excluded all of those who were ultimately cut.[24]

In this community a key tension is between old-timers and newcomers, and this difference in the community gets directly translated into the school.

Still another characteristic of smaller towns seems to be that the children of lower status families are more likely to be stigmatized. (Apparently in more urban situations other students have less information about family backgrounds.) This was evident in a Rhode Island community in which poorer students lived in the tenements of five nineteenth-century mill villages, which were becoming a suburb for the middle and upper classes.[25] In the small town in the Shenandoah Valley that was described earlier,[26] differences in dress and lifestyle were not that important for most students, but: "The status problem arose for those who could not afford to buy a pair of Levi's or Nike's. Those students … came from homes … under the poverty line. No names were given to these students, but one need not be labeled to feel an outcast … Movement from out of this group was rare.[27] Moreover, it seems likely that the inability to purchase the "in" status symbols is even more painful in a setting where the smallness of the school means it is inevitable that you will interact with more privileged students on a regular basis.

An additional kind of disadvantage is apparent in the descriptions. A student from a town on the Chesapeake Bay reports:

> Another group in school was the Bubbas.[28] They were a substantial minority, about fifteen percent of my school. My town is surrounded by water on three sides and many people in town earn their living by catching seafood. The Bubbas were the children of these watermen. They often did not have much money and [this] was reflected in the way they dressed. Ratty jeans and faded tee-shirts were the standard outfits. Any money they did have was put into their trucks. Bubbas drive huge four-wheel-drive trucks that look like they were out of a monster truck rally. The wheels were huge and the frame was lifted high above the tires. Trucks that looked like this were called Bubba trucks. These trucks were the Bubba male's pride and joy. A Bubba girl's status symbol within the group was how high her boyfriend's truck was above the ground. Bubba girls generally did not have their own transportation. Bubbas were mostly poor students and many simply planned on joining their fathers and work on the water after graduation. Other groups usually stayed away from the Bubbas due to their propensity to fight and lack of common interest with other groups.[29]

The last two descriptions make apparent that, in addition to economic disadvantages, poorer students were subject to well-institutionalized stereotyping and derogatory labeling. Reports from at least a dozen other schools indicated similar treatment of those variously termed "rednecks," "hicks," "kickers," "Bubbas," "cowboys," "farmers," etc. These terms are at least implicitly—and often openly—derogatory.[30] The students so labeled frequently adopted status symbols that further set them apart—for example, Western boots and hats. (In contrast, lower-class students in many larger urban and suburban schools are often even more preoccupied with the current status symbols portrayed in the national media than are their better-off peers.)

One other somewhat paradoxical characteristic of smaller schools is that students from different strata are more likely to have some significant contact with one another. The Shenandoah Valley boy quoted earlier reports that while subgroups were important, nearly everyone had friends from other groups. His comments on dating are especially revealing: "For the most part, the reasons behind why two persons started dating involved simple attraction ... This attraction could cross any of the various levels of status. This is due in large part to the fact that since the school was so small, people could not afford to be overly concerned with which group the date might come from ..."[31] He notes, "If you were to attend any school or social function, it would quickly become obvious that the differences were not too distinct. Most everyone would fit into at least two of the [cliques]. This was a fact of life in a school where the average graduating class was 80 students."[32] A student from a small town more than a hundred miles away says, "Interaction between the different status groups occurred quite often. Just because a person associated himself/herself with a particular group did not mean they could not be part of another group or talk with members of another group."[33] A student from a small-town school in Texas says, "Because of my high school's relatively small size, groups tend to overlap."[34] On the other hand, as we have seen, there are often strong tendencies to stereotype and isolate those at the very bottom. This was the case in the high school Hollingshead studied in the 1940s, at WWHS, and apparently at many, if not most, schools.

In sum, status systems in small towns tend to be more one-dimensional (and frequently emphasize good looks and traditional sports), more influenced by parents' ranks and status in the community, more likely to stigmatize those from the lowest socioeconomic strata, and more likely to involve significant contact between those from different crowds and different social strata.

SCHOOLS ON MILITARY BASES

The next two schools seem to have some of the characteristics of the small town, but also some distinct differences. These are schools run by the U.S. military for the children of military personnel. Those run within the U.S. or its territories are usually referred to as Department of Defense Domestic Elementary and Secondary Schools (DDESS) and those in foreign countries are usually known as Department of Defense Dependent's Schools (DODDS).[35] I have reports about two high schools associated with bases in the U.S.

A young woman, the daughter of an officer, who attended a school associated with a well-known military base, reports:

> The student body at "Fort X" High School can be broken down into a number of main groups based on specific characteristics … One of the most general, but at the same time most dividing, status characteristics, is the rank of the students' parents. The children of officers are automatically placed at a higher level on a hierarchical ladder than [a] child whose parent is enlisted … [O]nce a person has been designated one or the other his/her status is set. A child of a high-ranking officer is looked at as of the highest class and often can use their parent's high rank to influence or threaten other children.[36]

The other student says, "Officers' quarters were always separate from the … smaller and even more cramped housing that was assigned the enlisted soldiers. [This] is a definite metaphor for the mindset of the military community … It was this double standard that contributed to the social distinctions and resentments found later on in military high schools."[37]

Besides the direct effect of parent's rank, military rank is almost perfectly associated with the family's income.[38] These income differences further reinforce the status differences among children.

> [T]he norms of the officers' children kept them at a high status because they were unobtainable by children of an enlisted parent, usually because of money ... Officers' children tended to dress more elegantly; girls wearing skirts and sweaters and guys wearing collared shirts ... [of] such brand names as Guess, Express, or Liz Claiborne. The enlisted children could not afford these clothes and wore more trendy clothes in a hip-hop style (loose, baggy pants and tight or short skirts). The officers' children tended to have cars ... cars [that] were fashionable and expensive such as Volvos, Explorers, or jeeps.[39]

The other school was similar:

> ... emphasis was placed on outward appearances and especially on dress. The popular girls wore clothes from the specialty stores and shoes had to be trendy. Makeup was important ... Among guys status came from two sources. The first was the level of machismo a male possessed ... The other [was] the girls with whom he claimed association; the prettier and ... the more popular his female constituency, the higher status he was given.[40]

Parent's rank is also highly correlated with how students are academically tracked. Officers' children are much more likely to be in the more advanced academic tracks. Race played an important part in the dynamics of this school. The student reports, "Mixing between various races was negligible ... the racial divide was very distinct ..."[41] This led to a dualistic status structure that in some ways resembled the structure reported in chapter six, but there was much more ranking and open hostility between blacks and whites.[42]

I want to stress that these two schools are probably *not* representative of all or even most of the schools run by the military. Therefore, the point of this account is *not* to attempt to characterize all Defense Department schools.[43] Rather these two schools serve as some additional evidence that in smaller schools in relatively self-contained communities, parental status and other relatively inalienable and visible characteristics like race and gender are likely to have an especially strong effect on the status of students and on the formation of status groups within the high school.

In one respect these two schools are quite different from most small-town schools. Military personnel are transferred frequently and this probably further accentuates the effect of parents' formal military rank and other easily visible attributes. When students arrive in a new school, their relatively inalienable and visible status characteristics are parents' rank, race, gender, and physical appearance.[44] That these things would take on more significance in such schools is unsurprising.

CHURCH SCHOOLS AND THE EFFECT OF IDEOLOGY

Religiously oriented schools were founded to impart to their students a particular religious perspective and commitment to the values and beliefs associated with that world-view. Parents sometimes send their children to these schools because they share the world-view of the school and they want their children to also. Just as often they send their children to these schools in the hope that they can help protect them from being corrupted by what they see as some of the worst aspects of contemporary culture: drugs, alcohol, sexual promiscuity, incivility, violence, secularism, and low academic standards.[45]

This raises an interesting question. Does the generalized religious or ideological orientation of a school have a significant impact on the pattern of peer relationships? By generalized ideological orientation, I mean a well-developed and articulated philosophy of life and a mandate to inculcate this in their students. It would be desirable to study schools with a wide variety of ideological orientations: religious schools, atheist schools, socialist schools, etc. The reality is that in the U.S. very few non-religious schools have an articulated generalized ideological orientation. Consequently, I only have data from church-related schools. While I have reports from four Christian academies operated by relatively conservative Protestant groups and four reports from prep schools, three with ties to the Episcopal Church, the most reports—twelve—are from Catholic schools, and hence they will be the focus of this discussion.

Throughout much of American history the Roman Catholic Church has been committed to developing its own schools. Catholic parochial schools have been an important exception to the dominance of public schools in the United States. While the students that attend such schools make up slightly less than 4 percent of all students and about 4.5 percent of the high school students, Catholic schools have played an important educational role in many parts of the country. In 2001–02 there were 1,228 Catholic secondary schools enrolling 644,703.[46] Often they are held up as models of academic rigor and disciplined civility. There is some evidence to support these images. Catholic schools seem more effective in raising the performance of students, including urban minorities.[47] One study emphasizes the extent to which Catholic schools are a voluntary community and the effects of this not only on the morale of students and teachers, but on the educational process and its results.[48] As Coleman and others have noted, methodological difficulties make it hard to be certain about how much of the better performance of these institutions is due to what happens in the schools or is the result of the preselection and self-selection of the students who attend Catholic schools.

I have reports from twelve Catholic high schools located in eight states.[49] Five of these are girls' schools, three are boys' schools, and the remaining four are co-ed. These reports make one thing apparent: *Whatever the effects of these schools on academic performance, peer status relationships are not dramatically different from other schools.*

CLIQUES AND CROWDS

A female student from Holy Name High School,[50] a co-ed institution with 350 students, says:

> Subgroups within my high school were ... a perfect example of how cliques, money, and popularity played a major role in determining where one belonged and how one was treated. One would think that a Catholic school would be built upon values and morals that ensured an environment of equality and unity. However, at Holy Name the kids were too wrapped up in the "scene" to worry about whether or not everyone was included or accepted.[51]

She then goes on to describe the key groups as "the athletes," "the brains," "the sungods," and "the snobby Hispanics." The last two groups were essentially those associated with good looks, clothes, cars, and an after-school social life. She notes that students from most groups would cooperate with one another during class and on academic projects. But, she goes on to say, "Aside from these things, outside group meetings were clique-related."[52]

About halfway across the country is Bishop O'Sullivan High School. It is also co-educational, but twice the size of Holy Name and in the suburbs of a very large metropolitan city. A recent graduate[53] describes the clique structure in terms of "the popular crowd," "the alternative group"—which included the "potheads," "the academically gifted [who are] socially adept," and "the geeks" [who are not socially adept].[54] Higher ranked cliques tended to exclude outsiders: "The popular crowd was exclusive. Rarely did they associate outside their circle." This was despite the fact that the school was socially homogeneous:

> The school consisted mostly of rich upper- or upper-middle class white students. Minorities were almost obsolete [sic] ... out of our school of about 800, only six percent ... were other than Caucasian. I would not say at all that the student body as a whole was racist or prejudiced, but there were several people who I found myself shocked by [their attitudes on race]. The lack of minority presence was a definite hindrance to the educational process, and in terms of [peer] status, it was a moot point.[55]

One consequence of this relative social homogeneity is that in at least some schools students claimed, "Academic tracking did not make much of a difference. We did have Honors and Advanced Placement courses, but there was less emphasis on who took them. [T]he school was really competitive and we all tended to be focused on our education."[56] She goes on to note that social cliques were only weakly related to academic track.[57] She also notes that the impact of parents' status was weaker, and the nature of that status was less clear-cut.[58] The school's social homogeneity and metropolitan location undoubtedly contributed to this.

A student in the all-boys' Bishop Sanderson High School four hundred miles away describes a similar situation.

> The line between "Honors" kids and "regular" kids was ambiguous
> at best. The Honors kids were definitely a … mix—there were about
> forty of us … Outside of class, however, there wasn't a division between
> Honors and regular students. The line that had been established was
> purely arbitrary, a measure of academic proficiency, laid on us by the
> administration. In the student body, the most popular students were not
> the brightest.[59]

Uniforms were required at Bishop O'Sullivan and had to be purchased from a single approved source that provided a standardized product. Consequently, individual innovation had to take subtle and surreptitious forms: the type of tee-shirts or boxer shorts students wore under their uniforms, or whether girls tried to shorten their skirts by rolling them up at the waistband. Juniors and seniors wore a different color blazer from students in lower grades and this was a greatly prized privilege, which contributed to class solidarity: "There was little association between the blue coats and the green coats."[60] The student from Sanderson says, "Clothing was out [as a means of attaining status] due to the dress code … (sport coat, tie, slacks, dress shoes)." He notes that some students attempted to set themselves off by slight variations in dress and hairstyle, but that these were usually soon banned by the administration. At least some of these attempts at deviance were stimulated by the mass media. "Sideburns were very big. (None of us wanted to admit that our 'look' was inspired by [the television show] *Beverly Hills 90210*, even though it really was.)" It seems fair to conclude that the significance of clothes as a source of status differences was reduced though not eliminated.

In some schools cliques were quite insulated from one another. A student from Louisiana reports, "These cliques would stay intact exclusively—unless with an [outside] member of the opposite sex."[61] Predictably, in a very small rural school—only 59 students in the whole high school—this was much less the case. After describing six identifiable groups, the student says, "With the school being so small, most of the cliques would communicate together on a daily basis ... Outside of school ... different cliques would socialize with one another, as if cliques never existed."[62]

ALCOHOL, DRUGS, AND SEX

In the same metropolitan area as Bishop O'Sullivan High School is Pius X High School, a co-educational institution of approximately 1,200 students. A former student describes the usual hierarchical pattern of clique formation and status concerns. She also makes clear that alcohol, drugs, and sexual activity were the norm among popular students:

> Drinking and drug use was another source of status ... For both sexes, drinking was the foundation for being "cool." You did not have to get drunk, but you had to at least sip a beer, although males received more pressure to drink large quantities to be cool. Those who did not drink were teased or gossiped about or discarded as dorks.[63]

Norms concerning the use of drugs were more gender specific.

> Drugs were not acceptable for cool girls. Drugs, however, were acceptable and even encouraged for boys. I know one female who smoked pot, all the other cool females ostracized her, called her a 'druggie.' I know one guy who refused to try pot, and the cool guys called him a 'wuss' (that means wimp), and didn't ask him out to party anymore.[64]

In Center City Convent School, one of the most prestigious and expensive Catholic girls' schools in the country, a former student reports on the behavior of the popular crowd. "Common weekend activity spots included athletic events at all-boys private schools, house and 'field' parties and, later, bars. Alcohol played an important role in the social scene of the group ... Moreover, it seemed like their parents condoned and even encouraged alcohol use." She notes that some of the "weirdo" girls were into drugs. Many students, however, did not use alcohol or drugs.[65] Sacred Heart Academy, another old and exclusive girl's school, seems very similar. As we shall see later, Sacred Heart Academy was the most successful in reducing status competition among its students. Nonetheless a former student reports, "Being a Catholic all-girls school, Sacred Heart [students] had a reputation [for] being ... snobby and [having] promiscuous girls."[66] In a Gulf Coast town some of the students went to considerable ends to secure alcohol and drugs:

Some of the "partiers" were really smart and could have made good grades
… One of the main guys in this group was a big supplier of fake I.D.s in
the area. He and the rest of his group were the ones that supplied the liquor
and beer at most of the parties and brought pot or any other drugs that were
desired. Some of the guys in this group also tried making counterfeit money
along with fake I.D.s. Eventually the money was found to be bogus and
a couple of guys got arrested at school … and had to spend some time in
court but never went to jail.[67]

In these schools the stereotype of the "partier" was most accurate for the
most visible cliques, which on average included about one-third of the students.
With respect to sexual behavior, the student from Pius X reports:

For males it was considered cool to hook up or have sex with as many
females as possible (even if the females were low status or ugly). Since those
who were not of high status did not usually attend the parties (where the
majority of the one-night hookups and sexual encounters took place), they
did not engage in sexual activity as much as a high status student.[68]

As in much of American society, a double standard existed calling for
women to be more restrained in their sexual activity:

[M]ost females were selective and would not hook up with, let alone have
sex, with an uncool guy. Girls were expected to hook up (defined as sex acts,
but not intercourse), but not have sex.[69] Yet, high status girls could not hook
up too much, or they would be considered a slut. I would estimate that a girl
could hook up about two to four times a semester, and avoid being called a
slut or prude.[70]

She goes on to say that sexual activity was not an optional private activity
if you were going to be popular. "In order to gain status … [from] hooking up,
cool people had to know. Therefore, males and females told their friends about
their sexual experiences, and either reaped the benefits of status, or suffered
the punishment for nonconformity."[71]

Popularity—and presumably the behaviors associated with it—was not
restricted to a small number of students. The student observes: "In many status
arrangements, the high status group is small compared to the larger community. At
Pius X, there were many cool people. In fact, I would venture to say that one-third
to one-half of the sophomore, junior, and senior classes were accepted as cool."[72]

These patterns of behavior are not unique to this particular Catholic
school. At Saint Anne's, a girls' school of 700 students more than 1,500 miles
away, a student reports:

> The "fun" girls and the boys [of the boys' Catholic school nearby] considered the "crazy" girls as very popular. Their looks and urge to party and drink gave them such popularity … These girls were considered "crazy" because they drank, smoked marijuana, and loved to have a good time. [S]everal of them were kicked out of the Student Council because they showed up [at] a Christmas formal drunk and stoned.[73]

While the "crazy" girls were a relatively small social elite, the "fun" girls constituted a substantial part of the student body. "These were the type of girls that were involved in the Student Council, sports, National Honor Society, and other organizations. However, the 'fun' clique liked to drink, party, and have a good time, as did the 'crazy' girls."[74] The school also had "freaky" girls who "danced to a beat different than the rest of the cliques … They wore pale make-up with dark lipstick. They seemed to all have dyed hair colors and wore knee-high socks."[75]

Because church doctrine only recognizes the legitimacy of sexual relations between married heterosexual couples, homosexuality was a sensitive issue at Roman Catholic schools, especially in single-sex schools. The student from St. Anne's recalls that a "lesbian group 'came out of the closet' during my junior year … It was almost as if St. Anne's was in denial that girls were lesbians in an all-girls Catholic school … They were judged as outcasts by … the boys [at the nearby Catholic boys' school]."[76] The student from Bishop Sanderson says, "The community was very masculine and macho, perhaps a reaction to our status as an all-male community (and the resultant homophobia)." He goes on to describe how some students dealt with this atmosphere. "Proms were … the easiest way to ward off rumors about your sexuality. If a small freshman was getting picked on or getting harassed because he 'looked gay,' simply asking someone to go to a dance with him would (hopefully) dispel such rumors." But not just any date would do. "[A] universally-picked-on kid brought his cousin to the freshman semi-formal and [ended up] having to put up with jokes about it for the next few months. Making such comments about others was also an easy way to achieve status and prove that you weren't gay yourself."[77]

These behaviors are not restricted to Catholic schools. Reports from four schools established by conservative Protestant groups suggest very similar patterns.[78] One student who attended a "private, Baptist, college preparatory … Christian high school" in Florida begins her paper: "My high school was small compared to the local public high school. If you were not in a clique, you did not hang out with people from school. This made for unpleasant social situations. A constant feeling that you never belonged …" Another who attended a school run by a conservative Presbyterian church began her paper, "I disliked John Knox School because I felt the majority of students were catty and provincial …"[79] I have already reported how in yet a third Christian academy older boys hazed younger ones by sticking their heads in toilets and both men and women engaged in what the student labeled as "vicious" ritual insulting. Not surprisingly reports from four upscale Protestant prep schools—three with connections to the Episcopal Church—also indicate that the peer status structures are very little different from other schools except for the upper-class ambiance and the dynamics of smaller schools, often with an emphasis on year-in-school solidarity.[80]

SO WHAT?

What is the purpose of this description of church-related schools—primarily Catholic schools—that has focused on alcohol, drugs, and sex? It is *not* to suggest that the levels of status seeking, nastiness, drug use, sexual activity—or whatever—are especially high in religious schools. These issues receive attention because it is commonly assumed that these schools largely avoid or minimize these patterns of behavior. The reports from students in Catholic schools seemed to pay more attention to these issues—as well as homosexuality—than reports from other schools. I believe that this is the case not because the problems are more acute, but because the college students who recently attended these institutions implicitly sensed the gap between public perception and the reality they experienced.

From the descriptions that are available, both peer status structures and student behavior with respect to cliques, alcohol, drugs, and sex seem to be very similar to those found in comparable non-religious schools.[81] The key theoretical point is that peer relationships and behavior in these schools seem to be largely unaffected by their religious orientation. Stated in more general terms, the generalized ideology of an educational institution seems to have very little effect on the structure of peer relationships and the informal patterns of student behavior.

There are differences between religious and public schools. Most of the reports from students in religious schools seem to suggest that they meet higher academic standards. Most of the Catholic schools that were reported on specifically define themselves as selective college preparatory schools. Students did not report they felt unsafe. In at least one extensive study substantial evidence shows that students, parents, and faculty are much more likely to feel that their school is a community. However, the degree to which these desirable outcomes are due to the differences in the *content* of their ideology, or to the fact that they share *some* common values and ideals, is unclear.

Moreover, several other characteristics almost certainly play an important role. First and most obviously, since they are private schools, they can simply dismiss students who refuse to conform to the school norms. Relatively few students are dismissed from Catholic schools, but it seems almost certain that those who are most likely to be in serious trouble in public schools never get to Catholic schools. This eliminates an important set of problems that many public high schools have to deal with daily. Dismissing students from most public schools is a much more complex and problematic process. Second, while Catholic schools often provide substantial scholarship help to many students, the families of most students pay significant tuition.[82] This nearly always decreases the proportion of really low-income students in the school. Families who commit such resources probably also take an above-average interest in their children's education and schooling. Third, a number are single-sex institutions, though most have links to other opposite-sex schools. Fourth, most of these schools require that students wear a uniform. I mention these four factors because obviously these are not necessarily associated with being Catholic or religious per se, but they probably have implications for the peer cultures at these schools.

Let me be very clear about the political thrust of this section. It is not intended to be critical of church-related schools or to enter into a generalized debate about the relative virtues of private and public education. Nor is it to deny that there is considerable—but not definitive—evidence that by many measures Catholic schools are more academically effective than public schools.[83] Nor am I saying that religious participation and commitment does nothing to affect people's behavior; clearly some religious groups do raise adolescents who behave quite differently from most teenagers.[84] My aim is much narrower: to suggest that there are few differences between most religious schools and non-religious schools with respect to peer status relations—if the socioeconomic composition of their student bodies are roughly comparable. In both, intense status competition and "small cruelties" are the rule rather than the exception. In both, alcohol, drugs, and sex are key weapons in the adolescent struggles for status.[85]

A PARTIAL EXCEPTION—SACRED HEART ACADEMY

To argue that the informal status structures for students in most religiously oriented schools are very similar to those in other schools, is not to argue that they could not be different. The report from Sacred Heart Academy describes some differences in that school and suggests the possible reason for that difference. According to the former student, while "cliques and groups were still noticeable," they were much less prominent. "Although popularity was a concern at Sacred Heart, there were groups that girls associated with according to their interest with academics and social activities" and class (cohort) solidarity was relatively strong. In the introduction to her report she observes, "The goal of the administration was to break up cliques throughout our four years in high school so that we would all become friends." When she concludes her report and attempts to explain why her high school was different, she repeats the theme:

> I believe what set my high school apart from the rest was the administration. They tried to break up cliques and groups so that the class would be united. It succeeded by the time we were seniors. We had retreats that the whole class would go on to get to know each other, ourselves, and God. We also had intramurals between classes, which promoted class unity. This did not happen in public schools and I think that by forming a more united group of girls you, in return, have strong individuals confident in themselves. I also think that the all-girl school eliminated the popularity scale. This made the girls act themselves and not try to impress the guys. This way it was easier for them to make true friends and stick with them throughout school years.[86]

It would be a mistake to overemphasize the difference between this Catholic school and others on the basis of one report. The report, however, does not just claim the school is different but suggests specific structural reasons why this might be the case. It, of course, shares with a number of other schools such characteristics as being single-sex, requiring uniforms, and finding solidarity among seniors. What seems to set this school apart is that the administration actively tried to repress the formation of cliques and status groups and create class solidarity by special class events. This is, of course, another version of the mechanisms used in the "military model" described earlier.

I have already made clear that generalized ideologies, however valid and authentic, do not have much effect on high school peer relationships. The key point suggested by this description of Catholic schools is that these generalized ideologies must be embodied in organizational mechanisms that directly affect the formation of friendships, cliques, and crowds if they are to be effective in reducing status competition and differentiation. Whether the net effect of introducing such mechanisms is positive is an unsettled and debatable question.

The task of this chapter has been to describe schools that are different from most high schools, both in organization and student body, and in some cases peer status structures. The analytical task is to explain why each of these types of school is different from or similar to the schools described earlier. The theory of status relations draws attention to: the inalienability and inexpansibility of status, and conformity and associations as sources of status. Therefore, if the status structures of high schools vary, we should expect this to be due to variations in these factors, or things that affect these factors.

In "military-like" academies the significance of status groups, crowds, and cliques is muted by strongly encouraging class solidarity. This typically involves discouraging expressive relations with those of other classes, limiting variations in lifestyles and status symbols within classes, creating differences between classes, and creating broader school solidarity by requiring students to participate in sports activities. Moreover, most of these are single-sex schools; for heterosexual students this reduces the importance of expressive associations and competition for the attention of the opposite sex.[87] In theoretical terms, these mechanisms reduce individual variations in conformity and associations within a given class, and make year-in-school an important and relatively inalienable basis of status. A corollary is that this increases variations between classes. The result is a demotion in the importance of informal lifestyle as a basis for informal status groups.

The small private "total institution" for children of the local upper class tied admissions to an inalienable status characteristic (the "right families"), encouraged dress and other status symbols that were compatible with the upper-class culture, greatly restricted students' contact with young people in other schools, and maintained this isolation for their entire pre-college lives. In theoretical terms, differences in individual status were reduced first by selective admissions, second by restricting lifestyle norms, and third by restricting informal associations with those not part of the upper-class school culture.

Small-town schools usually have less multidimensional status systems; what counts is athletic accomplishment and good looks. Parents' status and influence in the community have a more direct impact on the student's status with their peers and how they are treated by school officials. Those at the bottom are likely to be subject to negative stereotypes and labels. Because the local social systems are relatively small, many boundaries are less rigid in the sense that the higher status students cannot be completely self-contained. Smallness also means behavior is more visible and gossip is common.

In small schools on military bases parent's military rank has a strong initial impact on student's status and in turn on conformity and associations. The rapid turnover of the student population accentuates the effects of relatively inalienable characteristics like parent's rank, race, and gender.

Church-related schools are often perceived by adults to be different from public schools, but this is rarely so with respect to student status systems, including sexual behavior and the use of alcohol and drugs. Generalized commitments to an ideology seem to have little impact unless specific mechanisms are used to reduce variations in conformity and associations and to encourage solidarity across crowds and cliques.

In sum, most of the differences between schools result from (1) reducing differences within a school with respect to lifestyles and associations, or (2) increasing the importance of certain relatively inalienable status characteristics, such as parents' status or military rank or year-in-school. These, in turn, may be affected by size of the school and community, control over admissions and expulsions, and restricting students' abilities to choose status symbols and associations.

SCHOOLS IN OTHER COUNTRIES: A BRIEF NOTE

A cross-societal comparison of peer status systems would require a separate book and is beyond the scope of this study. The information available on youth peer relations in other societies, especially middle-class youth, is relatively limited and uneven in focus and detail.[88] Nonetheless, an obvious question is: What are peer status systems like in other societies and would the theory of status relations be useful in understanding these?

In the course of preparing this book I made presentations of my findings in Italy, Britain, and Canada. In presentations I made in the U.S., there were often graduate students from other countries in attendance. A common remark was that the patterns that I was describing, and that were commonly displayed in the American mass media, were relatively unique to the United States. I remember one graduate student from Turkey remarking, "I always thought all of the notions about cliques and crowds, and the preoccupation with fashions that I had seen in American movies was the invention of Hollywood. Then when I came to the U.S. for the first time as an exchange student my junior year in secondary school, I was stunned to see that many of the images actually existed. There in the hallway of my new high school were the clusters of different crowds with their relatively distinctive styles." On another occasion when I had been discussing the importance of parties and proms, a professor from Germany said, "We don't have that kind of thing in our schools; we tend to business."

The point in recounting this very anecdotal information is to make one tentative observation and suggest a hypothesis to explain this. In a number of societies, competitive athletic activities are organized largely by private clubs and associations, and are largely unrelated to the school system. Similarly, schools seldom organize social activities such as proms or even extracurricular activities. To the degree that this hypothetical fact actually applies to a given educational system, the theory of status relations would predict that status concerns and peer groups would be less salient. To the extent that schools in other societies limit their responsibilities to largely instrumental activities and forgo organizing expressive activities such as sports and dances, the theory would predict that since associations in schools would be primarily instrumental, peer status concerns within the school setting would be lessened. If this hypothesis proves to be correct, it would move us beyond a vague pseudo explanation based on largely unspecified cultural differences such as "American schools are unique because we believe in individual freedom" or "German schools are highly structured because of deep strains of authoritarianism in the culture." Instead we would have a more concrete and testable hypothesis. This is not, of course, to deny that more general features of a national culture might not also have an effect on peer relationships within the school.[89] Obviously, more research and analysis is needed to adequately test the hypothesis, but a key purpose of theory is not simply to explain what we already know, but to suggest directions for new research.

Part IV

TEEN STATUS SYSTEMS AND CONSUMERISM

CHAPTER EIGHT

Creating Consumers

… man who had previously been free and independent, is now so to speak
subjugated by a multitude of new needs … [C]onsuming ambition,
the ardent desire to raise one's relative fortune less out of genuine need
than in order to place oneself above others, instills in all men a black
inclination to harm one another; a secret jealousy which is all the more
dangerous as it often assumes the mask of benevolence …'

—Jean-Jacques Rousseau, 1755

FROM THE LUNCHROOM: One thing I have forgotten to mention until now is the group's fascination with the very popular … television show "South Park." This is a very irreverent cartoon show, which is on cable television, and is much "worse" in terms of obscene language and violence than the much-debated "Simpsons" ever was. The boys especially seem to love the show. (Perhaps due to its violence and mild cursing, which resembles their own activity.) The other main topic … today was Sony Playstation games … [O]ne of the most popular seemed to be "Bushido Blade," an apparently VERY violent game involving one-on-one fighting.[1] Killing one's opponent was the "cool part," in Jacob's words.[2]

Red Hair described his Saturday night, where he and one of his male friends went to Country Retreat Center. "Man, we were the only people under thirty there! And all those old people were smoking up and shit. I mean, I was watching these people, and an old lady was like this (mimicked person smoking a joint furtively). Then she passed the joint to another lady and she was like this (mimicked her) … I couldn't believe all these old people were smoking pot." [Another boy] added, "Man, you'd be surprised at all the old people who toke." Red Hair replied, "Well, I've just never experienced it personally before, you know." I turned to Alan and Rebecca's group. They were discussing

their plans for spring break. Everyone in that group seemed to be
going somewhere. They were looking over ski brochures. One girl said
she was going to California.[3]

The focus in Parts II and III was on patterns of teenage behavior and variations
in these patterns. The theory of status relationships was used to explain the
patterns and variations observed. Here the level of analysis shifts. The focus is
on the link between teenage status systems and the broader society—and more
specifically consumer capitalism. Before I proceed, a brief discussion of the
nature of contemporary capitalist economies is required.

THE ECONOMY AND THE STATUS SYSTEM

In the early years of modernity the key economic problem was supply: to provide
the relatively basic commodities—food, clothing, housing, transportation—at a
price the masses could afford. Henry Ford knew that if he could produce cheap,
reliable cars he could sell them. His lack of concern about the details of consumer
demand is illustrated by his legendary quip about the Model T: "Any customer
can have a car painted any color that he wants, so long as it is black."[4] It was
largely because of his insensitivity to such issues that Ford lost its preeminence
to General Motors. As wealth increased, the limiting factor became demand—
which became closely linked to desire. As Bryan Turner notes, "Economic change
and restructuring have brought about fundamental shifts in the nature of labour
and its composition, which have also reorganized leisure and consumption ...
The labouring body has become the desiring body."[5]

Recessions and depressions occur because demand drops—not because of
an inability to produce and supply goods and services. In postmodern societies
maintaining consumer confidence and a steady demand is crucial. Disciplined
labor and efficient technology are still important, but eager consumers are
probably more important. The state contributes to this goal through the regulation of interest rates, taxes, and state expenditures.[6] Businesses do this primarily through marketing and advertising. Some of this is directed toward
providing people with information about the price and the practical utility of
particular commodities. Much more is directed at people's status concerns.
Goods and services become valued as much for the status they bring the owner
as for the utilitarian needs they meet. Rarely are new clothes bought because
the old ones no longer keep their owner warm; they are replaced because they
are "worn" or "out of style." SUVs are popular not because most people live
at the end of a long unpaved road, but because they are seen as "cool." These
status preoccupations and social pressures are different from the need to feed
one's family. They are nonetheless experienced as very real to those who live in
such a social context.[7]

Demand for consumer commodities must be created largely through obsolescence. Some obsolescence is created by innovation that makes new products and production technologies that are truly more efficient and effective than what was previously available. Computers are an obvious example. Making products that are designed to wear out is a second strategy. American car companies were accused of following such a policy from about 1950 to 1980. But this strategy has a fatal flaw: Others may produce quality goods and lure away your customers—as the Japanese did. A third tactic is to turn your product into a status symbol. Your glasses not only improve your vision; they are a "statement" about who you are; your identity becomes defined by the objects you display. Commodities vary in the degree to which they are valued for their practical uses and status value. A hammer has primarily a practical value. A designer gown has primarily a status value.[8] The more an item has status value, the more likely it is subject to the dynamics of fashion. Fashion automatically creates obsolescence: As soon as most people have a particular item, it loses its distinctiveness and hence its status value. In a postmodern consumer society this third factor has become central to sustaining consumer demand. Hence, for many businesses it is essential for people to be deeply concerned about their social status. Status must also be closely linked to the possession of consumer goods. This brings us to the link between high school teenagers and consumer capitalism.

BUSINESSES: PROFITING FROM TEENAGERS

Teenagers play a much broader and more important economic role than is usually assumed, but let us begin with the obvious ways they affect consumer capitalism—as a market for businesses.[9]

SCOPE OF THE TEENAGE MARKET

For reasons outlined in earlier chapters, teenagers often seek to maintain or enhance their status by the acquisition of fashionable status symbols. Children and especially teenagers are important consumers not only because they are potential customers in the present but also for two other reasons. According to Professor James U. McNeal in *Kids as Customers: A Handbook of Marketing to Children*,[10] there are three markets: children as a primary market spending their own money; as a significant influence on their parents' spending; and as a future market when they become adults.[11] All of these become more important as children develop into adolescents.

A caveat about the data on this topic is needed. For-profit research companies generate much of the available data. They probably exaggerate rather than understate the scope and potential of this market and their abilities to shape the preferences of this age group. A second key source seems to be journalistic accounts, which often express alarm about how children are being manipulated.[12] There seems to be very little careful research on marketing to adolescents published in peer-reviewed journals or by academic presses.[13] Nonetheless, while a critical attitude toward specific claims is warranted, teenagers are undoubtedly an important market. Businesses are clearly making serious efforts to shape the tastes and buying habits of children and adolescents.

Teenagers are a lucrative *current market*. While estimates of adolescent spending power vary from source to source, all agree that the level of spending by 12- to 17-year-olds is unprecedented. Peter Zollo heads one of the marketing research firms that focus on teenagers. He reports that America's 12-19 year-olds spent roughly $94 billion of their own money in 1998, up from $63 billion four years earlier.[14] Other estimates are as much as thirty-five percent higher than this.[15] To put these figures in perspective they are roughly comparable to the estimated direct initial cost of the U.S. invasion of Iraq in 2003. The youth market became apparent after World War II, but was accelerated by the strong economic expansion during the 1990s. Median family income increased from $29,077 in 1960 to $48,950 in 1999 in constant (1999) dollars—that is, real family income increased 68 percent.[16] Moreover, twenty-five percent fewer children per family meant that a higher proportion of the family income could be spent on each child.[17] Adolescents also began to earn significant amounts of additional spending money by working. Of the nearly nine million students enrolled in high school, forty-one percent, or 3.6 million of them, were employed in 1999.[18] Most of their income, as well as allowances from their parents, go for consumer commodities and services.[19]

Teenagers also *influence adult spending*. Advertisers have begun courting young consumers even for big-ticket items, such as cars, airline tickets, expensive family vacations, computers, and entertainment centers. Ford has ads in *Teen Magazine*, and BMW markets to adolescents as well. Hyatt Hotels and Resorts assembled a group of 12- to 17-year-olds to advise them about desired services at Hyatt Hotels as well as assist in decision-making for their new youth-oriented Camp Hyatt program. Minivan and sport utility vehicle producers advertised extensively in the children's magazine *Crayola Kids*—though obviously children do not directly purchase these products. Delta Airlines started a youth-oriented program, including a magazine and birthday greetings, as well as discounts for parents. While car, hotel, and airline companies do not see young people as the primary customer, they recognize that children have a major influence on which products their parents choose.

Perhaps most important, teenagers are seen as a crucial *future market*. As noted in chapter one, adolescence is the stage of life when people develop the sense of the identity they will draw on as adults. This includes tastes and preferences likely to last a lifetime. Music is an obvious example. Typically adults show nostalgia and loyalty about the music of their adolescence—even if they learn to appreciate a greater variety of musical styles. Marketers are aware of the long-term impact of habits and taste developed in adolescence and they are concerned to shape taste and brand loyalty during this seminal period.[20] A variety of firms, including airlines, banks, investment companies, and, of course, retailers invest in marketing to customers of the future.[21]

TAKING AIM AT TEENAGERS

Because of the three markets outlined above, teenagers have become the target of massive marketing and advertising campaigns. These campaigns shape their selection and use of a broad range of commodities. Advertising is also a core feature of the symbolic milieu within which young people grow up— and hence their very being and sense of the world are shaped by such ads. By the time American children graduate from high school they will have spent 18,000–22,000 hours in front of the television compared to only 13,000 hours in the classroom.[22] Children and adolescents spend more time watching TV and videos than any other activity besides sleeping.[23]

"Advertisers pay a premium to reach young viewers," according to *The Washington Post*. The article continues, "For example, although [the youth-oriented 'Dawson's Creek'] ranked only 76th among all viewers in the Nielsen survey, the WB network has charged advertisers about $250,000 for a 30-second commercial during the show. That's about what CBS charges for time on '60 Minutes,' which draws twice the number of viewers as 'Dawson.'"[24] Advertisers pay high rates to reach relatively small audiences because they are the most likely to consume their product. As Irma Zandl, marketing consultant, so aptly put it, "The people who are watching '60 Minutes' are not buying new fragrances and new jeans."[25] Teenagers are willing to experiment with new products and so companies see them as customers whose loyalty is up for grabs. As an article in the traditionally conservative *Economist* reported, the strategy is "Hook them on a brand today, and with any luck they will still be using it in the next century."[26] These companies not only advertise the nature of their products, but also attempt to associate their products with cultural images that appeal to children, including the Flintstones, Batman, and a whole array of Disney characters and various "superheroes." Most sport shoe and apparel companies have one or more celebrity athletes in their ads, which are aimed at teenagers. The Nike advertising campaign featuring Michael Jordan and his special line of athletic shoes is a classic example. Rock and rap music stars are also featured in ads aimed specifically at teenagers.

Very few ad-free zones exist for adolescents, as marketing permeates TV, the Internet, magazines, and even public schools. Others have written about the commercialization of school,[27] but I will give a brief overview of some of these trends. One of the most noted efforts at marketing in schools is Channel One. This is a TV program beamed by satellite to participating schools. It features ten minutes of youth-oriented news reporting and two minutes of advertising daily. Twelve thousand schools nationwide had opted to receive Channel One in 1993, serving over eight million teenagers, about forty percent of 12- to 17-year-olds enrolled in school.[28] Advertisers on Channel One pay $200,000 for a thirty-second spot.[29] This by no means exhausts the advertising in schools. According to Consumers Union, in some schools ads adorn bathroom stalls and wall space above urinals.[30] Nutritional posters depicting Rice Krispies cereal, compliments of Kellogg, fill hallways.[31] Ronald McDonald speaks at no charge to schools about self-esteem and other supposedly pertinent topics.[32] School districts now sell exclusive contracts to Coke and Pepsi for vending machine rights. Even Eli Lily, the pharmaceutical company that produces the antidepressant Prozac, spoke free of charge at a high school in Maryland, then handed out school supplies depicting Prozac insignia. School buses emblazoned with advertisements now serve New York City and Colorado Springs school districts.[33] Some educators are concerned that the results of advertising in an educational environment could have far deeper effects than other advertising. Advertising products in an "educational context may further heighten their credibility and impact."[34] In the terms of the theory of status relations, the legitimacy of advertisements is enhanced by their association with educational institutions.

In contrast, some postmodern theorists see advertising not as manipulation or even as a necessary nuisance, but as a central and legitimate part of contemporary popular culture. Marketing and advertising are seen as an absolutely central feature of the symbolic landscape in contemporary societies—as important in the lives of young people as books, music, and movies. They reject the assumption that labor and productivity are positive and associated with responsibility, while consumption is associated with self-indulgence. Consumption is not seen as a frivolous activity but something with "emancipatory potential."[35] It is a key aspect of personal and social identity formation.[36] In the postmodern world the core of one's identity is tied less to the job one does than to leisure activities. Marketing to teenagers is not simply a way to temporarily influence their purchasing preferences. More important, it is a means of shaping how they define themselves and what constitutes an appropriate lifestyle for that self—because choosing and creating one's own lifestyle is seen as the crucial form of "emancipation."

The more positive view of advertising seems to be gaining ground among the public in general. The marketing research firm Roper Starch Worldwide tracks people's attitudes toward advertising and says:

To say that the average American is exposed to a lot of advertising is like say-ing Antarctica has a lot of ice. It's a stupendous understatement. Given the lifelong barrage, it might seem that Americans would make up their minds once and for all what they think of advertising. But their feelings fluctuate. Positive feelings are currently in ascendance. Most adults agree "advertising provides useful information about products and services" and is "often fun or interesting." A negative statement that ranked in the top two during the 1980s and early 1990s has fallen to third place.[37]

In addition to advertising, specialized products, services, and stores are being created to appeal to children and adolescents. These include Helene Curtis's Suave for Kids and Proctor and Gamble's Pert Plus Shampoo and Dial for Kids. Even bottled water producers have kids' lines, such as Ozarka Spring Water for Kids.[38] Retail chains also have created entire stores focused on attracting children and adolescents, including Limited Too and Gap Kids. American Eagle Outfitters and Old Navy stores apparently see teens as a core market. Publishers have created *Teen People, teenStyle, Time for Kids*, and *Newsweek for Kids. Cosmopolitan* has created *CosmoGirl*, and *Vogue* has cre-ated *Teen Vogue*; both are aimed at attracting adolescents into their readership before other glamour magazines can claim them at a later age.

There is little doubt that marketers work hard to shape and influence the choices of teenagers, but their success is by no means automatic. Teenagers are not dolts totally manipulated by marketers and the media. Styles and products frequently fall flat; the "kids" simply do not think they are cool. In his excellent journalistic account of those who study what teenagers want, Malcolm Gladwell refers to these marketing research efforts as "the coolhunt."[39] This uncertainty about what will be cool is the primary reason that firms spend considerable amounts of money and time on such research. Pointing to these efforts is not to suggest that advertising and marketing are simply instruments of corporate manipulation. Neither, however, are they simply informational aids to con-sumer choice. Obviously all advertising and marketing is not bad and evil—but neither is it an innocent source of information. The crucial question is should these activities become an ever more central part of the experience and lives of our children and adolescents?

To the degree that adults are concerned about the consumerism of teen-agers, they usually blame the "usual suspects": the businesses that make products aimed at teenagers and the marketers and advertisers that attempt to persuade adolescents to buy these. But to understand both the reasons for teenage consumerism, and more generally the patterns of behavior char-acteristic of teenagers, we need to look beyond the "usual suspects" and consider the role of some "un-indicted co-conspirators": teachers, public officials, and parents.

TEACHERS, OFFICIALS, AND PARENTS: PROFITING IN OTHER WAYS

CONSTANT COMPLAINTS AND LAME LAMENTS

The very notions of "adolescence" and "teenagers" imply that this is "a diffi-cult age"—full of dangers and temptations for young people, and annoyance and frustration for adults.[40] In most societies adults bemoan younger peoples' lack of respect for tradition and their impropriety. Intergenerational conflict is not new, but it does seem more public and political than in previous peri-ods of American history.[41] Yet, despite a half century of adult complaints, and sometimes outrage, few changes have occurred in the way adults organize the lives of adolescents: They are sent off to schools for five days a week, sorted by age, and supervised by a few teachers. As school attendance and years of schooling increased, more and more young people have been kept in a state of postponed maturity for longer and longer. Clearly, this is likely to increase the importance of peers and decrease the significance of adults—resulting in behaviors that adults have long grumbled about. When those with real power complain loud and long about the behavior of subordinates—without really doing anything—we need to ask why.[42] Often those in authority have a vested interest in the very patterns they bemoan. More accurately, they are wed to patterns of social organization that make the forms of behavior they lament likely if not inevitable.

CUI BONO AND CO-DEPENDENCE

The Latin phrase *cui bono* asks, "Who benefits?" "Co-dependence" is defined as "mutual need: the dependence of two people, groups, or organisms on each other, especially when this reinforces mutually harmful behavior pat-terns."[43] (Note that this can refer to social dependence, not simply psycholog-ical dependence.) Both terms are relevant to understanding the social patterns associated with teenagers in American society. When patterns persist this is usually because the interests of various groups reinforce these arrangements. Most ways of organizing human beings result in both desirable outcomes and unwanted side effects. Typically the benefits are seen as the result of the wis-dom and efforts of one's own group; the undesirable consequences are attrib-uted to the failings of others. This is, I believe, the case for the behavior of contemporary teenagers. I will focus on three categories of adults that benefit from the existing patterns: parents, teachers, and public officials. Before con-sidering the role of these groups, however, we need to briefly look at the inter-est of those most directly concerned: teenage students.

Students: While many high school students are troubled and alienated, they are the minority. Most students report that they are reasonably content. They respect and appreciate their parents.[44] A small percentage of students work long hours to meet their school responsibilities, but the majority have a considerable amount of leisure time to spend with their friends. Students from low-income families often face real economic hardships, but most young people have a significant amount of money to spend on themselves. High school students may complain about the boredom of school and the constraints placed on them by adults, but for the most part they realize they have a pretty good life. Relatively few young people are pleading to be allowed to earn their own living or to take on the level of responsibilities that people their age faced in earlier historical periods. In short, there is little social pressure from most adolescents to change the fundamental social arrangement that shapes their lives: extended years in schools. This is not, of course, to deny that there are features of schools that many would like to see changed.

Teachers and public officials: Teachers, school administrators, and public officials are rarely in favor of shrinking or even radically changing the education system. Politicians find supporting education attractive because it is much easier to promise a better future than to actually improve the present. Even supporters of educational vouchers usually assume most young people will remain in school and that taxes will pay for this. In general, politicians, educational administrators, and teachers gain in power and influence when the scope of the school system is increased. Nearly everyone wants schools to be more effective, and most teachers work hard to accomplish this. Better teaching, revised curricula, and improved facilities may help. Such measures do not, however, address the issue of youth cultures, which frequently resist adult visions of what should happen in schools. Radically reducing adolescent autonomy, which makes youth cultures and resistance possible, would require a level of coercion and exclusion that is not available to teachers— even if they wanted to use it.[45] One or both of two things would be required. Schools would need to become more like prisons. Or, many students would have to be excluded from schools. Both the financial and the political costs would be enormous. The deinstitutionalization of the mentally ill has visibly impacted American cities by creating thousands of homeless people. Expelling all of the high school students who were not serious about their studies would have a much more dramatic and negative impact on both the job market and "law and order." In short, while our present schools often frustrate politicians, educational officials, and teachers, they are seldom in favor of a fundamental reorganization of education. Instead politicians, officials, educators, and citizens engage in their favorite activity: revising the curriculum.[46] Some of these revisions may actually change students' behaviors in modest ways, but they have little impact on the basic ways young people spend their lives. More commonly such reforms are taken in stride or ignored as young people go about the more important business of spending time with their friends.

Parents: First, let me affirm a legitimate truism: most parents love their children, want the best for them, and often make significant sacrifices on their behalf. But this does not mean that parents do not indirectly benefit from the social arrangements that cause the kind of adolescent behavior they criticize. One aspect of this might be called "*leaving children*." Raising children is very hard work and most parents—good, loving parents—are more than happy to see them go off to school for the better part of the day. Adults then have time to do other things with their lives.[47] In some families parents are working longer hours or different shifts from one another.[48] Divorces, single-parent families, geographical mobility, and families with fewer children are correlates of greater freedom for adults.[49] When both parents are working and commuting, and children have many after-school activities, family meals are more problematic. When they are possible, TV often competes with conversation. All of these are likely to reduce parent-child contact and increase age segregation. "Quality time" may create good emotional ties between parents and children, but it is not a substitute for a network of adults who know what their children and the neighbors' children are doing in the afternoon and evening.[50] Checking by phone helps, but not as much as being there. Many children and adolescents—good kids who love their parents—will still engage in risky behaviors if they can do so undetected. I am *not* suggesting that parents should stay home, but only that not doing so has significant consequences, not simply at the level of individual children and families, but at the level of the neighborhood, the community, and the society.

A second form of adult behavior might be called "*indulging children*." Parents' absence from their children's lives may be a source of guilt for a parent. One way to appease this guilt is by spending money on them. Joan Chiaramonte, vice president of a market research firm, states that because parents have such a limited amount of time with their children, they do not "want to spend it arguing over whether to go to McDonald's or Burger King," and so give in quickly to their children's demands.[51] Sometimes children become like little gods. David Bosworth[52] provides an especially vivid account of the near worship of children during a bar mitzvah in which the child and his peers were placed on a raised platform and were approached by adult men only when they were deferentially offering gifts of cash.[53] Parental concern and devotion to their children's welfare and status are expressed on bumper stickers such as "Baby on Board," "Have You Hugged Your Child Today?" and "My Child Is an Honor Roll Student at …" Instead of "housewives" preoccupied with their homes, we now have "soccer moms" (and dads) preoccupied with their children.

"*Using children*" to display the family's status is another way parents reinforce teenage behavior. Some parents attempt to demonstrate their wealth and status via their children. Until the middle of the twentieth century, men earned most of the income for the family, while women, as "traditional housewives," were responsible for providing services to family members and converting money into status.[54] This was seen most clearly in the value placed on neatness, cleanliness, decorations, and entertaining as lavishly as budgets would allow. These responsibilities spawned a whole industry of magazines, such as *Good Housekeeping, Ladies Home Journal, Better Homes and Gardens*, and *McCalls*. In general, today's adults are too busy earning income to attend to many of the subtle fine points of showing it off within local neighborhoods and communities. Increasingly children are their status symbols. Of course, parents in many societies and historical periods have spent considerable time and resources to improve their family status by enhancing their children's attractiveness to others—as terms like dowry, bride price, finishing school, and debutante ball suggest.[55] What is new is that the children are increasingly the key decision makers; they choose their peers and the commodities—including major purchases like automobiles—needed to enhance status among their peers and the family's status in the community.[56] For parents who have less time and opportunity to display their wealth in their neighborhood and local community, teenagers eagerly step in to take on this "responsibility." In this respect they are often the contemporary "housewives" of the professional and managerial classes.

Last, but not least, parents contribute the behavior they object to in adolescents by *copying teenagers.* Parents not only raise their own status by having successful, attractive teenagers; they raise their own status by being like their teenagers. In many societies the most prestigious social role was that of elder. With his usual biting hyperbole, the novelist Tom Wolfe claims this has all changed: "In the late nineteenth and early twentieth centuries, old people in America prayed, 'Please, God, don't let me look poor.' In the year 2000, they prayed, 'Please, God, don't let me look old.' Sexiness was equated with youth, and youth ruled. The most widespread age-related disease was not senility but juvenility. The social ideal was to look twenty-three and dress thirteen."[57] This is a caricature of adult life, but the reality to which it alludes is all too familiar. Fitness and sexual attractiveness are valued in all societies, but they are especially important in contemporary society—and they are associated with being young. A youthful body is the ideal.[58] It must be created, maintained, and improved through diet, exercise, regular health care, and plastic surgery. As Juliet Schor notes, "Even male executives, downsized, or downsizable, are getting blepharoplasty (to reduce droopy skin around the eyes) and other cosmetic surgeries to make themselves more marketable in a world where youth counts for everything."[59] Moreover, the "youthful" body must be shown to best advantage through clothing—or the lack thereof—and cosmetics.

If, however, parents gain status by being more like teenagers, it is difficult for them to exercise authority to change or shape the behaviors of those teenagers. Most parents try to responsibly cope with the dilemma they face:

maintaining their own status through displays of youthfulness and sexuality, and limiting and guiding the sexuality of their immature adolescents. This is, however, a fine and difficult line to walk. Many parents do this thoughtfully and skillfully. Some, however, have attempted to resolve this dilemma by helping their children to take on the characteristics of adults. Through dress, cosmetics, language, and body movements the children take on the symbols of sexuality at an early age. The result is the sexy sixth grader keenly attuned to the latest fashions and status symbols, and the juvenile parent preoccupied with the same concerns.

My intention is not to scold teachers, public officials, and parents, or to call into question their good intentions, sincerity, and hard work, but to suggest that understanding adolescents requires paying serious attention to the things adults do to create and sustain the teenage behaviors they lament.

CAUSATION AND CONSPIRACY

Good arguments are not improved by overstatement. Therefore I want to specify the nature of the causal relationships I am suggesting. My argument is that the structure of American secondary education—keeping teenagers in their own isolated world with little economic and political power or few non-school responsibilities—results in the status preoccupations of teenagers. These status concerns, in turn, play a significant contributing role in the development and maintenance of consumer capitalism.

Certainly other historical developments that have played a role in the development of consumer capitalism must be acknowledged. Historian Jackson Lears has shown that contemporary marketing and advertising, and the American consumer culture they have helped create, have their roots in the nineteenth and early twentieth century in what he calls "fables of abundance."[60] Central to this fable is a tension between the control associated with managerial professionalism and the enjoyment associated with the carnivalesque. Thomas Frank, a journalist and scholar of popular culture, has emphasized the importance of the transformation in marketing and advertising that both contributed to and resulted from the counterculture of the 1960s.[61] The symbols of the counterculture were co-opted and transformed into the tools of marketing.[62] Economist Juliet Schor has emphasized that people's base of comparison has been changed because of the mass media and the decline of social ties in neighborhoods.[63] They no longer simply try to "keep up with the Joneses" who live down the street; they don't know who lives down the street. Now they aspire to the lifestyles portrayed on television—images that disproportionately focus on the "rich and famous" or greatly exaggerate the standard of living of "typical" people. This increase in the level of aspiration has been further accentuated by growing income inequality and an extensive system of consumer credit. There are, of course, many other analyses of the roots of consumer capitalism, including the still relevant work of scholars such as Thorstein Veblen, Theodor W. Adorno and Max Horkheimer, John Kenneth Galbraith, and Jean Baudrillard.

Most of these analyses, however, tend to focus on broad historical and cultural transformations or they focus on the development of largely impersonal social institutions, such as consumer credit, shopping malls, chain stores, and the mass media. Yet there is a well-established line of theory and research that claims the influence of the mass media and other impersonal institutions is often mediated through concrete networks of interpersonal ties. Early research on voting, marketing, and the diffusion of ideas found that "opinion leaders" were crucial. Most people were not directly influenced by impersonal messages, but by the opinions of those they knew and interacted with.[64]

My argument is that the high school status system typically serves this role in the lives of teenagers. The "opinion leaders" who mediate the influence of the mass media are largely the peers in high school crowds and cliques. Their role is more than simply being the forerunners in the adoption of images from the mass media. They also create new styles. As we have seen, the producers for the adolescent market spend considerable time and effort observing and attempting to anticipate what high school opinion leaders will embrace as the next hot item, the thing that must be purchased in order to be cool.[65] Hence, without wanting to deny the importance of other influences on consumer markets, attention needs to be drawn to the crucial role that these adolescent status systems play in the broader economy and society.

One of the reasons that high school status systems are so important to this process is that they are virtually a universal experience for American youth. Of course, students vary in the way and the degree to which they participate in peer status systems. Virtually no American teenager, however, is oblivious to this aspect of his or her social environment. Moreover, this occurs at a key point in identity formation and for most people is one of their most memorable experiences. In *Broke Heart Blues*, Joyce Carol Oates's poignant novel about high school life and its aftereffects, one of the characters says, "High school life is our metaphor for life that devours what remains of the remainder of life."[66] Certainly this is literary hyperbole, but it telegraphically communicates the centrality of this experience for most Americans. This does not mean that high school life automatically transforms all Americans into mindless consumers. It does mean, however, that a strong desire to have the latest commodities and fashions is likely to be seen as "normal," rather than exceptional or objectionable. The pervasiveness of the pursuit of status and its link to consumer commodities become taken for granted.

I am not arguing that high school status systems are a necessary, much less a sufficient, condition for the emergence of consumer capitalism. Societies with quite different educational systems and adolescent subcultures seem to be embracing consumerism, though the U.S. is at the forefront of this development. As noted in the introduction, I see my argument as having parallels with aspects of Max Weber's famous argument about the role of Protestantism in the development of early capitalism. Briefly stated, Weber argued that Calvinistic Protestantism encouraged a form of self-discipline, hard work, savings, and investment that played a significant role in the creation of bourgeois capitalism in the seventeenth century. He is very clear that this was only one contributing factor, but an important one in the early stages of European capitalism. My argument is similar. In both cases, the claim is that important contributing factors have been identified.[67] I am suggesting that high school status systems have played an important role in the development of consumerism in the United States. More generally, I would say that there have been and continue to be strong elective affinities—to use Weber's term—between the interests of parents, schools, public officials, and businesses, and the status systems in high schools. Obviously, this is not a matter of simple one-directional causation. High school status systems did not cause consumer capitalism. Consumer capitalism and adolescents (who have the characteristics associated with American teenagers) are not inevitably linked. But they are highly compatible and mutually supportive of one another. Hence, they are very difficult to separate now that the pattern has emerged.

If the causation is multifaceted, the nature of the human agency that is involved is even more complex. I have tried to suggest ways in which adolescents, school officials, parents, and businesses all benefit from the present system. This is not to suggest that they anticipated these benefits and created the existing system with these in mind. It certainly is not the case that some shrewd "capitalist class" conspired to create the high school system in the anticipation that it would make an important contribution to the development of consumer capitalism.

Attempting to assign responsibility—and hence praise and blame—for the emergence of the present system is probably futile. This is less the case, I believe, when it comes to who is responsible for the continuation of the existing system. Currently, several stock villains are criticized. First and foremost we blame young people themselves.[68] This has, of course, been a favorite pastime of adults throughout most of history, and has become virtually a minor industry in the contemporary U.S.[69] Another villain in the standard plot are the school officials and teachers who shape the content of students' day-to-day lives—including the politicians who lay down policies and provide the funding for public schooling. Finally, "the media," and to a lesser degree the businesses and corporations that market to teenagers, are seen as corrupting influences. Certainly, young people, schools, the government, and the media can be legitimately criticized for many things. Nonetheless if we want to understand the sources of the problems we ascribe to young people and their schools, the analysis cannot stop there. It is like blaming a flood on the river. The explanation may be indisputably true, but throws little light on the fundamental causes of the problem.

If we want to understand the problems of teenagers and schools, we need to focus on how most adults behave in the context of our economic institutions. More specifically we must examine the relative importance and status attributed to different social roles. In advanced capitalist societies two roles are paramount: producer and consumer. If you want substantial respect and status, you must earn them in these realms. The first is reflected in a person's occupational prestige and the second in the lifestyles they live. Roles such as spouse, parent, community volunteer, citizen, or friend may be ritualistically extolled, but they are clearly seen as being of secondary significance. What counts is economic and professional success and the display of the status symbols associated with these. One simple indicator of this system of values is that many high status individuals—professionals and executives—would find being fired more embarrassing than being divorced or arrested for a minor offense such as driving while intoxicated. This would be especially so for men, but probably increasingly so for women, as jobs become more central to their identity. This is not because people think money is everything—usually they do not. Individuals may be conscientious spouses, parents, and citizens. They may try hard to teach their children the "right things." But no matter what they say to their children, the very organization of their lives communicates the fundamental importance of their roles as producers and consumers—and the secondary value of most other roles. The same can be said for the major organizations that shape our work-a-day world: businesses in general and corporations in particular. There are corporations who try to treat their employees well. Many make contributions to the arts, the sciences, and community institutions. Most local businesspeople and corporation executives genuinely care about these matters. But the fundamental concern of corporations is to make a profit and this requires that they encourage employees to be good producers and the public to be eager consumers. Everything else is secondary. Their employees know this and those who wish to prosper organize their lives accordingly. And their children get the message.

CHAPTER NINE

Consuming Life

Public education is not value-neutral; its values mirror our larger society. The vision conveyed in the public school is one of homo economicus: rational men and women pursuing their self-interest, seeking material pleasures, guided toward individual success. Without ... serious debate, this vision of the individual and the good life has been gradually adopted as the enculturation aim of public schools over the last century.
—Anthony S. Bryk, Valerie E. Lee, and Peter Holland, 1993

FROM THE LUNCHROOM: James and Charles brought up the topic of the preps who supposedly ate in Courtyard No. 1. This conversation quickly grabbed the attention of every boy in the group. Wilson talked about how, "The janitor had to put a garbage can ... where the preps ate each day because they always left their garbage there for someone else to pick up." The boys also commented on how the preps thought they were superior to everyone else. Charles said, "We should go beat them up right now. We can take them easily" ... Wilson remarks, "What do you have against all of them?" To which Charles answers, "It's not what I have against them, its what they have against me. They are always rude to me and act like they are superior to everyone else."[1]

Apparently everyone in this group drinks alcohol on weekends. [One male student] talked about a party that he had been to [at a fraternity at the local college] on Saturday night ... "Two hot girls were there but they left about half way through." Someone mentioned that a boy not at the table was having a party on Wednesday, and everyone commented on how stupid having a party on Wednesday was ... [O]ne boy started talking about all the accessories he was getting for his pickup truck. He pulled out a car magazine/catalog and showed off the chrome plating and other things he was getting ... [H]e and the boy next to him looked at it the [rest of the lunch period].[2]

181

An existing set of social institutions can seldom be completely delineated from what preceded it, or from their consequences. In this chapter, however, I will focus not so much on what led to teenage status systems or the linkages with consumer society, but rather on some of the consequences of these developments.

FROM ABSTRACT LABOR TO ABSTRACT DESIRE

As I indicated in chapter one, British sociologist Paul Willis uses the Marxian concept of abstract labor to understand the alienation of "the lads." For the working-class youth in industrial cities, most jobs required few skills that could not be learned on the job in a relatively short period of time. Most of the employment available involved low-skilled, highly repetitive manual labor. Labor had become abstract: one job was more or less like another; one low-skilled worker could easily replace another. Labor, a crucial factor of production, had been transformed into a standardized commodity. A pool of such abstract labor was an important prerequisite to low-cost production and profits.[3]

In many respects a parallel process has emerged in the realm of consumption. Many commodities are designed and marketed not to meet a particular concrete need or desire, but to meet a generalized, abstract desire: a desire for "more things," "the latest stuff," "what's 'hot'" or "what's 'cool.'" Objects are desired and acquired not for their direct use value, but for their status value—as means to enhance or display one's social standing. Of course, people have been concerned about status symbols in all societies, but for most of history only relatively decadent elites could put this at the center of their lives. Now this process is central to the experience of many people in developed societies and central to the experience of nearly all high school students in the contemporary U.S.[4] Advertisers increasingly market commodities by selling images of the self and the other: the self that we desire to be and the other that we desire. But the others that we desire and the selves that we desire to be are increasingly abstractions. Often celebrities epitomize the form our desire takes. Their public images are often carefully constructed abstractions. Not only is there little chance of any concrete relationship with such celebrities, but what we desire or desire to be is largely an illusory abstraction.

Sex is of course an elemental desire. As indicated at a number of points in earlier chapters, intimate associations—and especially sexual relationships—have an important impact on one's status. The reverse is also true; status tends to increase sexual attractiveness. Consequently, the desire for status and the desire for sex are often closely related. Advertisers and marketers have increasingly attempted to use this fact to market their goods and services. The use of beautiful scantily clothed women—and increasingly men—in a wide variety of advertisements is an obvious example. The implicit message is that you can be more like this "supermodel" if you own this dress or car, and hence you will be more sexually desirable. But like desire in general, sexual desire has tended to become more abstract. Instead of desire being stimulated by interaction with concrete real persons, sexual fantasies and ideals are often shaped by images of movie stars or super-models. The last term is telling. A model is an abstraction; in this case an ideal object of desire. Concrete real people seldom match this abstract ideal of a sexual partner. This contributes to dissatisfaction and a continuing search for a sexual partner who exists only as an abstract ideal. This mode of desire is a reversal of the situation in the mode of production. Abstract labor means nearly any worker will do; abstract desire means that no one will do. Of, course, humans have always had sexual fantasies, but in the past these fantasies have not been so tied to abstract models that virtually saturate the contemporary social environment. To point out the develop-ment of what I have called abstract desire is not to call for a return of sexual Puritanism or "family values." Certainly the developments in interpersonal relationships since the 1960s have included elements of what can legiti-mately be called sexual liberation. But when sexuality becomes abstract desire and sexual liaisons become another consumer choice, it is appropri-ate to ponder whether this constitutes liberation or a new form of social and personal alienation.

As I was writing this I thought perhaps my description exaggerates and is itself an abstraction.[5] I clicked on the home page of my Internet browser. In the upper right—traditionally where the lead story in a newspaper is—it read "Special Offers—Father's Day: Best Bets for Dad." I clicked on this and the shopping page appeared. The first ad was from the Gap chain of stores and read, "Spend $50 on our top summer picks and get 10% off at gap.com." I check their opening women's page and it began with "stock up on summer's sexiest styles" and continues, "more great shopping." The ad immediately below Gap on the Father's Day page said, "Best bets for Dad. Great ideas for what to give at Nordstrom.com." The ad from Banana Republic stores began, "Summer's here and so are the latest styles."

Note that none of these refer to a specific commodity. They suggest rea-sons for buying something and the reasons are not about concrete needs for specific items, but about being stylish and sexy, receiving a discount, stock-ing up, meeting the obligation to give a gift, or the shopping experience itself. Of course if you continue, specific commodities are offered, but almost never is the rationale for buying them some utilitarian need, but rather an implied need to improve or maintain one's status. This is made virtually explicit on the Guess (clothing) site. The first subcategory that can be selected is the "Hit List: top 10 sellers for men and women." The marketing assumption is that what people desire is determined by whether other people want it, because this is proof that it is a "hot" item—the key status symbol of the moment.

FROM ABSTRACT DESIRE TO PATRIOTIC CONSUMPTION

The centrality of consumption and its near sacral status became clearer following the terrorism of September 11, 2001, which killed nearly 3,000 people at the World Trade Center, the Pentagon, and the airline crash in Pennsylvania. Following this event a variety of public figures claimed that it was patriotic for individuals to spend money in order to stimulate the economy. Supposedly people had a duty to buy more, even if the events they experienced caused them to focus on personal, family, and political concerns rather than economic ones. An article appeared in the nationally circulated daily paper *USA Today* reporting on these exhortations to a new form of patriotism. Entitled, "Shoppers splurge for their country," it notes that Americans have long had numerous rationales for shopping. "But just weeks after the terrorist attacks that shook the nation, we are suddenly home to a new breed: the militant shopper ... It's the consumer, traveler or executive who is buying stuff right now, not just because he or she needs it, but also because the economy does." Several prominent politicians, including President George W. Bush, publicly made expensive purchases and urged others to do likewise. Getting back to normal was equated—or at least strongly linked to—shopping and spending. The article concluded, "And who can name one thing that's more intrinsically American than to buy something?"[6] This new version of social responsibility seemed to be a collective version of that old ironic quip, "When the going gets tough, the tough go shopping."

There was some dissent from this line of thought by a few intellectuals, but there was no visible public disapproval, much less any sense of moral outrage. While many might disagree that the essence of being an American is buying things, it is perfectly acceptable to suggest that this is the case, even in a time of national tragedy and mourning. In short, consumption has become an end in itself. We now have a moral duty, not only to be hard-working producers, but also to be fast-spending consumers. With only a little hyperbole it can be said that consumption has consumed life.

THE CULTURAL CONTRADICTIONS OF CAPITALISM

The emphasis on our roles as consumers, at the expense of other social roles, has contributed to a form of abstract desire and patriotic profligacy. Quite aside from what this has done to our inner selves and our interpersonal relationships, it also has led to a form of hedonism that has implications for the operation of the core institution of capitalist society, the market economy.

THE PROBLEM

In recent years Robert Putnam and others have drawn considerable attention to the decline of social capital: people's neglect of their roles as citizens in voluntary associations and non-economic interpersonal networks that constitute "civil society."[7] Others have pointed to the costs of the decline of marriage and family relationships.[8] The problem of consumer capitalism, however, is not only the pride of place given to producing and consuming—at the expense of other social roles. There is also a key tension between the roles of producer and consumer. Daniel Bell, renowned sociologist and once an editor of *Fortune*, refers to this as the cultural contradiction of capitalism.[9] His book argues that there is increasingly a conflict between the discipline and asceticism needed for efficient production and the hedonism and self-indulgence needed to maintain levels of consumption and market demand. Many have commented on this thesis. David Bosworth, an English professor and scholar of popular culture, gives his version of this argument:

> We live in a philosophy/economy that has long proceeded through separation and division, which has divided the classes, the sexes, and now the generations to enhance its own authority and multiply profits. So we shouldn't be shocked to discover that even that most valued of reifications, the Single Self, was also divided for exploitation. There was to be a Producing Self, and there was to be a Consuming Self; one set of ideal behaviors for behind the desk; another, and nearly opposite, for browsing in the mall. Each person was supposed to labor like a Calvinist and spend like an Epicurean.[10]

In less critical and more conventional terminology, the social ideal becomes the person who both works hard and plays hard. This has become a virtual philosophy of life among the professional and managerial classes. To be effective, ideologies must be sustained over time. How is such an ideology inculcated in the next generation?

THE SOLUTION: PREPPIES

I want to suggest that high school status systems are a key social mechanism for creating selves who incorporate these two roles. In modern high schools it is the prep who attempts to embody these two ideals. Preppies may or may not care about learning and ideas, but they are concerned about getting decent grades. They generally conform to adult expectations—at least enough to avoid being labeled a loser. They may not be like Weber's ascetic Calvinists, but they develop moderate amounts of self-discipline. The most successful students are often very disciplined and work exceedingly hard. But if they want to avoid being labeled a brain, or even worse a nerd, they must also learn how to "have a good time." This cannot be simply a private experience, such as appreciating fine art or beautiful scenery, though to show some knowledge and appreciation of these can be a subsidiary asset. One's commitment to a hedonistic good time must be publicly displayed. This is one of the reasons that partying is such a central feature of prep life. It provides an opportunity to publicly display your willingness and ability to "let go," to "go wild," to "get bombed." But this form of hedonism must be limited to weekends and special events if it is not to incapacitate the producing self. Hence, an additional type of self-indulgence is needed for "everyday," something that can be regularly combined with self-discipline. This takes the form of purchasing and displaying good quality fashionable clothes, cars, and other publicly visible status symbols. But these items must communicate both self-indulgence and self-discipline; hence, the expensive designer shirt—with the buttoned-down collar; the dress that is sexy and elegant—but not cheap in either the literal or figurative sense. In short, becoming a preppie is an effective way to learn to manage the two key roles required to be successful in a consumer capitalist society. Perhaps more important than the individual effects are the collective ones; the result is a substantial population of selves committed to the key requirements of a consumer society: high production and high consumption.

The cross-pressures of meeting these two sets of role requirements are even more intense for adolescents—because high school preps must hide both their ambition and their hedonism. As we have seen, to be openly preoccupied about doing well in school is to be labeled a brain or a nerd. But if ambition and self-discipline must be hidden from peers, hedonism must be hidden from adults. Purchasing and consuming alcohol—not to speak of drugs—is illegal for teenagers. They are expected and even encouraged to look and act sexy, but exhorted to refrain from sex. Even if everyone knows what is going on, it must not be made explicit. To do so would risk having parents restrict their activities or cut their allowances. They may lose the good opinion of teachers, who will write the all-important letters of recommendation during the college admissions process. Therefore, young people in general and preps in particular must learn to be less than candid. At times they are obliged to engage in outright deception and lying. When such behavior becomes routine—as it is in most high schools—it is hardly surprising that some students become systematically dishonest and deceitful.[11] Even more significant, it encourages a form of cynicism. For many students this becomes not merely an attitude, but an ideology—a public pose that is regularly displayed in the presence of one's friends and peers. The enormous popularity of the animated television programs "Beavis and Butthead" and "South Park" is an indicator of the prevalence of this mindset. Cynicism toward those in authority and each other is a central element of their content. These programs may reinforce such cynicism, but they are much more likely to be a reflection of this outlook rather than its cause. For some, cynicism becomes a world-view that is carried into adulthood. In its weaker form, cynicism is not the core of the cynic's world-view, but its close complements, irony and sarcasm, are abundant in his style of communicating.[12] These attitudes and styles are further reflected in the disillusionment of younger cohorts with politics and their low rates of voting. At the very least it becomes fashionable to express such indifference and cynicism about politicians and politics.

As I noted in chapter two, students who embrace some version of being "alternative"—whether punk, goth, hippy, or some other variant—are in part rejecting the hypocrisy that they perceive as inherent in the preppy lifestyle. In various ways they are more open about their hedonism. "Normals" are those who are unwilling or unable to both work hard and play hard to the degree that is characteristic of preppies. The various forms of "losers" are those who are undisciplined about both their work and play. They fail to get their schoolwork done and they play in ways that get them into serious trouble with their parents, the school, or the police.

The preppy lifestyle can also be seen in a more positive light. Preppies can be understood as the young people who are learning to deal with the complexities and moral ambiguities of the postmodern adult world. Hypocrisy can be seen as realism—as tact, discretion, and prudence. Young people with these attributes can be seen as having the sophistication needed to be the future leaders of our society.

But whether a negative or a positive interpretation is given to the preppy lifestyle, the key point is that it is not a world unto itself. Rather it is a diminutive version of the lifestyle of the managerial and professional classes of the adult world. More generally, the structure of high school status systems is not simply a transitory stage—a period of hormones and immaturity—unrelated to the adult world. For all of the separation from and contrast with the adult world, there are important parallels between the lives of teenagers and adults. These parallels both reflect and help create some of the key realities of the adult world in consumer capitalism.[13]

THE OUTCOME: BOURGEOIS BOHEMIANS

Many see alternating disciplined hard work and a genuine enjoyment of the good life as a high social accomplishment, a new, more balanced and creative culture. This ethos is the hallmark of the educated managerial and professional classes. This is the central theme of David Brooks's *Bobos in Paradise: The New*

Upper Class and How They Got There.[14] "Bobo" is the contraction of *bourgeois* and *bohemian;* such an amalgamated lifestyle is characteristic of the educated classes at the beginning of the twenty-first century. The social ideal is to be both a thoughtful, educated, disciplined professional and to maintain the bohemian appreciation of sensuality, the avant-garde, and egalitarianism. Bobos believe in individual freedom and choice. They also believe in social responsibility and strong communities. The style of Brooks's book is often ironic and playful; at points it seems superficial. For example he quips, "To calculate a person's status [in Bobo culture], you take his net worth and multiply it by his anti-materialistic attitudes."[15] Yet, this sometimes-flippant style is a way of communicating the irony, modesty, and pragmatism that he sees as characteristic of this world-view. This is a much more serious and thoughtful analysis than its mode of presentation sometimes suggests. He captures well many of the characteristics of the managerial and professional classes.

Brooks's description, however, suggests a very insular, even provincial social existence—not too different from the largely self-contained world of high school status groups. This bright, hardworking, environmentally concerned, and emotionally sensitive upper class has limited, and seemingly superficial, connections with the lives of less talented and less privileged people. "The thirty-one million Americans who officially live in poverty, not to speak of the eighty-five percent of the world's population with less than one-tenth of U.S. income levels, are largely invisible in this account.[16] This insulation of the Bobo milieu from other classes and cultures is a serious shortcoming in Brooks's view of social reality, and probably in the world-view of the classes he describes.[17]

American culture in general and Bobo culture in particular is certainly envied and copied around the world. Unquestionably, it has had a profound impact in shaping a global culture for the middle and upper classes of the world. But is it the "paradise" Brooks claims? Or is this socially structured oblivion? Of course, Brooks and all Bobos are not ignorant of those below them or of the wider world. Yet, Brooks's characterization of Bobos captures well what might be called a "cosmopolitan provincialism." It is not a provincialism rooted in a lack of knowledge, or even a lack of concern; their politics may very well be informed and support efforts to reduce poverty and inequality. Rather, it involves seeing little connection between the poverty of others and their own style of life. This form of oblivion helps to explain why members of this class (and those who try to copy them) are shocked and mystified by resentments expressed in the Oklahoma City bombing, the killings at Columbine High School, and the destruction of the World Trade Center.[18] Following the terrorism of September 11, 2001, comments by many people—especially Bobos, who are often the people that make comments in the public media—claimed that "their world" or even "the world" would "never be the same." These events were indeed awful and tragic. Compared to events experienced by many people

around the world, however, the consequences of September 11 were quite limited in terms of the number of people affected, the aggregate suffering experienced, and the sense of security people have. Americans in general and Bobos
in particular had joined "the real world."[19]

THE FUTURE: WHO DO WE WANT TO BE?

As we have seen, Brooks thinks that a combination of the bourgeois work ethic
and the bohemian enjoyment of life are a kind of paradise. Many more people
affirm the legitimacy of this way of life, though they would not identify it with
a heavenly kingdom. Though adult rhetoric often criticizes materialism and
hedonism, adult behaviors regularly affirm these values. But even if one accepts
the legitimacy of this world-view and lifestyle, it is not how most contemporary
young people will live their lives. First, the data presented in previous chapters seems to indicate that fewer and fewer adolescents even aspire to being
preps. (Preps joined by a few brilliant nerds and weirdos are the main source
of Bobos.) Whatever the virtues of the preppy lifestyle in preparing young people for success in the adult world, the majority of contemporary high school
students find it unappealing or unavailable. Perhaps various kinds of school
reform will convince young Americans to undergo the process of becoming
work-hard producers and play-hard consumers; citizens who eschew grand
visions of the future and are content to seek pragmatic solutions to concrete
problems. Even if this should occur there is another problem. As September
11, 2001, so tragically showed, significant segments of the billions of people
from less developed regions of the world are unlikely to leave our paradise of
pragmatism undisturbed.[20]

Our educational system plays a central role, not just in giving people technical skills, but also in molding their desires and ambitions. Life with one's
peers, in and out of the classroom, powerfully shapes people's world-views and
personalities. The peer status system is central to this process. Currently that
status system is an integral part of consumer capitalism; learning to consume
is one of the most important lessons taught in our high schools. The question
we need to face is whether this is the kind of education we want to give our
children and the kind of people we want them to become. The answer to that
question will be determined, in large measure, by how adults choose to organize their own lives.

A reminder is appropriate. Like all stories, my account has been selective.
Some people do live rather banal lives centered on the most crass forms of
status seeking and consumerism. Yet, the concrete lives of most individuals are
more complex. Many students are not simply preps, brains, weirdos, or whatever. Most adults see themselves as trying to be good employees, parents, and
citizens—not simply compulsive achievers and hedonistic consumers. Most of

us resist being categorized in any simple way; subjectively our lives feel more complex; the differences between others and ourselves seem subtler; and our motivations for adopting a particular lifestyle are many-faceted. The sociological models and arguments I have proposed do not capture the complicated motivations and myriad pressures that we sense shape our personal lives. That is not what they are intended to do. Their purpose is to point to processes and relationships that we tend to overlook, ignore, or repress as we go about living our day-to-day lives. The goal is to highlight things on the collective level that indirectly shape our individual lives—and to point out how our own interests and behaviors significantly contribute to this latent but ever more prevalent collective reality.

Let me recapitulate the arguments of this chapter. Maintaining high levels of consumption has become crucial to the economic prosperity of advanced capitalist societies, which can legitimately be characterized as consumer capitalism. Changes in fashion and more generally the desire to acquire status symbols have become central to maintaining high levels of consumption and economic demand. High school status systems play an important role in socializing people to be concerned about their status and more specifically the way this status is displayed through the acquisition of consumer commodities. "Learning to consume," not "learning to labor," is the central lesson taught in American high schools.

While most adults complain about teenagers' preoccupation with status and status symbols, adults support the basic institutions that encourage these adolescent behaviors because in certain important respects the grown-ups benefit from the existing social arrangements. Many businesses have become very self-conscious of how their economic interests are linked to the status preoccupations of adolescents. They have developed extensive marketing campaigns to encourage the preoccupations of both young people and adults with status, consumption, and the associated ideals of youthfulness, self-indulgence, and hedonism. Consumption now consumes much of life.

According to some analyses this produces a cultural contradiction within capitalism: the new exhortation to self-indulgence needed to maintain consumption potentially undercuts the self-discipline and commitment to work needed for efficient production. One partial remedy was to train people at a relatively early age to both work hard and play hard, to see their core identities as being linked to both production and consumption. The lifestyle of high school preppies incorporates both of these ideals. Being a preppy requires a level of deception that often produces cynicism. For this and other reasons the cultural dominance of the preppy lifestyle within high schools has declined and a more complex form of pluralism has emerged within many schools. In the adult world intellectuals have articulated explicit moral rationales for preppy-like behavior by adults. The emphasis is on a pragmatism that combines a bourgeois work

ethic with bohemian hedonism, a strong commitment to disciplined production and guiltless consumption. Whatever the moral legitimacy of this vision
for people in an advanced consumer economy, the resentment of the billions of
people around the world, who either reject such an ideal or see little possibility
in sharing its fruits, raises the question of whether this insular subculture can
be sustained as a *world*-view.

CHAPTER TEN

Conclusions and Implications

Only a people trained to accept the license of sheer fantasy could actually
believe that extending adolescence into middle age was a recipe for happiness.
—David Bosworth, 1996

FROM THE LUNCHROOM: [A girl complains], "When students have problems with other students, the teachers do nothing to stop the harassment." It is obvious from this comment that she is very concerned with
the way these individuals are treating her and that she feels like she has
no one to turn to.[1]

I immediately noticed a sour attitude among most of the girls as I sat
down. This was surprising because it was Friday, and normally they are
in a very good mood on Fridays ... I asked what was the matter ... Marcy
told me that Leesha and Penny had been caught returning to school from
Best Bagels by one of the administrators. They [had] asked the substitute [teacher] for a pass and said they were going "out" and wouldn't be
too long. They left in Leesha's car ... and picked up lunch for themselves
and for Marcy. As they were returning [to] school, one of the administrators saw them ... Marcy [said] that the administrator came up to her
and told her that her sister, Penny, had been suspended for two games of
softball. Leesha was worried that she would be suspended for two tennis
matches. They were trying to figure out how to get out of it. Leesha
decided that since the administrator had not seen them leave or come
back, but only returning with the Best Bagels bag, that they should deny
everything. The rest of the girls told her that this was not a good idea ...
Penny and Leesha had gone to talk to the administrator who turned them
in. They were very relieved [to find out] that he was just kidding ... He
hadn't reported them and just wanted to teach them a Lesson. I asked
them if they would skip again ... Both girls assured me that they would
not ... during tennis and softball season. Next semester they might.[2]

This book has had three key purposes. One is theoretical: to demonstrate the usefulness of the theory of status relationships. The second is more pragmatic: to increase our understanding of teenagers and the contemporary American consumer society. The third is to show that theory and pragmatics can and should be combined.

THE THEORY OF STATUS RELATIONS

The theory of status relations was originally developed to understand the Indian caste system and has been used here to analyze American teenage status systems. My claim is that the theory helps us understand the structure and operation of each of these social situations—even though the geographical location, cultural context, and historical development are very different. The theory is not only a set of categories for describing status groups and contrasting them to other types of groups, which is the main contribution of Weber, closure theory, and boundary work perspectives (see Appendix I). What it adds to these, as well as to the explanations provided by interaction ritual theory, is the logic behind status group formation and status behaviors.

As Weber noted, status groups (and quasi-status groups) have distinctive social properties that make them different from the economically based formations we call classes or the political formations we call parties. (Of course, the notions of classes, status groups, and parties are ideal-types that concrete groups more or less approximate.) A major contribution of the theory of status relations is that it explains *why status groups have the particular characteristics that make them different from other types of stratified groups*. For example, it explains why mobility is more problematic in status systems than in other types of stratified systems (i.e., inalienability and inexpansibility); why status groups are likely to have more complicated norms and rituals than classes or parties (i.e., elaboration); when these norms and rituals will be subject to changing fashions and when they will not; why deviance in status and religious systems are likely to involve retribution and the demeaning of outsiders and deviants (i.e., inexpansibility), than in more economic or political contexts; and why status, legitimacy, and sacredness are so closely associated (i.e., the inalienability of status).

The second, and closely related contribution is that it explains *why a relationship between two people or two groups may focus on status differences in one situation but ignore them in another*. That is, the theory of status relations helps explain when status differences will be important and when they will not be (e.g., when activities are expressive, and especially when they involve eating, sex, and other forms of intimacy; when interaction is highly visible; and when other resources are scarce).

In sum, my claim is not that all previous approaches should be abandoned, but rather that the theory of status relations, built upon a notion of resource structuralism, adds to our explanation of many of the details of status systems in social contexts as varied as the Indian caste system and American teenage culture.

An obvious next step would be to analyze teenagers in other societies. It should also help to throw light on the patterns of behavior characteristic of many aristocracies and many outcast groups. Not only people, but cultural objects have a status; some paintings are hung in museums, most are not. Preliminary work has been done on using the theory to explain the status of cultural objects such as public monuments, works of art, and social theories.[3] Potentially the theory of status relationships can be helpful in understanding any situation in which humans keep account of the expressions of approval and disapproval toward an actor, a group, or an object.

Calling this a "general theory" is not to assert that this is all we need to analyze and understand status systems. Nor am I suggesting that it identifies some of the "laws of human behavior." All theories, including this one, are shaped and limited by the historical and cultural context; all theories are abstractions that focus on some things and ignore others. But to acknowledge these points is not to accept the notion that all knowledge is concrete and local and that the only thing analysts can do is help outsiders see something of what insiders see. You do not have to be a teenager to understand much of teenage behavior, and perhaps to understand some aspects of adolescent life more thoroughly than those who are currently teenagers.

Generalizations useful for analyzing a variety of social situations are both possible and desirable. This kind of theory is not, of course, the only kind of knowledge that is needed to understand social life. In sum, my aim has been to show that this study of American teenagers and its findings further demonstrates the utility of this particular kind of knowledge and this specific theoretical perspective.

SOME POLICY IMPLICATIONS

The book has had a second key aim: to produce knowledge potentially useful for creating better schools and a better society. The transformation of research findings into fruitful policies is always a risky business. To discern order in the confusion and complexity of everyday life, we must focus on some things and ignore others. Even if we succeed in adequately understanding the causal connections between the factors we have analyzed and design policies that capture these insights, we are not home free. The things we have ignored have a nasty way of producing consequences we did not intend or anticipate. The acknowledgment of this limitation does not mean that research findings are of no practical value; the natural sciences face the same difficulty, though perhaps to a lesser extent. It does mean that when moving from findings to recommendations, considerable modesty and humility are appropriate.

Most of my analysis has focused on what goes on within the confines of the school and especially the peer culture of the students. Accordingly, I will focus on a few things that might be done at this level to improve the quality of school life. These suggestions will not be appropriate for all settings, but they are policies or changes worth considering in many contexts. The following suggestions are not a comprehensive list of needed reforms, but those suggested by these findings and the theory of status relations.

The theory of status relations has one key assumption and four elements. The assumption is that status becomes especially important when it is not reducible to economic or political power. The implication for the high school setting is that a key reason students are so preoccupied with status is because they are excluded from meaningful forms of economic or political power. Hence, one way to reduce the status preoccupations of students would be to decrease the extent to which their lives are centered on the opinions of their peers. We will return to some of the implications of this strategy later in the discussion.

With regard to the elements of the theory, two of these—conformity and associations—are the sources of status. If individual and group differences in conformity and association account for differences in the status of individuals and groups, then one way to reduce the importance of status differences is to reduce the differences in conformity and associations. At points in the discussion the significance of the inexpansibility and inalienability of status will also be considered. Many of the changes I will suggest require that teachers and school officials have sufficient power and influence to shape certain aspects of students' non-academic life.

CONFORMITY, NORMS, AND INEXPANSIBILITY

I will begin with a discussion of how differences between individuals' conformity to peer norms might be narrowed. Before discussing specific interventions, I need to clarify different aspects of conformity to norms that might be influenced or controlled. First, we can *reduce the possibilities of variations* in conformity. For example, putting only individuals of the same age in a group or class reduces the domination of younger children by older ones. You can reduce competition and differentiation in dress by requiring school uniforms. This strategy reduces status differences by reducing the possibilities of people differing by "outlawing" some kinds of variations. Second, we can *reduce the relevance of a particular kind of variation* in conformity and status by making other kinds of conformity a source of status. The significance of being a star football player is reduced if other sports and activities are also held in high regard. Third, we can *create norms emphasizing solidarity and equality* rather than inferiority and superiority. A core American value is that all citizens deserve basic levels of civility and respect. No one should be called "Lord Smith" or "your highness" nor called demeaning names, nor forced to bow to others; even convicted criminals are entitled to basic levels of respect. Fourth, we can *reduce the extent to which differences in economic power* are relevant to attaining status. Attempts to "buy" the title of class valedictorian would almost certainly be rebuffed. Even the significance of standardized-test scores would be significantly discounted if it cost $100,000 to take the test; everyone would know that a lot of smart people were excluded and a lot of rich (but probably not so smart) people were included. We already limit the use of economic and political resources to gain status in many areas of life, and perhaps this should be considered in the context of high school peer status systems.

SCHOOL UNIFORMS AND OTHER STATUS SYMBOLS

Requiring a standard school uniform is one way to eliminate the *possibility of variation*; nobody is in fashion or out of fashion. Public discussion about the virtues and vices of school uniforms has occurred before. My data and theory suggest that uniforms can blunt some of the most blatant and damaging forms of status competition among students. To work, this strategy must be implemented in a fairly rigorous manner. Requiring jeans and tee-shirts is not enough. This will simply shift students' concern to the differences between the latest designer jeans. A standardized uniform from sources that guarantee a high degree of uniformity are required. Nor will such a policy succeed if students are allowed to wear expensive jewelry and accessories, whether these are a string of pearls or a heavy gold chain. Clearly, such rules involve suppressing certain forms of individualism and creativity. Many students will complain bitterly about the violation of their "constitutional rights." I doubt, however, that such a policy would reduce intellectual and political individuality and creativity and turn people into unthinking automatons—though the subtle and unanticipated consequences should be carefully monitored. What such a policy will almost certainly do is threaten the economic interests of important sectors of manufacturing, advertising, and retailing. We should not expect too much of such a strategy. Of course, students will try to "cheat" and find subtle ways of differentiating themselves, but reducing both the centrality and the cost of the status competition associated with clothing and fashion is possible—at least in the context of the school itself.

Perhaps schools should consider regulating other status symbols. There are good reasons to consider limiting and regulating the use of cell phones and beepers on school grounds. While their significance as a status symbol will eventually decline, they are often used for drug-related activities and can be a disruptive distraction. Regulating the kinds of cars students drive is impractical—except perhaps in terms of the size of the parking space they take. On the other hand, the right to drive a car to school and park it on school property is not guaranteed by the U.S. Constitution. Discouraging the use of private cars as a means of transportation to school should be seriously discussed and debated; we should not unthinkingly assume that schools should de facto encourage the use of cars by providing parking.

My guess is that such regulations *by themselves* will not be very effective in reducing status preoccupations and will be seen as adult hypocrisy. When linked with other kinds of reforms it is possible they could play a useful role.

MANY KINDS OF STATUS

If there are multiple ways to gain respect this reduces the *relevance* of any one type of conformity. As we have seen, more multidimensional status systems tend to reduce the intensity of a "traditional" status hierarchy and contribute to pluralism. De-emphasizing traditional sports and cheerleading and channeling resources into a variety of sports and activities seem to contribute to this. Some blend of moving non-academic activities out of the school setting and distributing the resources more evenly to those that remain within the school setting should help reduce status differences and preoccupations. In the school that has well-funded programs in orchestra, chorus, drama, soccer, wrestling, lacrosse, and debating, fewer students will be preoccupied with associating with members of the basketball or football team and conforming to their lifestyle.[4] As the analysis in chapter six indicates, one way to reduce the inexpansibility of status is to create multiple status systems. So this strategy does not involve forbidding or repressing status differences, in the way requiring school uniforms does, but rather involves reducing the inexpansibility of status by multiplying the kinds of conformity that can be a source of student status.

FOSTERING CIVILITY

Teachers and administrators tend to see peer culture as largely outside of their realm of responsibility—unless school rules or laws are clearly violated. Educational "professionalism" includes the notion that teachers should shed their role as surrogate parents, policemen, or teachers of morality. It is unusual when a school administration creates educational programs to specifically discuss the different informal crowds and cliques and how they should treat one another. Even some of the most able and sensitive teachers we observed or interviewed at WWHS talked about which kids were "cool" and which were not, as if it was a given fact of life similar to gender or age. Never did we hear any discussion of how the informal peer culture might be shaped or transformed. Out of the more than three hundred reports from college students, only one indicated that school officials had specifically attempted to shape the peer culture. Of course, school officials commonly complain about and take actions against particular forms of behavior—smoking, drug use, and violence—that are associated with particular peer groups. But this is different from perceiving the informal stratification system of students as a structural problem requiring a planned and thoughtful response. The one exception was the report from the Catholic girls' school I have called Sacred Heart Academy, which did seem to be successful in lowering if not eliminating competition and hostility between different crowds.

This hands-off attitude concerning status group inequalities is quite different from the policies toward gender and racial inequality. It was not many years ago when open racism and sexism were an accepted part of high school culture. Blatant or open put-downs of those of another race or gender are now considered inappropriate and bring censure if not more severe forms of discipline. Black History Month is observed in many schools, and organized discussions of date rape and sexism are not uncommon. Of course, some students' surreptitious behaviors and attitudes still exhibit racism and sexism. But their public expression is likely to bring reproach rather than being something to be admired and copied. In the broader society, Americans have long had norms that discouraged airs of superiority or demeaning forms of deference. Would not similar norms in our schools be appropriate and useful? Such norms would have to be regularly expressed and affirmed rather than "buried" in some student handbook. Neither should there be a draconian enforcement of such norms. Just as the public expression of norms extolling academic excellence are appropriate and useful, the expression of norms extolling mutual respect and solidarity could play a constructive role. In theoretical terms this means that even when status is relatively inexpansible, attempts to raise your own status by publicly demeaning others would be considered a violation of the community's norms, rather than viewed as an acceptable way to raise your status and a routine feature of social life—as is now the case.

Would such norms restrain legitimate moral, political, and intellectual criticism and lead to a stifling form of political correctness? The stifling of disagreement and dissent is a legitimate concern. Often, however, the critique of "political correctness" is primarily a way to defend the inequities and injustices of the status quo. My theory and findings suggest that discouraging competition in consumer status symbols and encouraging civility would increase, not repress, debate. If it were considered bad form and poor taste to criticize people for the kind of jeans they wear or who their boyfriend or girlfriend is, the tendency to engage in criticisms and debate about significant moral and political issues would be increased, not decreased. That is, status competition could shift to matters more central to the explicit aims of an educational institution. While I believe schools should encourage civility and discourage obsessive one-upmanship with respect to fashions and academics, the goal is not to create some utopian community of harmony and consensus. Rather it is to shift conflict and competition to matters that are more central to the life of an academic community and a democratic society.

REDUCING THE POWER OF MONEY AND COMMERCIALISM

If we are concerned that our teenagers are too materialistic and too focused on momentary status symbols, turning schools into billboards and shopping malls makes no sense. We need to reduce the significance of individual differences in economic power as a means of gaining respect and status within our schools. The usual justification for allowing advertising in schools, on school buses, and at stadiums is because the schools need the money. Similarly, the members of bands, choruses, and other clubs are frequently pressured into becoming door-to-door salespersons for greetings cards, fruits, candies, and numerous other commodities so that their group can take school trips or buy needed equipment. The way to handle the cost of school activities is through better public financing, not through commercialization of the schools. One need not be a purist about this issue. Screening out all advertising on the Internet, forbidding the sale of hot dogs at football games, or outlawing student clubs from selling homemade fudge is not practical or even desirable. Some areas of life, however, should be largely free of things to buy and messages encouraging us to do so. Schools should be one of these areas. This does not mean that schools should be anti-capitalist or be advocates for asceticism, socialism, or radical egalitarianism.[5] But neither should they be adjuncts to the advertising and marketing industries.

On a much more fundamental level we need to call into question the value of economic activity and growth as *the* central concern of our civilization. The median family income in the U.S. in 1947 was $14,953 (in 1999 dollars). In 1999 it was $48,950. This means that real income (controlled for inflation) has increased 327 percent since the end of World War II. It is not self-evident that people today are three times happier or more satisfied with their lives. While there are good reasons to want to sustain modest economic growth and the expansion of material goods and services, should this be the de facto top priority of society? To reverse the famous mantra of the first Bill Clinton campaign, "It's *not* the economy, Stupid." For this political priority to change, individuals and families will have to change their priorities—and, more specifically, base their sense of community status and self-worth less on their occupational prestige and their economic standing. Clinton was right. To get elected, virtually all that mattered was convincing people that he could increase prosperity. Until that priority changes, our children are likely to become more materialistic and acquisitive—because that is what they have learned from us, and what they are learning in our schools.

ASSOCIATIONS AND INALIENABILITY

School authorities can probably influence interpersonal associations more easily than conformity to detailed norms; organizing who spends time with whom is simpler than controlling exactly what students do when they are not being observed. A variety of procedures could contribute to discouraging the insularity of certain crowds and cliques.

AGE-GRADED PRIVILEGES

Both the contrast between seniors and lower-grade students and between "military-type" schools and other schools, suggests that a system of increasing privileges (and responsibilities) linked to the year-in-school can increase the sense of community and reduce status competition between students. One problem with such a strategy is that the privileges and responsibilities have to be real—something the students care about. Moreover, such a system has its dangers, including the potential for intimidation and hazing of younger students. Nonetheless, I suspect that creating more elaborate age-related privileges could be a useful device in many situations.

RANDOM ASSIGNMENT OF STUDENTS

I reported on one girls' school that stressed age-graded privileges. This school also required all students to participate in intramural athletics, and randomly assigned them to teams. This forced them into cooperative efforts with those they would not have chosen to work with on their own. If students are assigned to sports or other performance-oriented teams, it is important to see that they are not on a losing team their entire high school experience. Perhaps creating some kind of handicap system—similar to professional sports—would be effective: the weakest teams are assigned (or choose) a limited number of the best players or performers for the next cycle of competition.

Individual choice is a highly rated value in our society, but I am not convinced that giving students "choices" is always an effective learning strategy. Frequently this is the way individuals cultivate their provincialism. I think it might be worthwhile to experiment with reducing "freedom" of choice in certain areas of school life—forcing students to associate with those they would avoid, left to their own devices. What would happen if students were randomly assigned seats in the lunchroom and these assignments were changed every month or so? This would probably be considered more tolerable if this system was used half of the month, every other week, even for a limited period during a term. The resistance might be reduced if this was made part of a graded educational process, for example, if students were required to interview and report on the cultural background of two students they had never talked with.

ASSIGNED STUDY TEAMS AND COLLECTIVE GRADES

For some activities, random assignments might be especially effective if students anticipated that they were going to have to work with a group of people over a sustained period of time, for example in a study team or group. "Team spirit" might be accentuated for academic activities by having some portion of the individual's grade be based on the team's average grade. Americans assume that it is "perfectly natural" for each individual to receive the "average score" in sports, that is, the won–lost record of the team. Even the most outstanding players do not proceed to the playoffs if their team has a losing record. Some firms link raises and bonuses to the profits for a particular period; all gain or lose depending on the success, performance, and luck of the whole organization. One of the things that adults often have to learn in the "real world" is that their long-term welfare is often dependent on cooperating productively with people they do not necessarily like. In contrast, suggesting that some portion of a course grade might be linked to learning such skills, as measured by the average grade of a study group, is considered some kind of bizarre collectivism. Both the taken-for-granted collectivism of team sports and the individualism of traditional forms of academic performance are essentially arbitrary social creations. It might be worth experimenting with more individualism in sports and more collectivism in academics. Our data show that sports teams are one of the most successful social sites for developing interpersonal associations across ethnic groups and lifestyle crowds. Perhaps study teams—in which the members were truly dependent on one another because part of their individual grade was based on the team performance—would provide another site for such ties.

GENDER SEGREGATION

I went to a men's college and I have long been strongly in favor of co-educational institutions. I think that this is still desirable during most of the high school years. But in talking with high school students and reading the literature about the status and sexual preoccupations of middle school students, I have become open to the possibility that single-sex schools might play a useful role for some age groups. As far as I am concerned this is not a matter of keeping students innocent or pure, much less suppressing knowledge about the intricacies of sex. The aim is postponing the peer pressure to compete for romantic and sexual relationships. Theoretically speaking, it would be another way of segregating instrumental and expressive associations and activities. Obviously, many teenagers are still going to be interested in romantic and sexual relationships, but these would be more separated from the actual educational process. This is not too dissimilar from the norms that are emerging for adults in the work situation: Romance and sex are fine, but not in the work setting.

Obviously several of these ways of manipulating associations (as outlined above) would also reduce the inalienability of a student's status—at least to the degree that status was based on associations. Arranging or requiring students to associate with a broader array of students or to reshuffle these associations occasionally would mitigate the tendency for students to be pigeonholed by others after the first year or so. Even emphasizing class solidarity and privileges provides everyone with a certain amount of upward mobility over time and reduces students being stuck in a low or demeaning status.

DECOUPLING EDUCATION, RECREATION, AND ROMANCE

Adolescents everywhere are concerned about how their peers evaluate them. American teenagers are, however, relatively unique in the degree to which peer status and peer groups are a central feature of school life. This is largely due to the fact that schools in most parts of the world do not provide extensive extracurricular or recreational activities. Throughout most of Europe, clubs and associations, which are quite separate from the schools, organize much of the athletic activity. Senior proms, homecoming, and the like are nonexistent or less central to school life. In short, schools focus on instrumental activity. Expressive associations and activity like recreation and romantic relationships take place primarily in other contexts. As the theory would predict, status preoccupations—at least the non-academic aspects of status—are less intense, though, of course, not extinct. Recognizing this is not to advocate that all schools do away with athletic and recreational activities. I believe it would be worthwhile, however, for some public schools to experiment with a version of the European model, and see if this reduced the significance of expressive associations and in turn increased the attention that students paid to academic matters. The goal is not to eliminate recreational and romantic relationships from young people's lives, but to see if we can find patterns of social organization that improve both the academic and non-academic experience. The way we are currently structuring young peoples' lives is neither "natural" nor necessarily the most effective mode of organization possible. Obviously, assuming that foreign patterns are necessarily better is also a mistake.

PROTECTING THE VULNERABLE

The inclusion of students with disabilities in comprehensive high schools was obviously a policy that attempted to manipulate student associations.[6] Supposedly "regular" associations between disabled and "normal" students should help to equalize differences in social status and self-esteem. Short of this, the handicapped would at least be identified with "regular" schools, rather than negatively labeled by the name of the school they attended. Integrating these students into ordinary social contexts is certainly a desirable goal.

In many schools, however, students with various kinds of disabilities seem to be especially subject to harassment and small cruelties. This policy of inclusion is of questionable value, as high schools are currently constituted. Perhaps an educational campaign to encourage "normal" students to be more sensitive and sympathetic to those with handicaps could help, but such a transformation will not be easy. As we have seen in many peer cultures the social pressures to put people down are very strong. Those who are least able to defend themselves are especially vulnerable. This problem makes even more urgent the creation and the effective enforcement of norms that make demeaning and harassing of others illegitimate. Unless this can be accomplished—and it will not be easy—the obviously desirable ideal of including the handicapped, held by many special education staff and activists, can become a rigid ideology that often consigns the most vulnerable to even more suffering and degradation.

REDUCING THE SIGNIFICANCE OF PEER STATUS

Up to this point the discussion has focused on reshaping the patterns of conformity and association within schools so as to reduce the importance of status differentiation and status symbols. Keep in mind that students' preoccupation with these matters is due to the fact that status is the only kind of meaningful power available to them. Now let us consider a few ways in which peer status might be made less central to the education of adolescents. The goal is not, and should not be, to make students indifferent to the opinions of their peers. I believe it is desirable, however, to both reduce the intensity of status pressures in schools *and* to make young people less isolated from other aspects of the society. Adolescents' near obsession with peer status is largely the result of how adults have organized young peoples' lives.

A LIFE WITH OTHER PEOPLE

Seeking to spend time with people of one's own age and developing some independence from parents is common across nearly all cultures. But societies in which adolescents lead a largely self-contained social existence are not common. One way to reduce teenagers' preoccupation with peer status is to give them more contact with non-teenagers and increase their economic and political power. This probably is going to require less differentiation among schooling, work, and the broader life of the community. More teenagers working longer hours in the fast-food industry (and other low-paying) jobs is not, however, the solution. They will only have more money to spend on status symbols, accentuating the problems we already have. Nor are rigid apprenticeship programs the solution; irrevocably channeling early teens into a particular craft or occupation creates more problems than it solves. Fortunately, these are not the only possibilities. Internships in which students spend time in work situations should be experimented with on a wider scale. We should consider requiring that a significant portion of any money earned during the school years in internships (or even in private sector jobs) be withheld and placed in an account for additional education or long-term investments. Employers already are required to withhold wages for Social Security and this proposal is no more administratively complicated or politically utopian than Social Security seemed when first proposed. We should experiment with lowering the voting age for those who can pass tests indicating they have a good grasp of the political process. Such a test could even be made as a prerequisite to a driver's license. Youth representatives on the boards of public and voluntary agencies should also be considered. Instead of trying to keep 19- and 20-year-olds from buying alcohol or having sex, we need to work harder at teaching young people how to responsibly deal with these aspects of life. In short, if we want our young people to stop being "a tribe apart," we have to stop organizing their education and their lives in a way that is almost certain to produce that result.

WHO SHOULD BE IN SCHOOL AND WHEN?

More flexible patterns of when teens are required to attend school might be another way to increase adolescents' integration into the broader society and decrease the significance of peer status. Encouraging young people to have extended experiences in settings other than schools also might contribute to their maturity and their education.[7]

In our postmodern knowledge economy "life-long learning" is a very fashionable concept. Despite its overuse as ritual incantation, I believe it is a helpful idea and ideal. But life-long learning does not have to mean that the first quarter to a third of one's lifetime must be spent in uninterrupted schooling. The information revolution is creating other ways to acquire knowledge. Even when schools are the appropriate vehicle for education, this does not mean that everyone should be required to be there continuously through most of their adolescence. Schools would work better and young people would be happier if they were assured long-term educational opportunity, but not all required to be in school more or less continuously.

We should seriously consider a universal national service corps that involves sending young people to places they have not been and performing needed work. Few people want to spend a lifetime keeping roadsides clean, assisting elderly people, or building trails in national parks. A year of this kind of experience can, however, be invaluable in helping youth to grow up and learn about people who are very different from them. Ideally these programs should involve both exciting and stimulating activities—for example travel to new places or learning to drive a truck or bulldozer—*and* a significant amount of routine and drudgery. Few things teach the value of education as much as extended periods of cutting weeds or emptying bedpans. The timing of when people fulfilled such service could vary, but for many, especially those alienated from schooling, some of the high school years might be ideal. A year or two of military service could be one option for those who could qualify. As with internship programs, a proportion of wages could be withheld for later education or long-term investments. Many will see such policies as overly coercive. I do not see why requiring young people to engage in a year of service activities is any more coercive than requiring them to attend school. As with military service there should probably be exemptions or alternatives for principled conscientious objectors.

Any alternatives to schooling must guard against several dangers. First, racial, class, and gender discrimination must be avoided, for example, channeling only disadvantaged boys into work camps. I am certainly not advocating a system in which an elite is given an excellent education and a substantial portion of other young people are prepared for routine low-wage jobs. This is one reason a service corps should involve universal participation. Second, we need to guard against people leaving schools without minimum levels of competency in reading, writing, and arithmetic. I suspect that many unmotivated students could develop these skills much quicker than they currently do if participating in or attending school sporting events, having a driver's license, purchasing alcohol, or being hired by an employer were contingent on demonstrating such competence—and they knew they could leave school for a while and participate in various alternative programs when they had demonstrated these competencies.

Perhaps the most important potential benefit of greater flexibility would not even be the effect on the individuals who enter alternative programs, but the effect it had on the educational atmosphere of our schools. That is, more flexible patterns might also decrease the alienation and deviance of those who were in school at a given time. Short of executions, corporal punishment, and imprisonment, the near universal means of controlling serious deviance is exclusion. Many pre-modern societies used banishment. Modern organizations fire employees. Often self-exclusion is even more effective—as when dissident members of a political party or voluntary association vote with their feet. In my judgment, the primary reason for the supposed superiority of private schools is their ability to exclude those not willing to abide by the basic rules of the institution. The right to expel students is important, but just as important is the right of students to leave. These mechanisms of social control are much less available to the typical comprehensive public high school. The alternatives to traditional schooling would also give this advantage to public schools and their students.

This does not, of course, mean that young people should be kicked out of school for trivial causes or be allowed to drop out at will. If we want our schools to work better, they cannot be a holding pen for the alienated or a way to reduce youth unemployment. High school should not be some kind of Spartan or Puritan training regime; but neither should it be a school for conspicuous consumption or criminal activity.

In short, we may be able to reduce the significance of peer status and accomplish other educational goals by giving individuals greater flexibility in the timing of their schooling. This must include constructive alternatives for some of their adolescent years, and giving them strong motivations to later return to school. All of these proposals are tentative suggestions; they are merely meant to illustrate some logically possible alternatives to the present system. Whatever the final details, we need a more flexible vision of both the timing and the institutional context through which people can participate in life-long learning.

SOME SPECULATIONS AND OPINIONS

Unlike the proposals above, the remarks in this section are not directly implied by my research finding or the theory of status relationships. They are, however, issues that are closely related to the matters I have analyzed.

ON MIDDLE-CLASS FLIGHT AND SCHOOL VOUCHERS

Currently middle-class parents reduce the number of unmotivated students in a given school by moving to areas that have few disadvantaged young people. Initially this involved primarily "white flight"—whites moving out of areas that had large concentrations of African Americans or other disadvantaged groups. This is still happening, but now middle-class blacks and immigrants are also joining this flight. Consequently, programs that allow alienated young people to leave school and enter alternative programs are unlikely to increase their disadvantages more than the current system. If urban schools were perceived to be safer and more academically rigorous, there would probably be less flight to the suburbs. Metropolitan areas might well be more racially and economically integrated and the perceived gap between urban and suburban schools would be reduced.

At the beginning of the twenty-first century in America, many critics of public education saw publicly funded school vouchers as the solution. These would allow students and parents to choose the school they think best fits their needs. The model is the shopper who buys from the store with the best products at the lowest prices. This strategy is intended to make teachers and school administrators more responsive and creative in meeting the educational needs of their students. If they fail to do so, families use their vouchers to send their children to another school that does provide what they want. Private and religious schools are presumed to be more effective and responsive to student needs because they are subject to such market pressures.

While this imagery and diagnosis of the problem may be partly accurate, it is seriously limited and flawed. Undoubtedly, there are many instances when entrenched school bureaucracies are unresponsive to students and parents, and are less innovative and effective than they should be. This is not, however, the main problem with our schools. The problem is not primarily unmotivated teachers and administrators, but unmotivated students. Obviously, it would be desirable to find ways to interest and motivate all students, but this seems beyond our grasp, and almost certainly is due to many factors outside of the school setting. Improved motivation was the aim of the "shopping mall" high school—something to interest everyone. The primary result was tolerable levels of student passivity rather than significantly improved levels of academic motivation. If significant numbers of students in a school are alienated, unmotivated, and primarily concerned with peer status and status symbols, creating a good academic program is a difficult if not impossible task.

The most likely outcome of a voucher system would be that the top students would be admitted to one set of schools, the middling students to another, and the poorest students to yet another. There might be some competition between the schools in each stratum, but few of the top schools would be competing with the poor ones to be allowed to admit weak students. This will certainly be the case if schools are allowed to charge families fees in excess of the value of the vouchers. Higher income families will simply outbid others for the best schools. Exclusive elite stores compete with each other, not with stores that serve the lower classes. I am not necessarily opposed to more experimenting with voucher systems, but the likely outcome is at least as problematic and uncertain as some of the things I have suggested.

PROTECTING STUDENTS FROM SMALL CRUELTIES

Bullies have always been a problem. Part of growing up is learning to deal with them. But this does not mean that young people should be without assistance in this regard. When adults move from being rude and aggressive to intimidation and violence, we call the police and expect them to protect us. Many high school students do not receive such support. On a number of occasions, students complained about teachers refusing to do anything about students who engage in physical intimidation. Even more frequently they are oblivious to the verbal and psychological harassment that some students receive. Teachers do intervene to stop fights—as our data show—but students can be and are harmed by harassment that stops short of open violence. In large part, teachers and administrators tend to ignore these more subtle forms of cruelty when they can because they lack the knowledge and power they need to deal with them. More specifically, the way schools are organized means it is hard for them to know what is going on in the peer culture and they have few effective sanctions to use against those who abuse others.

But why do teachers apparently do so little to control the "small cruelties" common in school life? The main reason is because they are unable to intervene effectively. To intervene ineffectively usually makes matters worse. To illustrate some of the limitations on teachers' power and influence, I will discuss a few factors that affect teachers' and officials' ability to shape and enforce norms.

SCHOOL SIZE

Our data seem to indicate that smaller schools tend toward more traditional forms of hierarchy. In schools located in small communities, family status is more likely to affect student status. In small schools, however, there was also more social contact between different strata and status groups; it was not practical for subgroups to remain self-contained in a small school. Unfortunately, very few small comprehensive high schools (less than 600) exist in urban and suburban areas. Hence, discerning the separate effects of school size and community size is difficult. What seems relatively clear, however, is that the informal social control systems that often work for smaller schools are less effective in larger schools. For example, it is much more difficult for a teacher to share the experience and knowledge she has about a particular student with the student's other teachers.[8] Moreover, in a large high school teachers will have students in class once, but virtually never see (or hear about) them again. The result is that the institutional knowledge that is available about many students is superficial, incomplete, and fragmented, or is restricted to overworked guidance counselors and assistant principals. The same is true of students' knowledge about one another.

It is not, I believe, accidental that most of the shooting rampages in schools have occurred in relatively large institutions. In many cases other students had heard the perpetrators threaten violent behavior well ahead of the event, but the information never reached anyone who took preventative action. The informal social networks were simply too large and fragmented for them to play a significant role in heading off trouble—even about the most horrendous possibilities. In contrast, a friend of mine—I will call him Miller—tells the story of an incident that occurred in his relatively small prep school. It seems a member of his own class had been bullying my friend's younger brother. One day the dean called Miller into his office and asked him whether he was aware that Rogers—the name I'll give the bully—had been beating up on his brother. He was not. The headmaster said, "Rogers will be headed into the class next door in just a moment. Why don't you 'speak to him' about this matter?" My friend stepped into the hall. When Rogers came by, he grabbed him, shoved him up against the wall and threatened to rearrange his anatomy if he didn't leave his little brother alone. Just as he was about to "underline" the point, the dean stepped into the hall and said, "Miller, what the hell are you doing? Get your hands off him and get to class." The harassment ceased. Whatever one thinks about this informally sanctioned use of threatened violence, the applicable point is how size affects the possibilities of informal social control. In a large school the dean would probably never hear about the problem, and it would be unlikely that he could work out an informal solution based on a "coincidental" meeting of the relevant parties.

There are, of course, genuine dilemmas with respect to the issue of school size. First, where there is residential segregation by race and class, small schools will usually result in segregated schools. Second, smaller schools tend to produce "traditional" status hierarchies rather than pluralism—unless school officials self-consciously try to counteract this tendency. Third, smaller schools mean fewer choices with respect to curriculum. Because these are often true dilemmas, I would not be doctrinaire about the issue of high school size. Linking smaller schools with a larger one that offered more specialized subjects is a potentially fruitful possibility. I would suggest, however, that instead of assuming that large high schools will remain the norm we should systematically experiment with a variety of smaller schools and carefully monitor the consequences.

TEACHER POWER

If one of the reasons teachers do not intervene is fragmented social knowledge, a second reason is that they have few effective sanctions against students, especially those indifferent about grades. In most schools teachers cannot—and most would not if they could—use corporal punishment. They cannot on their own exclude students from class. Troublemakers can be sent to a counselor or assistant principal, but the teacher who does this too often becomes defined as incompetent. Even administrators have few effective sanctions. Suspensions, not to speak of expulsions, are subject to appeals and legal action. The school that expels very many students is soon in trouble with higher level school and government officials. Larger school systems may have special schools for recalcitrant students, but they are often full and the numbers that can be sent are limited. Moreover, most teachers do care about their students—even the difficult ones—and do not want to expel them or send them to special schools if this can be avoided. A few teachers are simply collecting a paycheck, and we need better ways to help them rejuvenate their teaching or enable them to seek other employment. In contrast, a few teachers are extremely skilled or charismatic and can engage even very recalcitrant students. These are always a limited subset of the total staff. Schools as a whole have to operate with average people who are average teachers. The mean level of teachers' social skills can be raised, just as the mean level of their academic skills can—but in most cases such increments will be small. Just as churches need saints, schools need charismatic teachers. But both churches and schools, and virtually all other human institutions, must carry out most of their work with more ordinary folk. Hence, while honoring and rewarding outstanding teachers is appropriate, charisma can never be a generalized substitute for more routine forms of influence.

It may be possible to increase teachers' power by giving them additional positive and negative sanctions. The authority to confiscate students' driver licenses is one possibility; suspending students' rights to participate in sports and extracurricular activities is another. Positive sanctions are nearly always more difficult to come up with, but release time from class for those who already know the material might be one way to reduce boredom. The key point is that if we expect teachers to take more responsibility and better exercise the ones they have, they have to be given more effective power.

PATERNALISM/MATERNALISM AND AUTHORITARIANISM

Long-term socialization and education inherently involves asymmetrical power and responsibility. Obviously, young children would die if parents did not care for them and prevent them—often against their will—from hurting themselves. Certainly, by high school paternalism/maternalism should be declining and student autonomy increasing. But effective teaching means a significant degree of paternalism/maternalism and that student rights are limited and circumscribed—at least in the context of the school. The details of getting the right balance are a complex matter. My point is that our ideology about authority in schools must legitimate a form of teacher authority that involves significant levels of paternalism/maternalism and formally recognizes that students' rights are significantly more limited than those of full adults when they are at school or engaged in school-sponsored activities. Extensive restrictions on school officials' ability to search cars in the school parking lot— not to speak of school lockers—for guns or drugs are a design for trouble and tragedy. Ideological change emphasizing certain forms of teacher authority is not necessarily incompatible with also trying to increase student involvement and participation in decisions about both school life and educational activities. Orderly classrooms are more likely to facilitate rather than undermine more egalitarian forms of pedagogy. More effective teacher authority and social order within our schools is not inherently incompatible with more respect for students and increased student power. Any such changes will need to be linked to structural changes that make it possible for schools to exclude students who consistently disrupt educational activities or refuse to meaningfully participate in them. This is obviously tied to the suggestion that we develop more alternatives for letting adolescents grow up than forcing them to stay in school.

The notion that parents, teachers, and administrators should deliberately shape the informal peer culture of adolescents does raise a fundamental moral and political issue: How much of social life should those in authority attempt to organize and control? Everyone past infancy should have some level of personal and social autonomy. Totalitarian societies are those in which the state attempts to organize and affect virtually all aspects of life. What is frequently referred to as "civil society"—voluntary organizations and those informal aspects of social life largely autonomous from the polity and the economy—is crucial to a meaningful democracy. Is attempting to shape informal adolescent culture a subtle form of totalitarian authoritarianism? I take this question seriously. A serious answer has to address the degree to which adolescent "civil society" is usurped or manipulated by adults. Currently, it seems to me that the informal structures controlled by teenagers have at least as much impact on young people's lives as the formal school structures controlled by adults. The kinds of things I am proposing are intended to redress that balance. They are also linked to proposals that would add more flexibility to when adolescents would be subject to the formal education system, and would try to integrate young people into adult civil society rather than exile them to some youth culture. Thoughtful people of goodwill will disagree about how much control and how much autonomy is appropriate for adolescents. This issue needs to be broken down by the particular context that is under consideration; it should vary depending on whether we are talking about a public street, the school hallways, or the classroom. We need to debate this issue in ways that involve more than extolling the virtues of abstract notions such as "freedom," and "choice," or "respect for authority" and "responsibility." On a more concrete level we need to go beyond such things as raising the drinking age, calling for teenage curfews, or extending the length of the school year. Maternalism/paternalism can become authoritarianism, but that need not be the case.

THE LIMITS OF SCHOOLING AND EDUCATION

One of the great American fantasies is that schools can eventually solve almost any social problem. It is what I have called the "God, mother, country, and schools" theology—the four things all politicians and most Americans profess to believe in.[9] I have spent most of my life in schools and believe fervently in the value of education. Yet our attempt to solve all problems with education is for the most part an attempt to avoid dealing with difficult societal issues. If we are concerned about crime, drugs, economic inequality, residential segregation, cynicism—to name a few current issues—what we do in schools will have a limited impact if we leave the broader societal structures untouched. Most of the problems with young people in our schools are largely the result of what adults are doing outside of schools. Until we face up to this, the impact of school reform, whether of the curriculum or the peer culture, will have limited to modest effects. This is not to suggest that such reforms are useless. If, however, they are to have a major impact, they must be one part of a much broader commitment to a reorientation of what we think is important.

MIDDLE-CLASS POLITICS

This analysis has been focused primarily on the middle classes. If there are to be major changes in the way we organize not only our educational institutions, but also our economic and political institutions, the middle classes will have to support these changes. Poverty programs aimed at the disadvantaged— as needed and legitimate as these might be—are not going to fundamentally change the nature of the society we live in. Significant changes will come only if the middle classes become convinced that the products and services they are being given by advanced consumer capitalism are not worth the costs—in the way they spend their day-to-day lives, and the kinds of people that they and their children become. Certainly, the political discontent of lower classes— often expressed through crime and deviance—may contribute to an openness to change, but the aspirations and power of the middle classes will decide the future of consumer capitalism.

Some will see this emphasis on the middle classes as misplaced. They see the major features of contemporary society as shaped by a ruling class or a power elite. I certainly do not mean to deny the obvious fact that there are relatively small numbers of people who have highly disproportionate amounts of wealth, status, and power—and these inequalities have been increasing significantly. Nor do I deny that these people often use their power to advantage themselves and those similar to them. In contemporary Western democracies, however, with all of their flaws, the power and influence of elite groups require the cooperation and acquiescence of the broad middle classes.

The readers of this book will be largely from the upper-middle classes or students who aspire to be. If we are concerned about our children and the kind of world they are growing up in, we are going to have to change our own values and patterns of living. Meaningful change will require both individual and collective action. Of course, many aspects of our lives are and will be shaped by factors that are beyond our control. Even within the realm of human choices, some people and groups have much more power than others, and hence bear more responsibility for the construction of the collective reality that we share. None of us, however, are innocent or irrelevant. The crucial prerequisite to changing the lives of our children is for the adults who care about them to change their own lives.

Part V

FIFTEEN YEARS LATER

CHAPTER ELEVEN

Fifteen Years Later

This chapter will not try to deal with all the changes that have occurred since our earlier study, but it will focus on what seem to be several key alterations that have in various ways significantly impacted the content of teenager culture. We will focus on two obvious changes: an increase in concerns about students' measured academic performance, and new digital technologies such as cell phones and social media sites. I will argue that both an increase in academic pressure and the new kinds of technology are correlated with a more instrumentally oriented teen culture. For example, erotic relationships are less romantic and more matter-of-fact. This shift toward instrumentalism in teenage culture may well be part of a more general cultural change, and while it is difficult to specify causation these various trends are probably mutually reinforcing. A second key change is the impact of the new technologies on social visibility. Some things are more visible and some things are less so. Facebook pages make it more explicit who your "friends" are, but surreptitious texting can be carried on during classes. A related question is whether the new forms of technology and changes in social visibility are also contributing to more instrumental social relationships. As we shall see, the evidence about this is mixed. A third change is a decline in the link between teen culture and consumerism. None of this is to suggest that teenagers are merely the pawns of increased academic pressure or of the new technologies. Teenagers are also in part the creators of the new kind of youth culture that has emerged. The sections below attempt to elaborate on these themes.

ACADEMIC PRESSURE, POLARIZATION, AND AN INSTRUMENTAL PEER CULTURE

ACADEMIC PRESSURE

During the fieldwork on which the first edition of this book is based, students said relatively little about grades, quizzes, exams, homework, and academic pressure. Of course, many students worked hard and cared about their grades,

217

but these concerns were not commonly expressed and certainly were not central to most conversations at lunch. For the more popular groups it was bad form to say too much about your academic work. While on occasion students studied and did homework during their lunch period this was the exception rather than the rule.

As the young woman who was quoted in chapter four says, "Bad grades and fights with my mother were nowhere near as traumatizing as not being included in some social activity, a disagreement with a friend, or not having a date for homecoming." Keep in mind that this young woman was not some high school "airhead" dropout, but a college student in a quite selective university. The majority of students no longer show such nonchalance about their grades.

From our 2013–14 field notes at Woodrow Wilson High School:

7 white females, 1 African American female (mixed race) and 1 white male. All 9th grade. Kelly and Sabrina had been finishing a math exam so they were late to lunch. When Amber, Kelly, and Sabrina joined the table they all immediately take out classwork and start studying.

9 students, all in 10th grade, all Caucasian. 3 females and 6 males. All the students seemed to be very concerned about their grades and clearly were very invested in their courses.

3 white females, 1 Asian female; 11th grade; upper middle class. Samantha had an AP U.S. history review book out on the table and began leafing through it; Jenna observed that Samantha's class was using a different book than her class was. Samantha told her that she had bought this book as an additional study aid at Barnes & Noble.

5 white females (one may have been mixed race Asian); 1 male; middle/ upper-middle class. When I arrived at the table Chad was quizzing Luke on a music score and Theresa, Danielle, and Holly were talking about a chemistry quiz they had to take that day.

11 white females, 9th grade. SES: Upper middle class. Monica, Kathryn, and Allison were doing homework at the table, and left the table about 5 minutes into lunch to go to the library and study. Natalie was also working on her Spanish homework during lunch, but she continued to do her work at the lunch table instead of going to the library with the other girls.

Moreover, we could reproduce many other examples of this kind of behavior. These notes were made by two different observers and are drawn from dates shortly after one grading period ended and over a month before the end of the next grading period—so the great concern with grades is not because exams are imminent. In short, compared to the observations we made at lunchtime in 1997–99, our 2013–14 data show that there has been a significant increase in both the number of students who are concerned about their grades and the intensity of the pressure they feel.

Unsurprisingly, being "smart" became a source of status and snobbery. A girl from a high status public school in Washington, DC, reports, "Those outside of the AP class ... were looked down upon for taking the easy 'joke' classes or simply not being smart ..."

SOURCES OF ACADEMIC PRESSURE

Some parents exhort their children to do well academically and place high expectations upon them. "Ella said that her dad had yelled at her 'for like a half an hour' after her last biology test because she got an 89. Kaylee chimed in she was 'so bad' at Spanish because she had a 90 in the class." Of course, some students have always been concerned about grades, but why has this increased?

The greater academic pressure has multiple sources. An obvious one was the 2007–9 recession, the continuing poor job market and the high rates of unemployment through the end of our fieldwork in the spring of 2014. This reduced the inclination to drop out of high school or to enter the job market with a very poor academic record. Even fast-food employers require you to indicate the level of schooling you attended, whether you graduated, your degree/course, and your grade point average—and claim that they will assist you in getting additional education.[1]

A second source was the perception that it is much harder to get into high quality colleges. It is certainly the case that for the most selective schools a smaller percentage of the applicants are admitted than was the case in the past. This is in part due to online and standardized application procedures that have resulted in most applicants now applying to many more colleges than they did in the past. It is less clear whether on average it is harder to get into college (see, e.g., Urist 2014), but some students certainly perceive it as a problem.

> [Aleph] described his group in comparison with these other groups as "more calmed down" and focused on the "big picture of high school leading to college leading to a job leading to happiness." He then continued to say this can be an "unfortunate train of thought" because they sometimes put too much pressure on themselves and may have unrealistic expectations for their futures ...

A third related source of pressure was due to the increased enrollments in Advance Placement high school courses. According the College Board that certifies these courses, at the end of May in 2013, "more than 18,000 high schools completed over four million college-level AP® Exams in 34 subject areas ranging from math and science to history and world languages."[2] The increased enrollments in AP courses were partly due to students' attempts to be more competitive in the college admissions process. It was also seen as a potential way to reduce the rising cost of higher education by reducing the courses that have to be taken in college.

Fourth, the main source of pressure from many students' perspective is the trend toward requiring students to pass various standardized examinations in order to graduate from high school. Often these are called Standards of Learning or SOLs. There is heated debate over the usefulness of such exams (see, e.g., Zimmerman 2014).

GOOD AND BAD PRESSURE

Whatever the effect of these exams on actual academic skills, it is clear that they lower students' morale and make them more cynical about the educational process. Most students recognize that there is a legitimate role for testing and grades. "[Rachel] said she understands that adults need to be able to see what students are learning, but the current testing regime isn't working." Rachel is not alone in her disregard for the existing testing regime. Of the fourteen students we formally interviewed only one had anything good to say about the usefulness of SOL examinations; most were quite negative. Here are a few of the typical answers:

> As a ninth grader, Matt ... said most of his classes were oriented towards covering only the information on the SOLs, and he thought it made the classes worse because the teachers could not teach what they thought was interesting about the subject.

> [Jessica] said she knows they cause other students stress, but not her because she's "responsible and pro-active" about her school work ... "I get done what needs to be done in advance" ... . [S]he said the SOLs especially are useless ...

> [Brian] said he personally doesn't feel much pressure ... because he's exceptionally good at taking standardized tests. But, he enthusiastically added that "SOLs are bad and need to die in a fire"... [Teachers] end up teaching to the test and aren't as passionate about the material. He noted that his best high school classes were those that didn't have SOLs at the end.

Students were generally more positive about the value of SAT or ACT exams for the college admissions process, but several students thought that they measured a student's socioeconomic background as much as their ability. [Brian claimed that SAT exams] "were a 'class barrier' to college that weren't giving colleges the information about students that they need …"

Of course, students' comments about such matters are not unbiased. Most people are anxious about, or suspicious of, the procedures that are used to evaluate them. It is not news that most students don't like tests. Hence, these responses are certainly not the final word about the utility of standardized testing. Nonetheless it is troubling how negative most students are about SOLs and the deep skepticism that even good students express about the usefulness of this kind of pressure.

POLARIZATION

In 1986 Fordham and Ogbu published a paper entitled: "Black students' school success: Coping with the Burden of 'Acting White'." It was based on an ethnographic study of one high school in which most of the students were black. Their argument is often complex and subtle, but it suggested that one of the impediments to higher academic achievement of African Americans was the tendency of student peers to negatively sanction students who were too openly concerned about academic achievement—and defined this as "acting white." This argument stimulated almost continuous debate and considerable research.[3] Quantitative studies have usually found relatively weak evidence in support of this hypothesis. It should be kept in mind, however, that most of these studies are based upon answers that students give to questions about their expectations and goals—and in this regard most students from disadvantaged backgrounds are not dramatically different from more privileged (usually white) students in their hopes and aspirations (e.g., Jacob and Linkow 2011). What people say about their prospects for the future, however, does not always tap their actual feelings, much less the level of emotional energy and resources they have available to accomplish the expectations, and hence can lead to failure and disillusionment (Rosenbaum 2011). This is perhaps one reason ethnographic studies like this one have continued to find that some disadvantaged students seem, if not indifferent about grades and academic matters, at least less inclined to discuss their academic concerns in the context of peer groups and less committed to academic success. This was not true of all minority students, but a contrast in what students discussed was noticeable.

It was clearly the case that those most concerned about their grades were usually Caucasian students from middle to upper SES backgrounds. Certainly some African-American students cared about their grades and about "learning something." This is reflected in the conversation between two African-American girls who were students in the program that trained dental technicians at VOTECH [the vocational and technical education school associated with Wilson].

> Emma … started talking to the other two about their "senior portfolios" that were due soon. It sounded like this was a major assignment that included essays, a resume, and some other documents as well … . They chatted about the colleges they were applying to, with Felicia mentioning that she's applying to Howard and Longwood, among others. Emma remarked that Howard is a "good school."

> They talked a lot about a test they were going to have to take at [a university seventy miles away] … It sounded like a qualification test for some kind of medical certification … . Emma said that she hopes she passes this test, because "at least you get a certification out of it" and that it would make her feel like she "actually accomplished" something in high school … . Felicia got up to leave … Alexandra and Emma continued talking about their grades and a test they took last week. They talked about an instance where a teacher had to keep stopping class because "people were being stupid," which I took to mean acting out or trying to cheat during the test … . this worried her because "nobody's gonna learn anything."

These girls are obviously concerned about their academic work. In general, however, the students from lower SES backgrounds, who were often African-American or Latino, expressed less interest in academic pursuits and grades. This is reflected in the following conversation:

> 9 total at 2 adjacent tables. 1 female, 8 males. Race/ethnicity: 1 white male (Phillip), all rest African-American. Year: Juniors. SES: [probably mostly] working class—difficult to determine.

> Phillip … says that he bets their conversations are a lot different from the white students. He then mimics a white accent and says [in a funny, mocking way] "Josh, what did you get on that chemistry test? I got a 97. Isn't that terrible?" Phillip … says that he doesn't worry about his grades the way those students do, saying that if he got a 90 on a test "my parents would throw a parade!" He mentioned bringing his English score up from a 19 to a 22 by turning in essays (that he claimed he had a neighbor write for him) and his mom was really proud of him. Charles says he doesn't even want to think about his English grade.

In the earlier 1997–99 study there were certainly groups that were largely unconcerned about their academic accomplishments. The big change seems to be how much more many middle- and upper-class students are concerned about their grades.

If anything the pressure they feel may have reduced the academic motivation of many lower SES and minority students; the "competition" is so far ahead that it does not seem worth trying. This certainly is not true of all students from less advantaged backgrounds, but there seems to be a greater polarization of academic motivation and performance. It seems probable that the greater the gap they must overcome, the less likely it is that their expressed expectations will be fulfilled. It must be emphasized that this is a very impressionistic observation based on limited ethnographic data.

This polarization is not unique to Woodrow Wilson High School and there is some quantitative evidence that it is part of a national trend, probably not unrelated to the increasing inequality in the distribution of wealth and income. Sean F. Reardon of Stanford University looks at this issue for the period from 1940 to 2000. He summarizes his research question and findings in the following manner:

> As the income gap between high- and low-income families has widened, has the achievement gap between children in high- and low-income families also widened? The answer, in brief, is yes. The achievement gap between children from high- and low-income families is roughly 40 percent larger among children born in 2001 than among those born twenty-five years earlier (2012: 19).

A University of Chicago study finds a similar tendency using a different research design for the 1970–90 period:

> This study estimates the effect of changes in economic inequality between 1970 and 1990 on children's educational attainment. Data on individual children from the Panel Study of Income Dynamics is combined with other data on state characteristics. Growing up in a state with widespread economic inequality increases educational attainment for high-income children and lowers it for low-income children (Mayer 2001: 1).

These and other analyses of the relationship between socioeconomic background and academic achievement are complex and the precise patterns and mechanism of causation are not always clear. Such issues do not have to be resolved in order to note that if anything the increased pressure on students to improve their academic achievement may well have increased the differences between the top students and the lowest performing students rather than having reduced the gap.

A MORE INSTRUMENTAL PEER CULTURE

Has the student peer culture changed significantly because many students are more concerned about their grades than in the past? It certainly seems to be the case that students who are anxious about their grades are more likely to hang out with other students who share these concerns. In at least some respects these relationships have become more instrumental and less purely expressive. They have also become more competitive. An 11th grade Wilson girl:

> There was a lot of pressure to perform well on the SAT. She said most
> of this pressure came from herself and from her friends, because there is
> always competition within friend groups to see who performed the best or
> worst. She said she does not necessarily aim to do better than her friends
> (she claims they are all smarter than she is) but that nobody wants to have
> the lowest score, so there is pressure to "match" your friends' scores on the
> SAT. She also said that there is pressure from parents because it is impor-
> tant to do well on the SAT if she wants to go to college.

This kind of behavior was not unique to Wilson High. A girl from Pennsylvania reports: "[People] became friends with each other by taking the same level of advanced classes such as math and history, and became competitive with one another over grades and even trivial points on homework. This competition was … often shakily hidden with remarks like 'I got a 26/27 on that reading quiz last week. Oh, you got a 24/27? That's pretty good.' "

This is not to say that serious students who study together do not develop meaningful friendships, but in many respects many of these friendships seem narrower. Students who are working hard to keep their grades up are busy. Often they have complicated schedules and less time to simply hang out. One of the ways they compensate for this is to communicate with their friends via texting and social media. It seemed to me that the Wilson students of 2013–14 are less relaxed than the students of 1997–99. Admittedly this is a very impressionistic observation and it refers to a subtle change of ambiance rather than changes in the social categories or the explicit content of social roles. To be more concrete, the more academic students still have "best friends" that share secrets and anxieties. The difference is that it is not unusual—much less "weird"—that many of these shared anxieties are about grades or standardized exams. The description that Phillip above gives of "white students" being concerned about only making a 97 on a chemistry exam is of course a parody—but it is a parody that points to an important change in teenage culture.

ROMANCE, INTIMACY, AND PROFANENESS

I have suggested above that many teens feel under greater academic pressure and this has contributed to more instrumental orientations and actions.[4] The most obvious aspect of this is a greater concern with grades—at least for many students.

This move toward instrumentalism has not only affected the academic areas of school life, but more expressive realms. One aspect of this has been what one might call a decline in notions of romance. Dating—in the sense of one person expressing a romantic interest in another by asking them out to a specific event—is less common than in the past.[5] Instead, mixed gender groups hang out together, which may (or may not) include going to a specific event together. Instead of formal dating, couples "hook up." A fieldworker at Wilson reports, "I asked Ashley about the dating culture, and she said that there was not a whole lot of serious relationships at the high school. She said this was certainly the case within her own group, and thought it applied to most groups at the school as well. Ashley said most of the dating culture at the school consisted of 'pretty casual hook ups.'" The term "hook up" does not necessarily mean sexual intercourse per se, but usually implies some kind of sexual behavior. National survey data report that 18 percent of male and 13 percent of female high school students report that they have had sex with four or more people.[6] Nearly fifty percent of 15- to 19-year-olds report that they have had oral sex with an opposite sex partner.[7] Currier (2013) refers to the use of this term "hook up" as deliberate "strategic ambiguity." It offers more sexual freedom, but the ambiguity of the term helps protect the participants from being negatively labeled (e.g., "slut," "ho," "user," "SOB," "predator," etc.).

This "hook up culture" seems to have lessened the ideology of romantic relations and legitimized a more matter-of-fact and carnal attitude about such matters as sexual activities. This is certainly seen in the language on the Internet. Terms such as "friends with benefits" and "fuck buddy" are examples of the use of a more "profane" language. The online Urban Dictionary's definition of "fuck buddy" is, "All the benefits of being in a relationship minus the bullshit like not doing enough for Valentine's Day or her birthday, not spending 3 months salary on a stupid ring, and not spending enough quality time with her."[8] This is admittedly the entry of a single individual on an Internet bulletin board, but the language clearly shows not just a decline in romanticism, but contempt for such notions, as well as a more carnal and instrumental attitude toward erotic relationships. Such language would have been considered at best inappropriate even fifteen years ago.[9]

While we did not hear such language at Wilson, it seems clear sexual relationships have become more a matter of explicit exchange rather than implicit exchange; more of a short-term contract and less of a covenant—not only in fact, but with respect to the ideology and language used to describe such relationships. The degree to which there has been such a shift of course varies significantly for both individuals and groups.

This shift needs to be put into a broader historical and comparative context. Cultures and periods have varied significantly in what they considered was the appropriate and legitimate way to organize erotic relationships. For most pre-modern agrarian societies parents and other adult members of the family played central roles in arranging marriages and liaisons. Young people might be consulted, but sometimes they were not. Often marriage was a form of alliance between families entered into primarily for economic or political purposes. Hence it is important not to see hooking up as necessarily a cultural decline from a superior morality or to see "dating" as "natural." Illouz (1997: esp. chap. 2) has shown that "dating" was once a new social form that replaced "calling upon" young women at their family's home. It was closely linked to increasing levels of disposable income, the commercialization of entertainment, new forms of physical mobility such as the automobile, higher levels of individualism, and more generally to the rise of consumer capitalism. Similarly there are technological, social, and cultural sources of hooking up. It is also closely linked to a variety of ideologies such as gender equality, the legitimacy of pleasure and freedom of choice. These notions, especially the latter one, are closely associated with the taken-for-granted legitimacy of the market as the core institution of capitalist societies and the ideologies that defend this assumption.

To point out that these are alternative forms of intimacy is not to lapse into a complete relativism. The extreme version of an instrumental perspective on sexual intimacy is prostitution; physical intimacy is exchanged for money; intimacy becomes a commodity. In the overwhelming percentage of societies prostitutes are considered low status if not disreputable and even illegal.[10]

The key empirical point is that the ideology of what is considered as the "normal" intimate relationship for teenagers (and many young adults) has shifted away from romanticism and toward a more explicit instrumentalism.

INSTRUMENTALISM AND ABUSE

There is an increasing amount of research that shows how contemporary culture—and especially "hook up" culture—not only disadvantages women, but makes them subject to abuse, rape and violence (Armstrong et al. 2006; Currier 2013; Heldman and Wade 2010; Ronen 2010). Most of this research is based upon data from college students. While abuse certainly occurs in high schools, teenagers usually have much less autonomy and are less often in situations that lead to violence and rape—which is not to say that it does not occur. About ten percent of both female and male teens report that they experienced some kind of violence from a boyfriend or girlfriend.[11] Not only women but men are subject to sexual abuse. Rape seems to be increasingly common among gay men—and male rape is relatively frequent in jails and prisons—though even in prison women report higher rates of sexual abuse than men.[12]

Our project was not allowed to collect the kind of data that are needed to contribute to this kind of research. Rather, I will focus on changes in the way teens talk about sexuality and bodily functions. While the use of such language does not tell us much about actual sexual behavior, it does tell us something about the degree to which people are showing respect to one another—or at least variations in how respect is shown and not shown. It also suggests the degree that such respect is considered a quasi-sacred obligation rather than a profane quid pro quo. For example, the ideology associated with traditional Christian marriage is that it should be a sacred covenant binding the couple as long as both partners are alive. This is, of course, a Weberian ideal-type that actual marriages at best approximated. In contrast, one-time hook-ups approximate an ideal-type of profane quid pro quo exchange. In the latter case each partner is primarily an instrument for the other's momentary pleasure. Sacred or at least conventionally respectful language tends to be associated with the former, profane language with the latter. Hence, the use of profanity is one indicator of the degree to which human relationships are seen as profane and instrumental rather than sacralized expressive relationships.

To say that teenagers are more instrumental, less romantic and more profane and carnal is not to idealize the past; it can be argued that the new ways of acting and talking are more candid and honest. Nor is it to suggest that teens are more sexually active than in the past. We have no reliable data about how often Wilson students engage in sexual relationships. However, the national data that are available indicates that the sexual activities of 9–12th graders (e.g., the percentage that have had sexual intercourse) have been relatively stable for over twenty years, and have actually declined slightly. While Black/African-American teens are more sexually active than other groups, this has become less and less the case over time. In 2013 the percentage of 9−12th graders who reported they were "sexually active" was 33 percent for White non-Hispanics, 35 percent for Hispanics, and 42 percent for Black/African Americans.[13] Rather what seems to have changed are the norms about what it is appropriate to discuss and do in public—and the language that is used in discussions about sexuality and other bodily functions. Language that in earlier periods would have been considered inappropriate, vulgar, and verboten is more common.

THE PROFANE AND THE CARNAL

A fieldworker reports that a group of well-to-do students suggested that it was not unusual for them to use a considerable amount of profanity: "I approached the table of all girls, most of whom were dressed 'preppy.' When I asked them if I would be able to observe their table, Sasha asked if it was okay that they curse …" At a different lunch period: "An African American girl walked past the table to borrow something from Felix. Then Isaac said something (which I did not hear) to the girl and the girl responded by telling Isaac to 'shut the f*** up' … Isaac did not really care about the girl's insult and then turned to Terrance and said, 'Damn that girl has a big ass mouth.'"

The boy might have said something to the girl that was insulting—though this cannot be assumed—but the point is the kind of language she used to respond and the kind of language he used to describe her behavior.

In addition to profane language, discussions about sex seemed more common and matter-of-fact. The following is an example:

> Lucy was talking about how her grandmother, who lives with her, is funny
> and crazy and said that her grandmother was "twerking" in her house … . her
> grandmother complained that she had not had sex in a year. All the girls started
> laughing, and then Lucy said she even walked in on her grandmother having
> sex … All the girls were laughing a lot and talking about how gross it was … .
> Nora said "everything should be locked up after a certain age" and also said that
> her grandmother does not act "ratchet" around her.[14] Zoe said that she knows
> her grandmother still has sex because she is 63 and just got a new boyfriend … .
> [They mentioned an] older woman [who] was apparently a cheerleading coach
> and used to be a teacher at the school and is a "cougar" who has a much younger
> boyfriend.[15] All of the girls then began talking about this woman and how weird
> it is that she has a younger boyfriend and were laughing and making fun of her.

It is clear that these teen girls disapprove of the behavior of these older women, but it is telling that they share these descriptions of their grandmothers as "funny stories"—not as something that might be embarrassing to their families or themselves.

Four tenth grade African-American girls were talking:

> Jasmine told Erika she heard that Erika was holding hands with a boy who
> was not her boyfriend in the back of the bus. Erika did not deny it, and Mia
> added that she heard people were doing things they "shouldn't be doing" … .
> Erika said she would never do anything like that … because she knows they
> have cameras on the bus. All the girls laughed … because they interpreted
> her comment to mean she would be doing "things" … . if there were not
> cameras.

Whatever Erika might or might not do at the back of the bus she shows no embarrassment about "holding hands" with a boy who is not her boyfriend in a quite public place. This is incompatible with the traditional romantic notion of couples who are "in love" and "going steady."

The carnal is not limited to language about sex, but can be expressed in other kinds of actions:

> Torrie had a bag full of chocolate truffles … . At one point Lauren rubbed
> the chocolate truffle on a piece of paper, using the truffle to spell things … .

> Lauren and Daisy then decided to go to the bathroom and rub the truffle on
> a piece of paper and leave it … so that other people … would think it was
> poop left on the floor of the bathroom. All the girls were laughing and went
> to go see the bathroom stall.

This tendency should not be overstated. Most students probably avoid the use
of sexual or scatological language most of the time. Others, including teachers, are not, however, shocked or offended if they happen to hear the offhand
use of such language. There seem to be fewer and fewer "sacred" contexts in
which "profane" words are shocking or lead to students being punished in any
significant way.

CLARIFYING THE ARGUMENT

Several clarifications are required. First, it is certainly important to avoid being
nostalgic about the past. As noted earlier, historical periods and cultures vary in
the extent to which they are carnal and in how openly they express this. There
is, for example, plenty of "carnality" in both Chaucer and Shakespeare. I am
not suggesting that types of relationships that were less instrumental and more
expressive are necessarily better. When patterns of interpersonal relationships
change, however, it usually is because on average people perceive that the new
forms have advantages—given the social context in which they live.

Second, sacred and profane are not the same as religious and secular.
Even very secular anti-religious societies and institutions tend to have certain
symbols, values, and norms that they consider sacred. While profanity often
involves violation of religious norms this is not necessarily the case; demeaning
"The Revolution," "The Party," or "Our Great Leader" can be seen as slan-
derous profanity that can bring about severe sanctions.

Third, I am not suggesting that the increased academic pressure, and the
more instrumental attitude toward others that this can generate, is the only
source of the greater use of profane language by teenagers. Clearly some of
this comes from copying adult culture. The norms about how much profanity
and sexuality can be shown in movies and TV programs have changed significantly. Words such as "fuck" and "asshole" have become almost normal par-
lance—especially on programs that are not broadcast over the public airwaves.[16]
Granted an adult-to-youth imitation effect, it is hardly the case that teenagers
always copy adults, so it is likely that something in teens' own social situation is
also contributing to the greater use of profanity.

Fourth, this brings us back to whether there is a link between an increase
in instrumental relationships and profanity. The tendency toward more instrumental relationships is certainly not restricted to teenagers. One of the places
it is most obvious is in the relationship between employers and employees. The

conventional cliché has become that one is likely to have about seven careers in one's lifetime. It is certainly the case that a significant number of manufacturing, data entry, and call center jobs were moved overseas during the 1990s. This along with the recession of 2007–9 gave many employees a sense of insecurity. There is debate about whether or not jobs are more transient and less secure than in the past.[17] It seems clear, however, that the cultural assumption has changed.[18] The social expectation is not that one will join a company, be a loyal employee for one's whole career, and retire with an adequate pension. In short, employer–employee relationships have become more instrumental.

Of course, the point is not that greater academic pressure in high school is the only root of increased instrumentalism. It is, however, the most obvious, immediate, and concrete form of instrumental pressure that many high school students face. Such pressure is not the source of all the problems in the schools and the broader society. Rather, I want to suggest as a hypothesis that the particular kind of academic pressure that has become characteristic in our schools contributes to the decline of romance, a greater "carnality" about sexuality and bodily functions, and an increase in profanity—and that these are in part the result of a more general cultural trend toward more instrumental relationships.

This trend toward instrumentalism produces a complicated mix of benefits and costs. The problem is that it is usually easier to perceive the short-term gains than to grasp the longer-term costs and losses.

THE IMPACT OF NEW TECHNOLOGIES

Around the second decade of the twenty-first century the use of the Internet, cell phones, tablets, and social media expanded at a near exponential rate. The portability of phones makes them especially popular, and teens spend even more time on their phones than adults (Ling et al. 2012). This is not limited to those from more privileged backgrounds; one study indicated that 91 percent of African-American students had cell phones as did a substantial majority of Hispanic teens (Lee 2014).

Some phone use involves communication with others, but even more time is spent on the Internet utilizing various websites and phone-based applications (usually called "apps"). Here are some typical reports from observational field notes:

> Carole and Abby also spent a good amount of time on their cell phones. Abby spent more time on her phone, usually on Pinterest or Twitter. Carole and Abby both got on their phones during a discussion of Halloween costumes ... .

> For most of the lunch Rebecca and Madeline were on their phones, looking down and not engaging in much discussion.

> Fleur, an African-American female student, spent most of the lunch period …
> playing on her phone. Near the end of the lunch period she was joined by [two]
> African-American friends … . The girls did not talk a whole lot and mostly
> spent time on their phones while sitting [or] standing near bench #2.

Our field notes show dozens of similar entries.

How did these new technologies and new uses of the Internet affect the social relationships and peer cultures of teenagers? It was largely by increasing the frequency of communications and the social visibility (or invisibility) of these communications. These changes tended to affect the number and nature of social networks and the subcultures that often emerged from such networks. These in turn shaped the sources of social status and the nature of status relationships.

NETWORKS, PLURALISM, INDIVIDUATION, AND SUBCULTURES

NETWORKS

New technologies and social media have not only affected the behavior of individual students, but they have reshaped the broader social context. Casual observation and previous research on youth and the Internet makes it apparent that much more information is available to young people than was the case for earlier generations (boyd 2014; Ito et al. 2010). There are also new ways to form relationships with others. Young people play online games with people they have never seen; they are "pen pals" with youth in other countries; they keep tabs on what is going on in other schools in their area; they shop from national and international websites. This is in addition to keeping in more or less constant communication with their friends via texting and social media (Mesch and Talmud 2010, esp. chaps. 5–6).

PLURALISM

Social networks are not only larger, but they are more varied. Teenagers' video-game friends may be a different group than the ones with whom they play touch football, and these may be different from the individuals and networks they use to solve computer and social media problems. This is not to say that local face-to-face relationships are not important, but only that teenagers interact with others in a way that was simply not available to earlier generations. These more varied networks occur in a variety of ways. People and groups have separate e-mail lists for different audiences. They adjust their settings on social network sites (e.g., Facebook) to regulate who can see what portions of their web postings. They create subgroups and networks devoted to particular interests. These broader and more varied networks also increase the range of content and variety of styles that a given young person adopts or participates in. For example, one of the students from Wilson High noted, the "'preppy talkative' girls … . have started listening to 'thug' music like '2 Chainz' and 'A$AP Rocky,' which they never would have listened to earlier." A student at Wilson comments that, "she and her friends were 'art people' they were often looking at online interior decorating and design websites for pictures they found inspiring." Another female student reports, "Her group also plays a lot of games (e.g., 2048 and Candy Crush), and browses websites." A girl from an immigrant family reports, "Students in her group use their tablets to watch soap operas from their home countries."

Of course, people have always had different types of relationships—intimates, good friends, co-workers and casual acquaintances—and varied the nature and content of their communications to these different categories. The new forms of media have increased the variety of these groups. The greater variety of networks means individuals tend to participate in more networks—often simultaneously. For example, a fieldworker observes, "Tara was sharing her food with the other girls, [and yet] Tara and Chelsea were not very involved in the conversations and spent most of the time on their cell phones."

INDIVIDUATION

While peer groups still influence the kind of music people listen to, the ease with which people can listen privately via MP3 players, iPods and smart phones makes it possible for people to listen to a variety of styles without being criticized by peers. So not only are there more subcultures, there tends to be greater variation *within* groups at least with respect to the kinds of behaviors that are relatively private, such as listening to music, watching YouTube videos, and browsing on the Internet. A college student comments, "The favorite style of music varied *within* the group, but included Heavy and Stoner Metal as well as Punk music" [emphasis added]. At Wilson High: "Alex said within groups there tended to be a variety of types of styles, especially in terms of the type of music they listen to and the style clothing they wear." "Olivia said … that within different groups the students vary in their style and music and that she did not think the style of a particular student was a good indicator of what group they hang out with."

SUBCULTURES

This greater variety of networks tends to create varied subcultures. An interviewer records students' descriptions of these tendencies:

> [Randy] spoke of the "tech" kids, who he said were into video [games] and computers. He said these students dressed differently and often were carrying computers and "equipment," and were "weird."

> [Matt] thought that most groups had varying styles within their groups;
> with the exception of a few groups … . He said most groups had common
> interests in terms of their hobbies [;] … . some groups are more interested
> in sports or video games which is why they all hang out together.

> Brian said his group is "computer people," meaning that they're very into
> figuring out how to use, make, hack, and build computers and programs. He
> mentioned a friend of his at the table whose bedroom is littered with computer
> parts; he said, "you can't [take a] step without stepping on a motherboard."

"Hanging out together" is a key indicator. That is, the group shares not only a
particular interest, but their friendships and romantic relationships—that is,
their more expressive relationships—occur within this subgroup.[19] Before the
Internet "band nerds" and "drama geeks" were often seen as distinctive subcultures. The new technologies and media seem to have accentuated this tendency.
Some examples are video gamers, computer programmers, anime fans, and
Internet hackers. This is not to say that interest groups always become subcultures, but the same technology that serves as the basis for these interest groups
also increases the relative ease and frequency of communication between members—and the likelihood that they will become distinctive subcultures.

SEEKING VISIBILITY AND MONITORING OTHERS

Teens, of course, have multiple motivations for the intense use of phones,
tablets, and social media, but concerns about their status with other peers
are certainly central. A college student from Colorado reports: "At my high
school [social media was] a very big deal. Certain students were either Twitter
or Instagram 'famous' because they had a lot of followers. The amount of
'favorites' or 'likes' … received could determine their popularity."

The importance of social visibility is reflected in the remarks of a female
college student about her own high school experience:

> There were the star athletes, the dance team captain, the talented singer, the
> class comedian, the guy who threw parties every weekend, the girl who was
> arrested twice, and the girl who sent racy photos to the entire JV lacrosse
> team. *Those who stood out from the crowd, no matter how* they got the atten-
> tion, were those deemed popular [italics added].

The Colorado student's own remarks show that teens are well aware of social
visibility as a prerequisite for status:

> It was … easy for the popular crowd to advertise what they were doing at
> all times because they could simply post a picture or tweet and everyone

would automatically know about it. Students who weren't friends with
the popular crowd knew [of] their activities, drama, and friends ... . The
things that people would post on Twitter and Instagram tended to be
topics for gossip.

A student from Southwest Virginia is explicit about the importance of technology and social media in the concerns about visibility:

[T]he more outgoing students invested more time ... in keeping in touch
with their friends, social networking, and focusing on building relationships
... . Electronic communication played a crucial role in this constant communication ... . [I]t was utilized more often than face-to-face interaction. In an
average class, a "popular" student seemed to check their phone or send text
messages about once every five to ten minutes.

A student from New Jersey gives a similar account:

Instagram was definitely the most important reason to have an iPhone,
with Twitter at a close second. The "popular" clique was the most active on
social media [T]hey had to prove ... how much fun they were having at all
times. Partying with excessive amounts of alcohol was their favorite hobby
to broadcast. Their parties would be small and exclusive and half of the time
at the party would be spent taking pictures to post on Instagram. Four girls
would each post the same picture within minutes of each other [and] numerous other pictures that showed how "drunk-and-in-love-with-each-other"
they were. The captions would always be very boastful, such as "My friends
are better than your friends." Soon the entire news feed would be consumed
with pictures solely from this one party.

Trying to gain attention and popularity is not the only aspect of visibility
that is relevant. Students also try to keep track of those who are not especially popular but are perceived as competitors or enemies. The following
illustrates this: "Regina then mentioned that she friend requested the girl on
Facebook, even though she did not actually like her ... . in order to ... 'keep
tabs' on the girl and as a way of increasing visibility in to the girl's activities."
Another group gossiped about a girl at another local high school who had died
of bulimia. While a few of them had been at summer camp with the girl, most
of what they knew about the case they had gleaned from Facebook and other
Internet sites.

    A concern with gaining social visibility is not unique to teenagers, but it is
particularly salient to teens because of their relatively low and circumscribed

form of political and economic power and hence the centrality of status as a form of power.

Nor is seeking visibility a new phenomenon; the rich and the aristocratic have long hired poets and singers to proclaim (and exaggerate) their virtues and accomplishments. Press agents, publicists, and "spin doctors" have been a feature of Hollywood and Washington for years. What is new is the "democratization" of social visibility—and the unembarrassed explicitness of the effort to increase it. As I was drafting this section I received the following e-mail announcement from my own university:

> U.Va. Alumni, Parents & Friends
>
> Your Professional Online Presence: How to Build Visibility and Be Found
>
> Time: Dec 12, 2014; 12:00 PM – 1:00 PM EST
>
> Event Type: Webinars
>
> Presented by: XXXXX XXXXXX
>
> Educ '98
>
> Tags: Branding, Communication, Friday Forum, LinkedIn, Networking
>
> Register Now

Our employers have become "stage mothers" who expect us to become "celebrities." It is unclear whether teens are copying adults, or adults are simply continuing the practices they learned in high school.

PLURALISM QUALIFIED

Reports about how popular groups maintain high visibility suggest that the movement toward pluralism (discussed in chapter six) may need to be modified. In larger high schools of the recent past it was nearly impossible for the popular crowd to be visible to most people, much less for ordinary students to have a personal tie with them. This contributed to a more pluralistic status structure. With social media, however, the activities of the popular crowd can be made visible to everyone. It is possible for most students to have a "virtual relationship" with them, if not an interpersonal one. A college student recalls: "This technology can give popular students even more status and make them almost celebrity like." The popular peer becomes a mini media celebrity. This does not mean that the general trend toward more pluralistic status systems has stopped. There are still multiple groups with differing styles and subcultures, but for many the "popular crowd" has again become a focus of attention through social media. This does not mean everyone tries to copy them, much less become a member of the group. In some schools, however, they have an enhanced visibility.

BOUNDARIES, STABILITY, AND RIGIDITY

While the popular crowd may use social media to gain visibility, this is not its only use or consequence. More generally, it makes social boundaries more visible and more stable. One college student puts it this way: "As far as technology is concerned, the only real role within the high-school social-group community was to show exactly who associated with whom or who was part of a social group ... . Technology played the role of showing people where they belonged in high school and reassured people that the group they were in was most likely never going to change."

The greater visibility and stability of boundaries may or may not mean the boundaries become more rigid. Social media sites may make it clearer who is a member of a group and who is not, but they do not necessarily make clear who members of a group are communicating with. In our earlier study elementary school friends who are in different high school groups had to talk to one another "early in the morning or late after school" when the other members of their high school group were not present (see p. 89); now they can communicate almost any time online because of the invisibility of their interaction—a matter we will take up in more detail shortly.

On the other hand, making some relationships more visible may well make them more rigid. Romantic relationships are an interesting case of making interpersonal links and boundaries explicit. A male college student from upstate New York reports, "Before social media, if someone was dating they were official, but once the social media like Facebook came, a couple wasn't officially dating until they were 'Facebook Official.'" That is, they became "official" when they identified themselves as a couple on their Facebook pages. The same phenomenon is reported in the high school where we conducted observations and interviews: "Jane said ... being an 'official' couple usually entails being 'Facebook Official' in which a person's relationship status on their Facebook page will say they are in a relationship with [a particular individual]." This means that "everyone" knows who is official and who is not and the possibility of getting away with "cheating" on your partner is significantly decreased. "Official" relationships tend to involve a more serious commitment because they must be made publicly visible. Accordingly only a minority of students is engaged in such relationships. Stated another way, becoming Facebook Official has many similarities with becoming publicly engaged or married.[20]

INVISIBILITY

While the new social media make some kinds of behavior and relationships more socially visible, they make other things less visible.

In previous generations students often conducted illicit communications by passing notes. Passing a paper note, however, was a risky business; adults could often spot such behavior and confiscate the note and even make it public. Cell phones and text messages have made such communications harder to detect and police. One of the students quoted above indicates that popular students send a message every five to ten minutes. No student could get away with passing that many paper notes even if their content was innocuous. Students at Wilson are nearly uniform in reporting that students generally ignore the rules intended to discourage cell phone use:

> Matt said the existence of these rules does not actually stop his friends or any other students from using their phones.

> Julie's group does not usually follow the rules about technology use …

> Alex said there were no strict rules governing cell phone use in school. He said some teachers will attempt to implement no texting rules in class, but they rarely are followed by students.

One teacher attempted to deal with the problem by allowing students to have a couple of two minute phone breaks during his fifty minute classes. This apparently reduced the phoning during other times. This near obsessive phone use was not a peculiarity of Wilson High. A college student who went to a completely different school reports: "Technology was strictly forbidden [though] some teachers were more lenient and allowed cell phones, iPods, and computers during certain times … [S]tudents often found ways around the rules …"

The relatively low visibility of cell phone use also made it easier for teenagers to communicate with people that their parents might not approve of. This was especially the case for younger students who could not yet drive and hence often had trouble seeing people outside of school. Parents' great fear was of course "stranger danger"—especially older adults who might be trying to prey upon younger people. While this is, of course, a legitimate concern the probability of this occurring tends to be relatively low (boyd 2014, chap. 4). There has also been an outcry that the invisibility of young people's communications has contributed in all sorts of wild sexual activities such as sexting, that is, phone-texting all kinds of sexual messages and pictures to others. This relatively invisible form of communication has also contributed to an array of rumors and urban myths about increased sexual promiscuity. Best and Bogle

(2014) have surveyed many of the concerns that adults have expressed about "wild" kinds of sexual behavior by youth and found that many of these seem to be at best greatly exaggerated.

In addition to being able to communicate "invisibly" it is also relatively easy and common to make the content of social media sites invisible to parents and adults:

> Sally was going through her computer and showed the girl a list of people she was friends with on Facebook that she had to restrict their abilities to see her profile because she did not want them seeing everything. These people were mostly adults or relatives. Margaret said she did the same thing on her Facebook because she did not want many adults she is friends with seeing all her pictures. Michelle agreed, saying that there was one picture on her Facebook with a bottle of Patrón [Tequila] … . and that one of the adults she was friends with commented on the picture, so now she was going to increase her privacy on her page.

There was another more subtle form of invisibility that has occurred. A field-worker reports, "We also spoke with this teacher briefly about the study and he said that from a teacher's perspective technologies have made eye contact more noticeably absent from the classroom. He said that as a teacher, he really had to try to get students' attention to get them to look up." It is difficult to know whether the decrease of this form of visible face-to-face contact significantly decreases student learning, and to weigh this relative to the gains that cell phones and tablets contribute through easy access to the Internet. It is important not to be overly sentimental about old patterns being replaced by new ones. Nonetheless it seems highly unlikely that a decrease in this kind of interpersonal visibility is cost free.

ANONYMITY AND ABUSE

Another kind of invisibility involves posting messages on online bulletin boards either anonymously or by using false or pseudo identities. This allows people to say things publicly without having to take responsibility for what they say. A Wilson student reports, "some students use social media to post mean things about others [and this] created a new platform for influencing social relationships." Another Wilson student reports:

> An anonymous Twitter account was started called "our confessions" that allowed students to message the Twitter account a "confession" (involving everything from crushes on fellow students to accusations of student teacher relationships) and the Twitter account would anonymously "tweet" these

confessions out. Anyone who chose to follow this account could read these tweets … but … the trend soon fizzled out and the account stopped posting new messages.

There has been considerable discussion of cyberbullying.[21] The news media have reported a number of cases, some with tragic outcomes.[22] While students at Wilson mentioned this possibility and said it had happened to others, none of those we interviewed could come up with concrete examples. The cases they did mention were usually cases of public nastiness and conflict between individuals, but not the systematic harassment of a weak individual by a stronger one. This is not to suggest that bullying never occurs, but that most cases are more a matter of what students refer to as "drama."

INCREASED VISIBILITY AND DRAMA

In my earlier study of teenagers, "drama" was not a commonly used term—except in reference to the production of plays. Teenagers now use it to refer to unnecessary conflict and pettiness or treating a minor problem as a major tragedy. It is usually attributed to teenage girls.[23] Student reports suggest that they tend to see bullying as one form of drama:

> Jessica mentioned cyber-bullying specifically. I asked her to tell me a specific story about what she means when she uses the term. She said it's never happened to her, but to people she knows. She said the most common case is when someone doesn't like a picture someone else posts of them; they might get into a fight with the person who posts it until the person takes it down. She said it's not that big of a deal, but "causes more drama" than there would be otherwise.

> Tracy said she feels that using the technologies and social media platforms "makes drama worse" between friends. She explained that the little fights are now more public and "everyone knows about it" instead of before where only the people involved would know. She said she feels like this publicness makes "everyone wants to get involved, and say something about it."

So "drama" usually involves interpersonal conflict or harassment that has become socially visible—and social media accentuate this tendency. To use a bit of hyperbole, social media turn interpersonal conflicts into a "spectator sport." Ironically, this visibility may increase the proclivity toward disputes and conflicts. To avoid being a "nobody" some students seem to start public disputes in part to gain attention and visibility.

FASHION

For some groups clothes, shoes, and backpacks are still important items of fashion. While having the "appropriate" items may not dramatically increase your status, having the "wrong" items could certainly bring disdain.

> [Seven male and two female middle-class Caucasian sophomores] talked about a male African-American student's outfit, which they all thought was weird. The boys all made fun of the boy's vest, which was fleece and had animals and trees on it. They all were pointing at the boy, who was in the courtyard, and laughing. The girls turned to look at who they were talking about and laughed as well.

In general, however, stylish clothes play less of a role as a marker of status and popularity. The most common concern about "keeping up" is to be aware of the latest information that is available on the Internet, especially the local gossip about other students. As one Wilson student says, "people are constantly checking their phones for texts and different social networks because they are worried about getting left out. Students are always concerned with staying up to date with the latest news or gossip, and social media allows them to stay on top." That is, new forms of technology and social media are the key means of being "up on" the latest gossip, which is a key source of status. This has in many ways demoted—though not eliminated—the significance of other forms of fashion.

There is an additional way in which the new technology and media have affected fashion: having the latest kind of phone and using the newest cool Internet site or app can be more important than having the latest style shoes. Older forms of social media often became passé. Facebook largely displaced Myspace. Before long having a Facebook page was ordinary and no longer a key source of status. A student who was an 11th grader said, "Facebook is so 9th grade." This is hyperbole, but it indicates that the status of various social media can certainly vary over time. The relative importance of these different forms of fashion varies from school to school and among different peer groups in the same school. It seems clear, however, that this new form of "fashion" has affected most teenagers. One college student recalls what happened in her school when smart phones became available:

> Once the smart phones began to come out, it again took a huge toll on us … . [A]pps began to dominate the classes. Facebook became even more popular since it was an app on the phone along with Twitter, and Instagram. Between classes, instead of going to the computer lab, everyone would literally be look- ing down at their phones. Everything that was social became dealt with over

the phone. Twitter made students literally tweet every second of their lives and Instagram made them take pictures of every little thing they did.

That is, Internet technology and social media became a dominant focus of attention and an important source of status in the way that clothes or cars were for an earlier generation.

TECHNOLOGY AND INSTRUMENTALISM

Hugh did use his phone to keep him occupied and isolated from the girls' conversations throughout lunch. He only participated in a few moments of conversation, and when he wasn't [talking] he was focused on his phone in his lap.

Earlier I argued that academic pressure is correlated with and has probably been a contributing factor to a more instrumental orientation toward social relationships including erotic relationships. This raises the question of whether the new technologies and social media themselves contribute to more instrumentalism in a more direct fashion. It is clear school cultures are often preoccupied with these new technologies. A recent high school graduate from Roanoke, Virginia comments:

If there is anything all students could bond over it would be technology, television, video games, etc. [T]eachers and administration [sic] also under-stood that it could be used to unify students. [M]ost assemblies used some form of technology and administration even allowed the school to take part in the Lip Dub craze that swept across US high schools.[24] Overall, conflict comes out of technology but it also has a powerful unifying force that most likely could not be achieved by teachers and administrators alone.

Does using more technology make us more instrumental in the expressive realms of life? Young people are often ambivalent about this. A college student remarks, "Because of these sites, people can 'get to know' people on levels that they would not otherwise …" but she notes, "People become so wrapped up in life on their phones that they don't feel the need to branch out and make new friends." Of course, the question of whether a greater use of these new types of communication technology contributes to a more instrumental orientation toward others cannot be answered by a few examples from qualitative data. This ambivalence, however, suggests that at the very least people sense that there are costs as well as gains in these new patterns of communication.

There has been some previous research that looks at the effect of mobile phones, tablets, and social media sites on teen relationships. The results from these studies also suggest that technology's impact on social relationships is mixed.

> In 1987, 37.9% of incoming college students socialized at least 16 hours per week with friends while 18.1% spent five hours or less [socializing] … . By 2014, 18% of students reported spending at least 16 hours per week socializing with friends (an all-time low) … At the same time that students report spending less time socializing with friends and partying, they are increasing interactions through online social networks … . [T]he percentage of students dedicating six hours or more per week [to online social networks] increased from 18.9% to 27.2%.[25]

In small group experiments in which strangers were asked to discuss relatively trivial or meaningful topics, it was found that the mere presence of cell phones reduced participants' feelings of closeness, trust, and empathy when they were discussing meaningful topics; the presence of a paper tablet did not have this effect (Przybylski and Weinstein 2012). A troubling finding is that teenagers expect people to lie and be dishonest on the Internet. Hundley and Shyles (2010: 430–431) report:

> Our data reinforce [previous research about dishonesty on the Internet] and reveal that teenagers fully expect others to lie. We see this as a serious development that can have a potentially corrosive impact on traditional social cohesion and expectations about norms of acceptable behavior. While we do not view lying as something new, we see the justification of such behavior among teenagers on the internet as a cheapening of social expectations.

This is in part due to the potential invisibility discussed above, but it is not clear that this is the only source of such nonchalance about dishonesty. It is possible that the instrumental nature of the technology itself may contribute to a more general instrumental approach to life, a less qualified pursuit of self-interest, and to a proclivity to dishonesty if it serves those interests. A related factor is the creation of larger, multiple networks that is in some senses like urbanization. The number of people one deals with increases significantly, but the level of intimacy, solidarity, and candidness is relatively low. This propensity to be less than honest to others is certainly an indicator of a more instrumental orientation toward social relationships. The caveat emptor ("buyer beware") of the market place has been expanded to include a caveat lector ("reader beware") about the Internet—suggesting that all kinds of social relationships may drift toward the instrumentalism of the market place. These new technologies also seem to lead to several other kinds of negative consequences.[26]

Other studies, however, have reported that use of these devices and social networks is associated with the strengthening of existing friendships and romantic relationships (Subrahmanyam and Greenfield 2008; Xie 2014). Greater use of social network sites is also correlated with students' greater civic engagement and community participation and higher levels of some types of social capital (Ahn 2012). Other studies report a mixture of positive and negative effects (Campbell 2005). In short, digital technology and social network sites produce positive gains, but it is also clear that they have personal and social costs.

LOCAL CULTURE AND TEENS' AGENCY

Clearly, although these new technologies have affected students in nearly all high schools, the extent and nature of these effects may vary. Each school has a history of particular events. While generally high school peer culture has become more pluralistic and egalitarian in many respects, this is not true for all schools. Some still approximate the stereotypical clique structure portrayed in earlier movies. A New Jersey girl gives the following account:

> At Western Regional High School choosing whom to sit with at lunch on the first day of school is more stressful than any AP Physics test. Avoiding texts from those of lower status who weren't invited to the party was equally as stressful. Should you lie? Should you try to get them invited? Or would that lower your status and would you not make the cut next party? Social circles and cliques were so clearly defined by the time my senior year rolled around that it was impossible to steer clear of drama. The hostile social environment was the result of rigid social boundaries that consumed every sector of daily high school life. This prevalence would have not been possible without the dominance of social media.

There are significant differences between the hierarchical and rigidly differentiated school described by the New Jersey girl and the much more egalitarian Woodrow Wilson High School. It is very doubtful that these differences are due to variations in the availability of the new technologies. The new technologies have certainly created what will probably be long-term tendencies and trends, but these are channeled and shaped by variations in the cultures of local communities and specific schools.

Current patterns are not only shaped by new technologies and the traditions out of which they come, they are also shaped by the actions of contemporary social actors. The current generation of students use and adapt innovations and traditions in varying ways. Some examples: The ineffectiveness of teachers' efforts to restrict the use of phones in class leads to new rules that allow "phone breaks." It was not test-oriented educational reformers or advocates of sexual freedom that promoted a shift from romantic to more instrumental erotic relationships, but it was the way the teenagers adapted to the new pressures and opportunities that they faced. It has often been the choices of teenagers that largely decided which apps were going to be successful; examples include the shift from Myspace to Facebook and the rapid rise of Snapchat. As we shall see shortly, it was neither the creators of the new technology nor marketing specialists who decided to reduce the significance of teenage status systems as means for creating consumer demand; rather the new technologies led teenagers to redefine what "keeping up" meant. The obvious but key point is that teenagers are neither billiard balls that are moved solely by external forces, nor god-like free agents who simply choose new patterns of behavior. Their actions, which often trouble or annoy adults, are due to a combination of old structures, new opportunities, and their own choices.

SCHOOLS, CONSUMERISM, AND CONSUMER CAPITALISM[27]

RISE AND FALL OF THE PROTESTANT ETHIC

The link between high schools, teenage culture and consumer capitalism was a major focus of the first edition of this book. In chapter eight, I argued that there are parallels between Max Weber's analysis of the effects of Calvinism on the development of bourgeois capitalism and my arguments about the role of teenage status systems in the development of consumer capitalism. In both cases the analysis identifies an important contributing factor to the emergence of a major economic and cultural transformation. In the first case the ethic of ascetic Calvinist Protestantism helped to create bourgeois capitalism. In the second case the status concerns of teenagers with "keeping up" and "having the latest thing" contributed to the development of consumer capitalism. The development of such concerns was especially significant because it occurred at the stage of life when personal identities are being formed, and hence consumerism became a largely taken-for-granted feature of life.

But Weber's argument about bourgeois capitalism does not stop with its emergence. He goes on to make it clear that the religious ideology that played an important role in its creation is no longer crucial to the maintenance of that system. According to Weber, "Victorious capitalism ... no longer needs asceticism as a supporting pillar" (Weber 2009: 158). The dynamics of the market economy are largely self-sustaining and no longer require the religious motivations that helped to bring it into existence. In other words there was a rise and fall in the significance of what Weber called "the Protestant Ethic."

RISE AND FALL OF TEENS' INFLUENCE ON CONSUMPTION

In a parallel way teenagers' preoccupation with fashion and "keeping up" helped to create consumer capitalism; it is now less important to its continuation. While many teenagers are still preoccupied with having the latest shoes and jeans, they tend to be more concerned with the latest happenings and gossip. Being "in the know" has to some degree replaced "having the latest." Hence, I want to argue that the link between high school status systems and consumerism has in some respects declined. This is due to changes in the schools and to changes in other aspects of the society and culture.

CHANGES IN SCHOOLS

As previously discussed schools have tended to subject students to more academic pressure. While the concern with non-academic status symbols is still important, it is less significant than in the past. More of the lunchroom talk is about courses and grades and less is about the next football or basketball game or what the cheerleaders are wearing. There is still plenty of talk about sports, but the following conversation indicates the relative decline in the status of sports and more generally non-academic matters:

> Davina asked the other girls if they were going to the football game that
> night. Vivian yelled across to the table directly next to theirs to ask some
> questions about the football game that night (what time it started, who they
> were playing). When the boys at the next table couldn't provide satisfactory
> answers, all of the girls made fun of them. Davina explained that [they]
> were football players and it was "sad" that they didn't even know who
> they were playing.

This hardly denotes a student culture that is centered on local sports. Woodrow Wilson High School students were never as preoccupied with sports to the degree that some schools were—see for example the discussion of the small town in Texas (page 147). Nonetheless, it is very unlikely that members of the 1997–99 Wilson football teams would not know who they were playing on the day of the game.

Nor was the decline in the status of non-academic activities and consumerism unique to Wilson. A college student who went to a very different school reports:

> While material possessions are not an indicator of social status, other factors
> may be. For instance, different lingo was used between different groups
> which made the groups much more distinguishable. People who used correct
> grammar and walked with good posture belonged to one group, while those
> with a modified walk and language full of lingo unknown to those outside
> their group obviously identified as a separate social crowd.

Our observational field notes report on forty-three lunchtime groups at Wilson High. On only one occasion did a group of students discuss shopping for themselves; there were no references to trips to a mall. In the fourteen in-depth interviews we did shopping was mentioned only three times and two of the three times it was because the interviewer brought the topic up.

Certainly the decline in the concern with fashion and consumption varies for different schools and different peer groups. In some schools fashion and "having the latest" was still very important. In general, however, this concern seems less pervasive and intense, if for no other reason than because students spend so much time keeping up with gossip on the social media sites.

EXTERNAL FACTORS

There have also been factors external to schools that reduced high school students' consumerism. The "learning to consume" has shifted to younger ages through marketing to children using strategies such as McDonald's "Happy Meal" mascots or advertising embedded in children's cartoons.[28] Moreover, working adults are more accessible to advertisers via TV and the Internet.[29] In the past, few jobs exposed employees to TV ads for much of the day. In contrast, many employees as part of their legitimate work are subject to ads on the Internet, not to speak of those who manage to surreptitiously look at the latest fashions or shop from their work stations.

Other changes include the redefinition of holidays. These have shifted from being "holy days" to "shopping days": Black Friday, Black Monday, Presidents' Day Sales, Memorial Day Specials, etc. Hundreds and even thousands of adults camp out in front of stores to buy "doorbuster" specials, or the latest iPhone.[30] Moreover, shopping is not restricted to *days*; many stores have extended night time hours and some are now open "24/7"—as is online shopping.

People in general spend substantial amounts of time on the Internet and people are exposed to many more ads per day than in earlier periods. Another important development is that nearly all the major retailers now track the specific purchases of most shoppers. Consequently, they can target advertisements to meet the shopping preferences of specific people.[31] Marketing of consumer goods has become so central to so many aspects of individual and collective social life that "learning to consume" in high school is less central to maintaining high levels of market demand for goods and services.[32] Conversely, while having the latest fashions is still important to teenagers, it seems less central to high school life than it was in the past.

THE FINDINGS AND THE THEORY

There are both important continuities and changes in the nature of peer culture. Do the changes call into question the usefulness and the theory of status relations? I think not. Rather there have been important changes in contextual variables. These in turn change the strength of impact of the core variables of the theory: inalienability, inexpansibility, association, and conformity. I will not attempt to demonstrate this for all of the above observations, but rather to clarify how changes in what I call contextual variables affect the key elements of the theory.[33]

A key contextual variable for status systems is social visibility. If you are "invisible" to other actors in a status system you have no status—you are a "nobody." One of the key effects of the new technologies and social media sites is that they have made some things much more visible and other things more invisible. As we have seen it is easier to get away with sending text messages during class than to pass paper notes. More people can know what the "popular crowd" is up to if they post all their doings on a website than if others have to find out through face-to-face interaction. Because status is relatively *inexpansible*, when social networks become larger, a smaller and smaller percentage of their members can have significant visibility. So some become "celebrities" and some become invisible. The latter are motivated to create separate networks and status systems in which they are not "nobodies."

So in the context of the new technology and media, teens become less concerned about having just the right clothes and more about gaining visibility on the Internet by almost any means—even displaying videos of their intimate moments with a lover. Consequently, it is not that *conformity* and *associations* are no longer the source of status, but rather that the fight for visibility precedes and trumps traditional kinds of conformity. Great visibility also affects how *inalienable* status is. If you do something "stupid" when you are a freshman it is likely to be forgotten by the time you are a junior—unless it is recorded on a video and permanently posted on a website. If a couple becomes "Facebook Official" their relationship is considered more serious and stable. The key point is that the processes identified in the theory of status relations are still important, but the new technologies have changed the nature of visibility (and invisibility), which, in turn, has reshaped the way the elements of the theory work.

Another key change is the relative importance of instrumental and expressive *associations*. As students are pressured to perform well on various standardized tests, they become more instrumental and pragmatic about whom they spend time with. At least for many, similar levels of academic ability become a criterion for social *associations*. This does not mean that teens no longer form couples with those they find sexually and emotionally attractive, but it means that they are less romantic about the nature of these relationships; they "hook up" rather than "date" or "go steady." Stated another way, relationships in general tend to become more instrumental and less expressive. Hence, the norms about what constitutes an appropriate relationship change, which means what constitutes appropriate kinds of *conformity* changes; it is not shocking or scandalous if you are sexually intimate with someone you have not known very long.

Another contextual factor is how frequently people communicate. Before writing, communication usually required face-to-face presence.[34] Technology has slowly increased the speed and ease of communication. With cell phones, text messaging, and the Internet many people are almost constantly communicating. Hence, "keeping up" increasingly means having read the latest message rather than having the latest fashions. What is required to *conform* to the norms of the group and to have multiple strong *associations* is to be "in the know" by sending and receiving messages, pictures, videos, and postings. Again, the key point is that the theory still helps us to understand why status systems operate the way they do, *if* we take into account changes in the contextual variables that may affect the way inexpansibility, inalienability, conformity, and associations operate.

The Theory of Status Relations: Elaborations

This appendix is intended primarily for scholars and others interested in the analysis of status systems. Here I discuss various aspects of the theory of status relations that are not dealt with in the main text. The intention is both to clarify ambiguities, elaborate key points, and, at the end of this appendix, indicate how I see my theoretical perspective related to some of the previous work that concerns the operation of status systems.

BOUNDARIES OF THE THEORY

All theories make at least implicit assumptions about the context in which they are useful. Psychoanalytic theory assumes actors are capable of relatively complex forms of symbolic communication. While some might claim that they can provide psychotherapy to pets, no one would suggest that psychoanalysis is relevant to understanding the behavior of billiard balls or earthworms. Newton's laws of motion assume a perfect vacuum. When this condition is not met, variables not included in the theory must be taken into account to explain the movement of objects. The laws of supply and demand assume a perfectly competitive market, and when this condition is not met, economic theory must be modified and elaborated to understand how the interaction of supply and demand under non-competitive conditions will affect price.

Theories vary in how rigorously their boundary assumptions must be met in order for them to be useful. The laws of motion are quite effective in predicting the behavior of a cannon ball dropped from a tall tower, but much less successful in predicting the behavior of a feather dropped from the same tower. That is, the object's density and shape are additional variables that must be taken into account if the motion is not occurring in a vacuum. Similarly, the effect of supply and demand can still provide reasonably accurate predictions of the general trend in prices in many markets, even when these markets depart considerably from perfect competition. All this is to say, a theory may still be useful for some purposes even when its boundary assumptions are "relaxed" (not fully met), and especially if additional variables not included in the theory can be taken into account.

The key boundary assumption of the theory of status relations is that status is not reducible to economic or political power. When status is simply a function or reflection of these other forms of power, no separate theory of status relations is needed; theories of economics and politics are sufficient. A closely related secondary assumption is that there is some common recognition of the criteria of status.[1] A third assumption is related to the visibility of the criterion: Characteristics that are easily identified and relatively inalienable will usually serve as status criteria and affect group formation.[2] Gender, age, and race are examples of such characteristics (though these may or may not be important criteria in a particular situation). A pure status hierarchy is completely insulated from economic and political power and has a single highly visible criterion of what determines rank.[3] Just as there are no perfectly competitive markets, there are no pure status hierarchies, but it is a useful analytical concept for analyzing and comparing actual cases. But just as markets need not be perfect for economic theory to be useful, the theory of status relations can be useful in analyzing status systems that are not pure hierarchies. As we shall see, high schools vary significantly in the degree to which they approximate a pure hierarchy in contrast to a pluralistic system.

VISIBILITY, POPULARITY, AND STATUS

For others to express approval or disapproval of you, they have to be aware of your presence. Some minimum level of visibility is a prerequisite to status—negative or positive. The larger the social system, the more difficult it is to become widely known. Therefore, in even medium size social systems, such as large high schools, the relationship between visibility and status becomes a complicated one. If you have no visibility, you have no status. But many of the ways that people become visible, for example aggressiveness or exhibitionism, may be disapproved of and therefore would result in a negative status. But for some, even a negative status is better than invisibility. The old Hollywood press agent's maxim says, "There is no such thing as bad publicity."

Even if you gain visibility by means that people admire, and hence have a high positive status, this success sets in motion social processes that may undercut your status. First, others become jealous of success—even when they acknowledge that it is deserved.[4] Second, high visibility and high status usually mean that many others want to associate with you. Some of these overtures must be declined because of time constraints. This typically leads to accusations of snobbishness or elitism.[5] Of course, some who have attained high visibility and status are snobbish, mean-spirited people. Even the down-to-earth people usually ration their interaction with others and especially with those of low status. The exception to this is the very high status person who associates with those of low status at the expense of traditional elites. Jesus is a classic example, but populist religious leaders and politicians also approximate this model. Those who follow this pattern are often accused of being rabble-rousers or demagogues. Consequently, the attitude of others toward those with high visibility is frequently ambivalent. They might like very much to be like them, or to associate with them, but at the same time, they will often express hostility and disapproval—usually behind their backs. This is one of the reasons that gossip and backbiting are so commonly associated with status systems. This ambivalence about people who have high visibility is one of the reasons that the relationship between status and such terms as popularity, fame, and notoriety is often unclear. These latter terms implicitly focus on visibility, which may be associated with either approval or disapproval. Steinberg[6] has defined popularity as "how well-liked someone is" and defined status as "whether he or she is perceived as a leader—is associated with the ability to accomplish the things the group wants done." I find this distinction misleading. Both what Steinberg calls "popularity" and what he calls "status" result from receiving expressions of approval. Steinberg's "popularity" usually results from expressive leadership—"a fun person." What Steinberg calls "status" refers to instrumental leadership—"they can get the job done."[7] In my terminology both expressive leadership and instrumental leadership result in a kind of status, though the arenas of this status will be different. The "life of the party" and the "real brain" are admired for different reasons and their status is relevant in different arenas. The first is not likely to be asked to run the study group for the final exam and the second is not likely to be asked to organize the prom.

CONFORMITY-DEVIANCE, INNOVATION, ECCENTRICITY, AND STATUS

I have argued above that one of the sources of status is conformity to the norms of the group. Now I must complicate the argument a bit. Stated in economic terms, high positive status results from behavior that is in high demand and low supply. Star athletes are an obvious example. Usually this level of conformity is thought of as excellence. More easily attained types of conformity—even though they are considered desirable—do not bring high status. Playing ball with your children may mean you are seen as a good parent, but it will not give you the high status of the athletic star. Just as there is a range of positive levels of conformity there is a range of negative levels of deviance. Not paying your taxes might eventually land you in jail, but it does not bring the abhorrence and punishment of sexually molesting small children. In other words, conformity and deviance are to a significant degree two ends of a continuum. The top end focuses on what is *commended* and the bottom end on what is *condemned*. In both cases the focus is largely on deviation from the usual and expected, whether positive or negative.

The highest (and lowest) levels of status, however, do not come from conformity (or deviance) to the *usual* norms. Rather they come from redefining the norms and expectations. They involve not merely departure from the mean, but innovation in the content of the norms. St. Francis did not simply surpass his contemporaries in helping the poor; many have done that. By his example he inspired others to go far beyond the conventional notions of charity characteristic of his time and place. He redefined what was expected of a medieval monastic. Hitler is so reprehensible not simply because he violated conventional notions of human rights, but because he carried out atrocities that redefined the depths of human evil. Conversely, the early presidents of the United States are considered great, not because they were exceptionally skilled at conforming to the old norms governing monarchs, but because they set new precedents and established new norms for a new form of government. The high status of great artists comes neither from making replicas of masterpieces nor from simply creating something different. It comes from work that redefines the norms, that is, from *innovation*. Innovation by definition is socially influential. A departure from the norms that is neither condemned nor commended, and hence not socially influential, is an *eccentricity*. In the realm of informal, expressive behavior, those of relatively high status are most likely to be innovative or eccentric. Their higher status makes it possible for them to experiment without immediately incurring negative sanctions. Those of lower status seldom have this luxury.

STATUS AND STATUS-MARKERS

Simply attaching four gold stars to your collar does not make you a four-star general in the U.S. Army; writing "Ph.D." after your name does not make you an educated person. Clearly such insignias are *status-markers*, not the criteria and *bases of status*. In contrast, living in an expensive neighborhood can be a *basis of status*; you are admired by some people simply because you live in such a place. An expensive house can also be a marker of a more general status characteristic by suggesting that you are rich, which is a *basis* of status in most societies. One other complexity is important: Such markers vary in the degree to which they are themselves physical objects or symbols. The expensive house is clearly an object. The letters "Ph.D." are primarily a symbol; their physical aspect—the ink and paper—has little status or economic value per se. The commonly used notion of status symbol obscures these distinctions between the markers of status and the bases of status, and the difference between material and symbolic markers. These distinctions can be important to understanding how status systems work.

This is especially the case with respect to the inalienability of status-markers. Some status-markers can be acquired or shed much more easily than others. For most adults it is much easier to put on a tuxedo than an upper-class accent. On the other hand, if you are capable of switching accents, it can be done almost instantly. Physical status-markers vary in how easily they can be switched or changed. It is much easier to change an insignia on your lapel than a brand on your forehead, your clothes than your race or gender. Similarly, symbolic markers vary in their inalienability. It is easy to pick up a few "in" words and phrases, but nearly impossible for adults to fully master a foreign language. These differences in the accessibility and inalienability of status markers affect whether they tend to be used as signs of differentiation or means of solidarity.

STATUS, HONOR, VIOLENCE, AND FEMALE PURITY

Honor is a particular form of status. In cultures that place a strong emphasis on one's honor, the concept often implies that it is more basic than all other resources. The loss of money, political office, a battle, or even one's life is some-times seen as less disastrous than the loss of your honor—your "good name" or "reputation." A strong concern with honor is often associated with violence. Many military groups are concerned about their honor. The U.S. military's highest award is the Medal of Honor. Honor was also a key concern of the feudal nobility in Europe (and similar groups in other areas, such as Japan) who historically were a class of professional warriors. Anthropologists have identi-fied a category of societies that tend to be especially preoccupied with honor and shame.[8] Psychologists have explored the link between cultural variations and the use of violence and argued that people living in "cultures of honor" like the American South are more likely to react with anger and even violence to perceived slights.[9]

Honor is a central preoccupation of teenagers involved with gangs. They resort to violence more frequently than most adolescents. Violence occurs primarily when an individual or a group perceives that their honor has been publicly questioned or threatened. The present study has only limited and tangential data about this kind of behavior. The theory of status relations, however, suggests several hypotheses. First, like for most teenagers, individual and gang status is initially fragile but becomes relatively inalienable once it has been publicly established. A young person—usually but not always male—must be ready to defend his or her honor should anyone deliberately and publicly call it into question. As status becomes more established, he can shrug off all but the most blatant insults if he or she cares to do so. Second, fighting—an "inti-mate" association, like sex and eating—is most likely to occur between those who are more or less equal; starting a fight with a clearly weaker opponent is dishonorable; starting one with a clearly superior one is considered "crazy." Third, norms are often elaborated and complicated: Rules, etiquette, and style are developed to avoid unwanted fights. Fourth, the inexpansibility of status accentuates the likelihood of conflict because for someone to claim more honor usually requires reducing the honor of someone else. Fifth, groups preoccupied with honor are most likely to have few economic resources or to play down the significance of economic resources—at least in comparison to honor. Youth gangs exemplify the first and the feudal nobility the second. Hence, their most important resource is threatened when their honor is besmirched. For a good account of these processes in the context of Spanish-speaking youth gangs in Chicago, see Ruth Horowitz's *Honor and the American Dream.*[10]

Closely related to the honor of fighters is the honor of women in societies deeply concerned about male honor. My guess is that the preoccupation with the sexual purity of women (i.e., virginity and/or sexual loyalty to husbands) as a criteria and symbol of female honor is linked to violence in two respects. First, in social contexts where violence is common, rape is likely to be common, probably more common than actually killing women. Second, in such societies women are often defined as the property of males and hence an encroachment on women by violence or seduction dishonors the males associated with that woman. It is not accidental that dishonor in this context involves intimate expressive relationships whether or not violence is involved. When violence becomes less frequent and is monopolized by the state, the preoccupation with women's purity is likely to decline.

Varying notions of honor have relevance in additional historical context, but my reason for focusing on status rather than honor is that I see the latter as a particular form of status, especially associated with upper status groups in certain historical contexts.

RELATIONSHIPS OF THE THEORY TO PREVIOUS THEORETICAL WORK

I will begin with the very basic and broad issues concerning the relationship of social science to postmodernism. Next I will take up the broad issue of identities.

A NOTE ON SCIENCE AND POSTMODERNISM

Much of the language used in this book is drawn from the language of relatively traditional social science. For example, it uses the notions of variables, causal relationships, and generalizing theories. This language has been severely criticized by a number of writers who place themselves broadly in the tradition of post-structuralism and postmodernism, and especially by various forms of cultural studies.[11] This tradition tends to focus not on making generalizations about the empirical world, but rather in deconstructing and interrogating particular bodies of discourse. A key part of this involves being reflexive about a particular discourse's own social sources. It is especially important to be aware of the interests and commitments of the analyst and the social organization of the intellectual community of which she or he is a part.[12] "Discourse" usually means what passes for knowledge, as well as the language and assumptions that are involved in constructing and communicating that knowledge. Science is seen in large part as one of the important discourses that was created by those committed to the goals of modernity. The aim was not only human control over the physical environment, but also high levels of rationalized bureaucratic control of social relationships. Knowledge and power supposedly become largely inseparable.[13] The modern nation-state, especially those with colonial and neocolonial ambitions, is seen as a key locale of these developments. Many, postmodernists want to substitute the analysis—they would prefer to say the deconstruction or interrogation—of humanly created discourses for what they see as the pretensions of traditional social science.[14] Michael Foucault, for example, has written about the discourses that were created to define and deal with the mentally ill, criminals, and sexuality; he claims to show how these discourses and their related policies were not primarily rooted in new objective information, but rather were attempts at developing new forms of social control and dominance.[15] Various forms of this tradition have been applied to the analysis of young people from Stuart Hall to Nancy Lesko.[16] These analyses deconstruct the very notion of adolescence. They are especially critical of the assumption that there is some natural sequence of biological and psychological development, and of using this to legitimate the authority of adults over young people. I am sympathetic to many of the concerns postmodern analyses raise. In my judgment, however, many such analyses tend toward extravagant claims, opaqueness, and pretensions that are often the mirror image of the most arrogant forms of positivistic social science. It seems to me that calling into question the categories that we use to make sense of the world is a worthwhile project. In my opinion, however, this does not require abandoning efforts to make sense of a world "out there." Of course, our knowledge of that world is always mediated through the discourses and languages that we use. To acknowledge this does not require that we assume that there is no world "out there" or that discourse and its deconstruction is the sum total of legitimate analytical and political concern. Such an assumption can, in my opinion, be creditable only to intellectuals who have acquired very high levels of what Thorstein Veblen called "trained incapacity."[17] There are various languages of discourse that are useful, including those associated with science and generalization. It is primarily this latter language that I have chosen to use for this book.

IDENTITIES AND THEIR RELATIONSHIPS

In this section I will discuss a series of approaches that suggest issues that are probably important in understanding teenagers, but they are largely beyond the scope of my present endeavor. My focus is not chiefly about the effect of adopting a particular *social* identity on the individual's *personal* identity and self-image. Nor do I look at the psychological and developmental processes that make adolescents especially concerned about these matters. Psychologists, social psychologists, and those in the tradition of symbolic interactionism[18] are often interested in such micro issues; or they are concerned with how individuals draw on and customize social categories in concrete settings of social interaction. These are legitimate and important concerns, but they are not the primary focus of my analysis.

In recent years, attention has tended to shift from individual identities to the construction of social and cultural identities.[19] In addition to a continuing interest in the identities associated with nations and social classes, special attention has been paid to groups that have been discriminated against in various ways: ethnic minorities, gays and lesbians, and the physically handicapped.[20] These analyses often focus on the process of how boundaries and identities are created, and in mapping the relationship between groups and cultural categories. Zerubavel's "cognitive sociology" is an important contribution in understanding these processes.[21] Bourdieu's analysis of cultural capital and fields of power is one version of this kind of relational analysis, though he of course tends to focus on societal structures of power.[22] Alexander and Smith's strong program in cultural sociology would draw attention to the importance of carrying out a semiotic structural analysis of the cultural categories.[23] Adolescent peer groups and subcultures, and the relationships between these various cultural identities, could well be considered from this perspective. While I touch upon the issue of the power and semiotic relationship between different kinds of adolescent crowds, this is not my primary concern; such issues are largely bracketed.

Now I will focus on bodies of literature that are more obviously related to the analysis of status relationships.

MY EARLIER WORK

In earlier work I have written about how my theoretical orientation is related to Marx and Weber.[24] I will not repeat that here, except to make two key points. Like Marx, I think variations in the kinds of resources that are available in a given historical context help us to understand the nature of the patterns of social interaction and social structure that emerge. (I refer to this perspective as resource structuralism.) This is a provisional structuralism that is, I believe, a useful analytical strategy at this particular point in the history of sociology—rather than a final theoretical position that privileges structure over action and agency, or social structure over culture. This approach usually starts with a relatively macro, structural focus, rather than a micro focus, but this is only a provisional strategy, not a dismissal of the significance of more micro approaches.

Like Weber, I think we need to take into account not only the instruments and modes of production, but other kinds of resources as well, especially the importance of symbolic resources. (This is hardly an original or even eccentric position.) While Weber emphasizes the importance of differences in lifestyle in establishing status group identities and boundaries, he provides little systematic explanation about the patterns of behavior characteristic of status groups. My aim is to offer a more systematic set of explanations and predictions about the kinds of patterns that emerge when status is an especially central resource than was provided by Weber and other theoretical traditions since Weber. Let me briefly survey some of this work.

CLOSURE THEORY

Parkin and Murphy have drawn on Weber's notion of closure as a useful way of moving beyond the limitations of Marxism.[25] They have focused primarily on rethinking the notion of class in contemporary capitalist societies, paying special attention to property and credentials as mechanisms of closure and monopolization. While they are well aware of Weber's discussion of status groups and non-economic forms of power, this was not their primary focus. The degree to which closure is actually characteristic of contemporary class structures has been called into question by Kingston.[26]

REPRODUCTION THEORY

Bourdieu's reproduction theory has been a primary stimulus to taking more seriously non-material resources as sources of closure and exclusion, which in turn are important mechanisms in the transmission of power and privilege.[27] Bourdieu recognizes that accessibility to objective material resources and structural opportunities are important. His special emphasis, however, is to identify "cultural capital" and especially those relatively subjective aspects he refers to as "habitus." Much debate has occurred about the precise meaning of these concepts. It is clear, however, that on the one hand he is arguing that both culture and individual action have certain degrees of autonomy from existing structures, but, on the other hand, communities and individuals inherit certain tools and often absorb certain social dispositions from their social environments that shape their subsequent behaviors. These are not so much conscious values and preferences, but routine ways of behaving and responding—like the grammar that is unconsciously acquired as children learn a language. But if, under ordinary circumstances, the individual does not deliberately acquire the habitus, its creation and social transmission often involve deliberate efforts of privileged individuals and communities. Cultural "distinctions" of language, taste, and style are created to perpetuate and elaborate privilege. Habitus incorporates these and is a form of cultural capital. Supposedly it is every bit as important as economic capital in reproducing inequality, though just how strongly they shape outcomes is left rather vague. At least in his earlier work, however, such cultural capital is ultimately a means for controlling economic capital and labor; it is economic capital "misrecognized." Some version of reproduction theory has been used or drawn on by a number of analysts.[28]

Much disagreement exists about exactly what Bourdieu is asserting and the literature dealing with this is extensive.[29] Probably the most influential interpretation in American sociology is that of Lamont and Lareau.[30] They interpret cultural capital to mean, "institutionalized, i.e., widely shared, high status cultural signals (attitudes, preferences, formal knowledge, behaviors, goals and credentials used for social exclusion)."[31] Using their definition, Kingston has argued that despite the popularity of the notion and numerous attempts to use it in empirical research, the results are unimpressive.[32] He argues that there is a tendency to define cultural capital so broadly that it has little analytical or theoretical distinctiveness and, no matter how it is defined, the impact that it supposedly has on educational attainment is at best modest and often subject to alternative interpretations.

Reproduction theory was helpful in moving beyond the overly materialistic and deterministic tendencies of classic Marxism (and other extreme forms of structuralism). The work associated with this mode of analysis contains much to appreciate and admire, but unambiguous definitions of cultural capital and powerful and convincing empirical evidence of the broad significance and its effects on reproducing privilege are not among these. As I noted in chapter one, MacLeod's final conclusion seems to be that some overcome the handicaps of underprivileged backgrounds and some do not, but no one knows what produces these differences.[33] Lareau's thoughtful study of two elementary schools shows that children's educational experience is not only affected by the family economic resources or learned values and attitudes, but by the direct intervention of parents in school processes and activities.[34] While lower-class parents intervene less, it is not clear how substantial these differences are, nor is there any evidence that such intervention has long-term consequences for the children involved. Careful scholar that she is, Lareau's own conclusions only claim that these effects are "nontrivial."

In many respects reproduction theory has reached the point of rapidly diminishing returns—both intellectually and politically. I believe we need to move beyond studies that focus on how the upper classes maintain their privilege and how the lower classes are kept disadvantaged.[35] Reproduction theory and structural equation modeling of status attainment research made important contributions, but both have become an increasingly arcane and self-referential body of literature identifying very limited elaborations on previous work.[36] Reproduction theory is also guilty of grandiose claims of questionable merit, such that it has overcome the dualism of structure and agency, the objective and subjective, and so on. Both are in danger of becoming a kind of unproductive scholasticism. This does not mean, of course, that the insights they have provided should be ignored. Moreover, as I indicate in chapter one, I believe most reproduction theory makes the implicit assumption that the crucial social problem in contemporary societies is best understood as a lack of equality of opportunity, that is, as the intergenerational reproduction of privileges.

It is true that reproduction theory *could* bypass the issue of equality of opportunity and ask the question of how the structure of positions gets reproduced across time. There are two problems with this defense. First, it seems to me difficult to deny that the moral and political implications of most reproduction theory primarily focuses on reproduction of family background characteristics, and hence equality of opportunity. Second, the structure and culture in modern societies has been fairly dynamic with considerable changes over time in the occupational structure, the distribution of income and wealth, ethnic groups and their salience, the nature of the economy, and even basic cultural assumptions. The changes should not be overstated, but the primary argument of reproduction theory has not been about the static nature of the society, but rather the reproduction of privileges across generations. There are versions of reproduction theory that focus on the reproduction of fundamental assumptions and values. As Parkin notes, "There are also powerful forces in capitalist society that are more dedicated to the perpetuation of bourgeois values than bourgeois blood."[37] Even on this level, however, there have been notable changes such as the legitimation of consumption and hedonism, which have given rise to the arguments about the "cultural contradictions of capitalism," a matter that is taken up in chapter ten. None of this is said to defend the adequacy of contemporary capitalism, but rather to point out the limitations of reproduction theory.[38]

BOUNDARY ANALYSIS

Identification of boundaries has been a key concern in the Marxist tradition, e.g., who is in what class? Lamont's work has been influenced by Weber and Bourdieu in that she is concerned to identify how actors use cultural resources to define and maintain social boundaries.[39] She has, however, a healthy commitment to clarity and "the inductive method."[40] She maps the economic, moral, cultural, and racial boundaries that both professional and working-class strata of the middle classes create to distinguish themselves from those who are usually defined as above and below them. (The classes and types of boundaries that are emphasized vary somewhat for different analyses.) Her work makes important contributions to specifying a multidimensional view of contemporary social boundaries. More generally it describes various kinds of "boundary work" and identifies commonalities and differences for different societies and different classes within these societies. Like all empirical studies the work has both strengths and weaknesses related to its methods. Her conclusions are based on in-depth interviews, that is, what people say about their beliefs and actions rather than on observed behavior per se. Her work does not, however, provide a general theoretical argument about under what conditions particular kinds of boundaries will be particularly salient, such that we could make predictions about what kinds of boundaries are likely to be important in other situations and what kinds of boundary work are most relevant in different types of social situations. For example, it does not provide a general theoretical rationale about why members of the American working class place more importance on moral rather than other kinds of boundaries. This is not to be unappreciative of this work, but only to point out its limitations.

EXPECTATION STATES THEORY

There is an elaborate literature on status processes influenced by social psychology, small group experiments, and formal theory construction. Perhaps the best-known variety of this form of analysis is expectation states theory. The focus is on how individuals use information from their environment to develop their expectations about others and how these expectations in turn shape their behavior toward others. For a sampling of this literature and a sense of some of the questions it addresses, as well as its development over time, see Berger, Zeldich, and Anderson[41]; Webster and Foschi[42]; Ridgeway[43]; and Wagner and Berger.[44] Jasso's work is roughly in this tradition and similar in style and concern, but has often focused on issues of how people perceive and construct notions of justice.[45] While this tradition is impressive in its rigor and sophistication, it is, in my opinion, less impressive in the extent to which it has been able to convincingly explain the patterns of behavior in actual historic social structures. While I am hopeful that they will, in my opinion this is still an open question. The danger is that the theoretical and methodological tail will wag the empirical dog—at least the "dogs" that live in actual historic situations in addition to those who participate in small group experiments. My own approach is obviously less formal and rigorous and more closely tied to directly observable everyday patterns of behavior. I do not consider my approach as antithetical to this tradition, but rather as addressing a different level of analysis with a different style of analysis. It is certainly possible that some of the behaviors I describe are rooted in some of the micro processes that social psychologists and small group analysts highlight. It is, however, useful to work on the issues of status stratification from "both ends" so to speak, that is, from both a more micro perspective and from the more macro structural perspectives from which I begin.

THEORY OF INTERACTION RITUAL

Collins has devoted considerable attention to Durkheim's theory of ritual, as filtered through Goffman's micro analysis of face-to-face situated interaction, and has formulated a theory of interaction ritual.[46] His analysis includes more than status groups, but he has devoted explicit attention to status groups.[47] The theory draws attention to three independent variables: (1) social density, i.e., the degree of physical co-presence of other people, (2) common focus of attention and mutual awareness, and (3) common emotional mood. The greater these are, the more likely (1) membership is to be clearly defined and reified, (2) reactions to deviance, especially violations of what is considered sacred, involve righteous anger and are punitive rather than restitutive, and (3) attitudes toward non-members will be distrusting. Which of the independent variables has the strongest effect producing solidarity and reified membership varies depending on the type of group. According to Collins, "Full-blown Weberian status groups, recognizable by visible signs … can exist only when the round of everyday life is highly formalized." Less developed status groups, which he sometimes refers to as quasi status groups, rely more on common emotions: "the more informal or improvised rituals are, the more the need to be ostentatious, to make blatant appeals to emotion and to visible or highly audible action." He gives an example: "Those starved for institutional ritual status (e.g., black lower class, teenagers, and young people generally) tend to seek out means of intense situational dramatization." While I have certain quibbles (for example, the meaning and boundaries of certain key terms like "ritual," "scripted," "formal," and "reified"), I think this theoretical perspective makes an important contribution in helping to link macro Durkheimian theory with more micro processes, and in significantly adding to our understanding of actual historical variations.

THE THEORY OF STATUS RELATIONS

How does my theory differ from the above theories and what does it contribute that is not already captured by one or more of these approaches? Unlike Marxian class analysis or closure theory, I am not primarily concerned with redefining class or with the role that property, credentials, and status groups play (or do not play) in creating and maintaining class boundaries. In contrast to reproduction theory, I am not in the first instance concerned with how symbolic resources are used to reproduce the patterns of inequality across generations and time. In contrast to Lamont, my aim is not to map macro class boundaries with greater subtlety and sophistication. Nor am I concerned with the micro cognitive processes whereby individuals decide how to characterize themselves or other people and how to respond to others, which is the focus of expectation states and similar micro theories. There are some overlapping concerns between the theory of status relations and the theory of interaction ritual, but the theory of status relations makes additional contributions to our understanding in several ways. Collins takes religion as the model of ritual interaction, but the link between sacredness and status has been underdeveloped. In my earlier work the relationship between status and sacredness and the parallels between status processes and religious processes are clarified and specified.[48] (This matter has not been a focus of attention is this book.) Of more immediate relevance, the theory of status relations helps to identify and explain when interaction rituals are likely to be especially intense and why. Obviously, it would be desirable to more fully integrate the two sets of arguments, but that would be a different project and require a quite different kind of book.

For a summary of the contributions of status relations theory, see chapter ten.

Data and Methods

As already indicated, I draw on two main sources of primary data.

RETROSPECTIVE ACCOUNTS

The 304 descriptions of high schools and their status structures written by 300 college students are from 1,300 to 18,000 words in length with the average paper being about 7,150 words.[1] Students at the university where I teach wrote 146 of these; students who attended a large Southwestern university wrote 124 of them; and 34 were written by students at a medium size nationally known New England college. A copy of the instructions that were given to most students who wrote papers and a sample paper is reproduced in Appendix III. Students who wrote papers attended 251 different high schools in twenty-seven different states, eight foreign countries, and one U.S. overseas territory.[2] Obviously, the quality and reliability of these reports varies. Nonetheless, students who went to high schools in different states and who attended different colleges often describe very similar patterns of behavior, which I believe lends credibility to their accounts. Since college students wrote all these papers, they almost certainly are not a representative sample of American high schools, and clearly they report the perspectives of relatively "good" high school students. "Though I have a few examples of urban high schools in poor neighborhoods, they are underrepresented. My focus, however, is not primarily on inner city schools in low-income areas—which, if anything, are overrepresented in published ethnographic studies that have been conducted by social scientists. Rather, for the theoretical reasons outlined in the introduction, I have focused on the kinds of high schools that most middle-class American teenagers attend—on good students in relatively good high schools. I have tried to compensate for the underrepresentation of urban high schools by keeping in mind other studies that have focused on urban public schools and urban youth. Moreover, the data from Woodrow Wilson High School (WWHS) (the case study discussed below), looks at the full array of students in a high school that is both racially and economically diverse. Nonetheless, my particular focus and the limitations of my data need to be kept in mind.

CASE STUDY: WWHS

A second source of data comes from observations conducted in a single high school over parts of three school years. The observations started in the spring term of 1997, were continued during the fall term of 1997, and then conducted less intensely from the spring of 1998 until May 1999. The primary observations were conducted during the school lunch period, and secondarily at public events, such as assemblies, football games, the National Honor Society induction ceremony, and the junior/senior prom. These were the appropriate sites for the concerns of this research. Lunch periods were especially important in that it was a time when the whole school was together and felt free to choose their associations and—within broad limits—how their particular group would act toward one another and toward others. Neither classrooms or other school events, nor following individuals or groups through the day provides this kind of information. Virtually all WWHS students had the same 40-45-minute lunch period and were free to choose where in the school they would spend this period.

The primary observers were undergraduate university students enrolled in a course that focused on high school status systems. These were all first-year students and the majority of them were honor students admitted to a special program for outstanding high school graduates. They received training and ongoing tutoring in field methods and onsite supervision. Before they entered the field site, students received three lectures on method and techniques, and read and discussed a recent book-length school ethnography, paying special attention to the discussion of methods. After each fieldwork visit, they discussed what they had observed with the supervisor as the team returned to the university. They were repeatedly told, "Put down what you hear and see in as much detail as possible." Each week in class, observers reported on their experiences and compared their findings. In virtually all cases they were escorted to the observation site by me or one of three graduate students and supervised at the site. Most were initially randomly assigned to a lunchroom table and observed the behavior of those students. This was to ensure that fieldworkers did not all concentrate on the groups that appeared to be the most friendly or convenient to observe. Some students ate in the courtyards or locker areas and observers were also assigned to these sites. Due to club meetings, special exams, trips by teams, and so forth, on occasion a lunch table group might be absent or present only part of the period. Most fieldworkers spent this time observing one or two additional tables. After each lunch period (or other observation period) the student fieldworkers and the supervisor went immediately to the school library where everyone spent fifteen to twenty minutes writing initial drafts of field notes, or more accurately notes from which an account could be constructed later in the day. Within the next twenty-four hours students were responsible for completing their field notes and turning them in, to be commented on and graded. By the second semester we had worked out a computer-based system so that everyone's field notes were "turned in" by posting them on a site available online to everyone else in the class. This contributed not only to cross-fertilization and cross-checking of observations, but motivated students to take care that the quality of their notes were up to those of their peers. We stressed that they should always report data that contradicted our initial hypotheses or what other fieldworkers reported. (Finding pluralism instead of hierarchy, and segregation without conflict, were two examples of such unexpected findings.) We were unable to sound-record conversations in the lunchroom or other public areas. This school system requires that such recordings be preceded by the written permission of parents and the consent of students. Even when we might have gotten the consent of all of the students and parents at a particular lunch table, it would have meant that the moment another student approached—which occurs more or less constantly—the recorder would have to be turned off. Obviously, this would have been impractical and have produced data that would be almost impossible to interpret. The loud background noise in the lunchroom would also have seriously compromised the intelligibility of the recordings. Hence, we relied on the observers recording their recollections a few minutes after lunch was over.

Usually fieldworkers went to the site once a week in teams of three to four plus a supervisor. The schedule of teams was rotated so that teams were at the school most days of the week. All members of the research team were together once a week during the class period. In addition to discussing assigned readings, ample time was devoted to reporting initial research findings and conferring about any practical problems that had arisen. During the spring semester of 1997, eighteen undergraduates and two graduate students participated in this process. One woman graduate student and one undergraduate male were African American. In the fall of that year there were fifteen undergraduate students, including two black females and one black male. The black female graduate student continued on the project and another white male replaced the original white male graduate student. In the spring of 1998 a third black male undergraduate carried out observations for about seven weeks. (Two undergraduate observers were second generation Asian Americans, one male and one female, while the remainder of the observers were white.) During our first semester of observations I devoted most of my time to supervising, though I usually spent most of one lunch period at a student table. Starting in the fall of 1998, I regularly observed the same lunch group, who are described in chapter six. The fieldworkers generally felt that their presence had little effect on the way the students behaved; that is, in nearly all respects they did what they would have done if the observer had not been present.[3]

In additions to observation of behavior at public events, we interviewed thirty-five students in private using a standardized semi-structured schedule. A copy of the schedule is provided in Appendix III. Eighteen different interviewers conducted at least one interview. Of these eighteen, ten conducted two interviews each, two conducted three, and I conducted four. There were eleven females and seven males, and one African–American interviewer. The students interviewed had the following characteristics:

Class: freshmen 10, sophomores 8, juniors 9, seniors 5, unknown 3
Gender: females 18, males 17
Race: black 7, white 28

In addition, I carried out private interviews with six faculty members, including the director of the orchestra, the football coach, the chair of the English department, and two teachers from the vocational education department. I also had two rather lengthy interviews with the principal and at least a half dozen more informal conversations with him. I talked informally with the associate principal during at least half of my visits to the high school.

The interviews with students were the least successful of our data collection techniques. The main problem was that we had to get signed parental permission forms in order to interview students in private. While most students seemed willing to participate, we found it very difficult to get these signed permission slips, even though they were mailed directly to parents—often several times— and follow-up phone calls were made. We were more successful in securing signed forms from upper-middle-class white parents, though as indicated above we had seven interviews with African–American students. Students varied significantly in how articulate and thoughtful they were in the interview situation. This interview material provided useful supplementary data. I have, however, relied more heavily on the observational data.

Did these undergraduate students gather valid and reliable data? I believe the answer is yes. Obviously, they do not have much training and experience as social scientists. What they do have is the right amount of social distance from those they are observing. For the most part the high school students welcomed them or ignored them and went on about their business. One of the strengths of this method is that they were able to develop a rapport with the high school students that is difficult for older observers to achieve. On the other hand, they had not attended this high school and they had enough social distance from the situation to develop reasonable levels of objectivity. They were told not to try to become "friends" or "part of the crowd." The college student observers were forbidden to have any contact with the high school students other than as fieldworkers in the research setting. I am virtually certain that all observers honored this norm. A second important strength of this method is that it was possible to observe a considerable variety of groups during the same time period. On any given day the three or four fieldworkers who were at the school usually observed at least four different groups. Over the period of a week about three times that many groups could be observed. This meant that we were able to observe how particular cliques varied in their responses to school-wide events, such as a ballgame, an exam period, a holiday, a national event, etc. This is not possible with only one or two ethnographers, no matter how skilled and dedicated they might be. The weakness of this method is that most student fieldworkers only observed their group from four to eight times. However, observers [during] the second semester sometimes picked up on a group that had been observed the first semester.‡ To a limited degree I tried to compensate for relatively brief field contact of most observers by concentrating my own observations on the same group during the course of their junior and senior year. What this multiple fieldworker approach does provide is an *observed overview* of peer relationships that is difficult to gain by other techniques.

To my knowledge this particular blend of data collection techniques has not been used before. Most ethnographic work on schools has involved only a few observers who necessarily can only be in one place at a time and only at one or a few sites. On the other hand, survey research—for all of its virtues— necessarily misses the flow of social interaction over time and the unanticipated events that observers can record. My argument is not that this data collection technique is in any general sense superior to standard ethnographic or survey techniques, but that it is a valuable alternative to these that can be useful in some research settings. When this observational technique is combined with the retrospective reports from college students, it provides a rich base of qualitative data—but qualitative data that is not limited by the unknown eccentricities of one or two sites, or one or two observers. Moreover, it should be kept in mind that well-trained professional ethnographers, who are usually university faculty or graduate students, also have personal and structural biases. They are from a very selective subculture and there is a considerable social distance and age difference between the observers and the observed. This is not to be dismissive of professional ethnography, but only to argue that it is not the "gold standard" of methods any more than surveys, experiments, or historical documents are. In ethnography-based accounts it seems to be fashionable to claim that the actors' point of view and the meaning of events to the actors have been captured. (This is one of the key goals of various forms of symbolic interactionism.) It is, of course, important not to misreport the rationale behind peoples' actions, or the meaning they attribute to the action of others, but these goals can become a fetish. The degree of intersubjectivity (i.e., grasping the other person's point of view) required between the observer and the observed depends on the purpose at hand. Being someone's lover or psychoanalyst requires a different degree and kind of intersubjectivity than that needed to generate useful social science data. Moreover, the richness and depth of ethnographic data needed depends on the aims of the research.

I do not to claim that my methods provide an accurate representation of all high school experience, but rather that it adequately identifies and describes the forms of behavior relevant to understanding status processes in a wide array of settings. If it has a bias, the data probably overrepresents the views of good students from relatively good high schools. As I have said in the Introduction, the data collection strategy and the analysis deliberately pay special attention to the perspective of those from the middle classes. If my account seems to paint an overly pessimistic picture of high school life, it is unlikely that a more representative sample of students would provide a rosier view.

In order to honor the promise of confidentiality that was made to informants, all high schools and individuals have been given pseudonyms. In the few instances where this is not the case, it is because I am relying on press reports or other publicly available data. The WWHS school officials required that we get parents' permission to interview individual students; and declined to give us access to classrooms. In virtually all respects, however, they were open and helpful. They had no say about the content of the field notes or this book. While it would be methodologically desirable to give more detailed information about the school and its setting, this has not been done to honor our promise to students and officials that neither they nor the school would be identified.

FOCUSING ON STATUS

An initial working assumption of the research is that peer status was likely to be important to most high school students. I do not, nor does the methodology assume that all teenagers are equally concerned about it, nor did we refuse to consider other possibilities. It is true that the instructions to college students on how to write their papers asked them to describe status structures. A selected focus is, however, characteristic of virtually *all* questionnaires or instructions. Political polls ask people about political issues, not "how are you feeling?" or "what has been on your mind this week?" Certainly any research focus creates certain biases. It would, however, be much more questionable to have not asked students about status differences, and assume they were unimportant. If you ask people to describe their primary concerns, very few American whites will talk about race or racism, which does not mean it is not a crucial issue in our society. Therefore more open-ended approaches also have their biases and limitations.

Sample Research Materials

INSTRUCTIONS FOR TERM PAPER ON HIGH SCHOOL STATUS STRUCTURES

The Subject: You are to write a paper about status relations and groups in the high school you attended.

Due date: The paper is due at the beginning of class on [date]. It should be about ten pages long.

Some tips on how to proceed:

1. Identify and describe the most important sub-groups or cliques in your high school. Were they ranked? How? What was the basis of their ranking? If they were not ranked how did they relate to outsiders?

2. How did these groups and individuals attempt to display or symbolize their status and/or identity? Dress, music, style, language and vocabulary, walk and posture, etc., often serve as such markers.

3. Who talked to and hung out with whom and why? Did this vary during classes; in school but outside of classes; after school?

4. What were the sites and events where status was very important: lunchroom, dates, school dances, math class? Where were such differences less important? Why these differences? What were the big events and how/why were they important?

5. How much mobility and change was there? What did groups do to prevent such change? To what degree could the same individual belong to multiple groups?

6. It is especially important that you look for/recall behavior and patterns that are not explained by the theory of status relations or call the theory into question. Obviously, you do not want to ignore the data that supports the theory, but make a special effort to identify patterns that appear not to be explained by the theory.

7. The key to a successful paper is DETAILED DESCRIPTION. Do not say, "Dress was important." Tell what kind of dress was important in what context during your first year. Were there any significant changes or fads? Try to use specific, not hypothetical, examples: "Largely because of his good looks and ability to memorize quickly, my friend John managed to be a member of both the popular crowd and the drama group. I can think of six other people who spanned two groups. Probably five percent of the students fell into this category." IS PREFERABLE TO: "Some people had characteristics that enabled them to belong to two groups."

8. Avoid truisms, vague generalizations, and largely irrelevant autobiography: "High school is different for everyone." "Similar to society, the mainstream consists of a particular culture that has been developed and embraced by a majority of students." "When beginning to contemplate this paper, all I kept thinking about was that my high school experience was typical … nothing worth writing ten pages about." In short, avoid "filler." Virtually every sentence should convey specific information about your high school or community.

9. One way to approach this project is to imagine that you have a younger sibling and you want to advise them about how to get along when they arrive at high school, that is, think about who is who, what is what. Then take this description and think about how you would present it to the class as an example of sociological analysis.

10. While it should not be a part of this paper, you should be thinking about how the observations you make about your high school can help you to better understand American society in general.

Format and summary information:

1. Papers must be typed with double-spacing and one-inch margins; number all pages.

2. Use a cover page. In the center of the top of this page put your full name, Social Security number, e-mail address, your home (parent's) address, and phone number.

3. Two inches below this give the following information:
Name of school
Town and state (full address if available)
Setting: urban, suburban, small town, rural, etc.
Type of school: public, private, religious (indicate denomination), magnet, etc.
Size of school
Size of your class
Approximate racial/ethnic composition
Approximate gender ratio
Names of different academic tracks

Rate your overall my high school experience:

Pleasant   1 2 3 4 5 6   Unpleasant
Little stress   1 2 3 4 5 6   Great stress

Briefly explain your responses:

SAMPLE PAPER

[INFORMATION REQUIRED ON EACH COVER PAGE]

Public school with science and technology magnet program
School population: approximately 3,000 students
Class population: approximately 675 students
Racial/ethnic composition: approximately 40% white, 40% black, 20% Asian/other
Sex ratio: approximately 55% female, 45% male
Possible academic tracks: comprehensive, tag, science & tech
On a scale of 1–6, with 1 being pleasant and 6 being unpleasant, I would rate my high school experience a 2.
On a scale of 1–6, with 1 being little stress and 6 being great stress, I would rate my high school experience a 5.

Explain your responses:

> I enjoyed high school very much, though it was not perfect. I had many
> friends, had very interesting academic experiences, and had the opportu-
> nity to participate in numerous activities in which I may not have been able
> to take part were I at a smaller school. I did find it crowded at times, and
> I think the experience might have been more comfortable were the school
> not so densely populated. But on the whole, I think that the faculty and
> administration did amazing things with what they had, and I appreciated
> that and took advantage of what was offered me. In terms of stress, I was in
> a very academically challenging environment. I was in the Science and Tech
> program, which had rigorous requirements in terms of math, engineering,
> and science. In our senior year we had to do research in a local laboratory
> or facility of our choice, and write a five-chapter paper on that research.
> Assignments like this one, along with five AP classes, all honors classes,
> commitments to music, and a general wish to do well, led to a very valuable,
> but very stressful high school experience for me.

[TEXT]

Abraham Lincoln High School is a very large, diverse school, where a student
is almost guaranteed to find some group or organization to fit his or her major
interests. The status hierarchy is not so much a vertical one based on who is
more popular than who, but one where groups are based largely on interests
and activities. Because of this structure, the high status, medium status, and
low status are not always easily defined. As in most schools, certain groups are
labeled as "cool" or "nerdy," but there is not always a consensus on such labels.
Instead, mixing among groups occurs frequently, and those who look down
upon others are often the ones with whom most of the student body wishes not
to associate. In the following, I will attempt to make clear, to the extent of my
knowledge, how the status system is generally constructed. It is important to
note that in such a large school, I have not had close contact with many of the
social cliques and have much more information on certain ones than on others.
It is obviously not possible in this context for me to describe every social clique
of whom I am aware, but I will try to represent groups from various status
levels and from a variety of areas of interest. My explanation begins with one
group that cannot really be put into a category of high- or low-status, because it
contains so many people from different groups, but after that [I] will proceed in
the order that I perceive most schools would rank these social cliques in terms
of status.

SCIENCE AND TECHNOLOGY STUDENTS (AKA "TECKIES")

One of the most recognized groups at Lincoln is the teckies. This group is made up of students in the Science and Technology program. The Science and Technology program is a magnet program into which about two hundred students per year are accepted through a fairly competitive testing process. These students come from all over the county, and are usually coming from situations in which they were at or close to the top of their eighth grade classes. They come from public, private, and religiously-affiliated schools and from families of varying economic backgrounds. The Science and Technology program, unlike the school as a whole, is made up of white students mostly, but does have fairly large populations of Asians and blacks as well.

The purpose of the program is mainly to give academically-oriented students a chance to have more exposure to science and engineering, and to encourage those who have an interest, to pursue those subjects in college. The requirements for the program are very rigorous as high school programs go. Students must complete Biology, Chemistry, Physics, and one and a half years of Engineering Foundations, all courses designed specifically for Science and Technology students. Besides these base requirements, students must take at least three more years of science or engineering, including at least two advanced level courses, e.g., AP Physics, AP Chemistry, AP Biology, Microbiology, Production Systems, AP Computer Science, Organic Chemistry. The choices about which courses to take are based on the choice of a track, similar to the declaration of a major, in the students' junior year. Students must also complete four years of math, finishing at least through Pre-Calculus, and all of the normal public school requirements. Finally, in their senior year, students must conduct research, usually at a major research center, e.g., Goddard Space Flight Center, National Institutes of Health, Food and Drug Administration. They then have to take a full-year class called "Research Practicum" in which each learns basic statistics and scientific ethics, writes a five-chapter research paper on research done, participates in the science fair, and presents a poster at a symposium at the end of the year.

Science and technology students take many courses solely designed for people in the program. Because there is a very set schedule for the first two years, and somewhat in the third and fourth, as to what courses are taken when, the students end up spending a lot of time together. Many students meet people in classes in the first few weeks of school that are friends for all four years. This is not to say that these people necessarily all stick together. Most groups are based more on shared interests outside of school, and since science is mostly an academic interest, this large group does not dictate social groups. However, certain activities such as Computer Club, National Honor Society, and even band end up being predominantly teckies, partially because of the academic ability needed to participate in such activities. There are teckies on the football team and the cheerleading squad as well, but these do not make up as large a percentage of these organizations as in some other groups.

Besides sharing interests, some teckies become great friends because they share so many stresses. Though the program is a very admired one, from which most teckies will tell you they gained valuable knowledge and experience, it is overwhelming at times, and having people who can directly relate is often very helpful. This comes into play most often during senior year when conversations can be heard everywhere about the five hours spent the previous night writing the first section of chapter two for research practicum. It also brings about social activities, such as Calculus study groups at someone's house involving pizza and ice cream or large meetings of seniors at the local 24-hour Kinko's at 2 AM the morning three copies of the final RP paper are due in laser quality and bound.

Though the teckies do not all hang out together, they are very much a recognized group. My impression was that they generally are not disliked or made fun of by other students because of their academic achievements. Most students seemed to admire their efforts somewhat, pity their stresses, and besides that, not let it affect their friendships. I personally had many friends who were not teckies, and it was never a source of any tension between us. That is not to say that one would not occasionally hear a teckie being referred to as a nerd, but for the most part this was good-natured teasing, and most of it was not meant to cause hostility or major insult. To my knowledge, no one was ever shunned from any other group for being a Science and Technology student, and in fact, most of the group who considered themselves "popular" (this group will be discussed later in the paper) were teckies themselves.

THE NERDS BY CHOICE (AKA NBC)

NBC is a group rather unique to Lincoln, though it has come to my attention that one more chapter has been set up in a Virginia High School. Perhaps many schools have a group of people who, having experienced unpopularity, join together to form their own independent clique. What the group at Lincoln has done is to set up what they consider an independent organization. Though the school has not agreed to recognize it as an official club, NBC has managed to maintain itself as a well-known organization. They have found teachers who will let them hold meetings in their classrooms, have advertised on the Web, and have created quite a stir over the refusal of the administration to allow them to advertise in the school-sponsored newspaper or the yearbook. The general makeup of the group is about twenty or twenty-five students, including many in Science and Tech, but not all. NBC is one of the few groups I would classify as low-status and perhaps even isolates. The ambiguity comes in trying to determine if isolation is brought about by others, or by the members of the group themselves. As an outsider to this group, I would like first to present their advertised view of themselves, before giving the general impression the school has of them.

On their Web page, the group advertises itself as offering "unconditional social acceptance, period." Their goal is to "take someone who feels insecure with their social role … and bring them out of their shells." They go on describing in detail this mission. Another section explains the name, which is not meant to bring insult onto the group, but rather has been found to "mysteriously cease" name-calling from others. The remainder of the page is devoted to explaining the methods the group uses to bring people out of these "shells." These consist of "constant exposure to the 'free spirits that are already with the group,' and a 'mentoring program for all new members,' pairing each with a current member whom they believe to be 'easy to get along with.'" The group sounds very well intentioned and even seems to perceive that the "student body [is] quite receptive" to the idea of their advertising like a normal school group. However, many students to whom I have spoken have gained a very different impression of the people in the group as well as its structure. The people in the group generally seem to be very unhappy and unsociable people. They often wear dark clothes, rarely dress to look nice, and rarely talk to anyone outside of their group. I had classes with one member who was extremely overweight. My sophomore year I had Science and Technology Chemistry with him, and I immediately noticed that no one was talking to him. I was somewhat surprised. The people I had known at the school were usually not so petty as to shun someone for something like weight, which I will admit I automatically assumed was the reason for his isolation. Trying to be friendly, I went over and said hello and introduced myself. Patrick just sort of grunted and glared at me. Later, as that and other classes went on, I realized that Patrick was rude to everyone in the class and also to the teachers. He would read books during the lectures, would ask questions just to argue clear points made by the teachers, and he would deliberately fail to do assignments, though it was obvious he understood the material. It was not until my senior year that I saw Patrick be social with someone. We were in the same AP Biology class, and in the class before us was another member of NBC. Every day, this guy waited for Patrick to get there, and the two talked and laughed for the five minutes we had between classes. I found it really amazing to see Patrick happy, but as soon as class started, he was back to his old personality. Patrick was not the only case that I encountered. I often saw clusters of NBC members huddled together in a side corridor, obviously wishing to keep others out of their conversations.

Another of my impressions of this group that differed from their advertised assertions was the membership process and structure. From the Web page, one gets the impression that NBC is a club open to anyone who needs social support. However, walking home from my bus stop one day, I heard a very different version of the group's structure. I had just gotten off of the bus, and in front of me were members of NBC: Chris, and a Russian exchange student Vladimir. I heard Chris say to Vladimir something to the effect of, "I think you might be one of us." When Vladimir inquired about the meaning of this statement, Chris explained that he was a member of a group that accepted people like them and that if he could pass some sort of test, he might be able to join. I found it very odd that he was making it sound like this group was a refuge, but at the same time a competitive and selective organization. Though I was not accustomed to eavesdropping, as a freshman, I was very interested in hearing more about this strange group. When Vladimir asked about the test, Chris told him that he could not explain and that if he were truly one of them, Vladimir would agree to take the test without knowing its nature. At this point Chris realized that I was walking a few yards behind them. He told Vladimir to stop, and they let me pass. As I continued on my way home, I heard Chris say, "We can't talk in front of her. She's not one of us." I was completely baffled about this encounter until much later that year when I asked an upperclassman and they explained to me about NBC. Though this was a short and somewhat ambiguous encounter, it and many impressions I have gotten from other people and from observing members of the group, led me to believe that NBC, at least while I was there, was not the accepting refuge it claims to be.

THE BAND GROUP

Unlike many schools, the group of students associated with band at Lincoln is not, by any means, an unpopular group. This group interacts on a regular basis with other social cliques and has some members that are also members of other highly recognized groups. The "band group" is not made up of all band people in the school, as that would be about 300 students. Instead, there is usually one band group for each of the 10th, 11th, and 12th grades. This is made up of students from the Wind Ensemble, the most advanced of five bands at Lincoln, who spend a lot of time together outside of school, as well as a lot of time in the band room.

Specifically, I am going to discuss the band group of which I was a part, as I obviously know the most about this group. There were about fifteen people who considered themselves part of this particular clique. The group was pre-dominantly white, though a few minority students were part. This was a result of the makeup of the band being generally white, and not of any intentional segregation by the members. This group of people was characterized by other students by its spending inordinate amounts of time in the band room, whether for multiple music classes, student aide periods, extracurricular groups, or just hanging out. About half of the group had the same lunch period as the band

and orchestra directors and ate lunch with them in the band room every day (one should note that the cafeteria experience at Lincoln was a crowded and often unpleasant one). A few orchestra members occasionally joined in this ritual, but the directors limited this privilege mainly to the students in this group.

The band group was a fairly popular group in the school, mainly because of its high visibility and its general reputation for being very friendly. The people in this group were seen by the student body during concerts, which were usually very well attended, during the fruit sales the band had every month, and in the responsibilities and privileges given to these students. Members of the band group regularly answered the phone in the music office, conducted the concert bands when the conductors were not there, and ran errands to the office and other parts of the school. They were generally granted more freedom than many other students, both by the music directors and the administration and staff. The members of these groups came to be recognized and trusted in the main office. In one instance, I was sent up to get some chalk, and the secretary, who recognized me right away, gave me the keys to the stock room and told me to get whatever I needed. One must keep in mind that the stock room had packages of hall passes and attendance slips, which were hot commodities with many of the students in the school. The band group members, however, were well liked and very trusted, and I personally know of no time that trust was breached.

Another example of trust put into the students came on all-eastern weekend, when all of the music teachers would be away for an extended weekend at an annual conference. I was given the keys that unlocked every music room, including the office. I was asked to open the doors in the morning, stay in the room for as many periods as I could be excused from, act as director for any band period for which I could be there, and to arrange to have other band group members cover the times I could not be there. For two days, I had access to and control over all aspects of the music program, a program consisting of over 700 students. By these responsibilities and visible positions, the members of the band group gained status with both the adults and the students of the school.

The band group also gained some popularity through its reputation for friendliness. Since most of this group was in orchestra as well, many of the string players would visit in the band room with the band group, often expressing disappointment that the orchestra did not have the same kind of bond. Often, people not in the music program would stop by the band room in the mornings before classes, knowing that the group was there and seeing it as a social opportunity. Though in outside social activities the group often kept to itself, it welcomed visitors, and was definitely not a clique in the sense that it was exclusive or snobby. In fact, some outside social activities became quite popular with non-music students, such as late-night trips to Denny's after a big concert. Still others lent themselves to being kept within the group, such as small parties and coed sleepovers. Overall, the members of the band group found most of their best friends there, and much of the group's dating occurred within the clique. However, the group was known to others in the school, and always open to socializing with others.

DRAMA GROUP

The drama group was similar to the band group in that they were highly visible to the student body because of productions attended by most of the student body. They were a more diverse group in many ways. Racially, drama tended to have members from many minority groups. Also, the group was not split by grade levels at all, but instead was made up of all those people for whom drama was the major activity. This might be a result of the drama program being significantly smaller than the band program.

One major difference in the drama group was the frequency with which it was visited by outsiders. Many of the members of the drama group were members of other groups as well. However, when a group of drama students was sitting in the hallway (they tended to congregate in the hallway, while the band used the band room whenever it was opened), few outsiders were seen with them. This is not to imply that the drama people were not friendly, but only to point out that the nature of their gatherings tended to seem less accessible to other students. The reason for this is not clear.

As for social gatherings outside of school, the drama people often frequented the Denny's after performances as well (this was the only place in town open past midnight). They also had cast parties which were obviously more exclusive to the group, or at least to drama students in general. It was my general impression that there were not many less formal social occasions within this group, but I would not be able to say for sure.

MEN'S SOCCER

Lincoln has many athletic teams, most of which I am not that familiar with. I did, however, have several friends on the men's soccer team, and these seemed to form lasting friendships that continued through all of our years at Lincoln. The soccer team practiced every afternoon during the season. The games were fairly well attended by the student body. Many of the members of the team, especially those I would consider in this social group, were considered fairly attractive and liked by many of the girls.

This group spent a fair amount of time outside of school socializing. I heard many accounts from one of my friends about soccer parties, usually involving alcohol. My friend often spoke of he and his buddies getting really drunk after a big soccer game, "downing forties," and other popular party drinks. Beyond this, they hung out at school, but not on any regular schedule like the band or drama people. They of course socialized at practice, but beyond that I know very little about their everyday activities.

CHEERLEADERS

Unlike many schools, the cheerleaders were not necessarily considered the most attractive or the most popular girls in school. In the years I was there, the cheerleaders were a very diverse group, racially. Academically, most were comprehensive students (the regular track of study), though I knew of a few that were Science and Technology students. Many of the cheerleaders were from the immediate area, a result of most going to the school through the normal districting and not through the magnet program. Many of these girls were friends of mine when I was very young, as I grew up in [deleted]. Those whom I knew as a child were a very close-knit group and stayed that way through high school. In general they seemed friendly to me, but I again had little contact with them in such a large school setting.

The cheerleaders were very visible in the school, as they performed at all major sporting events. They did not, however, seem to gain unusual popularity from this. They were generally well-liked, though some, who were not in the group of friends referred to in the previous paragraph, were considered snobs. Having had no contact with the snobby cheerleaders, I could not make any generalizations about them.

THE POPULAR GROUP

There was one group at Lincoln my senior year who seemed to give off the impression of being the popular group, or at least of thinking of themselves that way. This was a group made up of about twenty students. Most of them were members of Student Government, Yearbook, or SADD (Students Against Drunk Driving). Individually, these were generally nice people. Yet, as a group, they tended to become very cliquey and were often criticized by other students for this behavior.

This group had many parties to which only a select group of non-core people would be invited. My best friend was often invited to these parties because of a middle school connection she had. She described the parties as having a lot of alcohol, and the people as being generally obsessed with putting forth images of maturity and popularity. There were certain people in the group who tended to act like she wasn't there at the parties, though some accepted her and encouraged her to become a more full-time member. The group was not outwardly mean to other students, but often acted as if outsiders were not there.

The group was made up mainly of white students, though there were one or two minority students. They were mostly Science and Tech students, but were all very active in at least one other high-profile organized group. Within these, many held executive positions or some other positions of leadership.

Overall, they are a harder group to categorize because they are not connected to one particular activity. They were, however, very well known in the school for having their own clique.

SUMMARY

Abraham Lincoln is a very hard school for one student to categorize and characterize. The student body was very diverse, yet many activities tended to be somewhat segregated. Because of this, I was unable to talk much about the mainly black or Asian social groups, though it should be noted that these did exist and played a major role in the makeup of the school.

There were a few general trends in the school that may not have been obvious through the descriptions of these few groups. First, no group of which I knew followed any particular style of dress. Some people preferred to wear a certain brand of clothing, but I was not aware of this playing a major role in anyone's social status. Secondly, the school was a fairly nonviolent place. Physical aggression between or within groups did not occur frequently, and when it did, the administration was very quick about expelling the aggressors. By a few weeks into the school year, one would see almost no fights. Lastly, there was not much racism in the school. Groups tended to be segregated based on different races generally participating in certain activities. For example, the step club was all black, while the swim team was mostly white. Yet, in classes, people interacted openly, and there seemed to be little wish by anyone to enforce any social segregation of races.

In conclusion, I would ask readers to forgive any inaccuracies or biases in this paper. These descriptions are based on the perceptions I got of different groups at my school, and many other groups of which I was aware I simply knew too little about to attempt to describe. If any reader has any specific questions about the information, I may be able to explain some generalizations more clearly in response to specific questions.

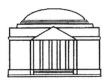

UNIVERSITY OF VIRGINIA
Department of Sociology

Murray Milner, Jr., Professor of Sociology
mm5k@virginia.edu

539 Cabell Hall
Charlottesville, VA 22903

Office: (804) 924-7293
Fax: (804) 924-7028

Xxxxxx XX, 1997

Dear Parent:

High school students are often influenced by one another at least as much as they are influenced by parents and teachers. Accordingly, with the permission of the school authorities, we are studying the informal status systems in your child's school—as well as in a number of other schools.

As part of this study we would like to interview your child. This interviewing will be voluntary and will be done during lunch and other times that would not interfere with your child's schoolwork.

All information gathered will be kept strictly confidential. In any reports that are produced, neither the actual names of the students nor the names of the schools will be used.

We would appreciate you giving your permission for your child to participate in this study by signing the statement below. Thanks for your cooperation.

Sincerely,

Murray Milner, Jr.
Professor

I give my permission for my child to participate in the study described above.

_____   _____   _____
(parent's signature)   (date)   (print parent's name)

_____
(names of all your children who can be interviewed)

INTERVIEW SCHEDULE

IVSCHD-xxx-F97.3   Notes in all CAPS are not to be read

1. Name: _____
   (last or family name) (other names including nick names)

2. Grade: Birthday: 3. Street Address:

4. How long have you been at [name of high school]?

5. Do you have a part-time job during the school year? _____

   If so, how many hours a week do you work on average? _____

6. What percentage of your spending money comes from your job(s)?

7. Considering your total spending money, what do you spend the most on?
   ____ CLOTHES   ____ MUSIC   ____ GOING OUT/PARTYING
   ____ CAR   ____ SAVINGS ____ OTHER (SPECIFY)

(OTHER COMMENTS RESPONDENT MAKES ABOUT MONEY)

8. Please list any extracurricular activities you participate in such as athletic teams, cheerleading, student government, clubs, etc. PROBE FOR
   LEVEL OF PARTICIPATION.

9. Students in many schools often divide themselves into different informal
   (STATUS) groups or categories. Could you tell me what the groups you
   think there are at [name of high school]? As you name these groups please
   indicate anything that is distinctive about them including differences
   in dress, slang, etc. PROBE FOR BRAND NAMES AND SPECIFIC
   PHRASES, ETC.

10. Could you rank the groups you already mentioned? ____

11. Do you think most students in the different groups would agree with
    these rankings?

12. Is there any tension or hostility between any of these groups? Which
    groups and why?

13. What determines the standing or status of a person or group? IF RESPONDENT DOES NOT MENTION "COOLNESS" PROBE ABOUT THE IMPORTANCE OF THIS NOTION.

14. How do dating or other romantic relationships affect the group or how does what group you belong to affect who you date, etc.?

15. Do you consider yourself to be a member of one of these groups? If so, which one? If not, why not?

16. How much influence do parents have on how high school students spend money, what they wear, who their friends are, etc.?

17. Some people would say there is quite a bit of segregation at [name of school] but very little open racial conflict. Would you agree with this statement? If so, why do you think this is the case? If you disagree, explain why.

18. Is there anything you would like to add before we finish up?

19. TO BE COMPLETED BY INTERVIEWER:
    Interviewer's name: Date of interview:
    Site of interview: Privacy of interview: H 3 2 1 L
    Respondent's   Sex: Race: AS: H 5 4 3 2 1 L*   RS: H 5 4 3 2 1 L**

 * *Interviewer's ranking of respondent's physical attractiveness*
** *Interviewer's ranking of respondent's reliability*

Data and Method 2013–14

An extensive description of the methods and data that were the basis of the original study are available in Appendix II and Appendix III. Here I will describe the nature of the data that were used in the "Fifteen Years Later" study.

First, I want to acknowledge that this follow-up study was much more limited in its time span and the number of observations made than the first study. This was due to both theoretical and practical considerations. Theoretically, there was reason to believe that the fundamental nature of status systems had not changed. Practically, I did not have the time or the resources to do a complete replication of the first study.

Second, let me outline how the second study was carried out. In addition to consulting existing literature and publicly available data, there were four types of data. One data source was ethnographic field notes reporting what was observed during the forty-three observation periods[1] at Woodrow Wilson High School—the same high school that was studied fifteen years earlier. Most of this fieldwork was carried out by a sociology graduate student and an undergraduate pre-med and sociology major who had served as a research assistant for a year and a half prior to this study. Unfortunately, our university's Internal Review Board (IRB), which must approve all research involving human subjects, would not allow us to talk to the students during the lunch period other than explaining the nature of the research and gaining their permission to sit with them at lunch. So the field notes consist of what the fieldworkers were able to see and hear during the lunch periods and at a few other public events such as a football game and a school assembly. The second source of data was a set of in-depth interviews with fourteen Wilson High students. Interviews were between twenty and forty minutes long. Interviewers were guided by an interview schedule, but asked a number of open-ended questions and probed for elaborations and clarifications when this seemed appropriate. As the interviews progressed we used a modified quota system to insure that we interviewed students from a variety of peer groups, racial-ethnic and economic backgrounds. A third source of data was papers written by fifty-eight college students from four different colleges and universities—usually first or second year students. The students were given a common set of directions that varied slightly depending on the college or university. They were asked to describe the student peer culture and its status system in the high school they attended—generally the same as the way this kind of data was collected in the earlier study. The fourth kind of data were interviews with the school principal, and more informal interviews and discussions with the assistant principals, and the police officers assigned to the school who were usually supervising the lunch periods. We also had informal interviews with about a half dozen teachers.

Since much of this data involves the students' perception of their social situation, it needs to be kept in mind that such perceptions are shaped by the social location of the observer. Those who are high status in a particular social system tend to perceive it more positively than those who feel left out or degraded. We do not have the kind of data that would be needed to measure such variations. We have tried to keep this limitation in mind by using quotes from a variety of different groups.

Finally, the aim of this second effort was not to completely replicate the first study but to identify key changes that had occurred.

All names used in the text are pseudonyms.

NOTES

A NOTE ON NOTES

• Citations to the literature are given in shortened form. For the full citation see the Bibliography. Many endnotes clarify or qualify points in the text, provide supporting data, or discuss connections with previous research.

• Three hundred and four papers written by college students describing their high school are one of the data sources used in this study. These are referred to as Student Papers, abbreviated SP. In order for the reader to be able to see both the variety of sources and when the same sources are being used again, each paper has been given a number. When that paper is quoted or is central to the discussion, its number is indicated in the endnotes, for example: "SP53."

• Field notes from thirty-five fieldworkers who participated in the study of a single high school, called WWHS, are also quoted. Each fieldworker has been assigned a number and this number is given in the endnote or in a parenthesis for a particular quote, for example: "FW16." About half of the students in this high school were African Americans. The race of the fieldworker might affect the nature of the responses and candor shown by students. Therefore, the numbers of African–American fieldworkers have been shown in italics, for example: *FW8*. Most of the time the context or the material itself makes evident the race of the students involved. I have not systematically indicated the gender of the fieldworkers, but this can often be discerned from the context.

PREFACE

1. My experience with the police is reported in Baker et al. (1969), *Police on Campus*. I was one of the six co-authors of this monograph.

INTRODUCTION: FIFTEEN YEARS LATER

1. MOOCs are likely to become more important, but they are not the core of the high school experience.

2. It is true that in principle their choices have expanded by the creation of special schools and programs in such subjects as arts and drama, science and math, vocational training, etc. In addition the intent of the charter school movement is to increase the choices that are available to families. For the most part this has given more choices to relatively well-off families who can afford to either transport their children to more distant schools or move to the neighborhoods where they exist. This still affects a very small proportion of students. In 2011–12, the latest year for which data is available, 4.2 percent of students were enrolled in charter schools (U.S. Department of Education National Center for

Educational Statistics: http://nces.ed.gov/programs/coe/indicator_cgb.asp; accessed 12/5/2014). The reality is that most students have little choice over which high school they attend.

INTRODUCTION

1. While the information about teenage "deviant behavior" is extensive and complex, let me outline a few of the facts about these matters. Homicide victimization rates and offending rates for teenagers (14–17-year-olds) and 18–24-year-olds rose dramatically in the 1980s and declined in the 1990s. "The homicides committed by 14–17-year-olds exploded after 1985, surpassing the rates of 25–34-year olds and 35–49-year-olds." Source: U.S. Dept. of Justice, Bureau of Justice Statistics, http://www.ojp.usdoj.gov/bjs/homicide/teens.him, January 2001. Rates of teenage alcohol consumption show that between 15–20 percent of eighth graders consume 5+ drinks in a row each weekend while over 30 percent of twelfth graders consume the same amount. Over 70 percent of eighth graders and 95 percent of twelfth graders say that it is "fairly easy" or "very easy" to get alcohol. See http://www.monitoringthefuture.org/data/00data/fig00_l0.pdf, January 2001. In the year 2000, 19.5 percent of eighth graders, 36.4 percent of tenth graders, and nearly 41 percent of twelfth graders admitted to using "any illicit drug" in the past year and nearly 25 percent of twelfth graders admitted to using illegal drugs in the past thirty days. See http://www.monitoringthefuture.org/data/00data.pr00t.pdf, January 2001. The 1998 teenage suicide rates in the U.S. from the American Association of Suicidology indicate that 15–24-year-olds make up 13.5 percent of deaths in the U.S., and 4,135 deaths in this age group were reported as suicides in 1998. See http://www.suicidology.org/index.html, January 2001.

2. As Schwartz and Merten (1967), "The Language of Adolescence," 459, noted some years ago: "Our informants almost instinctively measured their own worth against the standards of the youth culture. And the cardinal concerns of the youth culture are those domains over which they exercise direct control: friendships, relations with the opposite sex, and various types of expressive activities." They note, however, that the isolation of adolescents from adults should not be overstated.

3. SP220. [See above for an explanation of abbreviations in these endnotes.]

4. SP169.

5. SP235, FW5.

6. Michael W. Apple is the John Bascom Professor of Curriculum and Instruction and Educational Policy Studies, University of Wisconsin, Madison. The quotation is from the Forward to Dance (2002), *Tough Fronts*.

7. SP198.

8. Best (2000), *Prom Night*, 3–4.

9. For example, Best (2000), *Prom Night*; Giroux (2000), *Stealing Innocence*; Palladino (1996), *Teenagers*; Gladwell (1997a), "Annals of Style."

10. See, for example, Ogbu (1973), *The Next Generation*; Willis (1977), *Learning to Labor*; Fordham and Ogbu (1986), "Black Students' School Success"; MacLeod (1995), *Ain't No Makin' It*; Fordham (1988), "Racelessness as a Factor in Black Students' School Success"; Peshkin (1991), *The Color of Strangers*; Bettis (1996a), "Urban Students, Liminality, and the Postindustrial Context"; Bettis (1996b), "Urban Abstraction in a Central City High School"; Wells and Crain (1997), *Stepping Over the Color Line*; Christman, Cohen, and MacPherson (1997), "Growing Smaller: Restructuring Urban High Schools"; Finnegan (1998), *Cold New World*; Rathbone (1998), *On the Outside and Looking In*; Dance (2002), *Tough Fronts*. In addition, there are a number of other studies that contrast advantaged and disadvantaged students in particular schools. See Eckert (1989), *Jocks and Burnouts*; Foley (1990), *Learning Capitalist Culture*, and others that focus on young people in ghetto neighborhoods, for example, Horowitz (1983), *Honor and the American Dream*; Anderson (1999), *Code of the Street*.

11. See Massey et al. (2003), *The Source of the River*.

CHAPTER ONE

1. FW33, FW23.

2. Barglow (2000), [Review of] *The Nurture Assumption*.

3. See also Portes and Rumbaut (1996), *Immigrant America*. Harris's arguments have of course been criticized. See Lewis (1999), *Do Environments Matter At All?*; Gardner (1998), [Review of] *The Nurture Assumption*; Barglow (2000), [Review of] *The Nurture Assumption*; Gerstel (1999), [Review of] *The Nurture Assumption*.

4. Hulbert (2003), *Raising America*.

5. See Steinberg (2001), "We Know Some Things," for a measured defense of authoritative parenting—one of the concepts of appropriate child-rearing advocated by experts in recent years.

6. See for example, Anderssen et al. 2006, Ornelas et al. 2007, Scaglioni et al. 2008.

7. Park, Wallis, and Dell (2004); Dobbs (2012); Morris (2013); PBS Frontline (2002).

8. See for example, Johnson, Blum, and Giedd (2009), Johnson, Sudhinaraset, and Blum (2010), Jetha and Segalowitz (2012), Willoughby et al. (2014).

9. Bourdieu (1977), *An Outline of a Theory of Practice*; Bourdieu (1984), *Distinction*; Bourdieu (1986), "The Forms of Capital"; Bourdieu and Passeron (1990), *Reproduction in Education*. See Appendix I for a discussion of Bourdieu and reproduction theory.

10. In addition to Bourdieu, there are other important studies of the reproduction of the privilege of the upper classes through education. See, for example, Kingston and Lewis (1990), *The High-Status Track*; and Cookson and Persell (1985), *Preparing for Power*. I focus on the Willis and MacLeod studies of the lower classes because they have received so much attention from scholars and have been widely used in courses for students.

11. Willis (1977), *Learning to Labour*.

12. MacLeod (1995), *Ain't No Makin' It*.

13. Ibid., 147.

14. This does not strike me as a ringing testimony to the analytical power of reproduction theory. For a more extended discussion and critique of reproduction theory, see Appendix I.

15. Equality of opportunity is not a simple concept, as the whole debate over affirmative action has shown. See Coleman (1990), *Equality and Achievement in Education*, for his thoughts on these matters. He argues that complete equality of opportunity in the sense that background characteristics have no effect on outcome is impossible to obtain and hence should not be our goal. I would suggest that most public and political discourse is deliberately vague about this concept precisely to avoid having to acknowledge that this is the case. If it were openly acknowledged that equality of opportunity is impossible in a society that has significant degrees of inequality, this would oblige us to discuss the issue of how much inequality we should have. It is clear that most Americans believe in limits on the degree of political inequality (e.g., the president cannot hold office for life, make court decisions, or raise taxes) and status inequality (e.g., no one should be considered aristocracy or addressed as "Lord So-and-So"). In contrast, limits on economic inequality are considered by many to be "un-American." For an earlier statement on this issue, see Milner (1972), *The Illusion of Equality*.

16. This does not mean that the authors of these studies personally accept the legitimacy of the equality of opportunity model. Willis and MacLeod specifically are committed to social democratic societies that reduce the degree of inequality in addition to increasing equality of opportunity. But the analytical model they use to frame their work—reproduction theory—makes this assumption.

17. These studies can also be criticized on methodological grounds. It is hard to know how representative these groups are of even the sub-populations that they supposedly represent. Even more significant, the fundamental empirical assumption and findings are open to question. While it is clear that those from the bottom have a much lower chance of making it to the top (and those from the top are not likely to end up on the bottom), it is nonetheless the case that most people from the lowest and the

highest classes did not have parents from those strata. It is clear that in contemporary capitalist societies there is much inequality, but there is also much social mobility. For a book that provides an extensive review of the findings on these issues and argues that the notion of class is not useful in understanding the contemporary U.S., see Kingston (2000), *The Classless Society*. I am not going to directly address this issue, because my point is that no matter who is right about the "are-there-classes" question and the "is-class-position-reproduced" question, we need to move beyond these issues. To point out these limitations is not to be dismissive of these important studies, but rather to point out that our thinking needs to move beyond the issues that they highlighted.

For a very thoughtful and useful critique of "critical" approaches to the sociology of education, see Davies (1995), "Leaps of Faith."

18. I certainly do not mean that I am unconcerned about equality of opportunity or the impediments and barriers to learning by disadvantaged students, or that this is not *one* legitimate focus of analysis and social policy.

19. There are more recent and sophisticated neo-Marxian analyses that avoid economic reductionism, are sensitive to the issues posed by postmodern theory, and define "reproduction" more broadly than intergenerational transmission of privilege. Nonetheless there is a strong tendency to continue to place the primary focus on the organization of work and production and the role that schools play in creating a work force that in the end acquiesces to the constraints of a capitalist economy, even if they resist in numerous sorts of ways. See, for example, Apple (1995), *Education and Power*, esp. chap. 4.

20. For an elaborate set of research reports that document these trends see Duncan and Murnane (2011).

21. For an excellent introduction to the sociology of education and more specifically an overview of the evolution of schooling in America, see Brint (1998), *Schools and Society*, especially chapter 5. I have not tried to discuss all of the complexities and variations outlined by Brint because it would distract from the main focus of my analysis and is not necessary for the purposes at hand.

22. This does not mean that spending per pupil has declined; it has generally increased over time. But relatively collective spending has decreased. Since the 1970s the U.S. has spent around 6 or 7 percent of the GDP on education. The amount spent on elementary and secondary education has ranged from 3.5 to 4.3 with the highest levels in the early 1970s. Source: U.S. Department of Education (2000), *Digest of Educational Statistics*. The Social Security Administration reports that the total percent of GDP spent on education was 5.0 percent in 1970 and 5.1 percent in 1995. In contrast the percent of GDP spent on social insurance—mainly Social Security for the elderly—increased from 5.3 percent in 1970 to 9.8 percent in 1995. Source: U.S. Social Security Administration (2000), *Annual Statistical Supplement*, Table 3.A. Certainly the primary but not sole reason for the increase in spending on older groups is because they constitute an increasing percentage of the population. In 1970 there were about 20 million people, or 9.2 percent, over 65, while in 2000 there are about 35 million, or 12.7 percent. Source: U.S. Federal Interagency Forum on Aging (2000), "Older Americans 2000." For a detailed analysis of the history of expenditures on education, see Hanushek and Rivkin (1996), *Understanding the 20th Century Growth in U.S. School Spending*.

23. See Metz (1978), *Classrooms and Corridors*, for a discussion of the difficulties facing teachers and administrators in exercising authority during the 1960s in schools that were becoming more diversified and were having the traditional forms of authority, called into question. In many respects one of the junior high schools studied by Metz illustrates the factory model, while the other seems to be a proto form of the shopping mall school.

24. Powell et al. (1985), *The Shopping Mall High School*.

25. In 1929–30 there were 23,930 public schools with secondary grades; in 1997–98 there were 24,802 such schools. Total enrollments in grades 9–12 had, however, increased from 4.4 million to 13.1 million. In more recent years—since about 1980—however, the average size of all high schools has declined from 710 in 1982–83 to 699 in 1997–98. This drop has occurred primarily because of

the creation of specialized schools, such as those for the severely handicapped or those specializing in fine arts. Regular high schools increased from an average of 711 in 1987–88 to 779 in 1997–98. But averages are misleading. For example, schools with 1,000 students or more increased from 8.3 percent in 1982–83 to 9.8 percent in 1997–98. Many of these are much larger than 1,000. In my nonrandom sample of reports on 304 high schools, 70 were from schools of 2,000-plus and 20 of these had 3,000-plus students. Sources: U.S. Department of Education, National Center for Education Statistics, Statistics of State School Systems; Statistics of Public Elementary and Secondary School Systems; Statistics of Nonpublic Elementary and Secondary Schools; Private Schools in American Education; and Common Core of Data surveys (this table was prepared June 1999), http://nccs. ed.gov/pubs2000/Digest99/d99t090.html, March 22, 2001; U.S. Department of Education, National Center for Education Statistics, Statistics of State School Systems; Statistics of Public Elementary and Secondary School Systems; Statistics of Nonpublic Elementary and Secondary Schools (this table was prepared August 1999), http://nees.ed.gov/pubs2000/Digest99/d99t003. html, March 22, 2001. See Entwisle (1970), "Schools and the Adolescent," for comments on the effect of school size on educational effectiveness.

26. According to Powell, they have four types of curricula: the horizontal, the vertical, the extra curriculum, and the service curriculum. The horizontal curriculum offers a vast variety of subjects from Latin, calculus, and ancient history to auto repair, computer graphics, and cartoon comics as literature. The vertical curriculum refers to the fact that in core subjects such as math and English, courses are offered at two, three or even four levels of difficulty. It is not unusual for high schools to offer remedial, regular, honors, and advanced placement English.

27. William Lockhart (private communication) has suggested to me that large complex high schools are more like department stores rather than shopping malls since all of the subunits are under the authority of a single organization. This is certainly true, but the crucial point here is the increase in the diversity of "products" the school offers and choices that students can make.

28. In the factory-like high school, students who were performing poorly tended to be flunked out or allowed to drop out. There is now much more social pressure to keep young people in high school even when they are making little educational progress.

29. Like the factory, the metaphor of a shopping mall cannot be taken too literally. Arnstine (1987), "What High Schools Are Like," has pointed out that not all schools offer varied curricula and that once a student is channeled into a particular track or curriculum, there are often relatively few courses to choose between.

30. *The Digest* of *Education Statistics*, U.S. Department of Education (1999), National Center for Education Statistics, provides the following information about trends in students' performances: Reading proficiency for 17-year-olds was the same in 1996 as it was in 1971 (Table 112). The writing proficiency of 11th graders declined slightly between 1984 and 1996 (Table 118). For mathematics, "Performance of 17-year-olds declined between 1973 and 1982, but an upturn during the following decade returned average performance back up to 1973 levels" (Table 123). Science proficiency scores for 17-year-olds declined slightly between 1970 and 1996 (Table 131). "Between 1988–89 and 1998–99, mathematics SAT scores increased by 9 points, while verbal scores rose by 1 point (table 135)." "These are average trends for the total school population of the ages and grades indicated. There was considerable variation by age, gender, race, and region. Nonetheless the basic story seems to be one of little change over time.

31. Kaufman (2000), U.S. Departments of Education and Justice, National Center for Education Statistics.

32. Americans' confidence in public schools has been decreasing since the 1970s. When asked how much confidence people have in public schools in the U.S., 58 percent responded "a great deal" in 1973, compared to a much lower figure of 36 percent who responded the same in 1999. This data is from Public Agenda Online (Education) http://publicagenda.org/issues/pcc-detail.cfm?issue_type= education&list=2, February 15, 2001.

33. Only Steinberg actually wrote the book.

34. Biddle (1998), [Review of] *Beyond the Classroom*; Graubard (1998), [Review of] *Beyond the Classroom*.

35. 57.

36. 58.

37. 59.

38. 69.

39. 72.

40. 163–164.

41. 138.

42. 147–148.

43. Dance (2002), *Tough Fronts*.

44. This is not to deny that organization and leadership can improve the quality of schools. Research and implementation literature focuses on this process. See Bliss, Firestone, and Richards (1991), *Rethinking Effective Schools*; Hawley (2002), *The Keys to Effective Schools*. Most of this focuses on improving the quality of low-status urban schools and bringing them up to the quality of suburban schools.

45. Collins (1979), *The Credential Society*.

46. This may be especially so for students in elite schools who not only learn the skills of creating networks of peers, but actually create concrete social relationships with those who are likely to be able to help them secure and maintain power when they are adults. See Cookson and Persell (1985), *Preparing for Power*. This is an issue that I will only address in a brief way when we look at an elite private school. The focus of my analysis is more on the experience of the typical middle-class student.

47. Other studies of that attempt to disentangle the effect of schools from contextual factors such as family characteristics and neighborhood effects on a variety of dependent variables relevant to adolescent outcomes include Chen and Weikart (2008), Damron-Bell (2011), Gaviria and Raphael (2011), Jang (2002), Jang, Rimal, and Cho (2013) Perry (2009). These kinds of studies face significant methodological and complex statistical issues. For this reason it is important to recognize the tentative nature of our knowledge about these matters. Woolley and Grogan-Kaylor's remarks about their study apply to other examples of this form of analysis, "Results in the current study contribute to the accumulating evidence that the contextual aspects of school outcomes are complex to model and analyze. This complexity comes from both the multivariate nature of the school context and because different school outcomes are influenced by different factors within the family, school, and neighborhood microsystems."

48. Corsaro (1997), *Sociology of Children*; Corsaro and Eder (1990), "Children's Peer Cultures."

49. See Furstenberg (2000), "Sociology of Adolescence," 901–903.

50. See, for example, Portes and Zhou (1993), "The New Second Generation" for a brief discussion of the conflict between Haitian immigrant parents who are oriented toward education and upward mobility and their children, who are highly sensitive to the norms of their African–American peers. On the other hand, see Vickerman (1999), *Crosscurrents*, for an account of the racism that West Indian immigrant parents themselves experience and how it can blunt their initial aspirations.

51. See Boehm et al. (1999), "Teens' Concerns," who analyzed the calls made to peer counseling centers in each of four regions of the country. In all centers, peers' relationships were by far the most common topic (46 to 60 percent) of the calls.

52. See Card and Giuliano (2013), Albert and Steinberg (2011), Evans-Whipp (2013), Gaviria and Raphael (2001), Jaccard, Blanton, and Dodge (2005), Lundborg (2006), Megens and Weerman (2012), Sumter et al. (2009).

53. My point is not that parents, teachers, and curriculum do not matter. Much less is it that genes are more important than anything else. But we have enormous intellectual and organizational establishments devoted to the theory and practice of parenting, teaching, and the content of formal education—not to speak of departments of genetics and developmental psychology. Virtually every

school of education has one or more departments that deal with the first three topics and virtually every university has extensive programs dealing with the latter two subjects. Few schools of education have even a course, much less a whole department that focuses on the effect of peers. This is not to suggest that we need to create such courses and departments, but only to point out the relative emphases that these various factors receive.

54. Weber (1968), *Economy and Society*, chaps. IV, IX.

55. See my discussion of Randall Collins's terminology and discussion of status groups in Appendix I.

56. "Just Say No" was a phrase made familiar during Ronald Reagan's presidency by his wife, Nancy, when she advised young people about drug use.

57. Brown, Mory, and Kinney (1994), "Casting Adolescent Crowds in a Relational Perspective," have suggested a "relational perspective" of crowds that considers the significance of crowds for social identities, as channels for creating interpersonal ties, and as contexts that shape behavior and attitudes. I do not disagree with this, but partly because of my particular theoretical interests and partly because of the nature of the data I am using, I will not try to systematically deal with all of these aspects. I will primarily focus on status processes, which is not to deny that other factors shape the social organization of crowds.

58. In a five-school network study Ennett and Bauman (1996), "Adolescent Social Networks," found that cliques ranged in size from 3 to 10 members with an average membership of 5. Schools varied in the degree to which students were clearly members of a clique versus being isolates or "liaisons," but their study does not include a sufficient number of schools to show the sources of such variations.

59. Like many stereotypes this is probably generally true, but often exaggerated and misleading in specific cases. See for example Finnegan (1998), *Cold New World*, "book four" for a description of non-racist skinheads; and Soeffner (1997), *The Order of Rituals*, for an account of the emergence of punks and skinheads.

60. Even in the scholarly literature the use of such terms as status group, subculture, crowd, and clique varies. See Dunphy (1963), "The Social Structure of Urban Adolescent Peer Groups," for a seminal use of this distinction applied to Australian youth. See Steinberg (1993), *Adolescence*, for a standard discussion in a textbook on adolescents. Both types of units play important and somewhat distinctive roles. As Brown (1990), "Peer Groups and Peer Cultures," 184, notes, "clique affiliation indicates merely who an adolescent's close friends are; crowd affiliation indicates who an adolescent is—at least in the eyes of his peers."

61. These questions emphasize the relative uniqueness of American teenagers at the beginning of the twenty-first century. This is not to deny that the antecedent social processes of childhood are important or that there are no similarities between contemporary youth and earlier societies. But the reason teenagers in contemporary society are perceived to be a social problem is not because of the "eternal problems" of youth, but rather because of the particular characteristics at the beginning of the twenty-first century.

62. Ogbu (1978), *Minority Educations and Caste*, also draws on the notion of caste to analyze American high schools, but he primarily uses the term to describe discrimination against minorities. I will take up the issue of racial and ethnic segregation later. Here I am focusing on the distinctions that students create even when schools are racially and ethnically homogeneous.

63. Milner (1994), *Status and Sacredness*.

64. This is a very concise and oversimplified description of the Indian caste system. For a more elaborate characterization and analysis, see Milner (1994), *Status and Sacredness*, especially chaps. 4–6.

65. The intense racism of the American South allowed the milder forms of discrimination in the rest of the nation to be largely ignored for nearly a century. The residues of this history continue to be a central feature of the United States. The elitism of the British aristocracy and the patterns of privilege and deference associated with it still shape patterns of social interaction in Britain, even though they have had little formal political power for a century. This is not to say that these status patterns in the

U.S. and Britain have not been significantly weakened even within their core enclaves. Nonetheless the crucial point here is that these status systems, which were primarily restricted to a limited segment of the society, had reverberations for the entire society.

66. I have already outlined the debate about how much influence peers have. But there is also debate over how peers influence one another. Are members of cliques and crowds similar to one another because they pressure each other to behave in a certain way, or did those who had similar dispositions and inclinations simply come together? Studies seem to indicate that the latter process is stronger than the first, but this is certainly conditioned by the type of behavior that is involved. The extent to which peer influence is positive or negative—from the point of view of parents and other adults—is also unclear. See Brown (1990), "Peer Groups and Peer Cultures," 190–195, for an overview of these matters. See also Tolson and Urberg (1993), "Similarities Between Adolescent Best Friends." Despite these qualifications, as I have already indicated, I believe that in many areas of their lives adolescents are strongly influenced by peers and peer culture. For example, when fashions in clothing, music, and language change—sometimes relatively quickly and dramatically—and are almost universally adopted within a given clique or crowd, this change is due to mutual influence, not self-selection or parental influence.

67. Brown (1990), "Peer Groups and Peer Cultures," 179.

68. Younger children also see adults as controlling their lives and often resist this and increase their autonomy in various ways. See Corsaro (1997), *Sociology of Childhood*. Adolescents, however, are increasingly able to escape the supervision and control of adults and hence these processes are significantly accentuated. This growing autonomy is probably rooted both in changing cultural expectations—it is recognized that adolescents have a right of more privacy—and because their lives are more physically segregated from adults.

CHAPTER TWO

1. FW26.

2. For the benefit of those not initiated into the language of social science, let me say what I mean by social structure. Imagine that you lived in a world where social interaction and relationships were random: There was no correlation between whom you would talk with today and whom you had talked with yesterday or last week. That is, you were just as likely to talk with a perfect stranger as someone you had talked with many times before. In such a random world there would be no such thing as social structure. Social structure means there are predictable differences in how often people interact with one another and that these differences tend to persist over time. Of course, there are not only differences in how frequently people interact, but also in the content of their interaction. You are more likely to kiss or shout at the people you have kissed or shouted at in the past, than with a perfect stranger. With this in mind, the discussion of social formations can proceed.

3. In recent years the term *community* has often been used rather loosely for relatively abstract and diffuse categories, as in the "business community," the "black community," etc.

4. Considerable attention has been paid to the identification of social boundaries. See my discussion of closure and boundary theory in Appendix I.

5. Even though preferences for the gender of sexual partners may vary.

6. Sometimes groups try to increase their internal variation. At puberty, friendship groups often shift from single-sex groups to mixed-sex groups. Affirmative action programs recruit those from different backgrounds.

7. See the discussion of Appendix I for an elaboration of the relationship between my approach and more micro analyses of status and the issue of the construction and interpretation of symbolic meaning.

8. An anonymous pre-publication reviewer suggested that if this argument was correct it should produce the same outcome in retirement and nursing homes. Here is where I think stage of life and social competencies probably are important conditioning variables. First of all, unlike adolescents, older people have already developed a relatively stable self-image and social identity. Second, those who are

in relatively good health come and go more or less at will and participate only in those institutional activities they choose. Third, as their strength or health decline and they become more powerless and dependent, it is usually family members, not peers, who are most relevant to them in any attempts to resist or negotiate with the institution's staff. Moreover, at this stage they are often losing the energy and social competencies to maintain strong peer groups. Fourth, peer friendships probably are important in retirement communities for those who are in relatively good health. In such situations peers may organize to negotiate with institutional authorities. In short, I do not think more elaborate data from retirement and nursing homes is likely to invalidate the theoretical predictions.

9. This is a theme that has been a major focus of the work of Pierre Bourdieu especially in (1984), *Distinction*. For a more extended discussion, see Appendix I.

10. The classic sociological description of this process for adolescent boys is Cohen (1955), *Delinquent Boys*.

11. Associations are not, however, synonymous with friendships. The associations between adolescents vary considerably in their content, mode of communicating, and social and psychological significance. See Giordano (1995), "Wider Circle," for a contrast between close friends and wider circles. As Giordano points out, acquaintances who are not close friends or even members of one's primary clique or crowd can still provide important social support.

12. This is a theme that has been the focus of much of Michele Lamont's work in (1992a), *Cultivating Difference*, and Lamont (1992b), *Money, Morals, and Manners*.

13. For a more elaborate discussion of the link between status and rituals, see Appendix I.

14. Throughout most of the text I use the phrase "counterculture" or "counter norms" more frequently than "alternative" or "oppositional." The latter has become probably the more common usage in recent years. See, for example, Dance (2002), *Tough Fronts*. I prefer "counter" because the "alternative" implies no necessary connection with or reaction against the dominant culture, while "oppositional" implies self-conscious, organized opposition. It seems to me that neither of these conditions is necessarily or even usually the case. This choice of words is, as far as I am concerned, a matter of minor terminological preference and I have no serious objection to the use of the other terms.

15. Milner (1972), *The Illusion of Equality*.

16. Such moves may be only relative. Hence, if those at the bottom gain additional respect, it does not mean that anyone at the top will have to move to the bottom, but only that the distance between the top and the bottom will have been reduced.

17. Weber (1968), *Economy and Society*, esp. chaps. IV and IX.

18. Parkin (1979), *Marxism and Class Theory*.

19. Murphy (1988), *Social Closure*.

20. Bourdieu (1984), *Distinction*; Milner (1994), *Status and Sacredness*; Clark (1995), *States and Status*; Lamont (1992b), *Money, Morals, and Manners*; Lamont (1999), *The Cultural Territories of Race*; Lamont (2000), *The Dignity of Working Men*; Collins (1975), *Conflict Sociology*; Collins (1988) *Theoretical Sociology*; Collins (2000), "Situational Stratification"; Wagner and Berger (2002), "Expectation States Theory."

21. Weber (1949), *The Methodology of the Social Sciences*, 90–104.

22. Steinberg (1993), *Adolescence*, 181.

CHAPTER THREE

1. FW27.

2. FW17.

3. "Wannabe" is a slang contraction of "want to be." There are various spellings: wanabie, wanna-be, etc. It is defined as "somebody emulating somebody else: somebody who is trying to be like another person or to belong to a particular group (*informal disapproving*)." *Encarta World English Dictionary*. Microsoft. 2000.

4. SP54. Eder and Kinney (1995), "The Effect of Extracurricular Activities on Adolescents' Popularity," found that in middle school cheerleading could raise your visibility but also increase people's hostility toward you. While I have no systematic data on this issue, this tendency seems to be less the case in "traditional" high schools. As we shall see, in pluralistic high schools, the status of cheerleaders is often much lower. For a study of the relative prestige of different sports and extracurricular activities based on the opinions of college students taking an introductory psychology course, see Holland and Andre (1995), "Prestige Ratings of High School Extracurricular Activities." Suitor and Reavis (1995), "Football, Fast Cars, and Cheerleading," found that in the period 1979–89 the prestige of cheerleading had declined, but they did not have a nationally representative sample and it is likely that this varies by region and school. It appears that as cheerleaders have lost their traditional prestige as the "cool" and "hot" girls, there have been efforts to transform this activity into a sport or performance activity. Hence, in many schools cheerleaders execute rather complicated gymnastic and dance routines and are selected not only for good looks and "personality," but for skill in these activities.

5. SP235.

6. See Merten (1996b), "Burnout as Cheerleader," for an account of the role of cheerleaders and pep squads in a Midwestern junior high school and what happens when a low status burnout becomes a cheerleader.

7. SP98.

8. See Merten (1996b), "Burnout as Cheerleader," 56–58.

9. SP37.

10. Less information will be provided about the geographical location of Catholic and private schools since this might make it possible to identify the specific school being described.

11. SP230.

12. SP175.

13. See Kinney (1999), "'Headbangers' to 'Hippies.'"

14. As we shall see, there are both continuities and differences between schools in the particular mix and prevalence of various crowds. For studies of the prevalence, characteristics, and overlap of various crowds, see Youniss, McClellan, and Strouse (1994), "We're Popular, but We're Not Snobs," and Brown, Mory, and Kinney (1994), "Adolescent Crowds in a Relational Perspective."

15. The common noun referring to "a straight tool for measuring or drawing" is usually spelled "straightedge," but the websites and other references to these groups usually use "straight-edge." The name "straight-edge" and the original inspiration for the movement come from the song by that name recorded by the "hardcore" punk band Minor Threat in the early 1980s. The movement was originally associated with this type of music, though many now prefer other types of music as well. Sometimes there are disputes over whether being a straight-edge is primarily a matter of loyalty to a particular kind of music or whether it is primarily a commitment to particular ethical norms. (This is reminiscent of debates within religious groups over the relative importance of proper ritual and moral rules.) The symbol of straight-edgers is usually a black **X**, which they mark on various things, including their bodies. A common variation on this symbol is sXe. Another symbol is some version of XdrugXfreeX. The symbol probably comes from the **X** that is often stamped on the hand of someone too young to buy liquor when they go to dance clubs or bars (FW26). Straight-edgers are often relatively identifiable because of this symbolism and their strong sense of group solidarity. At the same time they claim to value individual thought, and in many respects do. This personal innovativeness must, however, be within the context of their broad world-view. They look with great disdain upon those who copy their style without embracing their values. Some students didn't like the straight-edge group because they were perceived to have a "holier-than-thou" mentality (FW33). In some areas they have a reputation for getting into fights with other groups.

16. SP304.

17. SP75.

18. It is possible that in some urban schools some of these gangs may have relatively high status, but these schools are underrepresented in our data. See Horowitz (1983), *Honor and the American Dream*, and Rathbone (1998), *On the Outside Looking In.*

19. Shrum and Cheek (1987), "Social Structure During the School Years."

20. SP206, SP166.

21. SP51.

22. SP106.

23. SP45.

24. My research is primarily interested in the role of adolescent status structures in schools and the broader society, not in how to get particular students to avoid one group or join another. Hence, I do not address the question of why particular students join particular crowds or groups. Past research suggests that there is both self-selection and mutual influence operating. That is, students with certain characteristics tend to seek each other out and then tend to reinforce and accentuate their common attributes. For example, why a group regularly uses drugs is partly a function of the students who are inclined in that direction joining together in a group and partly a function of mutual influence. See, for example, Kandel (1978), "On Variations in Adolescent Subcultures." See Brown (1990), "Peer Groups and Peer Cultures," for a discussion of the limits of our knowledge about this matter.

25. This is not to say that the importance of these factors is the same in all social settings, age groups, or periods. Tedesco and Gaier (1988), "Friendship Bonds in Adolescence," found that in choosing friends the importance of physical characteristics and achievement declined relative to interpersonal qualities as the students matured. Suitor and Reavis (1995), "Football, Fast Cars, and Cheerleading," comparing college students who had graduated between 1979 and 1982 with those who had graduated in 1988–89 found that there had been very little change in the significance of these factors in determining peer status. They did, however, find that in the later time period women received more respect for athletic achievement. We will consider these factors again when we look at pluralistic high schools in chapters five and six.

26. SP246.

27. SP253.

28. SP215.

29. SP215. The relationship between appearance and status begins in childhood. See Kennedy (1990), "Determinants of Peer Social Status," for an interesting analysis of the link between appearance and status for children in grades 2 through 8.

30. The terms "field observer," "fieldworker," and "observer" are used as synonyms in this book.

31. FW6.

32. Eder and Kinney (1995), "The Effect of Extracurricular Activities on Adolescents' Popularity," using both qualitative and quantitative data, found that this was the case for younger students in the 6th through 8th grades in middle schools.

33. SP277.

34. Goldberg and Chandler (1989), "The Role of Athletics"; Crosnoe (2001), "Athletes in High School."

35. See Eder and Kinney (1995), "The Effect of Extracurricular Activities on Adolescents' Popularity," for a more detailed analysis of the gender differences in middle schools. See Crosnoe (2001), "Athletes in High School," for how the effect of participating in athletics varies by gender with respect to grades and alcohol use. See Holland and Andre (1995), "Prestige Ratings of High School Extracurricular Activities," for analyses of how the status of students, especially that of women, is affected by the type of sport they are participating in and whether it is considered "sex appropriate."

36. SP277.

37. FW6.

38. SP125.

39. SP220.

40. SP304.

41. SP253.

42. SP205.

43. SP137.

44. SP254.

45. SP260.

46. SP142.

47. The Philadelphia student (SP254) reports that "JAPS" are on top of the status hierarchy and "the most well-liked clique ... What this high status truly came down to, however, was outward appearance."

48. SP224.

49. SP176.

50. SP277.

51. FW11.

52. SP106.

53. SP289.

54. Jackets are not, of course, an inherited characteristic, though there is probably some tendency for a strong commitment to athletic achievement to be passed on from parents to children.

55. SP215.

56. SP191.

57. SP235.

58. SP51.

59. SP137.

60. See Sanford and Eder (1984), "Adolescent Humor During Peer Interaction," for a study of humor in a middle school. They identify four types of humor: memorized jokes, funny stories, practical jokes, and humorous behavior. While we did not systematically record or code behavior by these categories, our data seem to indicate that funny stories are a more common form of humor among older adolescents and memorized jokes, etc., decline in significance.

61. Durkheim (1965), *The Elementary Forms of Religious Life.*

62. SP235.

63. SP177.

64. SP110.

65. SP25.

66. SP169.

67. SP87.

68. This is true since the development of mass media, but this was probably less the case in pre-modern societies.

69. For discussions of the degree to which music both unites and divides youth, as well as essays focusing on particular styles of music, see the essays in Epstein (1994), *Adolescents and Their Music,* particularly those by Berry, Gaines, Kotarba, Mohan, and Weinstein. For an interesting article that predicts musical preferences from people's location in a multidimensional social space, see Mark (1998), "Birds of a Feather Sing Together." While Mark's data show that age is the most powerful social predictor of musical preference, his data only deals with those over 18 years of age and therefore is not directly relevant to explaining the preferences of teenagers. Also see Best and Kellner (1997–99), "Rap."

70. These activities, which bring people together, center their attention, and involve emotion, are what Collins's (1988), *Sociology of Marriage and Family,* theory of interaction ritual focuses upon.

71. SP146.

72. SP300.

73. SP223.

74. Even for married couples with children under 18, the 1996 median income was $51,950. Whatever statistic is used to measure family resources, providing an adolescent with a "cool car" requires a substantial portion of most families' income. Source: U.S. Bureau of the Census 2000.

75. SP306.

76. SP220.

77. SP261.

78. I try to avoid language that uses male terms to describe populations that contain men and women. I did not find a suitable substitute for "freshman," "freshmen," and "upperclass-men," especially since the students themselves frequently use these terms. I tried using first-year, second-year, etc., but this created both awkward and confusing descriptions, given that these were not terms used by the informants themselves. The issue is further complicated by the fact that a "fresh person" means something quite different than a "freshman." A similar problem emerges in trying to use "upper-class students," which usually refers to their socioeconomic status rather than their year in school.

79. FW17.

80. FW17.

81. SP176.

82. SP94.

83. SP15.

84. SP169.

85. Cox, Cox, and Moschis (1990), "When Consumer Behavior Goes Bad."

86. MacCoun and Reuter (1992), "Are the Wages of Sin $30 an Hour?"; Vickerman and Philippe (1991), "Youth and Crime in an Inner City Neighborhood."

87. 38.

88. SP294. See Kinney (1993), "Nerds to Normals," 33, for similar findings.

89. SP43.

90. SP96.

91. Here are some additional examples: A student who attended one of the prestigious schools in suburban Washington comments, "If someone tried too hard in school or cared too much about grades they were outcast to the nerd groups. It was alright … to be smart, as long as they gave off an air of not having to try to get good grades" (SP215). A girl from a private Christian school in Tennessee reports: "There was a constant desire to appear to be getting away with something or pulling one over on the authorities … When one of the boys was kicked out of the school [at the end of his freshman year] his locker was made a 'shrine' in which people placed pictures and supportive notes. His rebellion was so greatly respected that he continued to have high status when he returned our senior year" (SP128). A girl who attended one of the nation's most prestigious church-related prep schools said, "There were also those who were just good enough [to] get away with breaking the rules without anyone knowing, and they were especially high status" (SP40). For most middle-class students the trick is to demonstrate resistance without getting into serious trouble or becoming defined as a "loser" or "screwup." As Jay Mathew's (1998), *Class Struggle*, makes clear, even many of the students in excellent schools often engage in behaviors that trouble or scandalize adults.

92. As Danesi (1994), *Cool*, 40, notes: "Coolness can be said to form a continuum, which ranges from an extreme form of 'slack coolness' at one end to an extreme form of 'rough coolness' at the other. Punk rockers … would be located at the rough end, exemplifying aggressive behavior, vulgar language, and so forth. Most teens, however, develop an average, or midcontinuum, form of coolness."

93. Willis (1977), *Learning to Labour*; Eckert (1989), *Jocks and Burnouts*; MacLeod (1995), *Ain't No Makin' It*; Rathbone (1998), *On the Outside Looking In*; Finnegan (1998), *Cold New World*.

94. FW24.

95. FW14.

96. Weber (1958), *The Protestant Ethic*.

CHAPTER 4

1. FW32.
2. FW5.
3. SP253.
4. SP215.
5. FW25.
6. FW25.
7. A girl who attended a Protestant school recounts: "One of my childhood friends … had been ridiculed in middle school and was largely ignored in high school. She was obsessively concerned with keeping me and her two other best friends close. If we didn't go to the mall or the movies every weekend she worried that I was 'social climbing.' She once accused me of deliberately avoiding eye contact with her in the hall, a sure sign that I was ashamed of our association" (SP128).
8. SP43.
9. SP235.
10. SP64.
11. SP15.
12. SP219.
13. SP216.
14. SP253.
15. Bettis (1996a), "Urban Students, Liminality, and the Postindustrial Context," 119.
16. Youniss, McClellan, and Strouse (1994), "We're Popular, but We're Not Snobs."
17. SP220.
18. Foley (1990), *Learning Capitalist Culture*, 33.
19. SP220.
20. SP279.
21. FW23.
22. SP125.
23. FW17.
24. FW25.
25. See Laursen (1996), "Closeness and Conflict in Adolescent Peer Relationships," for a developmental account—based on a version of exchange theory—of the changing nature of interdependence and conflict in adolescent friendships.
26. Merten (1996a), "Going-With." Merten studied junior high school students and from his account it is clear that most of these students have very weak emotional attachments. This is probably less the case for high school students, but even in this latter context, dating seems to be about social status as much as it is about emotional intimacy.
27. A more general issue is exactly what "dating" means. Furman and Wehner (1994), "Romantic Use," have suggested a typology of different types of relationships: simple interchanges, casual dating, stable relationships, and committed relationships. Moreover, they found that the prevalence of these varies across schools. I strongly suspect that this is related to the nature of the status structure, but my own data about dating are not detailed enough to identify such variations across schools.
28. SP215.
29. SP110.
30. FW26.
31. SP42.
32. FW26.
33. FW29.
34. FW6.
35. FW4.

36. While such inappropriate intimacy is rarely acted out behaviorally, it is a common form of verbal insult or way of describing a perceived hostile act. When someone is making demands or engaging in behavior deemed inappropriate, they are told to "piss off," or the response may even be, "piss on you." Interestingly, it is rare to even threaten defecation by saying something like "shit on you." It is, however, common to describe thoughtless and hostile treatment as having been "shit on." Apparently, defecation is perceived as such a hostile act that it is usually attributed to others rather than used as a threat. The broader theoretical point is that bodily functions that involve substances crossing the boundary of the body—eating, sex, urination, defecation—are all used in various ways to symbolize intimacy. Wanted expressions of intimacy increase solidarity. Conversely, inappropriate and unwanted acts or symbols of intimacy are powerful expressions of hostility. Symbols of "playful" hostility must be carefully chosen so as to symbolize some, but not too much, violation.

37. FW27.

38. Hersch (1998), *A Tribe Apart*, 124.

39. See Appendix II.

40. SP25.

41. FW11.

42. This entire section is heavily indebted to Merten (1999), "Enculturation into Secrecy Among Junior High Girls." While his work focuses on junior high girls, there are many similarities. On theoretical grounds I would predict that secrecy would be especially important to junior high girls since associations are so key to their status and that the importance of secrecy declines as other forms of intimacy such as dating and partying become more common.

43. There is a considerable literature on rumors as an aspect of collective behavior such as riots and panics, but this is beyond the scope of this inquiry. My focus is on more intimate relationships in the context of status groups.

44. FW13.

45. FW11.

46. FW32.

47. FW23.

48. SP294.

49. SP15.

50. See Best (2000), *Prom Night*.

51. While participation in sports does seem to increase social integration of minority students, previous research indicates that it does not tend to improve academic performance of these students. See Melnick, Sabo, and Nanfossen (1992), "Educational Effects of Interscholastic Athletic Participation on African–American and Hispanic Youth."

52. SP20.

53. SP45.

54. SP261.

55. SP137.

56. SP226.

57. SP201.

58. SP260, SP117.

59. SP28.

60. SP186.

61. SP74.

62. SP192.

63. I use the term "sex" rather than "gender" deliberately, because segregation is literally linked to the presence or absence of male or female genitalia, not to social or personal identities. Obviously, mixed-sex groups offer the opportunity for both heterosexual and homosexual relationships.

64. The common usage of homophobic language when referring to bands and drama groups is, of course, another aspect of status manipulation. Few students actually think most of the members of these groups are homosexual. Rather, it is a technique to justify denigrating these groups by associating them with a category that is assumed to have even lower status. The theory would predict that if homophobic language becomes less acceptable in high schools, the negative labeling of lower-status groups would take other forms. Obviously, the theory of status relationships could be used to analyze the status of homosexuals vis-à-vis heterosexuals in high schools, but this would be a large project in itself Given the widespread prejudice against homosexuals, the nature of our data collection techniques did not provide the kind of information that would be needed for such an analysis.

65. Students may begin lessons because of encouragement or pressures from parents, but if they continue the activity for an extended period it is usually because they find it gratifying.

66. This is a particular form of what sociologists have called "boundary work." For a discussion of this concept, see Appendix I.

67. This is referred to as the degree of physical co-presence of other people. It is unclear to what extent new forms of media, such as teleconferences, will reduce the significance of literal physical co-presence.

68. SP13.

69. SP93.

70. SP93.

71. SP235.

CHAPTER FIVE

1. FW24.

2. SP215.

3. Touchstone Pictures, 1987, starring Patrick Dempsey and Amanda Peterson, directed by Steve Rash.

4. SP261.

5. SP43.

6. SP253.

7. SP304.

8. SP149.

9. SP278.

10. One longitudinal study found that between the 7th grade and the 12th grade, more than 50 percent of the students changed crowds, though this may or may not be representative of most schools. Cited in Brown, Mory, and Kinney (1994), "Casting Adolescent Crowds in a Relational Perspective," 161. The data collected at two points in time by Franzoi and his colleagues (1994), "Two Social Worlds," indicates that there is very low downward mobility out of the highest groups and very little upward mobility out of the lowest groups, but considerable mobility between the middle groups and those above and below. The findings from Franzoi et al. are, however, built upon a sociometric measure of status that divides groups into the categories of popular, controversial, average, neglected, and rejected. It is doubtful, however, that the findings are solely due to this measure. The pattern that is reported roughly parallels what we know about occupational mobility in modern societies. See David L. Featherman and Robert M. Hauser (1978), "A Refined Model of Occupational Mobility," chap. 4. The rates of entry and exit to the top and bottom are even lower in high school status structures, which are rooted in inter-personal status differences and less tied to income and political power. This is what the theory of status relations would lead us to expect.

11. SP37.

12. In addition to the language often associated with symbolic interactionism, which often focuses on the social construction and interpretation of social and personal identities, most introductory

psychology textbooks have discussions of the "primacy effect," and other psychological mechanisms that bias actors' cognitions, attitudes, and behaviors. See, for example, Wortman, Loftus, and Weaver, III (1997), *Psychology*. These are probably some of the psychological and cognitive mechanisms that operate in the processes described by reproduction theory that reinforce restricted social mobility. I do not, however, mean to suggest that the social expectations or self-image of lower status students' personal identities are the key source of the low rates of mobility that could be remedied by various techniques aimed at increasing self-esteem.

13. SP57.

14. SP213.

15. SP213.

16. Danesi (1994), *Cool*, 49.

17. SP253.

18. SP220.

19. FW5.

20. SP128.

21. SP128.

22. SP128.

23. SP213.

24. SP277.

25. SP289.

26. SP169.

27. FW5.

28. SP170.

29. The most extensive studies of bullying have been carried out by Olweus (1993), *Bullying at School*, in Norway. He found that bullying is more common among girls than boys and that it declines with the age of the student. Between 5 and 6 percent of students in grades 7–9 reported being bullied, but nearly 12 percent of boys in secondary school reported that they engaged in bullying others. There was a clear tendency for smaller, weaker, and shy students to be victims. While Olweus did not find that academic competition led to bullying, he did not specifically look at competition for informal peer status. With respect to girls, see Simmons (2002), *Odd Girl Out*, and the journalistic account by Talbot (2002), "Mean Girls and the New Movement to 'Tame Them.'"

30. Adler and Adler's (1998), *Peer Power*, an account of behavior in the preadolescent years, portrays behavior that seems to be at least as mean and cruel as that characteristic of adolescents. It is clear from their account that most of this is rooted in the struggle for status and social relationships. What appears to be different is that the norms of "niceness"—which make the most blatant forms of nastiness counterproductive—are less developed prior to secondary school. This may well be due to the fact that the cliques and crowds are much more gender segregated than in high school.

31. See Eder and Kinney (1995), "Effect of Extracurricular Activities on Adolescents' Popularity," and Eder et al. (1995), *School Talk*, esp. chap. 4, for a discussion of the ambiguous feelings students have about those who are popular.

32. Merten (1997), "The Meaning of Meanness," has identified similar processes among junior high school girls and has discussed these in terms of "the meaning of meanness." See also Eder et al. discussion of "targeting the low end of the hierarchy" in (1995), "Effect of Extracurricular Activities on Adolescents' Popularity," 49–54. My discussion is certainly indebted to their work.

33. Allport defines scapegoating Allport (1948), *ABC's of Scapegoating*, as "a phenomenon wherein some of the aggressive energies of a person or a group are focused upon another individual, group, or object; the amount of aggression and blame being either partly or wholly unwarranted." See also Allport (1954), esp. chap. 15, "Choice of Scapegoats."

34. While scapegoating is often directed toward economic or political competitors, it is nearly always expressed in terms of status considerations. The discrimination against blacks by white workers

is usually justified in terms of the moral failings of blacks: They are characterized as lazy, dirty, immoral, unreliable, etc.

35. Children in many less developed countries who are physically deformed are severely teased and harassed. An organization named Operation Smile is specifically devoted to providing reconstructive surgery to children in such situations primarily because of the intense harassment they suffer from peers. Apparently this tendency of children and adolescents to attack the vulnerable is extremely widespread—cutting across cultures and historical periods. This does not mean that it is impossible to reduce the rates of such behavior.

36. Hollingshead (1975), *Elmtown's Youth*, 178.

37. Franzoi, Davis, and Vasquez-Suson (1994), "Two Social Worlds."

38. FW23.

39. Over the last quarter century, there has been a strong movement to integrate students with various kinds of mental and physical disabilities into the general school population. The intent, of course, is to reduce their isolation and sense of being "other." For a moving portrayal of the need to treat the mentally handicapped as "normal" human beings, see Edgerton (1993), *The Cloak of Competence*.

Given adolescents' (1) acute status consciousness, (2) judgmental attitudes toward most kinds of nonconformity, and (3) reluctance to associate with anyone of lower status, it is at least debatable whether this move toward inclusion of "special education" students in comprehensive high schools has increased or decreased the negative stigmatization they experience. As the above description indicates, such students can be aggressive in seeking attention and contribute to some of the very stereotypes that their integration with the general school population was intended to overcome. These comments are not intended to argue for the isolation of such students, but rather to point to the very mixed consequences of such policies—given the current structure of most high schools.

40. While my discussion focuses on different issues, it is highly indebted to Eder and Enke's (1991), "Structure of Gossip." Because we were not allowed to record conversations, I did not attempt to replicate or extend their approach.

41. FW21.

42. Guernsey (2003), "High School Confidential, Online."

43. Kinney (1993), "Nerds to Normals."

44. SP98.

45. FW17.

46. It is usually assumed that as adolescents mature, they are less insecure about their own personal identity, and hence less judgmental of others and less concerned about being exclusively identified with the "right" social group. It seems likely that this is the case. See Kinney (1993), "Nerds to Normals." This may be less important than is assumed. Brown, Eicher, and Petries (1986), "The Importance of Peer Group Affiliation in Adolescence," studied variation in attitudes toward crowd membership by age and gender. They found that the importance of the crowd declined as the students aged. However, the importance of crowd affiliation was *not* related to the students' sense of identity, but was related to their willingness to conform and their position in the crowd. This may suggest that social factors may have more impact on the importance of crowd affiliation than psychological attributes, though this is a very tentative hypothesis.

47. SP125.

48. FW7 and SP197.

49. Schwartz (1981), "Supporting or Subverting Learning."

50. SP149. Collins's (1988), *Sociology of Marriage and Family* theory of interaction ritual is again relevant here.

CHAPTER SIX

1. FW34.

2. FW23.

3. Lightfoot (1983), *The Good High School*, chap. 2; Peshkin (1991), *The Color of Strangers, The Color of Friends*; Kinney (1993), "From Nerds to Normals"; Bettis (1996a), "Urban Students, Liminality, and the Postindustrial Context."

4. The primarily quantitative work by Bradford Brown and his various colleagues on peer status systems has been especially influential. See Brown (1990), "Peer Groups and Peer Cultures"; Brown et al. (1986), "The Importance of Peer Group Affiliation in Adolescence"; Brown et al. (1993), "Parenting Practices and Peer Group Affiliations," and Clasen and Brown (1985), "The Multidimensionality of Peer Pressure in Adolescence." This impressive work moves substantially toward a more multi-faceted understanding of adolescent culture and its complex influence on the behavior of adolescents. Specifically, it argues that there are multiple adolescent peer cultures. Nonetheless, even the relatively recent work conceptualizes these different "crowds within a primarily hierarchical framework. Students are usually classified in terms of six groups (populars, jocks, brains, normals, druggies, and outcasts)." Though this conceptual scheme includes the bulk of students, approximately 30 percent fall outside these categories." See Brown et al. (1993), "Parenting Practices and Peer Group Affiliations," 470–472. Brown and his colleagues do not assume that the six groups can be unequivocally ranked on a single ordinal scale, or that individuals can be unambiguously assigned to one category or the other. They do, however, assume a form of hierarchy with the "leading crowd" of "populars" and "jocks" toward the top, the "druggies," "burnouts," "greasers," etc. toward the bottom, and others such as "normals" and "brains" some place in between.

5. Pescosolido and Rubin (2000), "The Web of Group Affiliations Revisited."

6. In previous literature, the term *pluralism* refers to a large set of loosely connected concepts. At best their interconnection involves a Wittgenstein-type family resemblance rather than a rigorous interrelated set of formal concepts or a distinct historical tradition. One tradition, beginning with Tocqueville and carried on by many political scientists, focuses on political pluralism and especially the presence of multiple political parties and pressure groups in the context of a democratic polity. A closely related tradition initiated by Robert Dahl (1961), *Who Governs?*, proposes pluralism as an alternative to the notions of ruling classes or power elites that had been posited by Floyd Hunter (1963), *Community Power Structure*, C. Wright Mills (1956), *The Power Elite*, and William Domhoff (1998), *Who Rules America?* A third strand is associated with Isaiah Berlin (2000), *The Power of Ideas*, and other philosophers and historians of ideas; this pluralism is often posed as an alternative to totalitarian regimes of the twentieth century. A fourth tradition that focuses more directly on race and ethnicity begins with J. H. Boeke (1953), *Economics and Economic Policy of Dual Societies*, J. S. Furnivall (1941) *Progress and Welfare in Southeast Asia*, and M. G. Smith (1965), *The Plural Society in British West Indies*. All of these observers draw attention to the fact that some nation-states are composed of multiple ethnic communities that are often integrated by little more than market relationships or coercive state power, rather than common values. A fifth tradition focuses on religious pluralism and on church–state relations as well as relationships between different religious communities, for example the recent work of Richard Wentz (1998), *The Culture of Religious Pluralism*, and Charles Lippy (2000), *Pluralism Comes of Age*. I draw on elements of these traditions to apply the notion of pluralism to the structure of student relationships in a high school. The two basic notions implied in our use of the concept are (1) there are identifiable groups, and (2) there is no clear hierarchy. There may or may not be various degrees of equality, mutual respect, and social peace between the groups. I have avoided the term *multicultural* because it frequently refers to the nature of the curriculum. A school can be ethnically homogeneous and have a multicultural curriculum, and vice versa. I am not hostile to the term or concept, but for the purposes at hand, it is less useful than "pluralism."

7. I am aware that this is in contrast to M. G. Smith's (1965), *The Plural Society in British West Indies*, influential definition of plural society, which emphasizes the dominance of one group over others. Whatever the merits of Smith's conceptualization for studying multiethnic developing societies, for the purposes at hand it would be misleading to include dominance as part of the definition of pluralism. Rather, the degree to which one group dominates another should be a variable.

8. *Encarta Dictionary* (1999).

9. "Race," "black," "white," etc., are of course socially and historically constructed categories, as are the perceptions of what is biologically inherited, what is culturally inherited, and what is a matter of "choice." When our ethnographic descriptions refer to an individual as "white" or "black," we mean that there is a high probability of them being classified as "black" (or "white") by strangers or casual acquaintances in the course of routine interactions.

10. The earlier discussion is on pp. 31 and 43. See Weber (1968), *Economy and Society*, chapter IX, section 6, and also Milner (1994), *Status and Sacredness*.

11. See Thorne (1993), *Gender Play*, for a good discussion of "border work" between boys and girls in elementary school. In many large high schools, the status group boundaries are less flexible and context-specific than is the case for gender boundaries in elementary schools.

12. Of course, disguising one's ethnic or racial background and "passing" does occur, but this is not the typical experience, especially when "race" is involved.

13. My definition of "relatively progressive" is rooted in the history of race and gender in local politics. Blacks are a quarter of the population. City council members are elected at large rather than by precincts. Mayors are elected by the city council. In the last thirty years, women have been elected to the council about as often as men have and there have nearly always been one or more black members on a six-member city council. Blacks have served as mayor three times and women have served as mayor at least four times. During the period of the fieldwork one of the representatives to the state legislature from an overwhelmingly white district was black. This is not, of course, to say that there is racial or gender equality or justice.

14. U.S. Census Bureau data reveals that the city in which WWHS resides has a median household money income of slightly under $28,000 as of 1993, and 24 percent (9,630) of the city's population is black as of 1996, the year before our study. In 1989 there were slightly over 9,000 people below the poverty line and approximately 6,300 were white and 2,300 black. There were slightly less than 700 blacks aged 15–19 in 1996, slightly more than 100 Asian and Pacific Islanders, and slightly more than 2,000 whites. (I have rounded these figures to protect the identity of the community. These figures give a general sense of the proportions of young people by age, but they do not give an accurate representation of those who are eligible to attend WWHS since some 18- and 19-year-olds have graduated. What the figures do suggest is that whites in WWHS are underrepresented relative to their numbers in the population of the city. This is probably because a number of whites go to private schools or enroll their children in the county school system.) Source: Government Information Sharing Project, Oregon State University; http://govinfo.library.orst.edu/index.html, 4/2/01. While some figures for the 2000 U.S. Census are available, I believe the earlier statistics are more relevant. Like many areas of the U.S., this area underwent considerable economic expansion at the end of the 1990s. However, the economic and demographic experience of this cohort of WWHS students was largely shaped before this economic boom and the 2000 Census. Hence, I used data that was collected before the study period.

15. Segregation is not, of course, unique to WWHS. In Hallinan and Williams's (1989), "Interracial Friendship Choices in Secondary Schools," study of interracial friendship choices based on large national samples of sophomores and seniors they found: "Friendships are eight times more common in sophomore black-black dyads as they are in sophomore black-white dyads. The ratio is slightly higher for black seniors. Whites are six times more likely to be friends with any randomly chosen white as they are with any randomly chosen black," according to Hallinan and Williams (1989), "Interracial Friendship Choices in Secondary Schools," 74. Ianni (1989), *The Search for Structure*, 33, reports that at the urban high school he calls Southside, territories are strictly segregated by race and ethnicity: "[E]ven the restaurant where Josie eats lunch is 'closed' to the white and Chinese students, who go to their own lunch spots to eat." On the other hand, Peshkin (1991), *The Color of Strangers*, describes a multiethnic school in which race and ethnicity play very little role in structuring student friendships including romantic relationships. WWHS falls in between these two cases.

16. FW33.

17. FW25.

18. FW32.

19. FW4.

20. The actual question was: "Some people would say there is quite a bit of segregation at WWHS, but very little open racial conflict. Would you agree with this statement? If so, why do you think this is the case? If you disagree, explain why."

21. FW32.

22. FW7.

23. FW5.

24. FW30.

25. FW2.

26. FW21.

27. FW26.

28. FW26.

29. FW31.

30. In Finnegan's (1999), *Growing Up in a Harder Country*, 253, a female immigrant from Mexico who was living in the Yakima Valley of Washington state declared:

> "What's needed here in *la valle* is something like *la plaza* in Mexico," Rosita declared. "Place where everybody goes to hear music, and says hello, and the men circle around in one direction, and the women walk together in the other direction. That would be much better than this endless cruising in cars!"

31. Visibility within a social context has been an important aspect in the literature on high school status. See for example Coleman (1961), *The Adolescent Society*, 296; Canaan (1987), "Comparative Analysis of American Suburban Middle Class, Middle School and High School Cliques," 392. For a discussion of the relationship between visibility and status, see: "A note on visibility and status," Appendix I.

32. FW6.

33. FW21.

34. FW2.

35. Of course, lower status groups are at times strongly territorial. The most obvious example is the behavior of gangs in defending their "turf." However, in these situations, neither clear pluralism nor clear hierarchy exists. Rather, gangs compete for both status and public territory—precisely because both public respect and private property are scarce. Hence, conflict for control of public areas—streets, parks, clubs, and sometimes bars and eating establishments—is common. Any attempt to encroach on a group's control of such territory is seen as an act of disrespect, and a failure to defend such territory is seen as a loss of honor, according to Horowitz (1983), *Honor and the American Dream*. This is not the situation at WWHS.

36. This difference in relating status to space—circulating versus territory—may also be related to differences in the significance of private property for different subcultures. The families of the privileged, who are mainly white, routinely own their homes and use these as a central status symbol. "Those from lower-class families are much less likely to use home or real estate as a status-marker—because frequently they cannot afford such markers. Rather, displaying highly visible consumer commodities, such as clothes and cars, are a much more viable strategy. More generally, spatial movement has often been associated with those who have high status and those who have low status. Ancient and feudal nobility often traveled widely, especially those interested in expanding and securing their empires. Historical examples of the tendency of lower status groups to circulate include vagabonds, drifters, hobos, gypsies, Okies, beatniks "on the road," and teenagers cruising the main drag (for example, in the movie *American Graffiti*).

37. FW1.

38. FW5.
39. FW14.
40. FW32.
41. FW23.
42. FW32.
43. FW16.
44. FW5.
45. FW32.
46. FW21.
47. FW21.

48. Because this raises important questions about my interpretation of WWHS as an example of pluralism, most of my correspondences with Mae are reproduced below.

Mae wrote:

> … coming from a foreign family, especially West Africans, and even for Bahamians, there is a general tendency to maintain a separation between their identity and that of the black race. We were true "African Americans," Creoles, in a sense, with a culture both American and foreign. I don't think this can be emphasized enough. It was this influence that allowed Melissa and I to make friends with whites more easily, and because I lived in a black neighborhood, I was able to make friends with a limited number of blacks (Maggie, Marsha, Elie). In this way, our table is less an example of what is possible for blacks and whites to be, because we don't truly count ourselves as "black"; we weren't raised in their culture, we have less of a tendency to look to the media to define us, because no "Creoles" of our type are in the media, and lastly many times, we are ostracized from black relations because we don't fit the norm. In this light, it makes sense we were able to defy the norms of "our" macro identities, and make lasting friendships with people of other races.
>
> It could be argued that Sue and Kim grew up in households that lacked those biases as well, making it easier for them to be friends with us, but, I think the reason they and the rest of our white friends were able to become friends with us was because they saw us as approachable individuals, as you mentioned in the book; but though they took a liking to us as individuals, they also saw us as "different" from "other blacks" (an issue with which most members of the non-American black Diaspora would agree, but with which we as 1st generationers would have a bit of a problem).
>
> I think that you are showing the readers that in order for interracial friendships to exist in a racially stratified environment, putting macro identities on the back burner is a must, and that is what we exemplify in your book. In a sense, we are ignoring the big issues of race, and that could be viewed as selfish or noble, negatively or positively.
>
> Perhaps we never discussed serious racial issues because we knew that if we were to, each one of us would have to assume a macro identity as a white, a black, an African, a Bahamian, a mixed girl (Maggie surely is "the whole world"), … we were not courageous enough to do that right way, at that time. Maybe there was no point to discussing it all, but one thing I know is, if we didn't know about each other as individuals, we wouldn't care for each other, and if we didn't ignore what was going on around us, we never would have.

I replied:

> I am sure your emphasis on the significance of the black members of your group coming from Creole backgrounds, which enabled them to "bracket" race issues, is certainly important. But I am not sure that this explains all of the interracial groups that existed. I give a list of examples just before the discussion of your group. While it is doubtful that many of these developed the same level of intimacy and trust that was characteristic of your group, they did persist over time and nobody seemed to care much one way or the other. Is this an accurate observation?

Mae replied:

> I'm making a concession, agreeing with you that there were other groups of interracial friends whose relationships persisted, even though they were not foreign, and generally no one cared.

> However, I'd like to mention that it also seemed these groups were generally of the lower socioeconomic level; it seemed to me they were among the social fringes (like the example you gave about kids making fun of rednecks). So being poor and/or living in the same area makes you friends, and that's the beginning of purer pluralism? Forgive me if I'm asking questions that seemed closed-minded, but I'm really trying to understand how everyone could one day come to respect each other mutually, and though I know that you'd like to present WWHS as coming close to that, and it may look that way from the outside, but to be in it (at least to me) feels like you are passing by ghosts in the hall; they can't feel you, and you can't see them. How do you think we can come to a greater acceptance and attain a mutual desire to deal with each other?

I would simply note, as I did in the main text above, that some of the other interracial groups drew African–American members from relatively middle-class and professional backgrounds.

49. Interview, FW24.

50. For a similar analysis of the effects of a lower class or rural background on the status structure in a middle school, see the discussion of "grits" in Eder and Kinney's (1995), "The Effect of Extracurricular Activities on Adolescents' Popularity," 40–46.

51. FW17; italics added.

52. The second student's full description as recorded in field notes reads:

> I casually asked [Stephanie] if there were many different groups at the school, and she answered quickly in the affirmative. Then she began to name them. Her listed included the preps, goths, yuppies, skaters, rednecks, jocks, freaks, homies, and drifters. She explained to me that the preps were just like the preps at any school where they dress in khaki pants and dressy button down shirts, usually Polo or Tommy Hilfiger, and wore leather shoes or boots rather than sneakers. "The goths," she explained, "always dress in black and like to keep to themselves" … [T]he yuppies [are] a lot like the preps, but on a smaller scale. She said that they dress in Gap, Structure, and Aeropostale clothing, wear Nike sneakers, and generally put a lot of effort into their appearance. The skaters … dress in the baggy jeans, Airwalk sneakers, and other loose-fitting apparel. They tend to be the more rebellious of the students, and tend to have arguments often with the freaks. Next come the rednecks, which she described as the group who listens to country music all the time. The jocks at Woodrow Wilson High School consist mainly of the football players and the basketball team. Stephanie said that, "The majority of the jocks are black, but there are several white individuals who are members of these teams and part of this clique." She further went on to say that the girls who are considered to be jocks are on the field hockey team. In addition, the homies are primarily the black students who dress in Tommy Hilfiger attire, black baggy down jackets, and sport thick gold chains. There are also the freaks who rebel against the established rules of the school, and tend to have the most problems with the remainder of the student body. The freaks frequently have disagreements with the other cliques, especially the jocks and the homies … "Drug use is a problem with a portion of the student body, primarily with the freaks" … She mentioned the drifters, who do not belong solely to one of the above groups, but tend to rotate among several of them. Stephanie went on to tell me that, "The students who are the most popular at this school are the ones who are not afraid to speak their mind. At this school, people like those who are willing to be unique rather than follow the behavior and viewpoints of others" (FW17).

53. It is a variant of "homeboys," which WWHS students considered an out-of-date term. The term is not necessarily pejorative, but neither is it necessarily complimentary.

54. While the term "wigger" was not specifically used in the two descriptions cited here, it was a commonly understood if not widely used term. Students used it more the first semester than the second semester of observations—perhaps reflecting the fact that the fights during the 1996 school year that had involved these students had faded from the collective memory.

55. FW3.

56. FW24.

57. FW26.

58. FW28.

59. FW28.

60. FW28.

61. FW33.

62. FW3.

63. "G-d" is a euphemism for "God damn."

64. FW26.

65. FW33.

66. See Dance (2002), *Tough Fronts*, for a discussion of the subtleties of the concept of "hard" and "hard-core." Her concept of "wannabe hardcore" is very similar to the notion of "pretend hoodlum" that will be mentioned shortly.

67. FW32.

68. Eckert (1989), *Jocks and Burnouts*. Jocks included all students who more or less cooperated with the school authorities and believed in the value of education. Burnouts were those alienated from the educational process and often engaged in various kinds of "deviant behavior."

69. FW34.

70. FW34.

71. FW4.

72. FW8.

73. FW8.

74. While we had confidence in his integrity and good intentions, we were at first concerned that the students he was observing were "putting him on." We kept a close eye on his work and are virtually certain his accounts are basically correct, though undoubtedly at times they are trying to impress or shock him.

75. FW14.

76. FW14.

77. Obviously, it is not possible to be certain about this without much more direct and detailed data than I have. This judgment, however, is parallel with available national data. National surveys since the early 1970s indicate that black females aged 15–19, for example, are significantly more likely to be sexually active (50–65 percent) than white females (25–40 percent) of the same age, though the differences narrowed during the 1980s. Brooks-Gunn and Furstenberg, Jr. (1989), "Adolescent Sexual Behavior," and Smith and Udry (1985), "Coital and Non-Coital Sexual Behaviors of White and Black Adolescents," found that blacks were more sexually active, and that the "preparatory period" of a relationship before first intercourse was shorter.

78. See Fordham (1988), "Racelessness as a Factor in Black Students' School Success," and Fordham and Ogbu (1986), "Black Students' School Success," for a portrayal of the dilemmas faced by black students.

79. FW8.

80. When one of Peshkin's informants claims, "Nobody makes you feel lower than what you have to do. And everybody just seems to socialize," he remarks, "This splurge of adolescent hyperbole overstates, but does not misrepresent the circumstances ..." See (1991), *The Color of Strangers*, 218. I would make a similar claim about our fieldworker's remarks. See also the description of "Wood High School" in Bettis (1996b), "Urban Abstraction in a Central City High School."

81. Such segregation is common. In addition to numerous ethnographic observations, a network study of 9th and 10th graders in five high schools found most cliques were homogeneous with respect to race, gender, and socioeconomic characteristics. See Ennett and Bauman (1996), "Adolescent Social Networks." Social scientists have frequently focused on the significance of the relative size of the groups as an explanation for segregation. Some have argued that numerical parity would do away with tokenism and increase integration, while others have suggested that small minorities were more likely to find friends in other groups. The results of research on this question are ambiguous, though in

schools numerical parity seems to increase certain forms of segregation. See, for example, Hallinan and Smith (1985), "The Effects of Classroom Racial Composition on Student Interracial Friendliness," and Hoffman (1985), "The Effect of Race-Ratio Composition of the Frequency of Organizational Communication." Hallinan and Williams (1989), "Interracial Friendship Choices in Secondary Schools," have pointed to the importance of tracking and other school policies. See also Schofield (1982), *Black and White in School*, Epstein and Karweit (1983), *Friends in School*. Yet, these factors, plus differences in student characteristics, account for only one third of the difference in probability that high school students will develop same-race rather than cross-race friendships. Another answer suggested by Tatum is that blacks need a safe space in which to negotiate identity formation in an unremittingly racist society. See (1999), *"Why Are All the Black Kids Sitting Together in the Cafeteria?"* 73–74.

82. Social scientists should not be too quick to completely dismiss at least some versions of the "natural inequalities" argument. Highly visible attributes, such as gender, age, beauty, and race are used as cognitive simplification mechanisms. That is, there may well be some very common tendency to assume that those who have the same visible physical characteristics are more likely to share similar personal and cultural characteristics. At the very least, it is likely to decrease the probability that you will be "put down" for possessing the particular physical characteristics, such as shortness, blackness, youth, etc. Such stereotypical simplifications may often be wrong, but they probably do increase the probability of finding other like-minded individuals. There is a significant technical literature on stereotyping. For two articles that point to the simplifying cognitive processes that are involved, see Bodenhausen and Lichtenstein (1987), "Social Stereotypes and Information-Processing Strategies," and Macrae, Milne, and Bodenhausen (1994), "Stereotypes as Energy-Saving Devices." Nevertheless, even if these stereotyping processes are part of humans' basic cognitive makeup, it is virtually certain that they are significantly accentuated or retarded by variations in individual socialization and the historical and cultural context.

83. Other social scientists have also pointed to this explanation. Ianni (1989), *The Search for Structure*, 33, in his study of a large interracial urban high school called Southside, notes, "There really is not much open conflict among the various ethnic and racial groups which come together in the school—at least not any more than happens within the various groups themselves. One reason for this, however, seems to be an informal but strictly adhered to pattern of territoriality for each of the various groups ..."

84. This is not to say that they may not have experienced racism from others. See Tuch, Sigelman, and MacDonald (1999), "The Polls—Trends," 124, for a careful analysis of the trends in the attitudes of American high school seniors about race relations. In summary, in the first half of the 1990s the attitudes of whites and blacks toward the other race became more similar, but this greater similarity was due to "blacks expressing less positive feelings about their interracial experiences and decreasing enthusiasm for interracial contact."

85. This process of sanctioning those who act too much like the "other" has been identified by several previous researchers. See Fordham and Ogbu (1986), "Black Students' School Success"; Bettis (1996a), "Urban Students, Liminality, and the Postindustrial Context," 119-121. In their study of black urban youth who had chosen to commute to suburban schools in the St. Louis area, Wells and Crain (1997), *Stepping Over the Color Line*, 194, observe, "The desire to escape the peer pressure of the inner-city adolescent world is one of the most prominent themes in the narratives of black transfer students we interviewed." To point to the tendency of blacks and other minorities toward voluntary self-segregation is not to deny that many whites, both deliberately and unintentionally, continue to engage in behaviors and assumptions that disadvantage and demean minority groups.

86. Peshkin's (1991), *The Color of Strangers*, discussion of "ethnic peace" pays special attention to the consistency and responsiveness of the school's administration. This is probably a necessary condition for peace, but it is not a sufficient condition for what he refers to as "mingling." My hypothesis is that in the present historical circumstances it is very hard to get most students to "mingle" when there are only two subcultures.

87. Schofield's (1982), *Black and White in School*, study of a magnet school emphasizes the importance of differences in academic achievement and the greater aggressiveness of blacks as sources of the segregation in the school she studied. These factors undoubtedly play a role, but it is doubtful that they are as important at WWHS as the situation she describes.

88. Some of the standard works that stress this point include Barth (1970), *Ethnic Groups and Boundaries*; Patterson (1975), "Context and Choice in Ethnic Allegiance"; Nagel (1986), "The Political Construction of Ethnicity"; and Nagel (1996), *American Indian Ethnic Renewal*.

89. I am not arguing that it is inevitable that students perceive these characteristics as inalienable, but only that this tends to be the case in most contemporary high schools. For some examples of students who see the contingency of ethnicity, see Lee (1996), *Unraveling the "Model Minority" Stereotype*.

90. SP224.

91. SP179.

92. SP37.

93. Most of the information and all of the direct quotes in this paragraph come from an article by Emily Wax, "Today's Titans Tackle World Challenges," *The Washington Post*, October 12, 2000.

94. Director: Boaz Yakin; Cast: Denzel Washington, Will Patton, Wood Harris, Ryan Hurst, Donald Faison, Craig Kirkwood, Ethan Suplee, Nicole Ari Parker, Hayden Panettiere (Walt Disney Pictures, 2000).

95. T. C. Williams High School Website http://www.acps.k]2.va.us/tew/index.html, November 2000.

96. SP122.

97. Pluralism is uncommon in lower-level schools, which, among other things, tend to be smaller. Adler and Adler (1998), *Peer Power*, 74, note that in the literature contrasting elementary peer groups with those in high schools, "This diverse differentiation has not been noted at the elementary level, where there is little variety in the types and rankings of groups available; instead, a unidimensional scale exists, with the popular clique located atop a hierarchy of friendship groups that descends in prestige and power." The "traditional" hierarchical high school is a form or extension of this phenomenon.

98. See Milner (1994), *Status and Sacredness*, 35–37, 39–41, for a discussion of how associations, and especially cross-gender associations, are a crucial determinant of status.

99. More accurately, the downward movement of the popular crowd reduces the social distance from at least some other crowds. The rank ordering of crowds and cliques may not change, but, to use a couple of standard imageries, the hierarchy is compressed or the pyramid is flattened.

100. For a thoughtful journalistic account of the complexities of the relationship between race and athletic participation, see Gladwell (1997b), "The Sports Taboo."

101. An aside is appropriate about why the activities of blacks are less multifaceted than whites. While few blacks participate in the non-traditional sports, it is not primarily because they are discouraged from doing so. Black students at WWHS are not reticent to vocalize their complaints about perceived slights or exclusions. We never heard any black students complain that they were discouraged from playing lacrosse, field hockey, or whatever. We do have one report of an African–American violinist saying she wished there were more blacks in the orchestra, but there was no hint that they were discouraged from joining. While interviewing a black teacher, I recorded the following:

> She said the norm is that you take up for your team members no matter what their race or
> background. She claimed that a similar tendency also occurred in band and orchestra. When
> I pressed her about the extent to which this was the case in orchestra, she said that … if there
> was a tendency for privileged kids to be concentrated in the orchestra it wasn't because of the
> [white] orchestra director's intentions or efforts.

This is not to say that the school has done everything it could or should have done to encourage black participation in a greater variety of activities. At this point in WWHS history, however, blacks' concentration in the traditional activities of football, basketball, and cheerleading is due primarily to their own actions. This is not, of course, to deny that a long history of racism may be shaping black students' preferences and choices, nor to suggest that all whites would warmly welcome black students into sports and other activities now dominated by whites. See Messner (1989), "Masculinities and Athletic Careers," for an analysis that points out how the structural limitations faced by black young men shape their preoccupation with athletics, even though it is clear that very few will benefit from this in the long run. It is highly likely that the high visibility of black football and basketball players in the national media also shapes students' preferences. This is gradually changing as professional black athletes come to prominence in such sports as golf and tennis, but these sports are not yet of great interest to most black teenagers. It is, however, important not to overemphasize the importance of either discrimination by whites or the preferences and choices of blacks—of simply blaming an exploiter or blaming the victim. Some cultural sociologists attempt to transcend this dilemma by emphasizing the importance of the cultural repertoires or scripts that are available to the various actors, see Lamont (1999): xi. Not only must there be new educational and economic opportunities, but the cultural tools and skills needed to actualize these opportunities must be neither too restrictive nor unavailable. While this adds a level of complexity and sophistication to the problem, it does not solve the issue of the relationship between structure and agency. Scripts are created—not simply found or inherited—and actors give their own interpretations to their role—not simply read their lines. Therefore, while the metaphors of and repertoires and scripts can be useful, it is not a substitute for further data and analysis.

102. Kinney (1993), "Nerds to Normals."

103. "Suburban high schools in 'good neighborhoods' are superior to center-city schools"—this is a common assumption in the U.S. and operated in this community at the time of our fieldwork. The students' awareness of the lower status of their school relative to others in the area may well increase solidarity and contribute to pluralism. Two other studies have found relatively egalitarian status structures in schools that were relatively low in status compared to other schools in their area. See Bettis (1996a), "Urban Students, Liminality, and the Postindustrial Context"; Peshkin (1991), *The Color of Strangers*.

CHAPTER SEVEN

1. FW35.

2. The concept of the military academy should not be taken too literally. Rather I am looking at certain features of social organization that are especially prominent in such organizations, rather than all of the features that are characteristic of such schools. For a useful, though rather abstract sociological analysis of military schools contrasted with Quaker boarding schools, see Hays (1994), *Practicing Virtues at Quaker and Military Boarding Schools*.

3. SP119.

4. SP125.

5. In contrast to this Pennsylvania school, another student account reports that in her academically oriented Catholic school academic tracks did not seem to have much effect on informal status and clique formation. Perhaps this difference is due to the fact that the Catholic school was restricted to those who had done well academically and hence the differences in tracks had less psychological and social significance. Research by Kubitschek and Hallinan (1998), "Tracking and Students' Friendships," indicates that who students are friends with is shaped by their academic tracks and that they seldom question their assignment to a particular track. Their analysis, however, is based on a national sample of sophomores in 1980. While it is hard to imagine that tracking would not have some effect, the extent of this effect may be significantly affected by the institutional and historical context. Lucas (2001), "Effectively Maintained Inequality," has argued that there has been a fundamental change in the form of tracking since the early 1980s. Instead of either being in or out of a particular track, students now choose different levels of difficulty for a given subject or course, for example, remedial, regular, and honors freshman mathematics. They may be in remedial math, but in honors history,

and regular English. While tracking still contributes to the reproduction of inequality, the process and the outcome are much more complex than previously thought.

6. SP197.

7. Goffman (1961), *Asylums*.

8. Cookson and Persell (1985), *Preparing for Power*.

9. SP206.

10. SP206.

11. SP206.

12. Cookson and Persell (1985), *Preparing for Power*. Cookson and Persell report that the amount of sex at boarding schools is "impossible to determine." Some former students claim it was common, others that "almost nobody did it. One suspects that sexual behavior varies by school, class, and clique.... Sexual frustration is common.... Masturbation ... seems to be the archetypical private solution ... but in boarding schools even this lonely activity can become part of a group effort. Lacking privacy and driven by sexual desire, mutual masturbation is not unknown at elite schools—'round-pounds' were a tradition at a number of former all-boys schools. This kind of sharing undoubtedly creates a quality of loyalty that is deeper than what verbal pledges of solidarity alone can provide" (142–143).

13. This overstates the matter a bit—no two people have the identical experiences—but there is a meaningful difference between sharing experiences and having similar experiences.

14. See Kingston and Lewis (1990), *High-Status Track: Studies of Elite Schools*, for an analysis of the role that elite preparatory schools play in relationship to elite colleges, graduate schools, and later life-chances.

15. SP289.

16. SP112.

17. This report is not from a "nerd" or "weirdo," but from a "jock" who was on both the football and basketball teams until he was virtually forced to choose one or the other.

18. 1975 [1949].

19. SP267.

20. The argument here focuses on the effect of parental social position on the child's social position in the peer status hierarchy within the school and local community. This is not the same question as whether parents' social position affects the child's educational accomplishments or social position when they become adults. (This is, of course, an issue that "reproduction theory" focuses on.) Though I know of no systematic quantitative data, it seems likely that the students' peer status at school is less closely linked to parents' status in contemporary suburban and urban schools than it was in the small town studied by Hollingshead.

21. Moreover, a re-analysis by Cohen (1979) of data collected by Hollingshead (1975) and Coleman (1961) shows that the situation in Elmtown itself changed between the 1940s and the 1950s, with the significance of parents' status having less effect on a student's status and peer relationships.

22. Lareau (2000) focuses largely on how parents influence the treatment of their children by teachers, vis-à-vis their academic work. Here I am focusing on the relatively direct effects of parental status on peer status and parental influence on opportunities to participate in extracurricular activities.

23. SP112.

24. SP45.

25. SP240.

26. SP289.

27. SP289.

28. A "bubba" is defined as "stereotyped Southern man: a term referring to a stereotype of rural Caucasian Southern men as uneducated and socially unadvanced (*slang, sometimes humorous, sometimes used as an insult*)." *Encarta World English Dictionary*. Microsoft, 2000. The students who used this term may have been making an allusion to the fisherman character in the movie *Forrest Gump*.

29. SP213.

30. There is a large body of literature on deviance and crime that stresses the importance of labeling and the literature on status generalization is also relevant, see Webster and Foschi (1988), *Status Generalization*.

31. SP289.

32. SP289.

33. SP30.

34. SP19.

35. In the last half of the 1990s there were about 150 DODD schools with a total enrollment of 80,000 plus. About 10 percent of these were in grades 9–12. In the same period there were about seventy DDESS schools enrolling 30,000 plus students and again about 10 percent of these were in grades 9–12. Source: Department of Defense Website, http://www.odedodea.edu/, October 10, 2000.

36. SP227.

37. SP298.

38. Many spouses probably have jobs that supplement family income. It would be very rare, however, for enlisted personnel to have spouses with incomes so high that their lifestyle would match that of officers.

39. SP227.

40. SP298.

41. SP298.

42. The student reports:

> "There were those such as myself, who had friends of different ethnicities. However, these were
> the types of friendships that solely existed inside the walls of the school. Different races simply
> did not hang out with each other … Harsh words were exchanged daily between members of
> the different "groups." [In the ninth grade] the other three whites and myself all sat together
> on one side of the room not by choice, but by a strange coincidence of alphabetical order …
> [W]e tended to be singled out for ridicule … I have a tendency to be friends with everyone …
> and therefore had few racial problems. The other three white students found themselves dealing
> daily with racial slurs and people trying to pick racial fights … (SP298).

43. While the identity of these specific schools can be protected, the identity of the Department of Defense and its school system cannot. About 70 percent of the students in Defense Department schools are in overseas schools usually associated with fairly large American bases. In contrast, the two accounts I have are from bases in the United States and are relatively small schools—one had only 170 students in the high school. I was concerned not to generalize about the entire system on the basis of two cases. Consequently, I posted an earlier draft of this description on several websites that were designed to keep alumni of these Defense Department schools in contact with one another. I received seventeen responses. The reactions were highly variable ranging from general agreement with the account to outrage at my gross misrepresentation of these schools. The following messages indicate the range of responses: "I am of the opinion that the written material is not factual at all. The experience I had was nothing like what was described. I went to a DODD School. Pete." "Dear Sir: I was recently forwarded your letter. As a former military/diplo-brat, I feel that I can speak with some authority on this topic. For the most part, it [Milner's description] was extremely accurate. However, in the schools I went to, race wasn't really a factor … Regards, K. [last name]." There seemed to be a significant difference in the experience of older generations and more recent generations and between overseas and domestic schools.

44. When the children of those whose parents have spent a full career in the military show up at a new post, they may well find other students that they know from previous assignments. At least in the two schools that are the focus of this analysis, however, that does not seem to have been a significant factor.

45. Data regarding non-parochial private schools show that the majority of parents, professors, and employers believe that private schools have "higher standards" than public schools in the U.S. Though public school teachers disagree, 68 percent of employers polled believe that private schools have higher

standards than public schools while 15 percent believe that public schools have higher standards and 8 percent believe standards are equal among private and public schools. See Public Agenda Online, Education; (http://publicagenda.org/issues/pcc_detail.cfm?issue_type=education&list=8), February 24, 2001; data collected by telephone interview October–November 1999. Data also show that the public cites the lack of parental involvement, drugs, undisciplined students, overcrowded classrooms, and violence/lack of school safety as the principal problems with public schools and perhaps are prime reasons for parents' choice to send their children to private or parochial schools. Source: http://publicagenda.org/issues/pcc-detail.cfm?issue_type=education&list=4, February 24, 2001, telephone interview of 1,422 adults, June 25–July 12, 1998 by ICR Survey Research Group, Sponsored by National Public Radio, the Henry J. Kaiser Family Foundation, and the Kennedy School of Government.

46. Figures derived from the National Center for Education Statistics (NCES), http://nces.ed.gov/pubs2003/digest02/tables/dt062.asp; November 2, 2003.

47. Coleman, Hoffer, and Kilgore (1982), *High School Achievement*; Coleman and Hoffer (1987), *Public and Private High Schools*; Grogger and Neal (2000), "Further Evidence on the Effects of Catholic Secondary Schooling."

48. Bryk, Lee, and Holland (1993), *Catholic Schools and the Common Good*.

49. There were reports from fifteen Catholic schools, but three of these were overseas and were excluded from this analysis.

50. All proper names of schools and persons are, of course, pseudonyms. Because there are fewer Catholic schools than public schools, I will provide less specific information about their location in order to protect their anonymity.

51. SP38.

52. SP38.

53. SP298.

54. Note that the student who wrote SP298 also gave a relatively unflattering account of the school she attended on a military base. I was concerned that the content of her accounts might be due to a particular personal tendency to be critical of her social environment, but the substance of her accounts seem to be confirmed by other accounts of the same kind of institutions.

55. SP298.

56. SP298.

57. See chapter six, note 80, and chapter seven, note 5, for citations of evidence that suggests the opposite.

58. SP298.

59. SP249.

60. SP298.

61. SP275.

62. SP177.

63. SP253.

64. SP253.

65. SP18.

66. SP149.

67. SP48.

68. SP253.

69. This student is not specific about exactly what "sex acts" means, but the flavor of the discussion certainly suggests that more is involved than kissing and caressing. A series of newspaper articles in the area's major paper, reported that oral sex was common among popular middle school students in this same middle- to upper-class community in which Pius X was located—though the newspaper report focused on the public schools.

70. SP253.

71. SP253.

72. SP253.
73. SP230.
74. SP230.
75. SP230.
76. SP230.
77. SP249.
78. SP12, SP128, SP210, SP295.
79. SP210.
80. SP40, SP71, SP206, SP296.

81. By "comparable" I mean schools with roughly the same socioeconomic and ethnic mix of students. I want to also stress that these conclusions are based on a very small number of cases. Nonetheless, it seems very unlikely that very many church-related schools have dramatically different peer status structures or patterns of behavior with respect to alcohol, drugs, and sex.

82. In 1993–94 the average tuition paid at Catholic secondary schools was $3,643. Source: U.S. Department of Education, National Center for Education Statistics, "Schools and Staffing Survey, 1993–94," August 1995. In December 1999, a check of the websites of the schools for which we have reports suggested that in the mid-1990s the tuition for the schools we will consider probably ran from about $4,500 to $6,500. Often there were additional fees for books, uniforms, transportation, and extracurricular activities that could easily total another $1,000. The higher-than-average fees of the schools studied means that much of the data on which this section is based are from the more expensive college preparatory Catholic schools.

The percentage of private elementary and secondary students decreased slightly, from 12 percent in 1988 to 11 percent in 1998, and the percentage of college students who attended private colleges and universities remained at 22 percent. In 1998, about 5.9 million students were enrolled in private schools at the elementary and secondary levels and 3.2 million students in institutions of higher education. The average full tuition for private schools was $3,116 in 1993–94. Schools with religious orientation charged significantly lower tuition than nonsectarian schools. Students at Catholic schools paid $2,178 on average and students at schools with other religious orientations paid $2,915 on average, compared with the average tuition of $6,631 for nonsectarian private schools. For private elementary school students the mean tuition was lower than that paid by students in upper grades, with Catholic school students paying $1,628. Students at schools with other religious orientations paid $2,606 and students at nonsectarian schools paid $4,693. Mean tuition paid for private secondary school students was substantially higher than that for private elementary school students, averaging $5,261 at non-Catholic religiously oriented schools, $9,525 at nonsectarian schools, and—as noted above—$3,643 at Catholic schools. See National Center for Education Statistics, *Digest of Educational Statistics* 1998, Table 62.

83. Grogger and Neal (2000), "Further Evidence on the Effects of Catholic Secondary Schooling."

84. For example, Weinbender and Rossignol (1996), "Lifestyle and Sexual Activity in High School," found that 24.3 percent of Seventh-Day Adventist teenagers in grades 9–12 were sexually active compared to more than 50 percent for the general population. What is of special interest for our purposes is that those who were active were much more likely to engage in milder forms of what the Adventists would consider deviant or questionable behavior—caffeine, smoking, computer games, etc. When the religious group was successful in affecting a wide arrange of behaviors this in turn affected such things as sexual activity and drug use. When religion leaves typical lifestyle patterns unaffected—as most religious schools do—it has much less effect on shaping adolescent behavior.

85. I am not the only one who suggests Catholic schools are not that different from other schools. Nancy Lesko's (1988), *Symbolizing Society*, 75, a detailed study of a Catholic school, found at least as much cliquishness and internal stratification as I have reported:

> One group of students, the "rich and populars," considered themselves better than other people, as demonstrated by not talking to classmates and often acting as if others did not exist, "looking right through people." "Rich and populars" talked only to others in their own clique. The assumed superiority and exclusiveness of this group was an important topic of conversation.

She goes on to describe students called burnouts who frequently violated the rules against smoking. At least some of these were almost certainly involved in other forms of deviance, including drugs. The popular girls did not openly use alcohol and drugs but admitted that they sometimes did in "private times." While some students were sexually active, this was apparently less common in Lesko's school—at least at the time she conducted the study—than in the schools described above. See Lesko (1988), *Symbolizing Society*.

In a cover article in *The New York Times* "Education Life" section, entitled "The Changing Face of Catholic Education," Timothy Egan, a national correspondent for the paper and a former student in a Catholic school, writes:

> [A]fter many educators had written them off for dead, Roman Catholic schools in America are in the midst of an extraordinary revival. Enrollment is up across the nation. Hundreds of new schools have opened. And more than 40 percent of all Catholic elementary and secondary schools have waiting lists for admission. More remarkably, Catholic schools, once staffed primarily by nuns, priests, and brothers ... are nearly devoid of clerics ... Ninety-three percent of the teachers are laity ... (28).

Egan notes that while religion classes are required and "the term 'social justice' is used a lot ... the intention is for the students to have an epiphany of the spirit [which is] an outcome that is not easily manufactured" (30). He reports that the staff at many schools claim that the schools are more Catholic than a generation ago. But he goes on to observe, "In some schools, Catholicism seems almost an afterthought." See *The New York Times*, section 4A, August 6, 2000.

Perhaps a personal note is appropriate here. It would be a mistake to see my claim that Catholic schools are not very different from other schools in the behavior patterns relating to status, sex, alcohol, and drugs as due to anti-religious or anti-Catholic sentiments. While I am not Catholic, I am an active member of a church. My two daughters both attended a Catholic school for one year when we were living in India and we were on the whole quite positive about their experience. I arrived at these conclusions by reading what students who had gone to such schools had to say. This does not necessarily make what I have said correct, but any inaccuracy is not due to initial biases against religion or religious schools.

86. SP149.

87. In the past most of these schools would expel students if it were known that they were homosexual so that has not been an important consideration in the publicly visible peer status structure.

88. See Brint (1998), *Schools and Societies*, for an overview of what we know, especially chapters 5 and 8. Michael Brake, a professor of social work, published a book comparing the youth cultures of America, Britain, and Canada. See Brake (1985), *Comparative Youth Culture*. The book, however, focuses almost entirely on highly alienated young people. For example, the chapter on middle-class young people is entitled "Trippers and Trashers" and focuses on cultural and political "rebels," such as the beats, the hippies, religious cults, and political movements. There is beginning to be some good comparative research, though it is often psychological in orientation. See for example, Alsakar and Flammer (1999), *The Adolescent Experience*.

89. Such factors as significant differences in geographical mobility, percentage of women in the labor force, degree of income inequality, residential and commuting patterns are likely to be relevant. For example, it is still common in much of Switzerland for all family members to go home for lunch. It would be surprising if this did not have effects on the significance of peer relations independent of the organization of athletic and extracurricular activities.

CHAPTER EIGHT

1. In November of 2000 the Playstation website listed nearly 1,000 video games available from this company alone, including "Bushido Blade" and "Bushido Blade 2."

2. FW13.

3. FW24.

4. Ford (1922), *My Life and Work*.

5. Turner (1996), *The Body and Society*, 2.

6. Here I am referring to a series of efforts that the modern state uses to level out the business cycle. Keynesian strategies manipulate taxes and public expenditures so as to increase demand during recessions and dampen it during booms. Monetary policy carried out by the Federal Reserve expands and contracts the money supply and hence lowers and raises interest rates, which in turn affects the proclivity to invest and consume. Also important but less discussed are the modern welfare state's attempts to provide minimum levels of income through welfare systems and minimum wage laws, and laws that protect the right of labor unions to organize and strike. These latter measures tend to redistribute income to those who are most likely to use it for consumption.

7. "Therefore I agree with those who argue that this is not simply a matter of false consciousness. Abercrombie, Hill, and Turner (1984), *The Dominant Ideology*, in their critique of the dominant ideology thesis, say: "We do not understand this kind of pragmatic acceptance as entailing the possession of any set of beliefs, attitudes or 'false consciousness.' Instead pragmatic acceptance is the result of the coercive quality of everyday life and the routines that sustain it." This is not, however, to say that people are simply exercising their "free choice" through the market. Rather, they are accurately conscious of the cost of deviating from the norms of a consumer society and are constrained by the social context that is in part created by the aggregate actions of individuals and in part by very deliberate attempts by businesses to shape the norms and assumptions of the society.

8. I realize that practical utility as well as status value is socially constructed and to some degree culturally variable. This is, however, a matter of degree. In virtually all societies clean water is valued for practical reasons even when it has little or no status value.

9. The attempt to transform children and teenagers into active consumers needs to be viewed in the broader context of changing social definitions of the relationship between younger people and economic activity. There is some irony in the fact that social movements to exclude or greatly limit young peoples' role as producers in the labor market marked the first half of the twentieth century. For a very useful analysis of this, and, more generally, of the social redefinition of the value and appropriate role of children, see Zelizer (1985), *Pricing the Priceless Child*. For an excellent historical sketch of marketing to children, attempts to regulate it, and the broader cultural change linked to these developments, see Cross (2002), "Values of Desire."

10. McNeal (1992), *Kids as Customers*; see also McNeal (1998), "Tapping the Three Kids' Markets."

11. The very fact that professors of marketing write on such topics is an important indicator of the extent to which marketing is specifically directed toward children and adolescents and the sophistication of the effort.

12. One of the most impressive journalistic accounts was a program broadcast by the PBS show *Frontline* entitled "Merchants of Cool," broadcast February 27, 2001. Following the broadcast an extensive website about the program and the topic was available at http://www.pbs.org/wgbh/pages/frontline/shows/cool/; November 30, 2001.

13. To an inquiry about available research, Professor James McNeal responded: "Thank you for your e-mail about research on adolescents. There isn't much that [is] publicly available. There is a group that I work with called EMR KidSay that does some good work, but it is mostly contract work. It has a website that you can look at." Personal communication, May 16, 2001.

14. Zollo (1999), *Wise Up to Teens*.

15. Packaged Facts, a research service of the Dialog Corporation, says teens spent $108 billion in 1996, including: $36.7 billion on clothing, $23.4 billion on entertainment, $16.7 billion on food, of which 24 percent was family groceries, $9.2 billion on personal care, $6.7 billion on sporting goods. See Stone (1998), "Teen Spending Keeps Climbing." The Rand Youth Poll "puts 1996 teen spending at $97.7 billion and believes that future growth is a certainty," according to Klein (1997), "Teen Green."

16. U.S. Bureau of the Census 2000. For married couples the increase was from $30,386 to $56,676. Historical data for this period for families with children under 18 is not available. It should be kept in mind that income did not increase equally for all social strata and that the income of the lower social strata tended to increase less than upper strata. Moreover, much of the increase was based on women entering the labor force, which increases family expenses as well as family income.

17. The average number of children per family for families with children under 18 dropped from 2.33 in 1960 to 1.85 in 1998. Source: U.S. Bureau of the Census 1998, Current Population Reports.

18. U.S. Bureau of Labor Statistics 1999. There is considerable debate about whether working has positive or negative effects on adolescents' grades, use of illegal substances, disruptive school behavior, criminal activity, etc. See Steinberg (1996), *Beyond the Classroom*, and Mortimer and Finch (1996), *Adolescents, Work, and Family*. The issue I am raising would be relevant, however this debate is resolved.

19. One small survey conducted for Merrill Lynch by International Communications Research— and presumably attempting to find out whether teens were a potential market for stocks, bonds, etc.— reports that teenagers save considerable portions of their resources. It is unclear for how long these savings are maintained. The data were released as part of Merrill Lynch's National Saving Month campaign, which began Wednesday, April 1, 1998.

20. This awareness has been noted in the academic literature on marketing for at least a quarter of a century. See Churchill and Moschis (1979), "Television and Interpersonal Influences," and the even earlier literature they cite.

21. For example, McNeal (1998), "Tapping the Three Kids' Markets," notes, "Delta knows that there are only two sources of new customers: those who switch from competitors and those Delta grows from childhood." Fidelity Investments has provided schools with "learning packages" on money management, even though it is obvious that those in school will make investments only in later years. See McNeal (1992), *Kids as Consumers*. Banks market credit cards for children and teenagers. Retailers create versions of their stores aimed at pre-adults, e.g., Gap Kids. McNeal (1993), "Born to Shop," estimates that "a lifetime customer may be worth $100,000 to a retailer, making effective 'cradle to grave' strategies extremely valuable."

22. Chen (1994), *The Smart Parent's Guide to Kids' TV*, see also Sherman (1996), "A Set of One's Own."

23. A study by the market research and consulting firm Roper Starch Worldwide reports that in the U.S. 32 percent of six- to seven-year-olds, 50 percent of eight- to twelve-year-olds, and 64 percent of thirteen- to seventeen-year-olds have a television in their own room. A similar study in 1996 indicated that nearly half of households with children under 18 had three TVs and more that half of the teenagers had sets in their own rooms. See Sherman (1996), "A Set of One's Own." Seventy-five percent of adolescents watch TV, videos, or play video games five or more times a week. Children watch TV and videos about forty hours per week. See Condry (1993), "Thief of Time, Unfaithful Servant."

24. Farhi (1998), "On TV, a Prime Time for Teens."

25. Ibid.

26. *Economist*, (1997), "Shop for Little Horrors."

27. For example, Giroux (2000), *Stealing Innocence*, esp. 94–101.

28. Johnston (1995), "Channel One." The company describes itself in the following terms: "ChannelOne.com is part of the Channel One Network, a PRIMEDIA Inc. company. The Channel One Network is a learning community of 12,000 American middle, junior, and high schools representing over 8 million students and 400,000 educators." See the website http://wwNv.channelone.com/eclubs/about us.html; May 22, 2001.

29. Hoynes (1997), "News for a Captive Audience."

30. Consumers Union (1995), *Captive Kids*.

31. Stead (1997), "Corporations, Classrooms and Commercialism."

32. Snyder (1995), "Ads."

33. Stead (1997), "Corporations, Classrooms and Commercialism."

34. Rossell and Bachen (1993), "Advertising on Channel One."

35. Firat and Venkatesh (1995), "Liberatory Postmodernism and the Reenchantment of Consumption." For an account that emphasizes the democratizing effects of consumerism, see Twitchell (1999), *Temptation*.

36. Elliott and Wattanasuwan (1998), "Brands as Symbolic Resources for the Construction of Identity."

37. Roper (1999), *The Public Purse*.

38. McNeal (1998), " Tapping the Three Kids' Markets."

39. Gladwell (1997a), "Annals of Style."

40. As noted earlier (p.18), the psychologist G. Stanley Hall (1969), *Adolescence*, popularized the concept of adolescence at the beginning of the twentieth century. The term *teenager* came into usage in the 1940s. See Hine (1999), *The Rise and Fall of the American Teenager*.

41. This is in part due to the changing institutional structure that has created a new kind of public realm. See, for example, Habermas (1994), "The Emergence of the Public Sphere," and Thompson (1994), "The Theory of the Public Sphere." This is accentuated because people's relationships to their social environments and to each other are increasingly mediated by the mass media, rather than by direct interpersonal interaction. These mass media are more publicly visible than interpersonal ties and hence intergenerational conflicts that might have been centered in the family at an earlier time, become public issues. The content of rap music rather than your children's friends becomes a point of conflict. The first is a public matter rather than a strictly family and private matter. The very creation of schools makes socialization less of a private or family matter and more of a public matter. Theorists as diverse as Durkheim (1925), *Moral Education*, and Althusser (1971), "Ideology and the Ideological State Apparatuses," have seen schools as key instruments for moral and ideological indoctrination, and hence a potential area of public discussion and conflict.

42. Certainly, the power of those with formal authority always has its limits. Even prison officials cannot prevent inmates from engaging in numerous forms of deviant behavior.

43. *Encarta World English Dictionary*. 1999. Microsoft Corporation.

44. Offer et al. (1988), *The Teenage World*; Brown (1990), "Peer Groups and Peer Cultures"; Brown, Mory, and Kinney (1994), "Casting Adolescent Crowds in a Relational Perspective."

45. See Willis (1977), *Learning to Labour*, 63–66, for a discussion of the limits of teacher authority in a British school.

46. In recent years revising the curriculum often includes adding various kinds of moral education. For a thoughtful analysis of various forms of moral education and an extensive critique of its limitations, see Hunter (2000), *The Death of Character*. While I am not quite as pessimistic as Hunter is about the utility of trying to articulate and teach "common values" in a pluralistic society, I certainly think such programs are at best a supplemental mechanism for teaching morality.

47. Men moved their place of work out of the home and abdicated routine child-rearing responsibilities much earlier, and still spend much less time on child-rearing. Since World War II, however, the key story has been the movement of women into the (officially employed) labor force. At the beginning of the twenty-first century more than 65 percent of all women in the U.S. (over 16 years old and not in school) were working or looking for work—and of these, 77 percent worked full-time or were looking for full-time work. For two-parent families, four out of five are two-income households, with both parents working and neither parent staying home with the children. Source: U.S. Bureau of Labor Statistics 1999.

48. The issue of whether people are working longer is a complex one. The average number of hours worked has remained relatively constant since 1960. But this disguises considerable variations between families and individuals, including a slight increase in the average hours worked by women. See U.S. Department of Labor (1999), *Report on the American Workforce*. Moreover, some studies find that changes in the time parents actually spend with their children has not changed as dramatically as the increase in women's labor force participation might suggest, and the changes are more complex than usually assumed, see Bianchi (2000), "Maternal Employment and Time with Children."

49. Between 1960 and 1998, children living in a single-parent home increased from 9 percent to 28 percent. Source: U.S. Bureau of the Census (1999), "Living Arrangements of Children Under 18 Years Old." This eliminates one parent from the child's immediate living environment and places a heavier burden on the remaining parent to earn an income, run the household, and provide emotional support and discipline. Certainly many single parents do a fine job of rearing their children, but on average, children and teenagers will have less contact with adults in their homes.

50. Mounts and Steinberg (1995), "An Ecological Analysis of Peer Influence."

51. *Economist* (1997), "Shop for Little Horrors."

52. Bosworth (1999), "The Spirit of Capitalism."

53. Here is his account:

> ... we were the ones destined to redeem the golden promise of the American dream: heirs not simply to the pursuit of happiness but to its purchase and possession. The extremity of that hope (and its secret folly) is one of the stronger memories of my own, mostly benign suburban upbringing. I recall especially a posh reception following a classmate's bar mitzvah during which we, his seventh-grade friends, were made to enter an enormous dining hall as though a wedding party or a royal procession. Two by two, a boy beside a girl, to the beat of a band's ceremonial music, we were marched up an aisle, parting a sea of damp-eyed adults, and then onto a raised platform where we ate, conversed, and later even danced, elevated above, yet surrounded by, the parents of suburbia hundreds in number.
>
> Occasionally, one of the men would slip up the steps, but then only briefly, to pass to my friend an envelope thick with congratulatory cash, as if only this, his propitiatory offering, gave him license to approach. Otherwise we remained there in exalted isolation, on perpetual display. And what I remember most now, beyond my own discomfort, was how the stares of the adults kept drifting up, from their plates of prime rib, to locate us; how they would touch and then hold the hem of the moment—this carefully composed, happy tableaux of "youth on the cusp" ... [E]ven then I sensed that there was something wrong in this reversal of status; something fundamentally (and frighteningly) false about the veneration we received in expressions that seesawed between proprietary joy and solemn awe ... What I see, when I glance back now, is the idolatry of childhood: the little god and goddess of Self-Esteem being raised on the altar of the secular dream.

54. See Collins (1992), "Women and the Production of Status Cultures." I am referring to relatively modern societies. Obviously, in many historical situations women have played a major role in the process of productions as well as consumption. Even when the "traditional" family was at its height, there were many women including widows who earned their own living or made significant contributions to the family income. Nonetheless the social ideal and to a significant extent the social reality was a gender division of labor in which men produced income and women converted it into family services and status.

55. For an accessible account of the issue of parents spending money to enhance the marriage prospects of daughters in contemporary village India, see Jeffery and Jeffery (1996), chaps. 3–4. For my own theoretical analysis of this issue, see Milner (1994), *Status and Sacredness*, especially chaps. 5 and 11. For a powerful novel that centers on this issue see Vikram Seth's (1993), *A Suitable Boy*. Many of Jane Austen's novels focus on this theme with *Pride and Prejudice's* Mrs. Bennet being a classic example of a parent preoccupied with marriages as a means of improving family status.

56. This varies somewhat by social class. The upper classes are still able to influence their children's choice of peers and the social contexts in which they meet by sending them to exclusive schools, camps, resorts, and social events. Lower classes have less influence because they have neither the social connections nor the financial resources to influence their children's consumption patterns. George Moschis claims, "Middle class adolescents appear to attain less independence in purchasing as they grow older than do adolescent consumers in lower and upper social classes ... attributed to middle-class families' greater consciousness of the normative standards of their class, and of their subsequent greater desire

to supervise their children's activities in an effort to socialize them into the class norms," in (1985), "Role of Family Communication in Consumer Socialization." But this greater influence is only relative to other strata.

57. Wolfe (2000), *Hooking Up*, 6.

58. In part, this is probably related to a decline in beliefs about life after death. Most world religions have concepts that parallel the Greek and Christian notions of body and soul. The individual's identity was closely tied to the notion of a soul that would survive the body. But as the salience of the afterlife declined, the link between the body and one's social identity has increased. This is not to say that beliefs in the afterlife have disappeared; they have not. But they are less central to the culture than when death rates were much higher and life expectancy shorter. Hence, the body has become an important human project. Among sociologists it is Bryan Turner (1996), *The Body and Society*, who has been most influential in pointing to the significance of the sociology of the body. He states its relevance for consumer capitalism in the following terms: "The consequences of postindustrial culture are important for a sociological understanding of consumerism, commercialization, and hedonism. There is obviously a strong commercial and consumerist interest in the body as a sign of the good life and an indicator of cultural capital. In addition to this theme of consumption there is a specific focus on the body beautiful, on the denial of the aging body and on the rejection of death, on the importance of sport and on the general moral value of keeping fit. In early capitalism there was a close connection ('an elective affinity,' as Max Weber described it) between discipline asceticism, the body and capitalist production, while in late capitalism there is an entirely different and corrosive emphasis on hedonism, desire, and enjoyment." See Turner (1996), *The Body and Society*, 3. We will return to the relationship between asceticism and hedonism later in the chapter.

59. Schor (1998), *The Overspent American*, 101.

60. Lears (1994), *Fables of Abundance*.

61. Frank (1997), *The Conquest of the Cool*.

62. According to Frank (1997), *The Conquest of the Cool*, 29–31, "the counterculture may be … understood as a stage in the development of the values of the American middle class, a colorful installment in the twentieth-century drama of consumer subjectivity." By associating hip consumption with rebellion "two of late capitalism's great problems could easily be met: obsolescence found a new and more convincing language, and citizens could symbolically resolve the contradiction between their role as consumers and their role as producers." But the kind of rebellion that was emphasized was not the violence of a political rebellion, but the much safer psychological and cultural rebellion of youth. Being young was transformed from an age category to "an attitude." And the attitude that business was particularly interested in encouraging was a quest for the new. "Unlike their parents, the hip new youth are far more receptive to obsolescence; buying goods for the moment, discarding them quickly, and moving on to the next." See Frank (1997), *The Conquest of the Cool*, 122. The concerns with status, newness, and fashion provided a marketing perpetual motions machine.

63. Schor (1998), *The Overspent American*.

64. One of the classics in this line of theory and research is Lazarsfeld et al. (1944), *The People's Choice*. For a recent study in this tradition, see Krause (2000), "Information Diffusion within the Electorate."

65. See Gladwell (1997a), "Annals of Style."

66. Oates (1999), *Broke Heart Blues*, 201.

67. In contrast to Marx's emphasis on how economic organization shapes ideology, Weber's work is often cited as an example of how ideology can shape the social structure. My argument does not emphasize this point, but rather points to the unexpected and unintended consequence of a non-economic institution (i.e., high school status systems) on economic activity. I am aware that Weber's argument is more explicitly comparative than my analysis in that he devotes considerable attention to non-Calvinist areas and religious traditions. The parallel would be to look at societies in which high school status systems were not present or much weaker. This was discussed in chapter seven.

68. Robert Wuthnow (1996), *Poor Richard's Principle*, 249, has noted this by referring to children as "the enemy within." "Focusing on the materialism of children can be a way of deflecting criticism from ourselves. Even those who seem to have children's interest at heart convey a mixed message when they speak as if children have become agents of undesirable economic forces."

69. The most amusing incidence of this tendency I have experienced involved a seminar I was teaching for freshmen. This was a group of eighteen honor students who had gone to high school in nine different states. I had given a brief lecture on the development of the American high school system and recent changes that had occurred. I asked them about changes they had experienced during the time they had been in middle school and high school. To my surprise the discussion almost immediately shifted to the "troubling changes in attitude" that had occurred among younger students. Younger cohorts were reported to "have no sense of responsibility," to be "obsessed with superficial matters," to be "disrespectful and even violent." What was striking about the discussion was that these students had only been out of high school a few months, and they already perceived the "younger generation" as "going to hell." Even though they had gone to different high schools, there was near universal agreement about the negative assessment of their juniors. To point out the strong tendency of older cohorts to criticize younger ones is not to suggest the younger generation is without their faults or that there are no real changes. Some young people have engaged in forms of behavior that are not only annoying and self-destructive, but also horrifying and reprehensible. My point, however, is that even if negative characterizations of the young are true, they are largely irrelevant to constructive social change. For the most part younger people have not created the basic institutional structures within which they live. They do "furnish them" with additions and elaborations that give each generation a certain distinctiveness. In certain historical situations they may play a major role in destroying or transforming the basic institutions. But it is usually a succession of older generations that have established the basic framework within which young people live their lives.

CHAPTER NINE

1. FW17.

2. FW23.

3. There is, of course, a debate about the degree to which contemporary work has become de-skilled and hence abstract labor in Willis's Marxian sense of the phrase. My concern here is not with the empirical adequacy of Willis's analysis, though it was probably accurate for the situation he studied, but rather to point to a parallel process in the realm of consumption.

4. This notion of abstract desire is, of course, very similar to Durkheim's notion of anomie. This term has been used to allude to many things, but for Durkheim its fundamental meaning was the absence of norms that placed limits on people's desires and expectations, and hence led to frustration and discontent. See Durkheim (1984), *The Division of Labor in Society*; Durkheim (1997), *Suicide*.

5. Saturday, June 2, 2001.

6. The article by Bruce Horowitz in *USA Today*, October 3, 2001, included the following passages:

> Even cheerleader-in-chief President Bush jumped onto the buying-as-patriotism bandwagon last week and Tuesday when he urged Americans to take to the skies. He also suggested that folks go to Disney World. Several big-shot politicians, and one former president, have recently been doing some high-profile shopping in New York City. Immediately after New York Mayor Rudy Giuliani urged New Yorkers to go out and spend money, former president Bill Clinton bought $342.79 worth of gifts for children of victims at the NBA Store in midtown Manhattan.
>
> Over the weekend, governors and mayors from several states flew to New York to do some very public consumption. They chowed down at the Carnegie Deli. They spent hundreds of dollars at Macy's. Several took in a Broadway performance of *The Lion King*.
>
> The rationale: Shopping has become a patriotic duty, and an economic necessity. The simplest way to make sure the terrorists don't have a nice day: Buy something. No matter if it's dinner at Sardi's, a sweater at Bloomie's or a round-trip ticket to Las Vegas. The economy needs it—or so the thinking goes.

7. Putnam, (2000), *Bowling Alone*.

8. For example, Nock (1998), *Marriage in Men's Lives*.

9. Bell (1975), *The Cultural Contradictions of Capitalism*.

10. Bosworth (1996), *The Georgia Review*, 451.

11. See introduction, note 1, for a brief summary of the prevalence of alcohol use among teenagers.

12. An example of this is the popularity of humorist Andy Borowitz, especially among well-educated young adults. He is a former president of the *Harvard Lampoon*, his writing appears in the pages of *The New Yorker, The New York Times, Vanity Fair, TV Guide*, and at Newsweek.com. He is a regular guest on CNN's *American Morning* and commentator for National Public Radio's *Weekend Edition*. The following is his satirical essay entitled, "Let's Give Thanks: A Thanksgiving List," Borowitzreport.com, published November 26, 2002:

> I'm thankful to the producers of "Stuart Little 2," for making a film that seems to have greatly reduced the chances of a "Stuart Little 3."
>
> I'm thankful to the executives of VH1 for pulling the plug on the reality show "Liza and David," since a program about Liza Minnelli's marriage couldn't really be considered a reality show.
>
> I'm thankful for the emergence of a public figure who finally justifies our trust—the Anaheim Angels' Rally Monkey.
>
> I'm thankful for the scientists at the Coca Cola Company, who turned mankind's long-elusive dream of a diet vanilla cola beverage into a reality.
>
> I'm thankful to Mr. and Mrs. Blix for naming their son "Hans," because I think "Hans Blix" is just about the coolest name I've ever heard.
>
> I'm thankful to CBS for airing the "Victoria's Secret Fashion Show," although I secretly fear that Fruit-of-the-Loom will demand equal time.
>
> I'm thankful for the urgent news alert crawl on CNN, which informed me that Rosie O'Donnell had taken her name off her magazine.
>
> I'm thankful for Kelly Ripa, who continues to be our nation's best defense against the return of Kathie Lee Gifford.
>
> I'm thankful to J. Lo and Ben Affleck for announcing their engagement, since the suspense was killing me.
>
> I'm thankful to Michael Jackson for making all of my parenting look perfect.
>
> I'm thankful for Winona Ryder, who showed that security measures seem to be working in at least one place in this country—Saks Fifth Avenue.
>
> I'm thankful for whoever came up with the term "perp walk."
>
> And finally, I'm thankful for how the election turned out—on "The West Wing."

It needs to be kept in mind that this essay focuses on a holiday that historically has centered on a genuine expression of thankfulness and the reaffirmation of traditional values; it was one of the least cynical occasions in the year. Note how the focus of the essay is on the banalities of the media and contemporary popular culture. My point is not to criticize this essay, but to use it as an illustration of the rise of cynicism as a common and perhaps even a dominant mode of expression.

13. Lamont's (2000), *The Dignity of Working Men*, especially 108–109, study of working-class men shows striking similarities between the criticisms that working-class men express toward those in the middle and upper classes and the criticisms that are expressed by high school students toward preppies. For example, working men often complain that members of the "upper half" are "two-faced," "engage in too much politicking," are "unreal" like "Barbie and Ken people." As "normals" and "alternatives" in high schools often reject grades and popularity as measures of self-worth, working-class men often reject economic and occupational ambition and success as the primary measures of moral worth. They frequently invoke other criteria that emphasize straightforwardness and thoughtfulness toward others. In contrast, "[F]ewer New York professionals and managers expressed alternative definitions of success, and most measured freedom by consumption, for instance, by being able to buy a house in a good neighborhood or to take off regularly for a weekend of skiing in Vermont." See Lamont's (2000), *The*

Dignity of Working Men, 116. In sum, working-class men's image of managers and professionals often parallels non-preppy students' perceptions of their preppy peers. While the behaviors and perceptions of adults are obviously shaped by more than their high school experience, it seems highly likely that these patterns are linked.

14. Brooks (2000), *Bobos in Paradise*. Brooks's argument is another version in a long line of theories of the "new class," though he does not connect his analysis to this tradition. See Dahrendorf (1959), *Class and Class Conflict*; Bell (1973), *The Coming of Post-Industrial Society*; and Gouldner (1979) *The Future of Intellectuals*, for a sampling of earlier versions of new class theory. See Brint (1994), *In an Age of Experts*, for a critique and specification of such arguments.

15. Brooks (2000), *Bobos in Paradise*, 50.

16. These figures are from U.S. Bureau of the Census estimates for 2000 and World Bank estimates for 1999. In the low- and middle-income countries, which contain 85 percent of the world's population, the per capita national income is $1,240, compared to $31,910 for the U.S., which contains 4.7 percent of the world's population. Even if one uses the "purchasing price parity" figures, which take into account differences in cost of living in different countries, the figures are $3,610 for the low- and middle-income countries and $31,910 for the U.S. Of those within most of the low- and middle-income countries, 25 percent are below the World Bank poverty line of earning less than $1.08 per day. Source: http://www.worldbank.org/data/wdi2001/pdfs/tabl-l.pdf; http://www.worldbank.org/research/povmonitor/index.him and http://www.census.gov/prod/2001pubs/p60–214.pdf; November 5, 2001.

17. There is also the question of whether the educated professionals and managers that compose most of the subculture Brooks describes are the "upper class." It could be argued that they are largely the employees of those who control large concentrations of property. Brooks's description includes people in this category, but it seems clear that most of those who compose the class have human and cultural capital, but do not own significant amounts of property. See the works of William Domhoff for an alternative view.

18. For a brief, eloquent characterization of this resentment, see Pamuk (2001), "The Anger of the Damned."

19. In the year 2000 alone there were forty armed conflicts in thirty-five countries. [An armed conflict is defined as a political conflict involving armed combat by the military forces of at least one state (or one or more armed factions seeking to gain control of all or part of the state), and in which at least 1,000 people have been killed during the fighting.] As of December 31, 2000, the U.S. Committee for Refugees estimated that there were 14,500,000 refugees throughout the world. In 2001 there were more than fifty major natural disasters. One of these, an earthquake in India killed nearly 19,000 people and left 600,000 homeless. This is not to suggest that events of September 11, 2001, were not horrible, but only that the rest of the world regularly suffers even greater natural and human-made disasters. Source: http://www.infoplease.com/ipa/AO878269.hind, accessed July 2, 2002.

20. Let me briefly discuss two problems which are beyond the scope of the present analysis, but which my conclusions point to. The billions of poor people around the world are likely to demand a significantly greater share of the world's resources and power. Worldwide income inequality has increased over a long period of time. This trend may have moderated, but currently about 70 percent of the income inequality in the world is due to differences between countries, not to differences within countries. See Firebaugh (2000), "Between-Nation Income Inequality," for a relatively conservative view of the extent and trend in international inequality. This structure of between-nation inequality means that, on average, being born into a poor (or rich) country has much more to do with your economic opportunities than anything you can do to improve your lot within that setting. The global media are making people increasingly conscious of this at the same time it is raising their desires for goods and services. In the political realm, it is obvious that with the collapse of the Soviet Union in 1989, military power became much more unequal, with the U.S. being the only world power. Moreover, whatever the justification, the U.S. invasion of Afghanistan and the two invasions of Iraq significantly raised fears

and hostility toward the U.S. in both the developing and the developed world. American supremacy in the areas of communication and culture production also increased. In countless villages without running water, people are well acquainted with American television programs and advertising logos. Many embrace American culture and consumerism, but many—sometimes the same people—fear and resent our spreading cultural dominance and the closely related consumerism. September 11 showed the lengths to which a relatively small group of fanatics were willing to go to express their resentments. Even when they admire and envy many things about the U.S., literally billions of people see American society, its government, and its culture, as a threat, and even an enemy. It is unlikely that any amount of military might or homeland security can protect Americans from such resentments.

The strategy of economic development and world trade via free markets holds out the hope that our consumerism can become sufficiently available to those in the rest of the world that their resentments can be alleviated. Yet, even assuming that this occurs, it leaves unanswered another increasingly pressing question. What would be the ecological consequences of spreading anything approximating American consumption patterns to the rest of the world? Even with the most optimistic of assumptions it is difficult to imagine how such a world economy could be sustained without dire consequences for the natural environment. Obviously, these issues are beyond the scope of this book and hinge on much more than the nature of peer status systems in high schools. My point is that high school status systems and their link to consumerism potentially contribute to even broader processes that are of fundamental importance.

CHAPTER TEN

1. FW17.

2. FW16.

3. Peterson (1999), *How Things Become Art*; Raphael (2000), *Sculpting Memory*; Milner (1999), "Explaining the Status of Brahmans, Nerds, and Social Theorists."

4. In many communities reducing the relative importance of traditional sports will not be easy because these are not simply a school activity, but a central community ritual that contributes to local solidarity and pride. This is not bad in itself, but should young people's educational experience be organized—and many would say, distorted—to meet this broader community need? This is not an easy question, but in my judgment we need to look for other ways to develop community solidarity and let schools focus on more specific educational tasks. This will usually require more multidimensional status systems.

5. It should, of course, be possible to discuss all of these ideas and ideals.

6. There has been a long and contested history of how to label people whose capacities are limited or different from the vast majority of people. The general trend has been to avoid terms that negatively stigmatize individuals. In the past such terms as "retarded," "disabled," "handicapped," and "challenged" have been in common usage. The current most common usage is people with "special needs."

7. See Furstenberg (2000), "Sociology of Adolescence in the 1990s," for a very useful summary of the changing nature of young peoples' experience in schools and the labor force.

8. I use the modifier "much" advisedly. As the size of a group increases arithmetically, the possible combinations and permutations increase geometrically.

9. Milner (1972), *The Illusion* of *Equality*.

CHAPTER ELEVEN

1. McDonald's online application site; https://gate.aon.com/Candidate/hiringtowin; accessed 2-10-2015.

2. https://www.collegeboard.org/releases/2013/more-11000-college-and-high-school-faculty-convene-score-more-4-million-college-level-ap-ex; accessed 11-20-2014.

To put this in perspective, in 2011 there were 27,000+ high schools and 16 million high school students in the U.S. Source: *Digest of Educational Statistics*, U.S. Department of Education, Table 2; http://nces.ed.gov/programs/digest/d12/tables/dt12_002.asp; and Table 5; http://nces.ed.gov/programs/digest/d12/tables/dt12_005.asp; accessed 11-20-2014.

The College Board describes itself in the following manner:

> The College Board is a mission-driven not-for-profit organization that connects students to college success and opportunity. Founded in 1900, the College Board was created to expand access to higher education. Today, the membership association is made up of over 6,000 of the world's leading educational institutions and is dedicated to promoting excellence and equity in education. Each year, the College Board helps more than seven million students prepare for a successful transition to college through programs and services in college readiness and college success—including the SAT and the Advanced Placement Program. The organization also serves the education community through research and advocacy on behalf of students, educators and schools.

3. For a mere sampling of the kind of research and debate that has occurred see Cook and Ludwig (1998); Farkas, Lleras, and Maczuga (2002); Fryer (2006); Hochschild (2014); and Wildhagen (2011).

4. There is certainly a parallel and overlap between the notion of instrumental—treating someone or something as an instrument or means to some other end—and Max Weber's notions of rationalization. Moreover, there is a similar parallel and overlap between the decline of romanticism and Weber's notion of disenchantment. The meaning of these Weberian concepts and terms is certainly contested among Weber scholars. I have avoided using them here because to do so would require a major tangent that is not necessary for the purposes at hand. There are a number of scholarly writings that attempt to clarify the meaning of rationalization and disenchantment and the implications these have for culture, politics, and economics (see e.g., Kalberg 1980; Seidman 1985; and Oakes 2003).

5. For example, the percentage of twelfth grade students who "date frequently" dropped from 34.2 percent in 1991 to 30.8 percent in 1999 (the year my earlier study was completed) to 17.9 percent in 2011. Source: "Dating," Child Trends, February 2013; Appendix 2; http://www.childtrends.org/wp-ontent/uploads/2012/05/73_Dating.pdf; accessed 12-9-2014. For U.S. government data source see "Trends in the Prevalence of Sexual Behaviors and HIV Testing National YRBS: 1991–2013"; http://www.cdc.gov/healthyyouth/yrbs/pdf/trends/us_sexual_trend_yrbs.pdf.

6. Child Trends, "Dating and Sexual Relationships," October 2013, Figure 3; http://www.childtrends.org/wp-content/uploads/2013/10/2013-04DatingSexualRelationships.pdf; accessed 12-9-2014.

7. Child Trends, "Dating and Sexual Relationships," October 2013, Figure 4; http://www.childtrends.org/wp-content/uploads/2013/10/2013-04DatingSexualRelationships.pdf; accessed 12-9-2014.

8. http://www.urbandictionary.com/define.php?term=fuck+buddy; accessed 1-23-15.

9. I use the term "carnal" instead of such terms as "vulgar," "profane," "crass," and "crude" because it is less judgmental. Perhaps it is too neutral a term because in most cultures there are words and phrases that are deemed inappropriate in more public settings—and that is the case with much of the profanity used by teenagers.

10. Prostitutes that are closely associated with rich and powerful men such as the courtesans of European royal courts or those associated with religious temples (e.g., ancient Canaan, Corinth in ancient Greece, or the *devidasis* of medieval South India) are honored in certain restricted religious contexts, but they tend to be treated ambivalently and largely excluded from conventional social relationships. In "societies of men" such as armies and boom towns, they may be considered valuable and "indispensable" members of the community, but their status is at best ambivalent and they are often abused or even enslaved.

11. Child Trends, "Dating and Sexual Relationships," October 2013; http://www.childtrends.org/wp-content/uploads/2013/10/2013-04DatingSexualRelationships.pdf; accessed 12-9-2014.

12. The U.S. Bureau of Justice Statistics carries out several kinds of surveys to determine the incidence of rape in prison, but the definition of concepts, the methodology and the findings are complex. To give a brief example of the findings, the analysis of the survey of prison and jail inmates in

2008-9 reported the following highlights: "Female inmates in prison (4.7%) or jail (3.1%) were more than twice as likely as male inmates in prison (1.9%) or jail (1.3%) to report experiencing inmate-on-inmate sexual victimization. Among inmates who reported inmate-on-inmate sexual victimization, 13% of male prison inmates and 19% of male jail inmates said they were victimized within the first 24 hours after admission, compared to 4% of female inmates in prison and jail." (U.S. Department of Justice 2010).

13. Data from Child Trends Data Bank; http://www.childtrends.org/wp-content/uploads/2012/07/23_Fig1.jpg; accessed 11-24-2014. These data are based primarily on U.S. Center for Disease Control biannual survey of high school students. For the CDC's wider array of data available on sexual behavior see http://nccd.cdc.gov/YouthOnline/App/Default.aspx?SID=HS; accessed 11-24-2014.

14. "Ratchet" or "ratchet girl" usually refers to a woman who uses sex to get what she wants and is overly sexual in her demeanor—though the exact meaning can vary from group to group.

15. "Cougar" refers to an older woman who has or pursues younger lovers.

16. An especially telling example of this is the HBO TV series *VEEP*. This is not a series about criminals, gangs, the police, the army or romantic relationships but it supposedly portrays behavior and language in the office of the U.S. Vice President. Yet profanity and sexual allusions are plentiful. My point is not that this is such an outrage, but that it is an indicator of the increased "carnality" of American culture.

17. See, for example, U.S. Bureau of Labor Statistics; http://www.bls.gov/nls/nlsfaqs.htm#anch41; accessed 12-9-2014.

18. See, for example, Lydia Saad, "U.S. Workers Still Haven't Shaken the Job Worries of 2009: Worry about being laid off has increased most for the low-income," Gallup: http://www.gallup.com/poll/164222/workers-haven-shaken-job-worries-2009.aspx; accessed 12-9-2014.

19. Ito et al. (2013: 15) distinguish between "friendship-driven" and "interest-driven" forms of participation, which is a useful distinction for their purposes. It overlaps with the instrumental-expressive distinction that I rely on, but I think the latter is more precise and theoretically useful. For example, a local bridge club or group of video gamers may appear "interest-driven" but be primarily an expressive, not an instrumental group—and this is likely to change the nature of the interpersonal relationships.

20. It should be kept in mind that in many pre-modern societies it was not usually the state that officially recognized marriage. Rather it was either recorded by religious authorities or remembered by those who witnessed the event. One of the reasons that weddings often involved inviting a number of people to the celebration was in order to make the event publicly visible and hence "official." The point is not that "Facebook Official" is the same as traditional forms of marriage in pre-modern societies, but rather the manipulation of social visibility is an important social mechanism for stabilizing a variety of social relationships.

21. Unsurprisingly the meaning of cyberbullying is contested. By this term I mean persistent harassment of a vulnerable person by another individual or group. I do not include disputes between those with roughly equal social power or the momentary put-down of a social inferior, such as a passing snide remark by an upper classmen toward a younger student. This is not to say that the latter kind of behavior is acceptable, but it does not constitute bullying in the sense that it is used here.

22. For one example see Alvarez (2013).

23. The online Urban Dictionary defines drama as: "Something women and especially teenage girls thrive on, consisting of any number of situations that have an easy solution, which would bring a fairly good outcome, but these girls choose another, shitty, bad way to deal with it, again consisting of backstabbing, blackmailing/gossiping/betraying their friends, or the all-too-common 'I want to break up with him but I still love him!' It drives men and what I like to call 'normal' girls nuts." Drama queen is defined as: "An overly dramatic person. [For example], Mary blows everything out of proportion! She's such a drama queen!" http://www.urbandictionary.com/define.php?term=drama; http://www.urbandictionary.com/define.php?term=drama%20queen; accessed 10-28-2014.

The terms "drama" and "social drama" have also been used by social analysts to refer to students' resistance to the authority of teachers and the social order that encompasses such authority (see

McFarland 2004). While the use of notions of drama in this sense has produced valuable insights, this is not the sense in which students use the term.

24. Lip Dub videos involve amateurs—usually the students and faculty of a particular school—being photographed mouthing the words of a popular singing group while acting out the various movements and motions of the original performers or making up other routines that are appropriate for the music being played and the particular school setting. Then the original professional recording is dubbed into the video of the amateurs performing so that it seems like they are both carrying out the motions and actually singing the recorded music. Some high school groups created elaborate videos with students, faculty, and even principals participating in what appears to be a highly professional music video. See, for example, https://www.youtube.com/watch?v=OX7TKY6VQvs; accessed 2-7-2015.

25. Eagan et al. 2014. Since the late 1960s a national sample of entering colleges freshmen have been asked about a wide array of matters relating to their experiences as young people. In 2014 over 1,500 colleges and universities participated in this data collection.

26. Excessive texting was correlated with higher levels of stress, poor academics, and poor sleep (Frank, 2011). In a study of middle-school students 39 percent admitted getting behind on schoolwork and 37 per cent reported losing sleep because of time spent on social network sites (Espinoza and Juvonen 2011).

27. The Merriam Webster online dictionary defines "consumerism" as "the theory that an increasing consumption of goods is economically desirable; also: a preoccupation with and an inclination toward the buying of consumer goods"; http://www.merriam-webster.com/dictionary/consumerism; accessed 12-3-2014.

In the first edition of this book, like Weber, I noted that there had been various types and stages of capitalism (e.g., booty capitalism, merchant capitalism, industrial capitalism, state capitalism). In an economy in which consumer spending makes up 70 percent of the GDP it is not inappropriate to characterize the economic system as consumer capitalism.

Unsurprisingly, there is debate about exactly what should be considered consumer spending. For example, does it include health care expenditures, many of which are paid for by various kinds of insurance including government programs such as Medicare? Despite such ambiguities consumer spending is at the core of most advanced economies and when it declines the overall economy tends to decline. Hence, it is appropriate to characterize this form of capitalism as consumer capitalism and to point out that consumerism—that is the desire of individuals and families to consume more—is a key to sustaining and expanding this kind of economy.

28. See, for example, Schor (2003) and Addato (2003). It is noteworthy that searches of library databases produced relatively few articles by social scientists on the use of cartoons to advertise to children, but produced literally hundreds of articles in marketing and business journals about this topic.

29. See, for example, Story (2007).

30. The intensity of the consumerism and its taken-for-granted nature is reflected in the term "doorbuster." The term comes from several events in which shoppers actually broke open the doors of stores before they had opened in order to buy items advertised at an especially low price. In several cases store employees and other shoppers were seriously injured and even killed in the stampede that occurred. Despite the dubious if not appalling nature of such events major retailers—even relatively traditional and staid ones such as J.C. Penny's—started to use the term "doorbuster" in their advertisements.

31. See, for example, *The Wall Street Journal* article that describes this, Angwin (2010).

32. Of course, people's economic circumstances affect their level of consumerism. During recessions consumer spending tends to decline. Because of the uncertainties and volatilities that seem increasingly characteristic of global capitalism, it is unclear whether consumer expenditures will continue to be the core of capitalist economies.

33. "Contextual variables" is used in a variety of ways in the social sciences, but it usually refers to some characteristic of the environment within which a more micro process such as interpersonal interaction occurs (see, e.g., Milevsky, et al. (2005) and Liska (1990)). My meaning refers to a factor that is assumed to be at approximately a certain value for the core elements of a theory to operate. For example, a key contextual variable for the law of falling bodies is a vacuum; the relationships between mass, distance, speed, etc. vary if the atmosphere (i.e., the context) does not approximate a vacuum.

34. Of course pre-modern societies used such things as smoke signals, drums, and flags, but these were quite limited in both the content they could contain and the distance and speed of the communication.

APPENDIX I

1. Common recognition may or may not imply consensual agreement. Blacks in the antebellum American South knew that most blacks were slaves, that no whites were, and that their overall social status was very much affected by this. This does not mean that they consensually agreed to the criteria imposed. On the other hand, in many status systems, common recognition and consensual agreement are closely related. See Cecilia Ridgeway (1998), "How Do Status Beliefs Develop."

2. The opposite of this would be for the characteristic to be socially invisible or constantly changing. Obviously such a characteristic would not be a very useful basis of social evaluation and differentiation.

3. The sole criteria of whether a U.S. high school student is a National Merit Semi-Finalist is the score they make on the Scholastic Aptitude Test (PSAT). Supposedly, family wealth, good looks, charm, work habits, or financial need are not considered. These factors, of course, may have had an indirect effect by shaping the cultural skills learned at home, the high school attended, or treatment by teachers, and in turn, the student's ability to score well on the test. That is to say, these various factors may have been partial determinants of the score that was made, but they were not the *criteria* of selection. In selecting the National Merit Finalist, other criteria such as financial need, extracurricular activities, and geographical location are taken into account.

4. Envy and the gossip and backbiting that can result, is, of course, an old story. A Biblical Psalmist observes: "How long will you assail a person … Their only plan is to bring down a person of prominence. They take pleasure in falsehood; they bless with their mouths and inwardly curse," see Ps. 62:4 NRSV. In the famous "Funeral Speech" in Thucydides, *History of the Peloponnesian War*, Pericles says, "Praise spoken of others is bearable up to the point where each man believes himself capable of doing the things he hears of: anything which goes beyond that arouses envy and disbelief," see 11.32.1.

5. See Merten (1997), "The Meaning of Meanness … ," for a discussion that outlines the difficulties and dilemmas of "managing popularity."

6. Steinberg (1993), *Adolescence*.

7. See Parsons and Bales (1956), *Family Socialization and Interaction Process*.

8. Péristiany (1966), *Honour and Shame*.

9. Nisbett and Cohen (1992), *Culture and Honor*.

10. Horowitz (1983), *Honor and the American Dream*; also see Anderson (1999), *Code …*

11. See Sarup (1993), *Post-Structuralism and Postmodernism* for a useful introductory overview.

12. For an important and provocative analysis of the sociology of the observer, see Fuchs (2001), *Against Essentialism*.

13. Foucault (1980), *Power/Knowledge*.

14. Derrida (1978), *Writing and Difference*.

15. See Foucault (1973), *Madness and Civilization*; Foucault (1978), *History of Sexuality*; Foucault (1979), *Discipline and Punish*.

16. Hall and Jefferson, (1976), *Resistance through Rituals*; Lesko (2001), *Act Your Age*.

17. Veblen (1992), *Theory of the Leisure Class*.

18. The broad perspective known as symbolic interactionism is rooted in the work of American philosophical pragmatism, especially the work of Charles Horton Cooley and George Herbert Mead, and given its classic articulation by Herbert Blumer. There are many versions and branches of this tradition. What they tend to emphasize is that social life, and hence sociology, is rooted in the observation of concrete social interaction, and central to this process is the creation and interpretation of meaning. The identities of individuals and the structures of social life are socially created and sustained (or changed) by means of human interaction that is shaped by past patterns of social life—but not determined by them. The focus of this type of analysis tends to be on the detailed analysis of interpersonal interactions based on direct observation or the relatively detailed accounts of social actors.

This approach is relevant to the present work in two important respects. First, status is primarily a matter of creating social meanings and evaluations. This is discussed in more detail in my *Status and Sacredness*. As is indicated there, my perspective is rooted in a social construction of reality tradition, which is closely related to symbolic interactionism. Hence, my approach is certainly not hostile to more micro traditions that focus on how actors create and interpret meaning during the process of social interaction. One of the virtues of my definition of status—the accumulated approvals and disapprovals received from others—is that it roots status, which is often a rather abstract and vague notion, in the concrete behaviors and interactions of individuals. As the discussion above indicates, this summation of approvals and disapprovals is located in the minds of other actors and hence is relatively inalienable. The symbols of status may be embodied or objectified in various objects—university degrees or the stars on a general's uniform—but these are worthless if other people do not recognize their meaning and respect what they stand for. Second, since my data are rooted in people's memories of their high school experience, the recorded observations and interpretations of fieldworkers, and high school students' responses to questions on interviews, the processes of the interpretation of meaning are central to my data. This issue will be discussed in Appendix II.

19. See Cerulo (1997), "Identity Construction," for a review of this literature.

20. See Berbrier (2002), "Making Minorities," for a recent example of this type of work.

21. Zerubavel (1991), *The Fine Line*.

22. Bourdieu (1989), *The State of Nobility*.

23. Alexander and Smith (1998), "Cultural Sociology or Sociology of Culture?"

24. Milner (1994), *Status and Sacredness*.

25. Parkin (1979), *Marxism and Class Theory*, and Murphy (1988), *Social Closure*.

26. Kingston (2000), *The Classless Society*.

27. Bourdieu (1984), *Distinction*, and Bourdieu (1986), "Forms of Capital."

28. For example, DiMaggio (1982), "Cultural Capital and School Success"; DiMaggio and Mohr (1985), "Cultural Capital, Education Attainment, and Marital Selection"; Lamont and Lareau (1988), "Cultural Capital"; MacLeod (1995), *Ain't No Makin' It*; Farkas (1996), *Human Capital or Cultural Capital*, Aschaffenburg and Maas (1997), "Cultural and Educational Careers."

29. See, e.g., DiMaggio (1979), "Review Essay on Pierre Bourdieu."

30. Lamont and Lareau (1988), "Cultural Capital."

31. Ibid., 156.

32. Kingston (2000), *The Classless Society*.

33. MacLeod (1995), *Ain't No Makin' It*.

34. Lareau (2000), *Home Advantage*.

35. For example, Bourdieu (1984), *Distinction*.

36. In many ways there are strong parallels between reproduction theory and status attainment analysis. See Blau and Duncan (1967), *The American Occupational Structure*; Jencks (1979), *Who Gets Ahead?*; and the related work in the structural equation modeling of academic outcomes in Entwisle, Alexander, and Olson (1997), *Children, Schools, and Inequality*. All three attempted to identify the processes that intervened between status or class origin and destination and the processes that shape

educational attainment. While reproduction theory was much more theoretically oriented and sophisticated, and much less quantitatively precise, it asked many of the same questions.

37. Parkin (1979), *Marxism and Class Theory*, 63.

38. Bell (1975), *The Cultural Contradictions of Capitalism*.

39. Lamont (1992a), *Cultivating Difference*; Lamont (2000), *The Dignity of Working Men*.

40. Lamont (2000), *The Dignity of Working Men*, 4.

41. Berger, Zeldich, and Anderson (1966), *Sociological Theories in Progress*.

42. Webster and Foschi (1988), *Status Generalization*.

43. Ridgeway (1998), "How Do Status Beliefs Develop?"

44. Wagner and Berger (2002), "Expectation States Theory."

45. See, for example, Jasso (2001), "Studying Status."

46. Collins (1975), *Conflict Sociology*; Collins (1979), *The Credential Society*; Collins (1988),
Sociology of Marriage and Family; Collins (2000), "Situational Stratification."

47. For a recent statement, see Collins (2000), "Situational Stratification," esp. 26–27; all quotes
[below] are from here.

48. Milner (1994), *Status and Sacredness*, esp. chaps. 12–15.

APPENDIX II

1. Two students attended and wrote about two different high schools. Two other students wrote
two papers about the one high school they attended: one general description and one more detailed
description about a specific aspect of high school life, for example, the homecoming event. Then a
number of students attended the same high school. This is the reason there are slight differences in the
number of students, the number of papers, and the number of high schools.

2. The states represented are Alabama, California, Colorado, Connecticut, Delaware, District of
Columbia, Florida, Georgia, Hawaii, Illinois, Louisiana, Maryland, Massachusetts, Mississippi, Nebraska,
New Jersey, New York, North Carolina, Ohio, Oklahoma, Pennsylvania, Rhode Island, South Carolina,
Tennessee, Texas, Vermont, and Washington. Reports on schools in Virginia and Texas are greatly over-
represented with 115 and 78 respectively. The eight foreign countries are Argentina, Cape Verde Islands,
India, Korea, Malaysia, Pakistan, Philippines, and Singapore, and the U.S. territory is Guam.

3. Here are some of the comments from fieldworkers:

> "The students seemed to be perfectly willing to let me sit with them but once I did, they pro-
> ceeded to ignore me. Once they asked me if I was going to ask them questions, but I told them
> that for right now I was only there to listen; they shrugged and proceeded to ignore me some
> more" (FW26).

> "They were indifferent to my presence at their table; their conversations did not seem
> affected by the knowledge that some college student was doing a 'study' on them. Thus, I was
> able to sit back and effectively observe the interactions between these students and the rest of the
> student body" (FW30).

> "I was nervous when I introduced myself and told them what I was doing. My voice even
> cracked slightly as I made this introduction; they found this very funny. Once I sat down, they
> basically ignored me" (FW33).

> "I generally felt ignored, and they seemed to be acting completely natural. I felt very invisi-
> ble for the most part" (FW31).

> "Both male and female all African–American … Initial reaction, greeted me, asked a few
> questions about me and then continued conversing among themselves. Seemed to behave in
> their usual manner" (FW4).

> "Gender composition of table mostly female with males dropping in and out. Racial compo-
> sition all African American. Age composition: one junior, one sophomore, two freshman (twins).
> I have spent one previous lunch period with this group. Friendly reaction to my presence, open
> to conversation" (FW4).

"I had never observed this group, but they told me that they had been studied before. They didn't seem to mind my presence and for the most part ignored me" (FW5).

"When they swore, they immediately turned to me and apologized; thinking that they were not allowed to do so. I guess this suggests that they still readily view me as an observer which seems logical since it is the first time that they have met me" (FW17).

A few observers reported difficulty in establishing rapport:

"This was my first observation of this group … I asked if I could sit down and some of the group looked at me with a look of contempt. I … started talking to the guy who looked like the leader, Martin. Most were not eating … Two in the group were working on schoolwork. Then when I really started to observe, most of the group got up and left." The same observer reports on a similar group: "I told them what I was doing and they accepted me right away and acted like I was just part of the group, introducing themselves to me." But later he reports: "this time the group seemed to be more apprehensive about my presence. They got into smaller groups and talked among themselves more—not allowing me to listen." Still later: "I felt they accepted my presence more this time …" (FW22).

"At some points there was no conversation at all at the table. I'm not sure if this was because of my presence or if that was how they normally act. Overall I think they were uncomfortable because I was there" (FW32).

4. After consultation with those who had participated in the fieldwork, the initial assignments of second semester students were to groups that had not been studied before, because we felt it was important to expand the variety of groups that were observed. Since most observers observed one or two groups in addition to their original assignment, some of the groups observed the first semester were also observed the second semester.

APPENDIX IV

1. During the first part of our re-study Wilson High had three separate lunch periods each day. Hence, if two fieldworkers observed students at each of the three periods this would result in six "observation periods." Later in the school year the school switched to only two lunch periods per day. Usually a fieldworker would spend the entire lunch period with one table of students. On some occasions, however, students might eat quickly and leave the lunchroom. In those cases fieldworkers usually moved to a different table and carried out observations for the rest of the period. At least two of the observation periods were not at lunch, but were a school assembly and a school football game. Interviews with students, teachers, and staff are a separate category of data and not included in the above estimate.

BIBLIOGRAPHY

Abercrombie, Nicholas, Stephen Hill, and Bryan Turner. 1984 [1980]. *The Dominant Ideology Thesis.* London: George Allen and Unwin.

Adatto, Kiku. 2003. "Selling out Childhood," *Hedgehog Review* 5:24–40.

Adler, Patricia A., and Peter Adler. 1998. *Peer Power: Preadolescent Culture and Identity.* New Brunswick, New Jersey: Rutgers University Press.

Ahn, June. 2012. "Teenagers' Experiences with Social Network Sites: Relationships to Bridging and Bonding Social Capital," *The Information Society: An International Journal* 28:2:99–109.

Albert, Dustin and Laurence Steinberg. 2011. "Judgment and Decision Making in Adolescence," *Journal of Research on Adolescence* 21:211–224.

Alexander, Jeffrey C. and Philip Smith. 1998. "Cultural Sociology or Sociology of Culture?" *Sociologie et sociétés* 30:107–116.

Allport, Gordon W. 1948. *ABC's of Scapegoating.* Chicago: Roosevelt College.

Allport, Gordon W. 1954. *The Nature of Prejudice.* Reading, MA: Addison-Wesley Publishing Company.

Alsakar, Francois D., and August Flammer. 1999. *The Adolescent Experience.* Mahwah, NJ: Lawrence Erlbaum Associates.

Althusser, Louis. 1971. "Ideology and the Ideological State Apparatuses," in *Lenin and Philosophy and Other Essays.* London: Verso.

Alvarez, Lizette. 2013. "Charges Dropped in Cyberbullying Death, but Sheriff Isn't Backing Down," *New York Times,* November 21, 2013.

Anderson, Elijah. 1999. *Code of the Street: Decency, Violence, and the Moral Life of the Inner City.* New York: W. W. Norton Co.

Anderssen, Norman, Bente Wold, and Torbjørn Torsheim. 2006. "Are Parental Health Habits Transmitted to Their Children? An Eight Year Longitudinal Study of Physical Activity in Adolescents and Their Parents," *Journal of Adolescence* 29:4:513–524.

Angwin, Julia. 2010. "The Web's New Gold Mine: Your Secrets—A *Journal* investigation finds that one of the fastest-growing businesses on the Internet is the business of spying on consumers," *The Wall Street Journal,* July 30, 2010.

Apple, Michael. 1995. *Education and Power.* New York: Routledge.

Armstrong, Elizabeth A., Laura Hamilton, and Brian Sweeney. 2006. "Sexual Assault on Campus: A Multilevel, Integrative Approach to Party Rape," *Social Problems* 53:4:483–499.

Arnstine, Donald. 1987. "What High Schools Are Like," *Educational Studies* 18:1:1–3.

Aschaffenburg, Karen, and Ineke Maas. 1997. "Cultural and Educational Careers: The Dynamics of Social Reproduction," *American Sociological Review* 62:573–587.

Baker, Michael, et al. 1969. *Police on Campus: The Mass Police Action at Columbia University, Spring, 1968.* New York: New York Civil Liberties Union.

Barglow, Peter. 2000. [Review of] *The Nurture Assumption* by Judith Rich Harris, *American Journal of Psychiatry* 757:8:1355–1356.

335

Barth, Fredrik. 1970. *Ethnic Groups and Boundaries*. Boston: Little, Brown and Company.

Belk, Russell W. 1988. "Possessions and the Extended Self," *Journal of Consumer Research* 15:2: 139–168, reprinted in *Consumption*, Daniel Miller, ed. 2001. London: Routledge.

Bell, Daniel. 1973. *The Coming of Post-Industrial Society*. New York: Basic Books.

Bell, Daniel. 1975. *The Cultural Contradictions of Capitalism*. New York: Basic Books.

Berbrier, Mitch. 2002. "Making Minorities: Cultural Space, Stigma Transformation Frames, and the Categorical Status Claims of Deaf, Gay, and White Supremacist Activists in Late Twentieth Century America," *Sociological Forum* 17:553–591.

Berger, Joseph, Morris Zeldich, Jr., and Bo Anderson. 1966. *Sociological Theories in Progress*, Vol. 1. Boston: Houghton Mifflin Co., chaps. 2, 3, and 12.

Berlin, Isaiah. 1998 [1997]. "The First and the Last," *The New York Review of Books*, May 14, 1998.

Berlin, Isaiah. 2000. *The Power of Ideas*, ed. Henry Hardy. Princeton: Princeton University Press.

Best, Amy L. 2000. *Prom Night: Youth, Schools, and Popular Culture*. New York: Routledge.

Best, Joel and Kathleen A. Bogle. 2014. *Kids Gone Wild: From Rainbow Parties to Sexting, Understanding the Hype Over Teen Sex*. New York: NYU Press.

Best, Steven, and Douglas Kellner. 1997–99. "Rap, Black Rage, and Racial Difference," *Enculturation* 2:2.

Bettis, Pamela J. 1996a. "Urban Students, Liminality, and the Postindustrial Context," *Sociology of Education* 69: 105–125.

Bettis, Pamela J. 1996b. "Urban Abstraction in a Central City High School," *The Urban Review* 28:4:309–335.

Bianchi, Suzanne M. 2000. "Maternal Employment and Time with Children: Dramatic Change or Surprising Continuity?" *Demography* 37:4:401–414.

Biddle, Bruce J. 1998. "[Review of] Beyond the Classroom: Why School Reform Has Failed and What Parents Need to Do," *Teachers College Record* 100:454–460.

Blau, Peter, and Otis Dudley Duncan. 1967. *The American Occupational Structure*. New York: John Wiley & Sons.

Bliss, James R., William A. Firestone, and Craig E. Richards. 1991. *Rethinking Effective Schools: Research and Policies*. Englewood Cliffs, NJ: Prentice Hall.

Bodenhausen, Galen V. and Meryl Lichtenstein. 1987. "Social Stereotypes and Information Processing Strategies: The Impact of Task Complexity," *Journal of Personality and Social Psychology* 52:5:871–880.

Boehm, Kathryn E., et al. 1999. "Teens' Concerns: A National Evaluation," *Adolescence* 34:135:523–528.

Boeke, Dr. J. H. 1953. *Economics and Economic Policy of Dual Societies: As Exemplified by Indonesia*. New York: International Secretariat, Institute of Pacific Relations.

Bosworth, David. 1996. *The Georgia Review*, L:3:441–459.

Bosworth, David. 1999. "The Spirit of Capitalism," 2000, *The Public Interest*, Fall [Archived Issue]. http://www.thepublicinterest.cow/archives/1999fall/article1.html; May 16, 2001.

Bourdieu, Pierre. 1977. *An Outline of a Theory of Practice*. Cambridge: Cambridge University Press.

Bourdieu, Pierre. 1984. *Distinction: A Social Critique of the Judgment of Taste*. Cambridge, MA: Harvard University Press.

Bourdieu, Pierre. 1986. "The Forms of Capital," in *Handbook of Theory and Research of the Sociology of Education*. New York: Greenwood Press.

Bourdieu, Pierre. 1989. *The State of Nobility: Elite Schools in the Field of Power*. Stanford: Stanford University Press.

Bourdieu, Pierre, and Jean-Claude Passeron. 1990. *Reproduction in Education, Society and Culture*. Second edition. London: Sage in association with *Theory, Culture & Society*.

boyd, danna. 2014. *It's Complicated: The Social Lives of Networked Teens*. New Haven: Yale University Press.

Brake, Michael. 1985. *Comparative Youth Culture*. London: Routledge & Kegan Paul.

Brint, Steven. 1994. *In an Age of Experts: The Changing Role of Professionals in Politics and Public Life*. Princeton: Princeton University Press.

Brint, Steven. 1998. *Schools and Societies*. Thousand Oaks, CA: Pine Forge Press.

Brooks, David. 2000. *Bobos in Paradise: The New Upper Class and How They Got There*. New York: Simon and Schuster.

Brooks-Gunn, Jeanne, and Frank E. Furstenberg, Jr. 1989. "Adolescent Sexual Behavior," *American Psychologists* 44:249–257.

Brown, B. Bradford. 1990. "Peer Groups and Peer Cultures," in Feldman and Elliot (1990).

Brown, B. Bradford, Sue Ann Eicher, and Sandra Petrie. 1986. "The Importance of Peer Group ('Crowd') Affiliation in Adolescence," *Journal of Adolescence* 9:73–96.

Brown, B. Bradford, Mary Jane Lohr, and Carla Trujillo. 1990. "Multiple Crowds and Multiple Life Styles: Adolescents' Perceptions of Peer-Group Stereotypes," in Muuss (1990).

Brown, B. Bradford, Margaret S. Mory, and David Kinney. 1994. "Casting Adolescent Crowds in a Relational Perspective: Caricature, Channel, and Context," in Montemayor, Adams, and Gullotta (1994).

Brown, B. Bradford, Nina Mounts, Susie D. Lamborn, and Laurence Steinberg. 1993. "Parenting Practices and Peer Group Affiliations," *Child Development* 64:467–482.

Bryk, Anthony S., Valerie E. Lee, and Peter B. Holland. 1993. *Catholic Schools and the Common Good*. Cambridge, MA: Harvard University Press.

Campbell, Marilyn A. 2005. "The Impact of the Mobile Phone on Young People's Social Life," Paper presented at the Social Change in the 21st Century Conference, 28 October, QUT Carseldine, Brisbane.

Canaan, Joyce. 1987. "A Comparative Analysis of American Suburban Middle Class, Middle School, and High School Cliques," in *Interpretive Ethnography of Education*. George Spindler and Louise Spindler, eds. Hillsdale, NJ: Lawrence Erlbaum Associates, pp. 385–408.

Card, David and Laura Giuliano. 2013. "Peer Effects and Multiple Equilibria in the Risky Behavior of Friends," *The Review of Economics and Statistics* 95:1130–1149.

Cartwright, Justin. 1998. *Leading the Cheers*. London: Sceptre.

Cerulo, Karen A. 1997. "Identity Construction: New Issues, New Directions," *Annual Review of Sociology* 23:385–409.

Chadwick, Bruce A., and Tim B. Heaton, eds. 1999. *Statistical Handbook on Adolescents in America*. Second edition. Phoenix, AZ: Oryx Press.

Chen, M. 1994. *The Smart Parent's Guide to Kids' TV*. San Francisco: KQED Books.

Chen, Greg, and Lynn A. Weikart. 2008. "Student Background, School Climate, School Disorder, and Student Achievement: An Empirical Study of New York City's Middle Schools," *Journal of School Violence* 7:3–20.

Christman, Jolley, Jody Cohen, and Pat McPherson. 1997. "Growing Smaller: Three Tasks in Restructuring Urban High Schools," *Urban Education* 32:1:146–165.

Christopher, E. Scott, and Susan Sprecher. 2000. "Sexuality in Marriage, Dating, and Other Relationships: A Decade Review," *Journal of Marriage and the Family* 62:999–1017.

Chung, He Len, Edward P. Mulvey, and Laurence Steinberg. 2011. "Understanding the School Outcomes of Juvenile Offenders: An Exploration of Neighborhood Influences and Motivational Resources," *Journal of Youth & Adolescence* 40:8:1025–1038.

Churchill, Gilbert A., Jr., and George P. Moschis. 1979. "Television and Interpersonal Influences and Adolescent Consumer Learning," *Journal of Consumer Research* 6:1:23–35.

Clark, Samuel. 1995. *States and Status: The Rise of the State and Aristocratic Power in Western Europe*. Montreal: McGill-Queen's University Press.

Clasen, Donna Rae, and B. Bradford Brown. 1985. "The Multidimensionality of Peer Pressure in Adolescence," *Journal of Youth and Adolescence* 14:6:451–467.

Cohen, Albert K. 1955. *Delinquent Boys: The Culture of the Gang*. Glencoe, IL: Free Press.

Cohen, Jere. 1979. "Socio-economic Status and High-School Friendship Choice: Elmtown's Youth Revisited," *Social Networks* 2:65–74.

Coleman, James S. 1961. *The Adolescent Society: The Social Life of the Teenager and its Impact on Education*. New York: The Free Press.

Coleman, James S., et al. 1966. *Equality of Educational Opportunity*. Washington, DC: Government Printing Office, HEW.

Coleman, James S. 1990. *Equality and Achievement in Education*. Boulder: Westview Press.

Coleman, James S., Thomas Hoffer, and Sally Kilgore. 1982. *High School Achievement: Public, Catholic, and Private Schools Compared*. New York: Basic Books.

Coleman, James S., and Thomas Hoffer. 1987. *Public and Private High Schools: The Impact of Communities*. New York: Basic Books.

Collins, Randall. 1975. *Conflict Sociology: Toward an Explanatory Science*. New York: Academic Press.

Collins, Randall. 1979. *The Credential Society: A Historical Sociology of Education and Stratification*. New York: Academic Press.

Collins, Randall. 1988. *Sociology of Marriage and Family: Gender, Love, and Property*. New York: Burnham Inc. Publishing.

Collins, Randall. 1988. *Theoretical Sociology*. San Diego: Harcourt, Brace, Jovanovich.

Collins, Randall. 1992. "Women and the Production of Status Cultures," in Lamont and Fournier (1992).

Collins, Randall. 2000. "Situational Stratification: A Micro Macro Theory of Inequality," *Sociological Theory* 18:1:17–43.

Condry, John. 1993. "Thief of Time, Unfaithful Servant: Television and the American Child," *Daedalus*, Winter 122:1:259ff.

Consumers Union. 1995. *Captive Kids: A Report on Commercial Pressures on Kids at School*. New York: Consumers Union Education Services.

Cookson, Peter W., and Caroline Hodges Persell. 1985. *Preparing for Power: America's Elite Boarding Schools*. New York: Basic Books.

Corak, Miles. 2013. "Income Inequality, Equality of Opportunity, and Intergenerational Mobility," *Journal of Economic Perspectives* 27:3:79–102.

Corsaro, William A. 1997. *The Sociology of Childhood*. Thousand Oaks, CA: Pine Forge Press.

Corsaro, William A., and Donna Eder. 1990. "Children's Peer Cultures," *Annual Review of Sociology* 16:197–220.

Cox, Dena, Anthony D. Cox, and George P. Moschis. 1990. "When Consumer Behavior Goes Bad: An Investigation of Adolescent Shoplifting," *Journal of Consumer Research* 17:2:149–160.

Crosnoe, Robert. 2001. "The Social World of Male and Female Athletes in High School," *Sociological Studies of Children and Youth* 8:89–110.

Cross, Gary. 2002. "Values of Desire: A Historian's Perspective on Parents, Children, and Marketing," *Journal of Consumer Resarch* 29:441–447.

Currier, Danielle M. 2013. "Strategic Ambiguity: Protecting Emphasized Femininity and Hegemonic Masculinity in the Hookup Culture," *Gender & Society* 27:5 (October): 704–727.

Cusick, Philip A. 1973. *Inside High School: The Student's World*. New York: Holt, Rinehart and Winston, Inc.

Dahl, Robert A. 1961. *Who Governs? Democracy and Power in an American City*. New Haven: Yale University Press.

Dahrendorf, Ralf. 1959. *Class and Class Conflict in Industrial Society*. Stanford: Stanford University Press.

Damron-Bell, Jessica. 2011. "The Development of Deviant Behavior in Adolescents: The Influence of Student Characteristics and School Climate." PhD Dissertation, Department of Educational and Counseling Psychology, University of Louisville.

Dance, Janelle L. 2002. *Tough Fronts: The Impact of Street Culture on Schooling*. New York: Routledge Falmer.

Danesi, Marcel. 1994. *Cool: The Signs and Meanings of Adolescence*. Toronto: University of Toronto Press.

Davies, Scott. 1995. "Leaps of Faith: Shifting Currents in Critical Sociology of Education," *American Journal of Sociology* 100:1448–78.

Deming, W. Edward. 1986. *Out of Crisis*. Cambridge: MIT Press.

Derrida, Jacques. 1978. *Writing and Difference*. Chicago: University of Chicago Press.

DiMaggio, Paul. 1979. "Review Essay on Pierre Bourdieu," in *American Journal of Sociology* 84:1460–1475.

DiMaggio, Paul. 1982. "Cultural Capital and School Success: The Impact of Status-Culture Participation on the Grades of U.S. High School Students," *American Sociological Review* 47:189–202.

DiMaggio, Paul, and John Mohr. 1985. "Cultural Capital, Educational Attainment, and Marital Selection," *American Journal of Sociology* 90:1231–61.

Domhoff, G. William. 1998. *Who Rules America?. Power and Politics in the Year 2000*. London: May field Publishing Company.

Dornbusch, Sanford A. 1989. "The Sociology of Adolescence," in *The Annual Review of Sociology*. W. Richard Scott and Judith Blake, eds. Palo Alto, CA: Annual Reviews, pp. 233–259.

Dreeben, Robert. 1967. *On What Is Learned in School*. Reading, MA: Addison-Wesley Pub. Co.

Duncan, Greg J, and Richard J Murnane. 2011. *Whither Opportunity?: Rising Inequality, Schools, and Children's Life Chances*. New York: Russell Sage Foundation.

Dunphy, Dexter. 1963. "The Social Structure of Urban Adolescent Peer Groups," *Sociometry* 26:2:230–246.

Durkheim, Emile. 1984 [1893]. *The Division of Labor in Society*. New York: Free Press.

Durkheim, Emile. 1997 [1897]. *Suicide: A Study in Sociology*. New York: Free Press.

Durkheim, Emile. 1965 [1915]. *The Elementary Forms of Religious Life*. New York: Free Press.

Durkheim, Emile. 1961 [1925]. *Moral Education: A Study in the Theory and Application of the Sociology of Education*. New York: Free Press.

Eagan, K., E. B. Stolzenberg, J. J. Ramirez, M. C. Aragon, M. R. Suchard, and S. Hurtado. (2014). *The American Freshman: National Norms Fall 2014*. Los Angeles: Higher Education Research Institute, UCLA.

Eckert, Penelope. 1989. *Jocks and Burnouts: Social Categories and Identity in the High School*. New York: Teacher's College Press.

Economist (U.S.). 1997. "The Shop for Little Horrors," July 5, 65.

Eder, Donna, and Janet Lynne Enke. 1991. "The Structure of Gossip: Opportunities and Constraints on Collective Expression among Adolescents," *American Sociological Review* 56:494–508.

Eder, Donna, Catherine Colleen Evans, and Stephen Parker. 1995. *School Talk: Gender and Adolescent Culture*. New Brunswick, NJ: Rutgers University Press.

Eder, Donna, and David A. Kinney. 1995. "The Effect of Middle School Extracurricular Activities on Adolescents' Popularity and Peer Status," *Youth and Society* 26:3:298–324.

Edgerton, Robert B. 1993. *The Cloak of Competence*. Revised and updated. Berkeley: University of California Press.

Egan, Timothy. 2000. "The Changing Face of Catholic Education," *New York Times*, August 6, 2000: http://www.nytimes.com/2000/08/06/education/the-changing-face-of-catholic-education. html; accessed 10/06/2015.

Elkin, Fredrick, and William A. Westley. 1955. "The Myth of Adolescent Culture," *American Sociological Review* 20:680–684.

Elliott, Richard, and Kritsadarat Wattanasuwan. 1998. "Brands as Symbolic Resources for the Construction of Identity," *International Journal of Advertising* 17:2:131–144.

Encarta World English Dictionary. 1999. [No location]: Microsoft Corp.

Ennett, Susan T., and Karl E. Bauman. 1996. "Adolescent Social Networks: School, Demographic, and Longitudinal Considerations," *Journal of Adolescent Research* 11:2:194–215.

Entwisle, Doris R., Karl L. Alexander, and Linda Steffel Olson. 1997. *Children, Schools, and Inequality*. Boulder, CO: Westview Press.

Epstein, Jonathan S., ed. 1994. *Adolescents and Their Music: If It's Too Loud, You're Too Old*. New York: Garland Press, Inc.

Epstein, Joyce Levy, and Nancy Karweit. 1983. *Friends in School*. New York: Academic Press.

Erikson, Erik. 1963. *Childhoods and Society*. Second edition, rev and enl. New York: W. W Norton.

Erikson, Erik. 1968. *Identity, Youth, and Crisis*. New York: W. W. Norton.

Espinoza, Guadalupe, and Jaana Juvonen. 2011. "The Pervasiveness, Connectedness, and Intrusiveness of Social Network Site Use Among Young Adolescents," *Cyberpsychology, Behavior, and Social Networking* 14:12 (December):705–709.

Evans-Whipp, T. J., S. M. Plenty, R. F. Catalano, T. I. Herrenkohl, and J. W. Toumbourou. 2013. "The Impact of School Alcohol Policy on Student Drinking," *Health Education Research* 28:4:651–662.

Farhi, Paul. 1998. "On TV, a Prime Time for Teens." *Washington Post*, October 21.

Farkas, George. 1996. *Human Capital or Cultural Capital*. New York: Aldine de Gruyter.

Farkas, George, Christy Lleras, and Steve Maczuga. 2002. "Does Oppositional Culture Exist in Minority and Poverty Peer Groups?" *American Sociological Review* 67:148–155.

Featherman, David L., and Robert M. Hauser. 1978. *Opportunity and Change*. New York: Academic Press.

Feldman, S. Shirley, and Glen R. Elliot, eds. 1990. *At the Threshold: The Developing Adolescent*. Cambridge: Harvard University Press.

Feldman, S. S. & Elliott, G. R. (1990). "Progress and promise of research on adolescence," in *At the Threshold: The Developing Adolescent*, eds S.S. Feldman and G. R. Elliott. Cambridge, MA; Harvard University Press.

Field, Tiffany, et al. 1998. "Feelings and Attitudes of Gifted Students," *Adolescence* 33:130:331–342.

Finnegan, William. 1998. *Cold New World: Growing Up in a Harder Country*. New York: Modern Library.

Firat, A. Fuat, and Alloadi Venkatesh. 1995. "Liberatory Postmodernism and the Reenchantment of Consumption," *Journal of Consumer Research* 22:239–267.

Firebaugh, Glenn. 2000. "The Trend in Between-Nation Income Inequality," *Annual Review of Sociology* 26:323–39.

Foley, Douglas E. 1990. *Learning Capitalist Culture: Deep in the Heart of Tejas*. Philadelphia: University of Pennsylvania Press.

Ford, Henry. 1922. *My Life and Work*. In collaboration with Samuel Crowther. Garden City, NY: Doubleday, Page, & Co.

Fordham, Signithia. 1988. "Racelessness as a Factor in Black Students' School Success: Pragmatic Strategy or Pyrrhic Victory?" *Harvard Educational Review* 58:1:54–84.

Fordham, Signithia, and John U. Ogbu. 1986. "Black Students' School Success: Coping with the Burden of 'Acting White'," *The Urban Review* 18:3:176–206.

Foucault, Michel. 1973. *Madness and Civilization*. New York: Vintage Books.

Foucault, Michel. 1978. *The History of Sexuality*. New York: Pantheon Books.

Foucault, Michel. 1979. *Discipline and Punish: The Birth of the Prison*. Harmondsworth, England: Penguin Books.

Foucault, Michel. 1980. *Power/Knowledge: Selected Interview and Other Writings, 1972–1977*. New York: Pantheon Books.

Frank, S. 2011. "Teens' Excessive Use of Texting, Social Media Linked to Risky Behavior," *American Public Health Association Newsletter* 13:4 (January):8–11.

Frank, Thomas. 1997. *The Conquest of the Cool: Business Culture, Counterculture, and the Rise of Hip Consumerism*. Chicago: University of Chicago Press.

Franzoi, Stephen I., Mark Davis, and Kristin A. Vasquez-Suson. 1994. "Two Social Worlds: Social Correlates and Stability of Adolescent Status Groups," *Journal of Personality and Social Psychology* 67:3:462–473.

Fryer, Roland G. 2006. "Acting White," *Education Next* 6:52–59.

Fuchs, Stephan. 2001. *Against Essentialism: A Theory of Culture and Society*. Cambridge: Harvard University Press.

Furman, Wyndol, and Elizabeth A. Wehner. 1994. "Romantic Use: Toward a Theory of Adolescent Romantic Relationships," in *Personal Relationships During Adolescence*, eds. Raymond Montemayor, Gerald R. Adams, and Thomas P. Gullotta. *Advances in Adolescent Development: An Annual Book Series*, vol. 6. Thousand Oaks, CA: SAGE Publications, pp. 168–195.

Furnivall, J. S. 1941. *Progress and Welfare in Southeast Asia: A Comparison of Colonial Policy and Practice*. New York: Secretariat, Institute of Pacific Relations.

Furstenberg, Frank E. 2000. "The Sociology of Adolescence and Youth in the 1990s: A Critical Commentary," *Journal of Marriage and the Family* 62:896–910.

Gardner, Howard. 1998. "Do Parents Count?" *The New York Review of Books* 45: http://www.nybooks.com/articles/archives/1998/nov/05/do-parents-count/; accessed 10/06/2015.

Gaviria, Alejandro and Steven Raphael. 2011. "School-Based Peer Effects and Juvenile Behavior," *The Review of Economics and Statistics* 83:257–268.

Gerstel, Naomi. 1999. [Review of] *The Nurture Assumption: Why Children Turn Out the Way They Do*, by Judith Rich Harris, *Contemporary Sociology: A Journal of Reviews* 28:2:174–176.

Giddens, Anthony. 2000. *The Third Way and Its Critics*. Cambridge: Polity Press.

Giordano, Peggy C. 1995. "The Wider Circle of Friends in Adolescence," *American Journal of Sociology* 10:3:661–97.

Giroux, Henry A. 2000. *Stealing Innocence: Youth, Corporate Power and the Politics of Culture*. New York: St. Martin's Press.

Gladwell, Malcolm. 1997a. "Annals of Style: The Coolhunt," *The New Yorker*, March 17, pp. 78ff.

Gladwell, Malcolm. 1997b. "The Sports Taboo: Why Blacks Are Like Boys and Whites Are Like Girls," *The New Yorker*, pp. 50–55.

Glazer, Nathan. 1997. *We Are All Multiculturalists Now*. Cambridge, MA: Harvard University Press.

Goffman, Erving. 1961. *Asylums; Essays on the Social Situation of Mental Patients and Other Inmates*. First edition. Garden City, NY: Anchor Books.

Goldberg, Alan D., and Timothy J. H. Chandler. 1989. "The Role of Athletics: The Social World of High School Athletes," *Youth and Society* 21:2:238–250.

Gouldner, Alvin. 1979. *The Future of Intellectuals and the Rise of the New Class*. New York: Seabury Press.

Graubard, Allen. 1998. "[Review of] Beyond the Classroom: Why School Reform Has Failed and What Parents Need to Do," *Boston Review* 23.

Green, Robert W. 1959. *Protestantism and Capitalism: The Weber Thesis and Its Critics*. Boston: D. C. Heath and Co.

Grogger, Jeffrey, and Derek Neal. 2000. "Further Evidence on the Effects of Catholic Secondary Schooling," *Brookings-Wharton Papers on Urban Affairs*, 151–193.

Grossberg, Lawrence. 1994. "The Political Status of Youth and Youth Culture," in Epstein (1994).

Guernsey, Lisa. 2003. "High School Confidential, Online," *The New York Times*, May 8.

Habermas, Jurgen. 1994. "The Emergence of the Public Sphere," in *The Polity Reader in Cultural Theory*. Cambridge: Polity Press.

Hall, G. Stanley. [1905] 1969. *Adolescence*. Reprint. New York: Arno Press.

Hall, Stuart, and Tony Jefferson, eds. 1976. *Resistance Through Rituals: Youth Subcultures in Post-War Britain*. London: Hutchinson.

Hallinan, Maureen T. 1980. "Patterns of Cliquing Among Youth," in *Friendship and Social Relations in Children*, eds. H. C. Foote, A. J. Chapman, and J. R. Smith. New York: John Wiley & Sons.

Hallinan, Maureen T. and Stevens S. Smith. 1985. "The Effects of Classroom Racial Composition on Student Interracial Friendliness," *Social Psychology Quarterly* 48:1:3–16.

Hallinan, Maureen T. and Richard A. Williams. 1989. "Interracial Friendship Choices in Secondary Schools," *American Sociological Review* 54:67–78.

Hanushek, Eric A., and Steven G. Rivkin. 1996. *Understanding the 20th Century Growth in U.S. School Spending*. Cambridge, MA: National Bureau of Economic Research, Inc., Working Paper Series.

Harris, Judith Rich. 1998. *The Nurture Assumption: Why Children Turn Out the Way They Do*. New York: The Free Press.

Hawley, Willis D., ed. 2002. *The Keys to Effective Schools*. Thousand Oaks, CA: Corwin Press.

Hays, Kim. 1994. *Practicing Virtues: Moral Traditions at Quaker and Military Boarding Schools*. Berkeley: University of California Press.

Hays, Sharon. 1996. *The Cultural Contradictions of Motherhood*. New Haven: Yale University Press.

Heldman, Caroline and Lisa Wade. 2010. "Hook-Up Culture: Setting a New Research Agenda," *Sex Research and Social Policy* 7:323–333.

Hersch, Patricia. 1998. *A Tribe Apart: A Journey Into the Heart of American Adolescence*. New York: Ballantine.

Hine, Thomas. 1999. *The Rise and Fall of the American Teenager*. New York: Avon Books.

Hoffman, Eric. 1985. "The Effect of Race-Ratio Composition on the Frequency of Organizational Communication," *Social Psychology Quarterly* 48:1:17–26.

Holland, Alyce, and Thomas Andre. 1995. "Prestige Ratings of High School Extracurricular Activities," *The High School Journal* 78:2:67–72.

Hollingshead, August B. 1975. *Elmtown's Youth and Elmtown Revisited*. New York: John Wiley & Sons.

Horowitz, Donald L. 1985. *Ethnic Groups in Conflict*. Berkeley: University of California Press.

Horowitz, Ruth. 1983. *Honor and the American Dream: Culture and Identity in a Chicano Community*. New Brunswick, NJ: Rutgers University Press.

Hoynes, William. 1997. "News for a Captive Audience: An Analysis of Channel One," *Extra* 10:3:11–17.

Hulbert, Ann. 2003. *Raising America: Experts, Parents, and a Century of Advice About Children*. New York: Alfred A. Knopf.

Hundley, Heather L., and Leonard Shyles. 2010. "US Teenagers' Perceptions and Awareness of Digital Technology: A Focus Group Approach," *New Media & Society* 12:3:417–433.

Hunter, Floyd. 1963 [c1953]. *Community Power Structure; A Study of Decision Makers*. Garden City, NY: Doubleday.

Hunter, James Davidson. 2000. *The Death of Character: Moral Education in an Age without Good and Evil*. New York: Basic Books.

Hupfield, Herman. 1934. "As Time Goes By," [Song lyrics], http://crydee.sai.msu.ru/public/lyrics/cs-uwp/h/hupfield.herman/as-time-goes-by; July 7, 2003.

Hurrelman, Klaus. 1996. "The Social World of Adolescents: A Sociological Perspective," in *Social Problems and Social Contexts in Adolescence: Perspectives Across Boundaries*, Klaus Hurrelman, and Stephen E Hamilton, eds. New York: Aldine de Gruyter.

Ianni, Francis A. J. 1989. *The Search for Structure: A Report on American Youth Today*. New York: The Free Press.

Illouz, E. 1997. *Consuming the Romantic Utopia: Love and the Cultural Contradictions of Capitalism*. Berkeley: University of California Press.

Isaacs, Julia B. 2007. "Economic Mobility of Families across Generations," Economic Mobility Project: An Initiative of The Pew Charitable Trusts, The Brookings Institute; http://www.brookings.edu/research/papers/2007/11/generations-isaacs; February 9, 2015.

Ito, Mizuko, et al. 2010. *Hanging Out, Messing Around, and Geeking Out: Kids Living and Learning with New Media*. Cambridge, MA: Massachusetts Institute of Technology.

Jaccard, James, Hart Blanton, and Tanya Dodge. 2005. "Peer Influences on Risk Behavior: An Analysis of the Effects of a Close Friend," *Developmental Psychology* 41:135–147.

Jacob, Brian A., and Tamara Wilder Linkow. 2011. "Educational Expectations and Attainment," in *Whither Opportunity*, edited by Greg Duncan and Richard Murnane. New York: Russell Sage, pp. 133–164.

Jang, Sung Joon. 2002. "The Effects of Family, School, Peers, and Attitudes on Adolescents' Drug Use: Do they Vary with Age?" *Justice Quarterly* 19:97–126.

Jang, Su A., Rajiv N. Rimal, and NamAuk Cho. 2013. "Exploring Parental Influences in the Theory of Normative Social Behavior: Findings from a Korean High School Sample," *Communication Research* 40:1:52–72.

Jasso, Guillermina. 2001. "Studying Status: An Integrated Framework," *American Sociological Review* 66: 96–124.

Jeffery, Patricia, and Roger Jeffery. 1996. *Don't Marry Me to a Plowman: Women's Everyday Lives in Rural North India*. Boulder, CO: Westview Press.

Jencks, Christopher, et al. 1972. *Inequality*. New York: Basic Books.

Jencks, Christopher, et al. 1979. *Who Gets Ahead?* New York: Basic Books.

Johnson, Sara B., Robert W. Blum, and Jay N. Giedd. 2009. "Review article: Adolescent Maturity and the Brain: The Promise and Pitfalls of Neuroscience Research in Adolescent Health Policy," *Journal of Adolescent Health* 45:3:216–221.

Johnson, Sara B., May Sudhinaraset, and Robert Wm. Blum. 2010. "Neuromaturation and Adolescent Risk Taking: Why Development Is Not Determinism," *Journal of Adolescent Research* 25:1:4–23.

Johnston, Jerome. 1995. "Channel One: The Dilemma of Teaching and Selling," *Phi Delta Kappan* 76:6:436f.

Kalberg, Stephen. 1980. "Max Weber's types of rationality," *American Journal of Sociology* 85:1145–1179.

Kandel, Denise. 1978. "Homophily, Selection, and Socialization in Adolescent Friendships," *American Journal of Sociology* 84:2:427–436.

Kandel, Denise. 1990 [1978]. "On Variations in Adolescent Subcultures," in Muuss (1990).

Kane, Mary Jo. 1988. "The Female Athletic Role as a Status Determinant with the School Systems of High School Adolescents," *Adolescence* 23:90:253–264.

Karabel, Jerome, and A. H. Halsey. 1977. *Powers and Ideology in Education*. Edited and with an introduction by Jerome Karabel and A. H. Halsey. New York: Oxford University Press.

Kaufman, P., et al. 2000. U.S. Departments of Education and Justice. NCES 2001–017/NCJ184176. Washington, DC; http://nces.ed.gov.

Kennedy, Janice H. 1990. "Determinants of Peer Social Status: Contributions of Physical Appearance, Reputation, and Behavior," *Journal of Youth and Adolescence* 19:3:233–244.

Kett, Joseph E 1977. *Rites of Passage: Adolescence in America 1790 to the Present*. New York: Basic Books.

Kingston, Paul W. 2000. *The Classless Society*. Stanford, CA: Stanford University Press.

Kingston, Paul William, and Lionel S. Lewis. 1990. *The High-Status Track: Studies of Elite Schools and Stratification*. Albany: State University of New York Press.

Kinney, David A. 1993. "From Nerds to Normals: The Recovery of Identity among Adolescents from Middle School to High School," *Sociology of Education* 66:21–40.

Kinney, David A. 1999. "From 'Headbangers' to 'Hippies'," *New Directions in Child and Adolescent Development* 84:21–35.

Klein, Matthew. 1997. "Teen Green," Forecast Newsdesk [of *Demographics*] posted December 1, http://www.demographics.cow/publications/fc/newsdesk/1201nd.htm, May 18, 2001.

Kornhauser, William. 1959. *The Politics of Mass Society*. Glencoe, IL: Free Press.

Krause, Granato J. 2000. "Information Diffusion within the Electorate: The Asymmetric Transmission of Political-Economic Information," *Electoral Studies* 19:4:519–537.

Kubitschek, Warren N., and Maureen Hallinan. 1998. "Tracking and Students' Friendships," *Social Psychology Quarterly* 61:1:1–16.

Lamont, Michele. 1992a. *Cultivating Difference: Symbolic Boundaries and the Making of Inequality*. Chicago: University of Chicago Press.

Lamont, Michele. 1992b. *Money, Morals, and Manners: The Culture of the French and American Upper-Middle Class*. Chicago: University of Chicago Press.

Lamont, Michele, ed. 1999. *The Cultural Territories of Race: Black and White Boundaries*. Chicago: University of Chicago Press.

Lamont, Michele. 2000. *The Dignity of Working Men: Morality and the Boundaries of Race, Class and Immigration*. New York: Russell Sage Foundation, and Cambridge: Harvard University Press.

Lamont, Michele, and Marcel Fournier, eds. 1992. *Cultivating Differences: Symbolic Boundaries and the Making of Inequality*. Chicago: University of Chicago Press.

Lamont, Michele, and Annette Lareau. 1988. "Cultural Capital: Allusions, Gaps and Glissandos in Recent Theoretical Developments," *Sociological Theory* 6:2:153–168.

Lamont, Michele, Jason Kaufman, and Michael Moody. 2000. "The Best of the Brightest: Definitions of the Ideal Self Among Prize-Winning Students," *Sociological Forum* 15:2:187–224.

Lancy, David F. 2008. *The Anthropology of Childhood: Cherubs, Chattel, Changelings.* Cambridge, UK: Cambridge University Press.

Landsheer, Hans A., et al. 1999. "Can Higher Grades Result in Fewer Friends? A Re-examination of the Relations between Academic and Social Competence," *Adolescence* 33:129:185–191.

Lareau, Annette. 2000. *Home Advantage: Social Class and Parental Intervention in Elementary Education.* Second edition. Lanham, MD: Rowan & Littlefield Publishers, Inc.

Lareau, Annette and Erin McNamara. 1999. "Moments of Social Inclusion and Exclusion: Race, Class, and Cultural Capital in Family-School Relationships," *Sociology of Education* 72:1:37–53.

Laursen, Brett. 1996. "Closeness and Conflict in Adolescent Peer Relationships: Interdependence with Friends and Romantic Partners," in *The Company They Keep: Friendship in Childhood and Adolescence,* eds. William M. Bukowski, Andrew E Newcomb, and Willard W. Hartup. Cambridge: Cambridge University Press.

Lazarsfeld, Paul, Bernard Berelson, and Hazel Gaudet. 1968 [1944]. *The Peoples' Choice: How the Voter Makes Up His Mind in a Presidential Campaign.* Third edition. New York: Columbia University Press.

Lears, Jackson. 1994. *Fables of Abundance: A Cultural History of Advertising in America.* New York: Basic Books.

Lee, E. Bun. 2014. "Facebook Use and Texting among African American and Hispanic Teenagers: An Implication for Academic Performance," *Journal of Black Studies* 45:2 (March):83–101.

Lee, Stacey J. 1996. *Unraveling the "Model Minority" Stereotype: Listening to Asian American Youth.* New York: Teachers College Press.

Lesko, Nancy. 1988. *Symbolizing Society: Stories, Rites and Structure in a Catholic High School.* New York: Falmer Press.

Lesko, Nancy. 2012. *Act Your Age!: A Cultural Construction of Adolescence.* Oxon, U.K.: Routledge.

Lewis, Michael. 1999. "Do Environments Matter At All?" *Social Policy* 29:34–43.

Lieberson, Stanley. 2000. *A Matter of Taste: How Names, Fashions, and Culture Change.* New Haven: Yale University Press.

Lightfoot, Sara Lawrence. 1983. *The Good High School: Portraits of Character and Culture.* New York: Basic Books.

Ling, Rich, Troels Fibaek Bertel, and Pal Roe Sundsoy. 2012. "The Socio-Demographics of Texting: An Analysis of Traffic Data," *New Media & Society* 14:2:281–298.

Lippy, Charles H. 2000. *Pluralism Comes of Age: American Religious Culture in the Twentieth Century.* Armonk, NY: M. E. Sharpe.

Liska, Allen E. 1990. "The significance of aggregate dependent variables and contextual independent variables for linking macro and micro theories," *Social psychology quarterly* 53:4:12:292–301, http://search.proquest.com/docview/61259992?accountid=14678 (accessed June 10, 2015).

Livy [Titus Livias]. circa 30 b.c. "History of Rome," 1.1, in *Readings in the Classical Historians,* selected and introduced by Michael Grant. New York: Charles Scribner's Sons, 1992.

Lucas, Samuel R. 2001. "Effectively Maintained Inequality: Education Transitions, Track Mobility, and Social Background Effects," *American Journal of Sociology* 106:1642–1690.

Lundborg, Petter. 2006. "Having the Wrong Friends? Peer Effects in Adolescent Substance Use," *Journal of Health Economics* 25:214–233.

McClelland, Kent A. 1982. "Adolescent Subculture in Schools," *Review of Human Development.* New York: John Wiley & Sons, chap. 22, pp. 395–417.

MacCoun, Robert and Peter Reuter. 1992. "Are the Wages of Sin $30 an Hour? Economic Aspects of Street-Level Drug Dealing," *Crime and Delinquency* 38:4:477–491.

McFarland, Daniel A. 2004. "Resistance as a Social Drama – A Study of Change-Oriented Encounters," *American Journal of Sociology* 109:1249–1318.

MacLeod, Jay. 1995 [1987]. *Ain't No Makin' It: Aspirations and Attainment in a Low-Income Neighborhood.* Boulder, CO: Westview Press.

McNeal, James U. 1992. *Kids as Customers: A Handbook of Marketing to Children*. New York: Lexington Books.

McNeal, James U. 1993. "Born to Shop." *American Demographics*, June.

McNeal, James U. 1998. "Tapping the Three Kids' Markets," *American Demographics*, April.

Macrae, C. Neil, Alan B. Milne, and Galen V. Bodenhausen. 1994. "Stereotypes as Energy-Saving Devices: A Peek Inside the Cognitive Toolbox," *Journal of Personality and Social Psychology* 66:1:37–47.

Males, Michael. 2009. "Does the Adolescent Brain Make Risk Taking Inevitable? A Skeptical Appraisal," *Journal of Adolescent Research* 24:1:3–20.

Marcel, Gabriel. 1952. *Man Against Mass Society*. Chicago: Regnery.

Mark, Noah. 1998. "Birds of a Feather Sing Together," *Social Forces* 77:2:453–485.

Martin, Karin A. 1996. *Puberty, Sexuality and the Self: Girls and Boys at Adolescence*. New York: Routledge.

Massey, Douglas S., et al. 2003. *The Source of the River: Social Origins of Freshmen at America's Selective Colleges and Universities*. Princeton: Princeton University Press.

Mathews, Jay. 1998. *Class Struggle: What's Wrong (and Right) with Americas Best Public High Schools*. New York: Times Books.

Mayer, Susan E. 2001. "How Did the Increase in Economic Inequality between 1970 and 1990 Affect Children's Educational Attainment?" *American Journal of Sociology* 107:1 (July):1–32.

Mayer, Susan E. 2010. "Revisiting an old question: How much does parental income affect child outcomes?," *Focus* 27:2 (Winter):21–26.

Melnick, Merrill, J., Donald E Sabo, and Beth Vanfossen. 1992. "Educational Effects of Interscholastic Athletic Participation on African–American and Hispanic Youth," *Adolescence* 27:106:295–308.

Meltzer, Bernard N., John W. Petras, and Larry T. Reynolds. 1976. *Symbolic Interactionism: Genesis, Varieties and Criticism*. Boston: Routledge & Kegan Paul.

Merten, Don E. 1996a. "Going-With: The Role of a Social Form in Early Romance," *Journal of Contemporary Ethnography* 24:4:462–484.

Merten, Don E. 1996b. "Burnout as Cheerleader: The Cultural Basis for Prestige and Privilege in Junior High School," *Anthropology and Education Quarterly* 27:1:51–70.

Merten, Don E. 1997. "The Meaning of Meanness: Popularity, Competition, and Conflict among Junior High School Girls," *Sociology of Education* 70:175–191.

Merten, Don E. 1999. "Enculturation into Secrecy Among Junior High Girls," *Journal of Contemporary Ethnography* 28:2:107–137.

Mesch, G. S., and I. Talmud. 2010. *Wired youth: the social world of adolescence in the information age*. London: Routledge.

Messner, Michael. 1989. "Masculinities and Athletic Careers," *Gender and Society* 3:71–88.

Metz, Mary Haywood. 1978. *Classrooms and Corridors: The Crisis of Authority in Desegregated Secondary Schools*. Berkeley: University of California Press.

Meyer, John W. and Brian Rowan. 1977. "Institutionalized Organizations: Formal Structure as Myth and Ceremony," *American Journal of Sociology* 83:340–363.

Milevsky, Avidan, Kylie Smoot, Melissa Leh, and Amy Ruppe. 2005. "Familial and contextual variables and the nature of sibling relationships in emerging adulthood," *Marriage & Family Review* 37:4:123-141, http://search.proquest.com/docview/59997126?accountid=14678 (accessed June 10, 2015).

Mills, Michael W. 1974. "The Student Movement and the Industrialization of Higher Education," in Karabel and Halsey (1974).

Mills, C. Wright. 1956. *The Power Elite*. New York: Oxford University Press.

Milner, Murray, Jr. 1972. *The Illusion of Equality: The Effects of Education on Opportunity, Inequality, and Social Conflict*. San Francisco: Jossey-Bass.

Milner, Murray, Jr. 1994. *Status and Sacredness: A General Theory of Status Relations and an Analysis of Indian Culture*. New York: Oxford University Press.

Milner, Murray, Jr. 1996. "Geeks, Weirdos and Cool Kids: Status Among American Adolescents." Presented at American Sociological Association Annual Meeting, 1996.

Milner, Murray, Jr. 1999. "Explaining the Status of Brahmans, Nerds, and Social Theorists." Presented at American Sociological Association Annual Meeting, 1999.

Milner, Murray Jr. 2013. "Paradoxical Inequalities: Adolescent Peer Relations in Indian Secondary Schools," *Sociology of Education* 86:4:253–267.

Montemayor, Raymond, Gerald R. Adams, and Thomas P. Gullotta, eds. 1994. *Personal Relationships During Adolescence*. Thousand Oaks, CA: SAGE Publications.

Mortimer, Jeylan, and Michael D. Finch, eds. 1996. *Adolescents, Work, and Family: An Intergenerational Developmental Analysis*. Thousand Oaks, CA: SAGE Publications.

Moschis, George P. 1985. "Role of Family Communication in Consumer Socialization of Children and Adolescents." *Journal of Consumer Research* 11:4:898–913.

Mounts, Nina S., and Steinberg, Laurence D. 1995. "An Ecological Analysis of Peer Influence on Adolescent Grade Point Average and Drug Use," *Developmental Psychology* 31:915–922.

Murphy, Raymond. 1988. *Social Closure: The Theory of Monopolization and Exclusion*. Oxford: Clarendon Press.

Muuss, Rolf E. 1990. *Adolescent Behavior and Society: A Book of Readings*, Fourth edition. New York: McGraw-Hill.

Nagel, Joane. 1986. "The Political Construction of Ethnicity," in *Competitive Ethnic Relations*, eds. Susan Olzark and Joane Nagel. Orlando: Academic Press.

Nagel, Joane. 1996. *American Indian Ethnic Renewal: Red Power and the Resurgence of Identity and Culture*. New York: Oxford University Press.

National Center for Education Statistics. 1998. Digest of Educational Statistics, Table 62.

Nisbett, Richard E., and Dov Cohen. 1992. *Culture of Honor: The Psychology of Violence in the South*. Boulder, CO: Westview Press.

Nock, Steven L. 1998. *Marriage in Men's Lives*. New York: Oxford University Press.

Oakes, Guy. 2003. "Max Weber on Value Rationality and Value Spheres," *Journal of Classical Sociology* 3:27–45.

Oates, Joyce Carol. 1999. *Broke Heart Blues: A Novel*. New York: Dutton.

Offer, Daniel, et al. 1988. *The Teenage World: Adolescents' Self-Image in Ten Countries*. New York: Plenum Medical Book Co.

Ogbu, John U. 1973. *The Next Generation: An Ethnography of Education in an Urban Neighborhood*. New York: Seminar Press.

Ogbu, John U. 1978. *Minority Educations and Caste: The American System in Cross-Cultural Perspective*. New York: Academic Press.

Olweus, Dan. 1993. *Bullying at School: What We Know and What We Can Do About It*. Oxford: Blackwell Publishers.

Ornelas, I. J., K. M. Perreira, and G. X. Ayala. 2007. "Parental Influences on Adolescent Physical Activity: A Longitudinal Study," *The International Journal of Behavioral Nutrition and Physical Activity* 4:3.

Palladino, Grace. 1996. *Teenagers: An American History*. New York: Basic Books.

Pamuk, Orhan. 2001. "The Anger of the Damned." *The New York Review of Books*, November 15, 2001.

Parkin, Frank. 1979. *Marxism and Class Theory*. New York: Columbia University Press.

Parsons, Talcott, and Robert E. Bales. 1998 [1956]. *Family Socialization and Interaction Process*. In collaboration with James Olds, Morris Zelditch, Jr., and Philip E. Slater. London: Routledge.

Patterson, Orlando. 1975. "Context and Choice in Ethnic Allegiance: A Theoretical Framework and Caribbean Case Study," in *Ethnicity: Theory and Experience*, eds. Nathan Glazer, and Daniel Patrick Moynihan. Cambridge: Harvard University Press.

PBS Frontline. 2002. "Inside the Teenage Brain," http://www.pbs.org/wgbh/pages/frontline/shows/teenbrain/; accessed 09/06/2015.

Péristiany, Jean G., ed. 1966. *Honour and Shame: The Values of Mediterranean Society*. Chicago: University of Chicago Press.

Perrow, Charles. 1986. *Complex Organizations: A Critical Essay*. Third edition. New York: Random House.

Perry, Lorraine J. 2009. "Student-Teacher Relationships: The Impact of Students' Relationships with Teachers on Student School Engagement, Academic Competence, and Behavior." Ph.D. dissertation, Department of Psychology, Syracuse University.

Pescosolido, Bernice, and Beth A. Rubin. 2000. "The Web of Group Affiliations Revisited: Social Life, Postmodernism, and Sociology," *American Sociological Review* 65:52–76.

Peshkin, Alan. 1991. *The Color of Strangers, The Color of Friends: The Play of Ethnicity in School and Community*. Chicago: University of Chicago Press.

Peterson, Karin Elizabeth. 1999. "How Things Become Art: Hierarchy, Status, and Cultural Practice in the Expansion of the American Canon." Ph.D. thesis, University of Virginia.

Portes, Alejandro, and Min Zhou. 1993. "The New Second Generation: Segmented Assimilation and Its Variants," *The Annals of American Academy of Political and Social Science* 530:75–77, 81, 92, 96.

Portes, Alejandro, and Ruben G. Rumbaut. 1996. *Immigrant America: A Portrait*. Second edition. Berkeley: University of California Press.

Powell, Arthur G., Eleanor Farrar, and David Cohen. 1985. *The Shopping Mall High School: Winners and Losers in the Educational Marketplace*. Boston: Houghton Mifflin Co.

Powell, Walter W, and Paul J. DiMaggio, eds. 1991. *The New Institutionalism in Organizational Analysis*. Chicago; London: University of Chicago Press.

Przybylski, Andrew K., and Netta Weinstein. 2012. "Can You Connect with Me Now? How the Presence of Mobile Communication Technology Influences Face-to-Face Conversation Quality," *Journal of Social and Personal Relationships* 30:3:237–246.

Putnam, Robert D. 2000. *Bowling Alone: The Collapse and Revival of American Community*. New York: Simon & Schuster.

Raphael, Edith Nan. 2000. "Sculpting Memory: The Making of Public Commemorative Monuments." Ph.D. thesis, University of Virginia.

Rathbone, Christina. 1998. *On the Outside Looking In: A Year in an Inner-City High School*. New York: Atlantic Monthly Press.

Reardon, Sean F. 2012. "The Widening Academic Achievement Gap between the Rich and the Poor," *Community Investments* 24:2 (Summer):19–39.

Reese, Shelly. 1998. "KIDMONEY: Children as Big Business," *Arts Education Policy Review* 99: 3.

Ridgeway, Cecilia L. 1998. "How Do Status Beliefs Develop? The Role of Resources and Interactional Experience," *American Sociological Review* 63:331–350.

Riesman, David, Nathan Glazer, and Reuel Denney. 1953. *The Lonely Crowd: A Study of the Changing American Character*. Garden City, NY: Doubleday.

Risman, Barbara, and Pepper Schwartz. 2002. "After the Sexual Revolution: Gender Politics in Teen Dating," *Contexts* 1:16–24.

Ronen, Shelly. 2010. "Grinding On the Dance Floor: Gendered Scripts and Sexualized Dancing at College Parties," *Gender and Society* 24:3:355–377.

Roper Starch Worldwide. 1999. *The Public Purse*, January. http://www.roper.com/; 4/14/01.

Roper Starch Worldwide. 1999. "Money is a Good Thing," *The Public Purse*, April. http://www.roper.com/; 4–17–01.

Rosenbaum, J. 2011. "The Complexities of College-for-All: Beyond Fairy-Tale Dreams," *Sociology of Education* 84:2:113–117.

Rossell, Christine, and Christine Bachen. 1993. "Advertising on Channel One: Are Students a Captive Audience?" *High School Journal* 76:2:100–109.

Rousseau, Jean-Jacques. 1755 [1990]. "Discourse on the Origin and the Foundations of Inequality Among Men," *Second Discourse in The First and Second Discourses together with the Replies to Critics and Essays on the Origin of Languages*. New York: Harper & Row.

Sanford, Stephanie and Donna Eder. 1984. "Adolescent Humor during Peer Interaction," *Social Psychology Quarterly* 47:3:235–293.

Sarup, Madan. 1993. *An Introductory Guide to Post-Structuralism and Postmodernism.* Second edition. Athens: University of Georgia Press.

Savage, J. S., J. O. Fisher, and L. L. Birch. 2007. "Parental Influence on Eating Behavior: Conception to Adolescence," *Journal of Law and Medical Ethics* 35:1:22–34.

Scaglioni, Silvia, Michael Salvioni, and Cinzia Galimberti. 2008. "Influence of Parental Attitudes in the Development of Children's Eating Behavior," *British Journal of Nutrition* 99:1:22–25.

Schofield, Janet Ward. 1982. *Black and White in School: Trust, Tension, or Tolerance?* Praeger Studies in Ethnographic Perspectives on American Education, General Editor, Ray C. Rist. [New York:] Praeger Publishers, CBS Inc.

Schor, Juliet B. 1998. *The Overspent American: Upscaling; Downshifting, and the New Consumer.* New York: Basic Books.

Schor, Juliet B. 2003. "The Commodification of Childhood: Tales from the Advertising Front Lines," *Hedgehog Review* 5: 7–23.

Schwartz, Frances. 1981. "Supporting or Subverting Learning? Peer Group Patterns in Four Tracked High Schools," *Anthropology and Education Quarterly* 12:99–121.

Schwartz, Gary, and Don Merten. 1967. "The Language of Adolescence: An Anthropological Approach to the Youth Culture," *American Journal of Sociology* 72:453–468.

Seidman, Steven. 1985. "Weber's Turn to Sociology: A Reply to Horst Helle," *Canadian Journal of Sociology* 10:202–206.

Segalowitz, S. J., D. L. Santesso, and M. K. Jetha. 2010. "Electrophysiological Changes During Adolescence: A Review," *Brain & Cognition* 72:1:86–100.

Seth, Vikram. 1993. *A Suitable Boy.* New York: Harper Collins.

Sherman, Steve. 1996. "A Set of One's Own: TV Sets in Children's Bedrooms," *Journal of Advertising Research* 36:6:RC9(4).

"Shop for Little Horrors," *The Economist,* July 5, 1997.

Shrum, Wesley, and Neil H. Cheek, Jr. 1987. "Social Structure During the School Years: Onset of the Degrouping Process," *American Sociological Review* 52:218–223.

Shulman, Elizabeth P., Laurence D. Steinberg, and Alex R. Piquero. 2013. "The Age–Crime Curve in Adolescence and Early Adulthood is Not Due to Age Differences in Economic Status," *Journal of Youth and Adolescence* 42:848–860.

Simmons, Rachael. 2002. *Odd Girl Out: The Hidden Culture of Aggression in Girls.* New York: Harcourt.

Smith, Edward A., and Richard Udry. 1985. "Coital and Non-Coital Sexual Behaviors of White and Black Adolescents," *American Journal of Public Health* 75:1200–1203.

Smith, Joe. 1988. *Off the Record: An Oral History of Popular Music* [stories told to] Joe Smith; ed. Mitchell Fink. New York: Warner Books.

Smith, M. G. 1965. *The Plural Society in British West Indies.* Berkeley: University of California Press.

Snyder, Susan. 1995. "Ads: Ring Around the Curricular Collar." *Morning Call* (Allentown Pennsylvania), November 19.

Soeffner, Hans-Georg. 1997. *The Order of Rituals: The Interpretation of Everyday Life.* New Brunswick (U.S.A.): Transaction Publishers.

Spethmann, Betsy. 1992. "Young Travelers Exposed to Hyatt Touch," *Advertising Age* 63:6:56.

Stead, Deborah. 1997. "Corporations, Classrooms and Commercialism." *New York Times.* January 5.

Steinberg, Laurence D. 1993. *Adolescence.* Third edition. New York: McGraw-Hill.

Steinberg, Laurence D. 1996. *Beyond the Classroom: Why School Reform Has Tailed and What Parents Need To Do.* New York: Simon & Schuster.

Steinberg, Laurence D. 2001. "We Know Some Things: Parent and Adolescent Relationships in Retrospect and Prospect," *Journal of Research on Adolescence* 11:1:1–19.

Steinberg, Laurence. 2008. "Social Neuroscience Perspective on Adolescent Risk-Taking," *Developmental Review* 28:1:78–106.

Steinberg, Laurence, Ilana Blatt-Eisengart, and Elizabeth Cauffman. 2006. "Patterns of Competence and Adjustment Among Adolescents from Authoritative, Authoritarian, Indulgent, and Neglectful Homes: A Replication in a Sample of Serious Juvenile Offenders," *Journal of Research on Adolescence* 16:1:47–58.

Stone, Bill. 1998. "Teen Spending Keeps Climbing," Forecast [of *Demographics*], January; http://www.demographics.cow/publications/fc/98_FC/9801_fc/9801F0l.htm; May 18, 2001.

Story, Louise. 2007. "Anywhere the Eye Can See, It's Likely to See an Ad," *The New York Times*, January 15, 2007.

Subrahmanyam, Kaveri and Patricia Greenfield. 2008. "Online Communication and Adolescent Relationships," *The Future of Children* 18:1 (Spring):119–146.

Suitor, J. Jill, and Rebel Reavis. 1995. "Football, Fast Cars, and Cheerleading: Adolescent Gender Norms 1978–1989," *Adolescence* 30:118:265–272.

Sumter et al. 2009. "The developmental pattern of resistance to peer influence in adolescence: Will the teenager ever be able to resist?" *Journal of Adolescence*, 32:4 (August):1009–1021.

Talbot, Margaret. 2002. "Mean Girls and the New Movement to Tame Them," *The New York Times Magazine*, February 24, pp. 24ff.

Tatum, Beverly Daniel. 1999. *"Why Are All the Black Kids Sitting Together in the Cafeteria?" and Other Conversations about Race*. New York: Basic Books.

Tedesco, Lisa A., and Eugene L. Gaier. 1988. "Friendship Bonds in Adolescence," *Adolescence* 23:89:125–135.

Thompson, John B. 1994. "The Theory of the Public Sphere: A Critical Appraisal," in *The Polity Reader in Cultural Theory*. Cambridge: Polity Press.

Thorne, Barrie. 1993. *Gender Play*. New Brunswick, NJ: Rutgers University Press.

Tolson, Jerry M., and Kathryn Urberg. 1993. "Similarity Between Adolescent Best Friends," *Journal of Adolescent Research* 8:3:274–288.

Trost, S. G., J. R. Sirard, M. Dowda, K. A. Pfeiffer, and R. R. Pate. 2003. "Physical Activity in Overweight and Nonoverweight Preschool Children," *International Journal of Obesity & Related Metabolic Disorders* 27:7:834–839.

Trow, Martin. 1961. "The Second Transformation of American Secondary Education," *International Journal of Comparative Sociology* 2:144–165; reprinted in Karabel and Halsey 1977.

Tuch, Steven A., Lee Sigelman, and Jason A. MacDonald. 1999. "The Polls—Trends: Race Relations and American Youth, 1976–1995," *Public Opinion Quarterly* 63:109–148.

Turner, Bryan S. 1981. "Weber and the Frankfurt School," in *For Weber: Essays on the Sociology of Fate*. London: Routledge and Kegan Paul.

Turner, Bryan S. 1996. *The Body and Society*. Second edition. London: SAGE Publications.

Twitchell, James B. 1999. *Lead Us Not into Temptation: The Triumph of American Materialism*. New York: Columbia University Press.

Ueda, Reed. 1987. "The Origins of High School Youth Culture," in *Avenues to Adulthood*. Cambridge: Cambridge University Press, chapter six.

Urist, Jacoba. 2014. "Is College Really Harder to Get Into Than It Used To Be?" *The Atlantic* (April 4); http://www.theatlantic.com/education/archive/2014/04/is-college-really-harder-to-get-into-than-it-used-to-be/360114/.

U.S. Bureau of the Census. 1998a. Current Population Reports, P20–515, "Household and Family Characteristics: March (Update)" and earlier reports; http://www.census.gov/population/socdemo/hh-fam/htabFM-3.txt.

U.S. Bureau of the Census. 1998b. Current Population Reports, P23–196, Special Studies. "Changes in Median Household Income: 1969 to 1996," by John McNeil.

U.S. Bureau of the Census. 1999. "Living Arrangements of Children Under 18 Years Old: 1960 to Present," Internet release date: January 7, 1999; http://www.census.gov/population/socdemo/ms-la/tabch-1.txt; May 21, 2001.

U.S. Bureau of the Census. 2000. "Historical Income Tables-Families, Table F-7, Type of Family (All Races) by Median and Mean Income: 1947 to 1999, Revised October 30, 2000"; from March Current Population Survey; http://www.census.gov/hhcs/income/ histinc/fD7.html; May 18, 2001.

U.S. Bureau of the Census. 2001. Current Population Reports, P60-214, *Poverty in the United States: 2000*, by Joseph Dalaker; http://www.census.gov/prod/2001pubs/p60–214.pdf.

U.S. Bureau of Labor Statistics. 1999. "Labor force status of persons 16 to 24 years old by school enrollment, educational attainment, sex, race, and Hispanic origin," October; http://www.bls.gov/news. release/hsgec.t02.html; May 18, 2001.

U.S. Bureau of Labor Statistics. [n.d., circa 2000] "Labor Force Statistics from the Current Population Survey." Table No. 1: Work experience of the population during the year by sex and extent of employment, 1998–99. http://stats.bls.gov/news.release/work.t01.htm, January 11, 2001.

U.S. Department of Education. 1999. National Center for Education Statistics, *Digest of Education Statistics, 1999*; http://nces.ed.gov/pubs2000/Digest99/Chapter2.html; August 1, 2001.

U.S. Department of Education. 2000. National Center for Education Statistics, *Digest of Education Statistics, 1998*, Table 37–4; http://nces.ed.gov/pubs2000/digest99/d99t031.html; June 7, 2001.

U.S. Department of Education. 2003. National Center for Education Statistics, *Digest of Education Statistics, 2002*; http://nces.ed.gov/pubscarch/pubsinfo.asp?pubid=2003060; July 1, 2003.

U.S. Department of Justice Bureau of Justice Statistics. 2010. *Sexual Victimization in Prisons and Jails Reported by Inmates, 2008-09.*

U.S. Department of Labor. 1999. *Report on the American Workforce*. Washington, DC.

U.S. Federal Interagency Forum on Aging. 2000. "Older Americans 2000: Key Indicators of Well-Being," Table 113. http://www.agingstats.gov/chartbook2000/tables-population.html#Indicator 1; June 7, 2001.

U.S. Social Security Administration. 2000. *Annual Statistical Supplement, 2000*; http://www.ssa.gov/ statistics/Supplement/2000/; June 7, 2001.

Veblen, Thorstein. 1992 [1912]. *The Theory of the Leisure Class*. New Brunswick, U.S.A.: Transaction Publishers.

Ventura, Stephanie J., and Christine A. Bachrach. 2000. "Nonmarital Childbearing in the United States, 1940–99," *National Vital Statistics Reports* 48:16, Hyattsville, MD: National Center for Health Statistics.

Vickerman, Milton. 1999. *Crosscurrents: West Indian Immigrants and Race*. New York: Oxford University Press.

Vickerman, Milton, and Jimmy Philippe. 1991. "Youth and Crime in an Inner-City Neighborhood," paper presented at the American Sociological Association.

Vidich, Arthur J., and Joseph Bensman. 1958. *Small Town in Mass Society: Class, Power, and Religion in a Rural Community*. Princeton: Princeton University Press.

Wagner, David G., and Joseph Berger. 2002. "Expectation States Theory: An Evolving Research Program," in *New Directions in Contemporary Sociological Theory*, eds. Joseph Berger, and Morris Zeldich, Jr. Lanham, MD: Rowman and Littlefield, pp. 41–76.

Warner, W. Lloyd. 1963. *Yankee City*. New Haven: Yale University Press.

Wax, Emily 2000. "Today's Titans Tackle World Challenges," *The Washington Post*, October 12.

Weber, Max. 1949. *The Methodology of the Social Sciences*. New York: Free Press.

Weber, Max. 1958. *The Protestant Ethic and the Spirit of Capitalism*. New York: Scribner's.

Weber, Max. 1968. *Economy and Society*. New York: Bedminster Press.

Weber, Max. 2009. *The Protestant Ethic and the Spirit of Capitalism with Other Writings on the Rise of the West*, Fourth edition, translated and introduced by Stephen Kalberg. New York: Oxford University Press.

Webster, Murray, Jr., and Martha Foschi, eds. 1988. *Status Generalization: New Theory and Research*. Stanford, CA: Stanford University Press.

Weinbender, Miriam L.M., and Annette Mackay Rossignol. 1996. "Lifestyle and Risk of Premature Sexual Activity in a High School Population of Seventh-Day Adventists: Value-genesis 1989," *Adolescence* 31:122:265–281.

Wells, Amy Stuart, and Robert L. Crain. 1997. *Stepping Over the Color Line: African–American Students in White Suburban Schools*. New Haven: Yale University Press.

Wentz, Richard E. 1998. *The Culture of Religious Pluralism*. Boulder, CO: Westview Press.

Whyte, William H., Jr. 1956. *The Organization Man*. New York: Simon and Schuster.

Wildhagen, Tina. 2011. "What's Oppositional Culture Got to Do with It? Moving beyond the Strong Version of the Acting White Hypothesis," *Sociological Perspectives* (September 2011) 54:403–430.

Willis, Paul. 1977. *Learning to Labour: How Working Class Kids Get Working Class Jobs*. Westmead, Farnborough, Hants, England: Saxon House.

Willoughby, Teena, Marie Good, Paul J. C. Adachi, Chloe Hamza, and Royette Tavernier. 2013. "Examining the Link Between Adolescent Brain Development and Risk Taking from a Social–Developmental Perspective," *Brain and Cognition* 83:3:315–323.

Wolfe, Tom. 2000. *Hooking Up*. New York: Farrar Straus Giroux.

Woolley, Michael E., and Andrew Grogan-Kaylor. 2006. "Protective Family Factors in the Context of Neighborhood: Promoting Positive School Outcomes," *Family Relations* 55: (January):93–104.

Wortman, Camille B., Elizabeth E. Loftus, and Charles A. Weaver, III. 1997. *Psychology*, Fifth edition. New York: McGraw-Hill.

Wright, Erik Olin. 1985. *Classes*. London: Verso.

Wuthnow, Robert. 1996. *Poor Richard's Principle: Recovering the American Dream through the Moral Dimension of Work, Business, and Money*. Princeton: Princeton University Press.

Xie, Wenjing. 2014. "Social Network Site Use, Mobile Personal Talk and Social Capital among Teenagers," *Computers in Human Behavior* 41: (December):228–235.

Youniss, James, Jefferey A. McClellan, and Darcy Strouse. 1994. "We're Popular, but We're Not Snobs," in Montemayor, Adams, and Gullotta (1994).

Zelizer, Viviana. 1985. *Pricing the Priceless Child: The Changing Social Value of Children*. New York: Basic Books.

Zerubavel, Evitar. 1991. *The Fine Line: Making Distinctions in Everyday Life*. Chicago: University of Chicago Press.

Zimmerman, Jonathan. 2014. "Why Is American Teaching So Bad?" *The New York Review of Books*, December 4, 2014; http://www.nybooks.com/issues/2014/dec/04/; April 7, 2015.

Zollo, Peter. "Talking to Teens," *American Demographics*, November 1995.

Zollo, Peter. 1999 [1995]. *Wise Up to Teens: Insights into Marketing and Advertising to Teenagers*. [NL] New Strategist Publications.

INDEX